MEDIEVAL GERMANY
1056–1273

Medieval Germany
1056–1273

Second Edition
Alfred Haverkamp

translated by Helga Braun
and Richard Mortimer

OXFORD UNIVERSITY PRESS

1992

Oxford University Press, Walton Street, Oxford OX2 6DP

Oxford New York Toronto
Delhi Bombay Calcutta Madras Karachi
Petaling Jaya Singapore Hong Kong Tokyo
Nairobi Dar es Salaam Cape Town
Melbourne Auckland

and associated companies in
Berlin Ibadan

Oxford is a trade mark of Oxford University Press

Published in the United States
by Oxford University Press, New York

© C. H. Beck'sche Verlagsbuchhandlung (Oscar Beck),
Munich 1984
This translation © Oxford University Press 1988, 1992
Reprinted 1990

British Library Cataloguing in Publication Data
Haverkamp, Alfred
Medieval Germany, 1056–1273.
1. Germany, ca 1050–1200
I. Title   II. Aufbruch und Gestaltung.
English
943'.02
ISBN 0–19–822132–0
ISBN 0–19–822172–x (Pbk)

Library of Congress Cataloging in Publication Data
Haverkamp, Alfred, 1937–
Medieval Germany, 1056–1273.
Translation of: Aufbruch und Gestaltung.
Deutschland, 1056–1273.
Bibliography: p.
Includes index.
1. Germany—History—To 1517.   I. Title.
DD126.H3813   1988   943'.02   88–5141
ISBN 0–19–822132–0
ISBN 0–19–822172–x (Pbk)

Printed in Great Britain by
J. W. Arrowsmith Ltd, Bristol

To Ida, Eva, and Anita

PREFACE TO THE ENGLISH EDITION

The original German version of this book was published as the second volume of a series appealing to a fairly wide readership. This is the reason why its plan is not that of a typical German textbook, which usually describes the state of research in greater detail. Nevertheless it was my intention to integrate the results of recent research into my narrative. Moreover, the book aims at making the reader as familiar as possible with the historical sources handed down to us. In order to make even complicated facts easier to understand I have frequently resorted to quoting the actual wording of the sources.

I have attempted to base my narrative on as broad a point of view as possible. This does not apply only to the aspect of geographical range which is to be discussed later. I have also aimed at taking into consideration all the essential spheres of life: modes of political action and the structure of government, economic facts and activities, the state of the church and the forms of piety, the levels of education and the manners of perception, social groups and communities. At the same time I have sought to grasp the intense interrelationship between those spheres, respecting, however, their individual features and specific dynamics. Interrelated as these spheres were, they determine the arrangement of the main sections as orientation-marks of the whole and as a guide to the reader. A socially differentiating approach forms an integral part of such an arrangement. At any rate I intended to pay special attention to all groups and strata of society from the higher nobility down to townsmen, peasants, and serfs, from the high ecclesiastical lords down to the monks and the heretics and, last but not least, the Jews, thereby discussing the relationship among each other and their characteristics and limitations. This ideal, which I have striven for, manifests itself in the fact that each of the three main sections ends with a chapter on the structure of society, thus giving a certain synopsis.

The arrangement of the book also shows that I have tried to

describe the course of German history in the more than two centuries as being a part of western culture and the Latin world, which expanded during that very period, receiving new impulses and undergoing considerable change.

In systematically considering the European context I by no means intend a complete change of paradigm from the long-prevalent national historiography to the pan-European approach. I am concerned rather with emphasizing that the German countries, which were in themselves very different, had been very much affected by their contacts with the neighbouring, highly cultivated countries and by the events in the broader European environment over this long period of time. Above all, many inspirations from the Romance countries in western and southern Europe were taken over in Germany and especially in the regions of early settlement, promoting there innovations in important areas.

The subtitle of the German edition was *Aufbruch und Gestaltung*. A period of time in which such processes, strongly influenced by external factors and supported by internal forces, had far-reaching effects on the course of German history may justly be characterized as an age of new departures (*Aufbruch*). At the same time it must be emphasized that the German countries where these changes took place in extremely different forms experienced a configuration (*Gestaltung*) which was— unlike all previous developments—of fundamental importance for German history far into modern times. Hence both terms, *Aufbruch* and *Gestaltung*, are inseparably connected as characteristics of the period under discussion.

I am glad to say that the book has been very favourably received both by my colleagues and by the public at large. All the more I appreciate its being now directly available to the English reader. Perhaps it can thus contribute to a deeper interest in a fascinating epoch of German history located in its European context.

In the present edition all mistakes that have been detected have been eliminated. I have updated the references to primary sources and literature. Some passages of the first part of the German text have been omitted as containing matter well-known to the English reader. The map once again records only the chief places mentioned in the text.

My thanks are due to many people and many institutions, above all to the Oxford University Press for taking the book into their publication programme and to the 'Inter Nationes' foundation for granting a generous allowance for the translation expenses. I am particularly indebted to Ms Helga Braun and Mr Richard Mortimer for their translation of a text rich in difficulties.

A.H.

Trier, New Year's Eve 1987

PREFACE TO THE SECOND EDITION

Fortunately, this book aroused so much interest that as early as the summer of 1990 a reprint was necessary. For this second revised edition I have altered the text in a few places, above all inserting some additional material. These textual changes include the removal of a few misunderstandings from the translation. The versions of most of the newly inserted passages are the work of the translator, but extra work on the English text was carried out by my research assistant, Christoph Cluse, to whom I am most grateful.

Bibliographical details have been brought up to date, most of the changes adding recently published titles, but also discarding a few older publications. For their assistance in this work my colleagues, Dr Margit Müller and Dr Friedhelm Burgard, deserve my thanks. It was not possible fully to consider the three volumes of *Die Salier und das Reich* [no. 338] published in the last few weeks. More volumes are in the press, to coincide with a planned exhibition on the Salians.

In an appendix a genealogical table has been added. The map still shows only the chief features. A special problem is fixing the boundaries of the empire, for these changed over and over again in the course of the high Middle Ages. So little was the exercise of power within the German kingdom, founded on the importance of personal connections and the diffusion of lordship rights, guided by firm borders, that imperial boundaries were unimportant if they were established at all.

For this new English edition I must repeat my thanks expressed in the dedication of the first German edition: for Ida, Eva, and Anita.

A.H.

Trier, New Year's Eve 1990

PREFACE

This book presents the interim results of my teaching and research on the high Middle Ages. It is not a reference-book, nor a bibliographical survey. It is intended to be a reading-book designed to portray, as vividly and in as many aspects as possible, a fascinating period of German history in its European connections and to offer hints for further engagement with the thought-provoking events of this great age.

Trier, early summer, 1984   A.H.

CONTENTS

NOTE ON REFERENCES

Figures in square brackets within the text refer to the numbered entries in the Bibliography; they are followed by a colon, the volume-number in roman figures, and the page-number in arabic. Thus [14: xi. 518] refers to entry no. 14 in the Bibliography, vol. xi, p. 518.

Introduction

THE date limits of the period of more than two hundred years from 1056 to 1273 derive from the course of political history in the German empire. The first date is determined by the beginning of Henry IV's reign, after the early death of his father Henry III (5 October 1056), when his widow Agnes assumed the regency for the emperor's son, then only six years old. The other limit is the election of King Rudolf of Habsburg (1 October 1273), after the death of Richard of Cornwall (2 April 1272). With this the struggle for the throne, which had continued in the German empire since 1257 between the brother of the king of England and King Alfonso of Castile, both of whom could claim a close relationship with the Staufen ruling family, was ended. Towards the end of the following year, at an election which the hitherto unsuccessful Castilian had vainly tried to thwart, the electors chose Rudolf of Habsburg (1273-91).

The election and subsequent coronation of the Habsburg in Aachen buried all hopes, particularly among Italian supporters, of continuing in the Staufen family in the person of the emperor's grandson, Frederick of Meissen-Thuringia. In fact, a decision against a succession in the male line of the Staufen house had been made at the latest on 29 October 1268. On this day Charles of Anjou, who had been crowned king of Sicily at Epiphany 1266 in St Peter's, Rome, had the sixteen-year-old Conradin—the son of Conrad IV and the grandson of the Emperor Frederick II—beheaded in the Piazza del Mercato in Naples. A few months previously (23 August 1268) Charles had defeated the Staufen army near Tagliacozzo in the Abruzzi.

With the death of Conradin, the last of the legitimate male successors of the Emperor Frederick II, the right of the German electors was freed from the claims of hereditary title. This right held its own in subsequent elections, with a constant change of

dynasties up to the election of King Wenzel, the son of the
Emperor Charles IV, in 1376. From this point of view the
events of 1272-3 are more of a break than those of the year
1125. In this year the Saxon Duke Lothar of Supplingenburg
was elected king after the death of the childless Salian Emperor
Henry V, and thereby the hereditary candidacy of the Staufen
Duke Frederick II, a nephew of the Salian emperor, was thrust
aside. After the death of Lothar III (1125-37), who had intended the Welf Duke Henry of Saxony and Bavaria, his son-
in-law and the most powerful duke in the empire, to succeed
him on the throne, the Staufen candidate Conrad III (1138-
52) finally managed to gain possession of a generally acknowledged royal title through a renewed election by the German princes. The long struggle for the throne (1198-1218)
between the Staufen and the Welfs after the death of Henry
VI, only interrupted for four years (1208-12), also eventually
led to an undisputed reign by the Staufen Frederick II. This,
however, only lasted until the emperor's deposition by Pope
Innocent IV at the Council of Lyons in 1245.

The struggles for the succession to the throne considerably
affected the capacity for action of the German emperors. In
Germany this capacity was closely related to the increase in
power of the secular and ecclesiastical princes. Furthermore,
the papacy influenced the struggle for the throne directly or
indirectly and used it to improve its political position. The
above-mentioned interruptions in the succession to the throne
were landmarks on the way to the establishment of the right of
election, which had received its greatest boost in the election
of the anti-king Rudolf of Rheinfelden at the height of the
investiture dispute in 1077. At about the same time hereditary
right was consolidated in the Norman kingdom of Sicily, among
the Capetians in France, and finally also in the Anglo-Norman
kingdom. This varying development of election and hereditary
right in the succession to the throne indicates the different
positions of both the ecclesiastical and secular princes—particularly the bishops and the high nobility—in the western
kingdoms, as participation in the act of election manifested the
kingship's dependence on the princes, and strengthened the
consciousness of equality with the kings, particularly among
the great noble families.

If we bear in mind the length of time dealt with here, for which the limiting dates only serve as reference points, it equals about the period from the second half of the eighteenth century to the present. This playing with time not only sharpens our sensitivity to time, which tends to compress and shorten past ages more the further away they are from our own experienced history; it is also instructive in that Germany between the second half of the eleventh century and the last quarter of the thirteenth century experienced far-reaching changes such as were not exceeded until those of the last two centuries. The changes are equally fundamental. This applies not only to Germany but also to the other European countries.

Thinking of our period with a European perspective in mind shows it to be the most important age of change between the ancient world and modern times. In German history the foundations laid earlier were strengthened; other important characteristics of development were now created. Germany moved from the periphery into a central position, having close contacts with the surrounding European countries. From the cultural point of view the German territories received the strongest influences from the south and west, the variations in culture between south and north and between west and east thereby being more evened out.

Although the beginnings of a national consciousness can be noticed in Germany from the twelfth century, imperial policies reaching far beyond Germany remained decisive. From the second half of the twelfth century these policies assumed a stronger universal concern, going beyond the closer interest in Italy out to the wider Mediterranean area. Direct access was thereby gained to the highly developed Mediterranean cultures. In this area too the Crusades were concentrated—the strongest religious–political movement in Latin Christendom at this period, which can with good reason therefore generally be characterized as 'the age of the Crusades'. As well as in the Mediterranean area, the crusading movement was used for pushing back paganism in continental central Europe. In this way the area of the *regnum teutonicum* was also expanded further eastwards.

Because of this expansion in the Mediterranean area and in continental Europe, which still more or less lagged behind the

Mediterranean in civilization, new dominions and states came
into existence which limited the effectiveness of universal policies. At the same time the tendencies towards the concentration of power became stronger. They were in close correlation
with the creation of new co-operative forms of organization—
particularly communes—and were also limited by them. The
expansion and intensification of states and governments
occurred in connection with a considerable increase in population, with a great spreading of new settlements, and with
the consolidation of settlements into urban centres, as also
happened in the towns that already existed. These processes
were in turn inseparably connected with the extension of the
agricultural area and more effective forms of agricultural production, and with a spatial, qualitative, and quantitative extension of trade, commerce, and the use of money, which was
followed by a considerable increase in the division of labour.
It was not only in this respect that closer contact with the
Mediterranean gave important impulses to the area of the
German empire and to the other European regions.

   Such far-reaching changes presupposed a greater physical
mobility in broader circles of the population, as could be seen
in the Crusades, in the pilgrimages and merchants' journeys,
in the migration to new and frequently distant settlements,
and also in the migration into towns. By this the constraints of
the traditional social order were weakened even further, and
new formations became possible. In the crusading movement
the noble ruling class gained a new knightly ethos, which at the
same time favoured the acceptance of new men. Such an opening also resulted from the competition between rulers and the
widening and intensification of the power of lords. At least in
continental European countries and those further north, only
now did there come into existence those classes of peasants and
town-dwellers which were so fundamental in later European
history. The forms of personal dependence in general became
looser, so that the legal consequences of unfreedom—as far as
these remained in existence in the older forms—lost importance
in determining social position.

   The political controversies between Church and State were
accompanied by theological, philosophical, and legal controversies concerning the ordering of, and the relations between,

the Church and the world, which favoured new forms of argumentation and new approaches in thought. The revival of thoughts buried for centuries, such as the philosophy of Aristotle, was furthered not least by cultural contacts in the Mediterranean area. Certainly the exchange of thought was hastened and deepened by the busy and often distant wanderings of students and teachers. The birth of influential schools, and ultimately of the first universities in the West, added a great deal to this. They started, or were founded, in the larger cities. The spiritual and religious life which hitherto had in general had its most important centres in the rural monasteries and secular churches, at least in the areas outside the Mediterranean, was now increasingly concentrated in the towns. Behind this lay the advance of literacy, mainly in urban circles even outside the Mediterranean countries south of the Alps, and thereby an increase in its spread amongst lay people, who also needed this form of culture more and more in their daily lives. In this way the laity won for themselves direct access, no longer necessarily with clerics as mediators, to traditions fixed in writing and above all to the Bible, the decisive source for the organization of life.

Independent access to the basic truths, from which the way of life in the here-and-now was to be deduced and on which eternal life depended, was forced upon the laity all the more because the Church reformers themselves questioned norms which until then had been largely unquestioned. The 'age of Church reform', which can roughly be limited to the period between the middle of the eleventh and the first third of the twelfth century, left behind many unsolved questions to which the answers slipped threateningly out of the control of the official Church in the following period. Out of this there developed heresies, at times widespread, the greatest danger to the official Roman Church before the Reformation. The danger was only averted when, at the beginning of the thirteenth century, the papal Curia brought itself to develop new forms of the cure of souls. Only now, and primarily with the help of the mendicant orders, did it manage to reintegrate into the rich and powerful official Church those religious mass movements which had grown up mainly in the big cities of the western

Mediterranean and part of which had deviated considerably from Church dogmas and ways of life.

Although the German empire was touched and influenced by the religious, philosophical, and theological disputes of the time outlined here, it remained a backwater also in this aspect of world history, which still had its nerve-centre in Mediterranean culture. Germany was still a 'developing country', which received its most important influences from the centre of gravity in the Mediterranean and beyond that from the West, and which made them fruitful to an astonishing extent. The Mediterranean area was then, so to speak, the meeting-place of world history. There the Roman, Graeco-Byzantine, Arab, and Jewish cultural streams merged. It was also the centre of political, religious, and economic activity. The south apart, it was mainly the West which was significant for German history. Towards the north and east the German empire itself grew into a mediating role. Therefore it was only natural that imperial politics more and more concentrated on Italy and the Mediterranean area. It was not accidental that Italy played a leading role in German history in the high Middle Ages: a period which can reasonably be thought to end when the Norman-Staufen dynasty leaves the stage.

It is thus necessary to point out the most important basic conditions and sets of connections in which German history in the high Middle Ages is embedded. With the help of this pattern, which is determined by relations of differing importance between north and south, and east and west, it should become clearer in what ways and in which areas German history was influenced by events and trends in neighbouring countries as well as those in other areas of Europe and the Mediterranean lands, and how it influenced those areas in turn. This is the aim of Part I of the book.

This approach, differentiating various areas, is also to be applied in the subsequent sections on a smaller scale to the presentation of German history. Here the most important difference is that between the more densely populated areas of old settlement in the west and south, with their ancient connections with 'Romania', and the later-developed areas in the north and east and in the north-east, where influences converged between 'Slavia' and 'Germania'. The border was marked by the Elbe and Saale, and further south-east by the western slopes of the Upper Palatinate and Bavarian forests. Among the old settlement areas linking up with the west, the country along the great rivers, especially the Maas, Moselle, Rhine, Danube, and Main, had the highest degree of development. Given this disparity, at the beginning of our period they were markedly in advance of the new settlement areas, not only in their settlement but also in their economic infrastructure, with towns and markets, as well as in Church organization. Only in the course of the twelfth and thirteenth centuries were these differences at least partly evened out. At first the most important political controversies concentrated on the nucleus of the old settlement areas.

Research into local history, which in recent decades has done much to further our knowledge of certain aspects and to define the problems, has been of great help for this study. Admittedly it often restricts its view to rather too limited areas and often neglects the wider connections. On the whole it is also an advantage that the high Middle Ages have for long been a favoured area of historical research in Germany, so that there is a rich literature on many detailed questions and from many points of view. This is especially true for research into political events and processes, for imperial and ecclesiastical history, and in general for constitutional, legal, and intellectual history. The research situation for economic and social history is less favourable, influenced partly by the availability of sources. This also makes it difficult to include the activities and sufferings of wider circles of the population. The quantity and character of the sources themselves once again represent the cultural realities of the different areas, as will be pointed out in the last chapter of Part I.

Alongside the cultural and geographical approach, the following work attempts to depict as fully as possible the manifold activities and sufferings of the people. To bring out the connections and correlations in time between events in this broad view, the great length of time of the period here dealt with has been divided into two phases in Parts II and III of the book. The periodization has again been taken from political history.

I
THE AGE IN EUROPEAN
PERSPECTIVE

The Expansion of the West in the Mediterranean Area

[a] THE SHIFT IN THE CENTRE OF GRAVITY OF IMPERIAL POLITICS TOWARDS THE SOUTH

From Henry IV to Conrad IV and Conradin, every ruler visited the kingdom of Italy in person, including Conrad III, whose stay in Italy from 1128 to 1130 while anti-king must be considered here too. Under Henry VI this north–south axis was extended as far as the heartland of the South Italian–Sicilian kingdom, which the Welf Otto IV after his coronation as emperor (1209) also moved into. Frederick II's major field of action was his inherited Norman kingdom of Sicily. From this centre of Mediterranean culture, saturated in tradition, the emperor reached out, contrary to the direction of previous action, towards the northern kingdoms, amongst which imperial Italy played a key role. Frederick's illegitimate son Manfred, who had himself crowned king of Sicily at Palermo in 1258, only crossed the borders of the kingdom into imperial Italy in a few campaigns before the battle of Benevento (26 February 1266), which he lost to Charles of Anjou and where he also met his death. Compared with this north–south orientation, which at its longest extended about 3,000 kilometres, the Burgundian and Provençal *regnum Arelatense*, as the rulers' itineraries show, remained in the lee of imperial politics, from which it only emerged at times under Frederick Barbarossa.

[b] CRUSADES AND *RECONQUISTA*

The Crusades also aimed at the areas of old culture in the Mediterranean, which thus became more and more the centre

of activities of the Staufen emperors—but also of the Welf
Emperor Otto IV. As early as 1063 and 1064, before the First
Crusade (1096–9), Pope Alexander II had granted remission
of sins to the Christian warriors fighting against the Muslims
in Spain and Sicily, and thereby, and in other ways, justified
the politically motivated wars against the heathens.

In the First Crusade, summoned by Pope Urban II (1088–
99) at the synods of Piacenza and Clermont-Ferrand, the idea
of an armed pilgrimage, which appealed to broad circles of the
population, was pushed into the background by the urge for
conquest of the 'Frankish' knights and lords who took part.
They created largely independent lordships in the county of
Edessa and the Norman principality of Antioch, to which in
1109 the county of Tripoli was added as a bridge between the
Franks in Syria and Palestine. After the capture of Jerusalem
(15 July 1099) and the death of Duke Godfrey of Lower Lorraine, who had adopted the title of 'Protector of the Holy
Sepulchre' only, his brother Baldwin had himself crowned king
on Christmas Day 1100 in the church of the Nativity at Beth-
lehem by the Latin patriarch of Jerusalem, Archbishop Daim-
bert of Pisa. The Italian trading ports of Pisa, Venice, and
Genoa, which had already received trading privileges in the
Byzantine empire, and on which the crusader states were dependent for conquering and securing the coastal towns and for
the transport of supplies, gained huge economic advantages for
their fleets in the merchant towns of the Near East.

With the *reconquista* in Spain, the expulsion of the Muslims
from Sicily, and the hardly anticipated successes of the First
Crusade, the papacy increased the area of its authority considerably. In the crusader states this happened by the creation
of a Latin hierarchy and the subordination of the patriarchates
of Antioch and Jerusalem. The conquest of southern Italy by
the Normans had already considerably circumscribed the authority of the patriarch of Constantinople in favour of Rome.
More important, however, was the fact that the Byzantine
empire had finally been expelled from Italy, and in the following period was almost constantly threatened by the new
power in southern Italy and Sicily. The crusading movement,
which Pope Urban had at first intended to use in favour of the
Byzantine emperors, developed into an almost continual source

of danger for the eastern empire. It is significant that the Norman Duke Bohemond, when lord of the principality of Antioch, was able to persuade Pope Paschal II in 1104 to have a holy war preached against Byzantium.

The expansion of Latin Christianity at the expense of Islam and the Eastern Church remained closely connected with the politico-religious crusading movement after the First Crusade as well. The fall of Edessa in 1144 was followed by the Second Crusade (1147-9), which was unsuccessful despite the participation of two kings—Louis VII of France (1131-80) and the Staufen Conrad III. The even greater participation of western kings in the Third Crusade, for which the Emperor Frederick I and the kings Richard I of England (1189-99) and Philip II of France (1180-1223) set off in 1189 and 1190, was a reaction to the most severe defeat that the crusader states had yet suffered. Only a few months after his complete victory at Hattin in Galilee, the Sultan Saladin in October 1187 even captured Jerusalem, a holy city for Islam too. Following the recapture of Acre, which happened with the help of French and English crusaders in July 1191 after a two-year siege, King Richard won further victories and finally gained a truce (2 September 1192) in which Saladin guaranteed free access to Jerusalem for pilgrims.

Henry VI's crusading campaign, which was in any case strongly influenced by his expansionary Mediterranean policies, led in October 1197, not least because of his early death, only to the occupation of the towns of Sidon and Beirut, which nevertheless were strategically important. Neither the Fourth Crusade (1198-1204) nor the Fifth (1217-21) advanced as far as the Holy Land. The Emperor Frederick II, excommunicated by the pope, was the first to achieve success. Through his marriage to the heiress Isabella in 1225, he had gained a claim to the kingdom of Jerusalem. On a diplomatically well prepared crusade (1228-9), which the pope had forbidden, he succeeded by a treaty with the Sultan al-Kamil in winning back Jerusalem together with a piece of land between the holy city and the coast. Frederick II's government soon met with bitter resistance from the barons in the kingdom of Jerusalem, where, since the birth of his son Conrad IV (1228), he was looked upon only as regent. A mere five years after the expiry of the treaty, fixed

for about ten years, Jerusalem was finally lost to the Muslims
(1244). The crusade of the French King Louis IX (1226–70)
which took place between 1248 and 1254 was not able significantly to change the balance of power.

[*c*] THE CONQUEST OF CONSTANTINOPLE:
THE SUCCESSORS OF THE BYZANTINE EMPIRE

After the Norman Duke Bohemond's planned crusade against
Byzantium already mentioned (1104), and a pact between the
Norman King Roger II (d. 1154) and the French King Louis
VII which had been directed against the eastern empire, during
the Third Crusade Frederick Barbarossa also for a while considered the conquest of Constantinople. Along with the kingdom of Sicily, which he took over in 1194, Barbarossa's son
Henry VI acquired the traditionally anti-Byzantine policy of
his Norman predecessors. The marriage of Henry's younger
brother Philip to Irene, the daughter of the Emperor Isaac II
(1185–95), gave the Staufen a legal justification for intervention in the eastern empire. Only a few days after the
marriage Isaac II had been deposed and blinded by his brother
Alexius III (1195–1203). Because of a papal veto, Henry VI
to begin with contented himself with the extortion of a high
annual tribute of 1,600 pounds of gold from an eastern empire
weakened by inner conflict and external threats.

In the crusade which Innocent III (1198–1216) announced
only a year after the death of Henry VI, the pope intended to
keep away the West European kings, and particularly the
Staufen Philip, in order to strengthen his own claims to leadership. But in the event Enrico Dandolo, the doge of Venice,
succeeded in using the *c.*10,000 crusaders assembled in the
merchant city to the advantage of Venetian policy. Against
postponement of their debts for the intended crossing, the doge
persuaded them to capture the town of Zara in Dalmatia. In
Zara, which was conquered in November 1202, envoys of the
German King Philip and his young brother-in-law Alexius IV,
who in 1201 had escaped from prison, succeeded in persuading
the crusaders to reinstate on the throne the Emperor Isaac II —
i.e. Philip's father-in-law and Alexius IV's father.

On 17 July 1203 the Byzantine capital, which for some nine centuries had resisted numerous attempts by Persians and Arabs to conquer it, fell to the crusaders. Isaac II was reinstated as emperor with his son Alexius IV as co-emperor. They were, however, incapable of keeping the grand promises made in Zara—ecclesiastical union with Rome, huge sums of money to the Venetians and crusaders, and the reinforcement of the crusader army with 10,000 soldiers. When in January 1204 they fell victim to an uprising and the son-in-law of Alexius III ascended the throne, the doge of Venice and the crusaders put into practice a plan possibly made as early as 1202. On 13 April 1204 Constantinople was once again conquered. Many inhabitants of the town, which, at that time, with more than 100,000 residents, was the most populous urban centre in Europe, were murdered. A large number of monuments or works of art, which had been made or collected there during almost a thousand years of Constantinople's history, were destroyed or captured as loot. Relics, reliquaries, and pictures were much in demand. From that time on the loot conveyed to the people of the Latin West a tangible perception of Byzantine culture, which had long evoked both admiration and disdain. More than ever particular forms and motifs of Byzantine art were since then taken over, transformed in part or syncretically re-worked. These artistic impulses from the East supplemented classicizing trends, which, to varying degrees in different parts of the West, formed part of the wide-ranging Renaissance of the twelfth century and were to have a lasting influence.

Like the booty, which alone was worth 400,000 silver marks, the Byzantine empire was distributed amongst the conquerors according to the treaty made previously. While Venice laid the foundations of its colonial empire along the lifelines and at the heart of the Eastern Roman Empire, the other lordships which were built on the ruins of Byzantium were hardly viable in the long run. Besides the Latin empire, two Greek ones sprang into existence on Byzantine soil, and to them was added the Bulgarian tsardom, which the emperor had recognized towards the end of the twelfth century (1187).

With the dismemberment of the Byzantine empire, this power which had linked Europe and Asia was eliminated as a

major authority and active partner in the power politics of
Europe. From the 1240s, however, the Emperor John Vatatzes,
later canonized, considerably expanded and strengthened the
empire of Nicæa, which unlike neighbouring states was spared
the attacks of the Mongols. Its resurgence could not even be
halted by the Staufen King Manfred of Sicily, who allied himself with the despot of Epirus and the Latin powers in Greece.
In 1261, the Emperor Michael VIII of Nicæa (1259/61–82)
made a pact with Venice's rival Genoa; and in the same year
he put an end to the Latin empire with the conquest of Constantinople. His family maintained its hold on the imperial
throne until the fall of Constantinople in 1453. The recreated
Byzantine empire consumed, and even dissipated, its forces in
defensive wars against the West lasting decades, and in constant
wars in the Balkans. It subsequently degenerated into a minor
power.

The papacy became more and more dependent on the French
kingdom, so that the gap between its universal claims to authority and its actual influence widened. The western empire
lost its anchoring in the Mediterranean area, with which the
Staufen in particular, and Frederick II *par excellence* among
them, had buttressed their superior power and authority. This
expulsion, not only due to the papacy, from the central areas
of the contemporary world, in which Italy had long played an
unchallenged mediating role, cut the western empire off from
its oldest and strongest roots. But the effects of events in the
Mediterranean area on German history in the later Middle
Ages are only a reflection of the great importance the Mediterranean nerve-centre of the contemporary world had for Germany in the period which concerns us most. The Italian
interests of the German rulers and the actions of imperial policy
from the end of the twelfth century, which went even beyond
Italy, as well as the participation of German kings and emperors, high nobility and clergy, knights, and other groups of the
population in the Crusades, are all expressions of the key position of the Mediterranean region in this period.

2

The Spread of Latin Christendom in Continental Europe

Only a few decades after the First Crusade had led to the first climax of expansion in the Mediterranean area, a renewed and in the long run successful expansion of the Roman Christian sphere of influence towards the east began in continental Europe too, after about a century of set-backs, or at least of stagnation. While the attacks in the Mediterranean area were directed towards old cultures, against Islam as well as the Orthodox empire of Byzantium, those on the continent were mainly directed against the Slavs and other still pagan peoples in the as yet thinly settled regions east of the Elbe, which still to a great extent practised a natural economy. In contrast to the Mediterranean, where the various attempts at conversion almost without exception met failure, the pagans in the lands north-east of the Elbe and Saale as far as the Prussians (between the lower Vistula and the mouth of the Niemen) and the inhabitants of the Baltic countries were, with the exception of the Lithuanians, converted to Christianity in the course of the twelfth and thirteenth centuries. At the time the last bastions of the crusader states fell to the power of Islam, the spread of Christianity in Europe was completed and secured.

In this last phase of the Christianization of continental Europe, the motives of mission and conquest were again connected in a complex, inseparable symbiosis. This religious–political amalgam found its clearest expression in the application of the idea of crusade to the conversion of the pagans in north-east central Europe. This probably happened for the first time around 1107–8, in a summons to the bishops and secular lords from east Saxony. In this the call to Christianize pagan territory was connected with the promise of taking possession of the best land for settlement. In this respect the Second Crusade saw a considerable advance. In 1147 mainly Saxon lords who did not wish to participate in the crusade to the Holy Land joined forces 'in the same way, under the sign of the cross', in order, as a contemporary description continues, 'to put an end to the wicked encroachments of the Slavs living on the other side of the Elbe'. A decade after this Slav crusade, which was on the whole militarily unsuccessful against the Obodrites and Liutizi, the Swedish king began the conquest of Finland with a crusade. In the area between the Elbe, Saale, and Oder, however, the policy of military mission and conquest retreated. Thus here, and later also in the areas between the Oder and the Vistula, a generally peaceful conversion and settlement could be carried out.

[*b*] THE KNIGHTLY ORDERS: BATTLE AND MISSION

The crusading movement was highly effective in converting and subjugating the Prussians and Courlanders, Lithuanians and Letts, and Livonians and Estonians on the far side of the Vistula after the turn of the thirteenth century. This is evident not only from the numerous crusades. Thus Albert of Buxhövden, consecrated bishop of the Livonians in 1199, organized a crusade as early as the turn of the century, which made possible the foundation of Riga in 1201. Further crusades against the Prussians followed as early as 1218 and 1221-3. The Livonian order of the Knights of the Sword (*Fratres militiae Christi de Livonia*), which was founded in 1202 by the Cistercian monk Theoderich, put itself under the command of the bishop of Riga. This order, which was wholly concentrated on fighting the pagans in the wider Baltic area and played a large part in the subjugation of Semigallia, Courland, Estonia, and the island of Oesel, adopted the rule of the Templars. In doing so it placed itself in a tradition that reached back to the first decades of the twelfth century, to the genesis of the orders of knighthood in the Holy Land, and which was in essence laid down by the great Cistercian abbot Bernard of Clairvaux, the most important initiator of the Second Crusade. Among the orders of knighthood newly come into existence in the Baltic area, there was also the Knights of Christ of Dobrin; this order was founded in 1228 by Bishop Christian of Prussia, formerly also a Cistercian abbot, together with the Polish Duke Conrad of Mazovia and the bishop of Plock. Alongside these new orders of knighthood the Templars and Hospitallers, which had both come into existence in the Holy Land, also participated in conquering the pagans of the Baltic area; in doing so they were able to draw on their settlements and rich possessions in Western Europe, which had rapidly expanded in the mean time. In Pomerelia even the knights of the order of Calatrava, which had originated in a Cistercian monastery, founded a settlement. Thus one of the orders of knighthood whose main aim was the reconquest of the Spanish peninsula for Christianity took a part, though admittedly a small one, in the conquest of pagan lands in the north-east of Europe.

Much the most effective in this were the Brothers of St Mary's Hospital of the Germans in Jerusalem (*Fratres hospitalis sancte Marie Theutonicorum Ierusolimitanorum*), who for short also called themselves the Teutonic Order (*Ordo Theutonicorum*). The prehistory of the order probably reaches back to a hospital founded in Jerusalem by some Germans as early as 1143, around which there gathered a brotherhood of lay people to cater for the mainly German hospital inmates. At any rate it confirmed its independent development with the foundation of a camp hospital near Acre by merchants from Lübeck and Bremen in 1189 or 1190, i.e. at the time of the Third Crusade. In the following years it seems to have been actively promoted by German nobles and princes, until in 1198 it chose as one of its duties the fight against the pagans, and in 1199 it was raised by Innocent III to an order of knighthood on the model of the Templars. The order soon acquired many establishments in Palestine, Armenia, Cyprus, Greece, Italy, Spain, and France as well as in Germany. Besides its main tasks in Palestine and Syria, in 1211 the Teutonic Order took over the protection of the region of Burzenland in Transylvania against the pagan Cumans, on the basis of a contract with the Hungarian King Andrew II. In 1225, however, the king drove the order out by

military force because of its attempts at political independence.
Only a few months later, Duke Conrad of Mazovia offered the
Teutonic Order a new field of action against the pagan Prussians. No doubt remembering his experiences in Burzenland,
the grand master of the order, Hermann of Salza (1209–39),
had himself granted far-reaching privileges by the Emperor
Frederick II in the Golden Bull of Rimini of March 1226. This
secured for the Teutonic Order, in the area offered by the Polish
duke and in the regions which were still to be conquered from
the pagans, power as independent as that which the princes
of the empire had meanwhile obtained. When Frederick II's
crusade ended (1228–9), the grand master began the further
securing and realization of this ambitious plan, so that in the
mean time the Polish duke felt bound to found a new order of
knighthood; this, like the Knights of Christ mentioned above,
was incorporated into the Teutonic Order only a few years
later (1235 and 1237). Not until 1234, when the order had
already gained its first successes in battles on the far side of the
Vistula, did Hermann of Salza reach an agreement with the
papal Curia about the legal position of the Teutonic Order in
the countries to be conquered.

    The Teutonic Order was not able to complete the conquest
of Prussia until 1283, with the strong support of crusaders
mainly from Germany and Poland, and only after fighting
numerous wars and suppressing dangerous rebellions (1242–9,
1260–74). Lithuania continued to escape the expansion of the
order, and survived as a pagan principality. Estonia remained
under Danish government until 1346. The grand master's
change of residence from Acre to Venice (1291), and from the
Adriatic merchant city to Marienburg in 1309, marks the retreat of the Teutonic Order from its original centre in the
Holy Land and the eastern Mediterranean and its enforced
concentration on the development of a state of its own in north-
east central Europe, where, however, towards the end of the
thirteenth century the limits of its expansion had been reached.

3

The Creation of New Kingdoms and Forms of Lordship

[a] KINGDOMS AND DUCHIES ON THE PERIPHERY OF EUROPE

As a result of the expansion of the West in the Mediterranean many new kingdoms and independent principalities of different sizes and types came into existence. One need only think of the kingdoms of Castile-Leon, Aragon-Catalonia and Portugal on the Iberian peninsula, the crusader states with the kingdom of Jerusalem, the new creations on the soil of the Byzantine empire conquered in 1204, and the Norman principalities in southern Italy and Sicily.

The Normans, emigrating in small groups from the north of France from the turn of the eleventh century, had succeeded in imposing themselves as a small governing class in the south of Italy and in Sicily, and it was their state-building more than any other that influenced the politics of the German emperors. This holds true already long before 1194, when the Norman kingdom was united with the empire under Henry VI, against the persistent opposition of the papacy. The papacy had had a supporter against the empire ever since 1059, when the Norman dukes had been legitimized as papal vassals for their conquests up to then on the mainland and for Sicily, which was then still under Islamic rule. The enfeoffment itself already passed over the legal claims of the Roman emperor. The papacy, however, had to make further concessions to the Norman dukes if it wanted to secure their support. Urban II (1088–99) had allowed independent powers in Church matters, even renouncing the appointment of a legate, to Duke Roger,

who led the conquest of the island of Sicily and there erected a
regime almost entirely free of aristocratic collaboration.

When by the end of the 1120s Roger's son Roger II (1101–
54) had succeeded in uniting the various Norman duchies in
his own hands by conquest or inheritance, he exploited the
outbreak of a papal schism and had himself crowned king in
Palermo on Christmas Day 1130, with the agreement of the
anti-pope Anacletus II, whom he supported. Roger II finally
compelled the grant of the royal crown as a papal fief from
the opposing pope, Innocent II, whom he defeated and took
prisoner near Monte Cassino in July 1139. As early as 1140
Roger II, in the Assizes of Ariano (*c.*30 kilometres east of Benevento) had a law-book put together for his thereby legally
based hereditary monarchy; this marked the resumption of
systematic legal codification in high medieval Europe. Taking
over rules of Roman law and the common law of the Norman-
French ruling class, as well as elements of Greek and Arabic
law, though to a lesser extent, the code reflects the heterogeneous composition of the population of the kingdom, which
also counted a considerable number of Jews. In a clever calculation of his advantage Roger II pursued a policy of tolerance
towards the Greek Orthodox Christians, towards the Muslims,
and also towards the Jews. By incorporating Byzantine and
Arab traditions, the monarch was able to stabilize his auto-
cratic form of government on the basis of an effective administration in which Arab civil servants also worked. The real
opponents of the kingdom were the Norman aristocrats on the
mainland, who had had wide independence under Roger's
predecessors. Their power was again openly demonstrated only
a few years after the death of the first Sicilian king. Under the
government of William I (1154–66) and even more during the
minority of his son William II, who died childless at the age of
only 36 in 1189, the nobility gained an at times decisive influence in the kingdom, even in Sicily.

In spite of signs of decay this hereditary kingdom, with its
key position in the Mediterranean, with the great wealth of
its cultivated lands and cities, and with the highly developed
abilities of its population, belonging to different cultures and
religions, offered an attractive inheritance to be fought over

with might and main; and it was no accident that the competition between empire and papacy concentrated on it for decades. After long conflicts, mainly directed against the aristocracy, Frederick II recovered and strengthened the centralizing roots of the Sicilian monarchy. He tried to impose the forms of government forced through there on imperial Italy too. In this, however, he finally ran aground on the resistance of the papacy and the anti-imperial city communes. Now and again in the Staufen period the southern example of the 'civil servant state' may have had an influence beyond the Alps in the German empire, but on the whole the attempts at governmental and institutional consolidation there were independent of this model.

Among the European realms the Anglo-Norman kingdom, founded by Duke William of Normandy in 1066, showed the most similarities to the Norman–Staufen monarchy. One of the most important reasons for the relative similarity is most probably the common home of the conquerors, who pushed forward into such different countries and who ascended to kingship in totally different ways. But in this respect the decisive fact was that both kingdoms were based on conquest. In contrast to south Italy and Sicily, a centralizing feudalism became the mainstay of royal power in the Anglo-Norman monarchy.

The rise of the Capetian kingdom from a rather provincial position in the Île-de-France to unchallenged power in France and finally to the equal of imperial authority in western Christendom was firmly based on the inner structure of royal government. From the reign of Philip II Augustus (1180–1223) at the latest, hereditary right in the royal succession was indisputable. With the relatively late take-over of the duchies and counties of the crown vassals—especially those of the English kings—the Capetians made use of the successes their predecessors had achieved in the acquisition of territories and in building up administrative institutions. In the crown domain Philip II started by instituting larger administrative districts (*baillages*, or later in the south *sénéchaussées*) which were headed by officials (*baillis* or *sénéchaux*), and subordinated to them were *prévôts* (*praepositi*). The efficiency of the royal administration, particularly in military matters, was thereby increased and a more effective control of the *prévôts* made easier. At the same time the monarchy secured itself a high income in money. The Capetians also enforced high reliefs for succession to crown fiefs. A large role was played by the cities, to which Philip II granted generous privileges primarily for fiscal reasons. In the course of the thirteenth century the monarchy also subjected the larger cities to stricter financial control. The money income, amongst other destinations, was used to pay officials, and was needed not least to recruit mercenaries, who were to supplement the limited and altogether insufficient army service obligations of the vassals.

In comparison to the south and west, constitutional development in north and east central Europe remained archaic in spite of the far-reaching changes which took place there as well. In Denmark, Poland, and Hungary, countries which in contrast to the duchy, later kingdom, of Bohemia lay outside the borders of the empire, this fact can be seen in the regulation of the succession to the throne. In Denmark the archaic military kingdom, which in peacetime left the king with little power, continued in operation until late in the twelfth century. Until the accession of King Valdemar I (1157-82) there were frequently three rival kings at the same time. In Poland Boleslav II had himself crowned king as the third of the Piast dynasty at Christmas 1076, but his successors had to renounce the royal title. The attempt of Duke Boleslav III (d. 1138) to secure the supremacy of the oldest of the Piast family over the other members endowed with principalities, by introducing a seniority rule, was a failure—even in the first generation there was heavy fighting for the post of senior. The splintering of Poland into several independent duchies (Greater Poland, Lesser Poland, Mazovia, and Silesia) thus begun, was continued by division among co-heirs. By 1163 the duchy of Silesia had split into the duchies of Upper and Lower Silesia; in 1248 the duchies of Breslau, Liegnitz, and Glogau came into existence in Lower Silesia. In Hungary, after fighting lasting decades within the Arpad royal family, unity was restored, after thirty years of division, in the reign of Ladislas I (1077-95). Awareness of the unity of the kingdom was also strengthened by myth-making around the figure of the first Hungarian king, Stephen (997-1038), who was canonized in

1083, but struggles for the throne broke out again and again later on. Nevertheless they were dammed up for the time being by the growing influence of the aristocracy and the Church.

Conflicts within the ruling families in these three kingdoms frequently offered the German kings and emperors the opportunity to intervene. Sometimes vassalage ties with the German rulers resulted from this. The frequent armed expeditions undertaken by the latter did not aim at conquering the country. On the other hand the kings of Hungary, and also of Denmark, directly influenced imperial politics, mainly at times of crisis in the German kingdom. The Byzantine imperial court, particularly under the Emperor Manuel I Comnenus (1143-80), tried to obtain decisive influence over Hungary, situated between the two empires, both by supporting pretenders to the throne and by military action, but without lasting success. An important reason for the hostile situation between Hungary and Byzantium was the south-western expansion begun by Ladislas I towards the Adriatic Sea. The cousin and successor of Ladislas, King Koloman (1095-1116), managed to incorporate Croatia and Dalmatia into the Hungarian kingdom; both countries lay at the crossing point of the interests of the Byzantine empire and the trading republic of Venice. The expansionary policy of the Arpad dynasty under King Andrew II (1205-35), which already under Andrew's brother and rival for many years King Emerich (1196-1203) had aimed at enforcing feudal sovereignty over the Balkan lands, had its climax in the attempt to win the imperial crown of Constantinople. The 'knightly king' Andrew, however, also failed in this attempt, despite the fact that mainly on this account he had taken part, at great cost and with a large army, in the unsuccessful Fifth Crusade (1217-18), which he then cut short at an early stage.

For the duchies and kingdoms of Denmark, Poland, and Hungary, themselves Christianized only towards the end of the tenth and the beginning of the eleventh centuries, the wars against the pagans and the missions closely connected with them were of extraordinarily high political importance. With his participation in the conquest of the pagan Wends along the south coast of the Baltic Sea, King Valdemar I initiated a far-reaching expansionary policy by the Danish kings. After

considerable successes, which in 1219 even led to the conquest
of Estonia, this phase of expansion was ended with the defeat
of King Valdemar II (1202–41) by north German dukes and
the cities of Bremen, Hamburg, and Lübeck at Bornhöved in
1227. The Polish Piast dynasty were denied long-lasting success
in their fight against the pagan Prussians. From the time of
Ladislas I, who was canonized in 1192, the Hungarian kings
had fought defensive wars against the attacks of various Turkic
peoples (Pechenegs, Uzes, Cumans), who, being mounted no-
mads, were difficult to bring under control. The Hungarian
kings only gained successes against the Cumans in the 1220s,
when they themselves were pressed hard by the Mongols and
suffered a severe defeat along with the Russians. In 1227 the
Cuman chief Barc submitted to the overlordship of the king of
Hungary, who had previously furthered the Dominican mission
among the western Cumans, and he had himself and 15,000
Cumans baptised.

The Mongol attack which King Bela IV (1235–70) had long
feared, and the aims and effects of which were generally underestimated in western Christendom, concentrated, after the conquest of the Russian duchies, on the kingdom of Hungary. The
campaign of the Mongols against the Poles also served this aim.
It ended with the disastrous defeat of Duke Henry II of Lower
Silesia at the battle of Liegnitz (9 April 1241), in which many
Germans fought at the side of the Piasts. Two days later the
Hungarian army was crushed by Batu Khan near Mohi. The
Mongols' pursuit of the fleeing King Bela IV caused further
devastation in Hungary. Because of the news of the death of
the Great Khan the Mongols gave up their aim, and thus freed
central and western Europe from a great danger for which it
was not prepared. In Hungary, it is believed, about one-half of
the population fell victim to the Mongols; the more densely
settled western areas of the kingdom, however, suffered less.
The Mongols left deep traces in eastern Europe, which reinforced the contrast between the development of central Europe and the regions further east in later centuries.

[b] CONSTITUTIONAL TRENDS

The expansion of the West in the Mediterranean area and
in eastern central Europe was accompanied in most western

kingdoms and principalities by political purposes and activities which went far beyond existing borders. The crusading movement in its early history and its various later forms gave the most important impetus for this and at the same time provided an essential justification. This was not only used for the wars against the pagans and the Muslims, but also for the campaigns against heretics and against Orthodox Byzantium, and was finally used by the papacy in the conflicts with the last Staufen rulers. The expansionary trends were accompanied by tendencies towards rounding off, towards the stricter organization and institutional consolidation of existing dominions. They showed themselves at very varying levels, in the building-up of administrative centres of local or regional range as well as in the institution of central offices and councils. These measures aimed at a more effective fulfilment of military, legal, and fiscal aims, on an official or authoritative legal basis. They were usually accompanied by attempts to strengthen the personal ties and service dues of the lay and often also of the ecclesiastical lords towards the kings or princes, for which feudal law offered a starting-point. Such trends, however, could only be exploited in the Anglo-Norman and Capetian kingdoms, though in different ways, with more or less success, and often after decades of struggle to strengthen the kingship, and without having thereby put an end to opposition, particularly that of the nobility. In other countries, in contrast, the dukes and high nobility, and partly also the bishops, with very similar methods maintained their positions to various extents *vis-à-vis* the kingdom, which again and again was decisively weakened by struggles for the succession to the throne; sometimes they even improved their position, so that they at least managed to enforce a right of consultation.

The political expansion, the sharpened competition between the traditional holders of power, and the enforcement of new forms of territorial government favoured the rise of social groups which up to then had had little political influence. Among them especially were those who were now more intensively used for military and administrative tasks. But not least in this complex interconnection of functions, in which economic changes also played an essential role, was the encouragement given to the creation of co-operative communal institutions. Long before the middle of the eleventh century greater urban centres developed in the Mediterranean countries. There, already before this period, several of them had a greater political range of action, especially the cities engaged in sea-borne trade. But only from the end of the eleventh century did they develop more solid forms of communal constitution, which were the precondition for lasting self-government and political independence.

Despite the usually less favourable economic framework and the far more slender foundations of urban tradition, the development of city communities in the northern countries began at almost the same time. But only in those areas where the power structure remained weak, and where at the same time a higher level of urbanization was reached, could the city communities in the twelfth and thirteenth centuries achieve greater political independence. Both conditions were present to an exceptional extent in imperial Italy, and in a lesser way also in the old settlement areas of the German empire. In contrast, even the bigger cities of southern Italy and Sicily, of the Iberian peninsula, and of France and England stood under the effective control of the princes or the kingdom. But the development of communities in most areas of southern, western, and central Europe also covered smaller urban and even rural and agricultural settlements, which none the less were able to take on more or less limited tasks of self-government. Not the least important function of this development was opening up new areas for settlement. In its varied forms and effects it clearly showed the far-reaching changes in the structure of power and society during the high Middle Ages. Urban, rural, and village communities in fact were only one manifestation, though politically the most important one, of those co-operative and corporative forces, now becoming effective on a wider basis, which had fundamental importance for later European history.

4

Population Increase, Settlement Density, and Economic Growth

[a] POPULATION INCREASE

The importance of population levels for government practice, economic conditions, and the living circumstances of most of the people is quite apparent. Unfortunately the history of the population of Europe in the high Middle Ages can only be determined very approximately, from few sources of only regional value as evidence, and from individual findings in settlement history. Nevertheless it is generally accepted that the period from the eleventh century to the end of the thirteenth represents the climax of European population expansion in the Middle Ages. This fact is all the more striking as from the beginning of the fourteenth century the population of large parts of western, central, and southern Europe stagnated, and from the middle of the same century even underwent a considerable decline—up to about one-third. In some regions, the population density of the high Middle Ages was not exceeded until the nineteenth century.

The scale of the medieval population expansion was apparently different in the various European areas. In the Mediterranean countries, where around the year 1000 a relatively high level had been reached, the figure is reckoned to have doubled at the most in three centuries, and the population figure for Italy at the end of the thirteenth century is calculated at seven to nine million. For the Slav countries and also Hungary, where the Mongol attacks in the second third of the thirteenth century were partly responsible for considerable losses, the increase, at c.50 per cent, is estimated at even less, from 9.5 to 13 million. For the west of central Europe, northern

Europe, and France, there are good reasons to assume a treb-
ling, from *c.*12 to *c.*36 million. Within the larger areas again
one has to reckon with varying growth rates, which especially
in the as yet unsettled areas led to increases from a low level at
a considerably higher rate of growth. For the country which
was later called Saxony, it has been estimated that the population increased tenfold between 1100 and 1300.

[*b*] EXPANSION AND MULTIPLICATION OF SETTLEMENTS

The increasing settlement density caused by the unusually high
population growth showed itself, with regional differences, in
the strong expansion of existing settlements and in the foundation and growth of numerous rural and urban centres, as well
as in the spread of agricultural exploitation even in regions
which up to then had only been sparsely settled. This increase
in the settled area can best be observed in the bigger towns. In
the Lombard metropolis of Milan the settled area of 133 hectares protected by the Roman city walls had been insufficient
since the tenth century. With the new walls begun in 1157 this
area grew by a further 100 hectares without being able to cope
with the subsequent increase in population, which reached
nearly 100,000 by 1300. For Piacenza, which was medium-sized
by the standards of imperial Italy, a doubling of the population
to 15,000 between the tenth and the late twelfth century can
reasonably be suggested; in the course of the thirteenth century
it grew again at around the same rate to *c.*30,000, the walled
area of 45 hectares being extended to 65 hectares around the
middle of the twelfth century and again to 75 hectares between
1218 and 1232. Such extensions of city walls, which were undertaken primarily for political and military reasons, became
numerous in the towns of imperial Italy from the middle of the
twelfth century, in French towns between about 1180 and 1250.
  Parallel to these processes, which to varying degrees and at
different rates also took place in other western and central
European countries during the twelfth and thirteenth centuries,
were the transformations of what up to then had been agricultural settlements into urban centres, generally walled towns,
and new foundations of fortified settlements. In imperial Italy,

however, only very few towns were founded after the middle of
the twelfth century (where a town is defined as an episcopal
city). New urban creations here, predominantly through the
initiative of larger city communes, mostly took the form of
numerous castle settlements (*castra* and *burgi*). They were concentrated in border areas disputed for territorial and political
reasons, and on otherwise geographically important communication centres. Only a few attained the status of *civitas*
(episcopal city). In France, similar processes manifested themselves in varying regional forms and at different times in the
burgi and *salvitates*, in the *villeneuves* and *bastides*. In contrast to
imperial Italy, which was exceptional in this respect, in France
they were initiated and furthered by secular or ecclesiastical
lords and by the kings. For most of these foundations it is
difficult to decide on the basis of their legal position or economic
development whether they should be called villages or towns.
This is also true for the *poblaciones* in central Spain. These settlements are a part of the resettlement of unsettled areas within
the context of the *reconquista*.

[c] EXPANSION AND IMPROVEMENT OF THE
AGRICULTURALLY EXPLOITED AREA

The resettlement of central Spain, in its range and results,
represents an extreme case in the settlement of south-western
and southern Europe. It can best be compared to the development of huge and thus far only thinly settled areas or
wildernesses in northern and eastern central Europe. In the
other old lands of Roman culture, which in contrast to the
Iberian peninsula had not been afflicted with centuries of fighting between Muslims and Christians, the reserves for settlement
were far more limited and relatively soon exhausted. Here, as
for example in the Po valley, the expansion of the agricultural
area was to a great extent only possible by draining swamps
and by creating terraces in hilly country. In Mediterranean
countries with dry summer months—especially Spain, the
south of France, and Italy—yield was also considerably increased in the twelfth and thirteenth centuries by the improvement of irrigation systems. The level of agrarian culture,

already high anyway, allowed only few large improvements in the lands around the Mediterranean.

In western and central Europe, on the other hand, not only could broad areas be developed more intensively, but there were also large areas of forest, grass, heath, and swamp available close to the old settlement areas into which agriculture and settlement could be expanded. From the eleventh to the thirteenth century these opportunities were exploited so intensively that, particularly in western continental Europe and the British Isles, by about 1300 even high uplands had been reached, posing great risks for grain-growing agriculture. With insufficient fertilization of poor soil, signs of exhaustion quickly appeared. On fertile soil, through the advance of the three-field system the yield of grain, the staple food of the time, could be increased considerably. In this the use of more effective agricultural implements, like the iron plough with mouldboard, and the harrow, helped a great deal. Tractive power was increased by using a collar for horses and a head-yoke for oxen. At the same time the faster and more enduring horse was increasingly used on peasant farms alongside oxen. Hence greater distances between the farm and the agricultural land became economically acceptable, and thus concentration in village settlements would have been favoured. Further progress in supplying the expanding population was made by growing protein-rich pulses.

The huge expansion of settlement and cultivation and the far-reaching clearance and reclamation of other marginal soils in western, central, and northern Europe during the high Middle Ages was, the results of recent research suggest, favoured by a long-term improvement in the climate. From about the end of the tenth century to the thirteenth, apparently, important preconditions for agricultural expansion over these large areas were created by higher temperatures, with generally warmer summers and milder winters, and on the whole decreased precipitation. For eastern Europe on the other hand more negative climatic conditions are posited. The decrease in rainfall should have made the drainage of marshes easier in the Mediterranean countries; at the same time the unusually strenuous efforts to improve irrigation gain particular significance. With the help of such measures, yields could be reached there which were very exceptional north of the Alps. Thus the scholarly and much-travelled Bishop Otto of Freising characterizes northern Italy around the middle of the twelfth century as a 'pleasure-garden' (*hortus deliciarum*): 'The land is irrigated by the Po . . . and other rivers, and because of the fertile soil and the mild climate it bears grain, wine, and oil in such quantities that it almost produces forests of fruit-bearing trees, especially chestnuts, figs, and olive-trees.' [3: xvii. 306 ff.].

Greater fertility in the Mediterranean countries contributed considerably to the fact that during the high Middle Ages far fewer famines occurred there than in northern areas, where they are reported particularly often in the eleventh and the first half of the twelfth century. North of the Alps harvest yields in cereals, which in these areas were irreplaceable as the staple diet, were on average hardly more than three times the seed sown. Harvests were also far more dependent on the weather. Loss of a great part of the harvest, which could also be severely damaged by wars and feuds, often quickly forced the population of the affected regions to eat their seed-corn. In this way a scarcity in one year could quickly create a period of famine. Means of transport and general traffic conditions, which meant that bulky goods could only be transported by ship, complicated the import of cereals into continental Europe from distant areas producing a surplus. Under these circumstances only one solution was left to the starving, to go themselves to those places where they could expect relief. In the extensive trade of the Mediterranean, on the other hand, cereals in large quantities had been transported since the eleventh century. Furthermore the city communes, especially in imperial Italy, from the twelfth century on took measures to secure the cereal supplies of their population.

In processing agricultural products water and windmills were used increasingly and with improved technique. The manifold possibilities of water as an energy source were vividly described at the beginning of the thirteenth century by a monk of the Cistercian monastery of Clairvaux: 'One of the arms of the river flows'—as was the case in many other Cistercian monasteries—'through numerous workshops of the abbey and is highly valued everywhere because of its good services . . . The water, regulated by walls, first plunges into the mill. It uses its power to grind the grain with the millstones and to separate bran from flour with a fine sieve ... Next to the mill are the fulling-mills. Useful earlier on for the monks' food, so it is now for their clothes ... The water alternately lifts and drops those mallets and hammers, or in other words wooden feet, as this word describes the jumping action of the fullers better. In this way it frees the fullers from hard work ... From there it goes to the tannery, where the necessary materials for the brothers' shoes are being prepared and where great industriousness is displayed ...' [11: 185, cols. 570ff.]. It was calculated that one of these mills actually replaced the work of forty people. Windmills were considerably improved from the eleventh/twelfth century by mounting the wheels and the free-moving works on to an axis. A 'machine' of this type, which up to then was only known in the West, was constructed for the first time in Syria during the First Crusade. In the thirteenth century, there were about 120 windmills in the country near the west Flemish town of Ypres.

[d] TRADE AND INDUSTRY

The close correlations between the politico-religious expansion of the Latin West and the broadening and deepening of trade between Orient and Occident have already been mentioned, as has the leading role played in Mediterranean trade by the Italian cities, especially Venice, Genoa, and Pisa, from the end of the eleventh century. Since the First Crusade they had had direct access to the trade routes from Asia. After the end of the Byzantine empire (1204) the Venetians in particular considerably increased their trading activities in the north-eastern Mediterranean area, which the competing city of Genoa succeeded in doing only later (after 1261). Via the Black Sea the Italians had access to the trade routes into southern Russia, with the main centre at Kiev, where trade routes from the west as far as Regensburg, from the north as far as Novgorod close to the Baltic, and from the east crossed. Seaborne trade was made much easier by the use of compasses. These had been used in western Europe by sailors and also miners since the twelfth century, and in the thirteenth were greatly improved, so that they were then much more precise than those which had been in use in China as early as the eleventh century.

Until the 1270s, when the first Genoese galleys made direct contact through the Straits of Gibraltar with the harbours of the North Sea, and especially with Bruges in Flanders, trade between the Mediterranean and continental Europe was completely dependent on the generally difficult overland route. The most important link between the Mediterranean trade and the north-eastern area, where Flanders and the Maas–Schelde region were from the eleventh century the most highly developed industrial areas, led along the river valleys of the Rhône, Saône, and Maas. Commerce between northern Italy and France, as well as with the German empire, which increased greatly from the twelfth century, went over the various passes of the Alps.

After the middle of the twelfth century a large part of the commerce between the Mediterranean countries and northern Europe was transacted at the fairs of Champagne. From the last quarter of the same century merchants from northern and central Italy were active there. These fairs, which in the mid thirteenth century became the centre of the European money and credit business, owed their immense success to the protection of the counts of Champagne and later to the safe conduct of the French kings, and to an effective control by commercial judges. The most important objects traded at these fairs were the various kinds of cloth originating mainly from England, Flanders, and northern France; particularly precious textiles made from silk, spices, sugar, alum, laqueurs, and dyes were mainly sold by Italian merchants, who for their part chiefly took back cloth into the Mediterranean trade. Merchants from neighbouring countries to the east, i.e. especially from the German-speaking lands, were attracted to this, the turntable of world trade at the time.

In comparison to the clearly dominant south–north axis of long-distance trade, the exchange of goods between north-western and north-eastern Europe gained in prominence only with the beginning of German settlement in the east and the urbanization connected with it. Because of this northern Germany acquired a mediating role. The high level of trade and business in north-western Europe offered favourable conditions for this bridge-building as far as Russia.

The far-reaching changes which can be observed in European trade from the eleventh century mainly originated in the expansion of Mediterranean trade and in the rapidly proceeding urbanization which from the same period also occurred outside the Mediterranean countries and beyond the borders of the old Roman empire; new markets in economically more developed countries were thereby opened up for the large-scale exchange of goods. The growing or newly founded towns, as well as the pre-urban market-places, gave long-distance trade a strong structure of markets on which the local or even regional exchange of goods was concentrated. A very important consequence was that trade, which in Latin Christian western Europe had for centuries been restricted to luxury goods and therefore had been directed only to the needs of small, politically dominant groups, was expanded to distribute articles which were needed and bought by wider classes of the population, especially by town-dwellers. Long-distance trade was now more and more determined by industrial production, originating mainly in the towns. It gained a new dimension in the interplay between the import of raw materials for industrial processing and the export of finished products. Hence the closeness or even identity between the merchant's and craftsman's professions: the same man both produced the goods and participated in trade with them or the raw materials necessary to produce them.

Short- and long-distance trade as well as the growth of towns promoted craft specialization. It started, however, from very different levels in different local and cultural areas. In the bigger cities of the Mediterranean as early as the eleventh century it reached far beyond the primitive forms of division of labour between baker, butcher, smith, potter, weaver, furrier, and so on. But in the smaller towns, especially in new settlement areas in the east, this level was not even generally exceeded by the end of the thirteenth century. In both places division of labour reached its highest level in the big export businesses. As a model craft export town one could cite the Spanish city of Cordoba, which already in Islamic times was famous for its leatherwork, so that for example in Trier in the thirteenth century the equivalent craftsmen were called 'corduanarii' (cordwainers); or the Tuscan city of Lucca, which from the middle of the twelfth century developed as a well-known centre of the silk industry. Such export businesses in general developed in several places and towns of an area at the same time. This for example held true for woollen cloth production in Flanders, which developed far beyond the county, and also in England. In many towns of northern Italy and Tuscany the production of cotton cloth and 'Barchent' (cotton flannel, from the Arabic word *barrakan*) gained in importance from the second half of the twelfth century.

In the twelfth and thirteenth centuries many innovations were tried out and applied in industrial technique. Important technical innovations were introduced in architecture, as the major Gothic cathedrals bear witness to the present day. The great technical achievement in the rapid construction of Chartres cathedral, which introduced the High Gothic manner, is comparable to the building of the Pyramids or the Roman viaducts [no. 292]. From the turn of the thirteenth century, rationalization of operations—both standardization of structural parts and prefabrication of building materials—in great Gothic buildings moved on quickly. This also became apparent in the preparation of plans to scale, so that here, too, written records proliferated and the transfer of designs and prototypes was encouraged. The building boom of the high Middle Ages, which still dominates the face of a large number of old European cities, gave the architects a high reputation which was increasingly also based on their distinction as designers, and which they manifested in their artistic self-expression. Lombard master masons, who already in the early Middle Ages worked as experts in continental Europe, may even have influenced the spread of brick building in northern Europe from the middle of the twelfth century. As the production of bricks presupposed a high degree of division of labour and keeping of stores this process was also influenced by the advance of the money economy.

[*e*] THE DEVELOPMENT OF THE MONEY ECONOMY

Regional variations in the level of development of trade and industry, and thus of the division of labour and of professional specialization, are reflected in the monetary system and the money economy. While in the Roman Christian West gold currency had played no role since the early Middle Ages, in the Byzantine and Muslim Mediterranean it remained predominant, or at least in existence. This was doubtless an expression of the economic inferiority of the Christian West. Here only silver was still used as the basis of a money economy which had anyway in many regions been almost completely pushed out. The old urbanized country of imperial Italy and southern France in the tenth and eleventh centuries had a clear advantage over the other countries of Christian western Europe, of which the areas east of the Rhine and even more those east of the Elbe and Saale were dominated by a natural economy. In spite of the great progress which was achieved in the following period north of the Alps, imperial Italy until the end of the thirteenth century and even beyond was the most highly developed country from the point of view of a money economy, and by then even led the Mediterranean region in this respect. The change to gold coinage should be seen against this background; this was introduced, after some earlier attempts, around the middle of the thirteenth century by the city communes of Florence and Genoa (1250 and 1252). In doing so they took over the model of the gold 'augustal', coined supposedly for prestige reasons on the pattern of ancient imperial coins by the Emperor Frederick II since 1231—i e. in connection with the Constitutions of Melfi. The florin was imitated as early as 1266 by the French king, though initially with little success. Later than in other European countries it became the leading currency in Germany too, in the middle of the fourteenth century. The spread of high-value gold coins in western Europe offered a favourable means of payment especially for long-distance trade, as meanwhile in most countries silver coins had constantly deteriorated through declining silver content—the sterling of the English kings after the mid twelfth century being an exception.

Italian merchants and businessmen were the first to develop modern forms of trade organization and credit systems. Those great financiers from inland cities like Siena, Florence, and Piacenza, who in general were excluded from sea-borne trade, from the thirteenth century used their financial resources for credit transactions with ecclesiastical and secular lords. The rich citizens of Arras (Artois) acted in the same way, though more restricted to northern France and Flanders. From about the middle of the thirteenth century in the towns of western central Europe money-changers from Piedmont ('Lombards') and south-west France ('Cahorsins') appeared, who, with special permission and with a great financial return to the lords of the towns, carried on small loan businesses. These Christian 'usurers' competed with the Jews.

5

Poverty, Penitence, and Heresy

[a] POVERTY AND WELFARE

The overall economic upturn, the expansion and intensification of agriculture, the increasing specialization of craft production, the advance of money into the everyday life of wider classes of the population, the progressive urbanization, and the increase in population which was connected with these processes between the middle of the eleventh and the second half of the thirteenth century, by no means had a positive effect on all population groups and classes at all times. Although greater geographical mobility could open up new opportunities for broader population groups, these were often attended by high risks. It must not be forgotten that departure from the home region and the usual environment was often enough caused by a real emergency. For people without means, life in a foreign country was fraught with immense effort and danger. Building up a new existence, even in neighbouring cities or in developing new lands, was often connected with unpredictable hardships, changing economic conditions and supply difficulties, and with physical threats. In addition, traditional social securities in the circle of one's own family, relatives, and further manorial ties— such as the *familia*—fell away in the foreign country, and had to be created afresh.

Supply difficulties in times of famine and high living costs only made widely apparent and generally obvious the widespread destitution in the towns, where, simply because of enormously increased immigration, the traditional forms of alms-giving were no longer sufficient. The crusade-preacher and cardinal Jacques de Vitry (d. 1254), who was acquainted with the East as well as the West, defined the poor (*pauperes*) as those who earn their living working with their hands, without thereby being able to supply more than their daily food. The *pauperes* came to be virtually at home in the larger industrial towns. The weaving trade especially, in which the percentage of dependent labourers was high because of its particularly well-developed division of labour, brought into the towns many people who could not save out of their wages for famines or times of scarcity. These and other manual and paid workers, in contrast to the craft masters, could not unite in guilds and other brotherhoods and therefore could not safeguard themselves against emergencies. But this often also affected the restless intellectual élite which since the beginning of the twelfth century had studied and taught at the new intellectual centres. Thus Arnold of Brescia, who after the departure of Abelard wanted to continue his master's school, suffered so much from poverty together with his pupils that they had to go from house to house begging for alms.

New efforts were made to ease material poverty, from the end of the eleventh century, mainly in the centres of social change—along the trade and pilgrimage roads, and in the towns. The merchant and craft guilds, organized like brotherhoods, in their religious and charitable aspect aspired to mutual support for their members, especially in times of real need. The new and rising hospital fraternities and also the knightly orders primarily took on the task of supporting pilgrims and caring for the sick. At the same time the regular canons also furthered the development of hospitals. Even the older Benedictine monasteries renewed and strengthened their activities in this field in the twelfth and thirteenth centuries. Members of the urban ruling classes also participated in the form of brotherhoods in extending hospitals caring for the poor and sick, to the point of founding leper houses.

[*b*] FOLLOWING CHRIST IN VOLUNTARY POVERTY

Against the social background of mass poverty, poverty voluntarily accepted for religious reasons gained a new emphasis. In Benedictine monasticism it was kept as a norm, although in reality the monks lived a life of material security in the old, generally rich monasteries. After some earlier attempts in Italy the radical way of life in imitation of Christ gained towards the end of the eleventh and the beginning of the twelfth century a new fascination, unknown up to then in the Middle Ages, especially among clerics and lay people in France. The movement, spread by hermits and wandering preachers, led to new forms of monastic life; but with them were also interwoven sharply anticlerical and even heretical ideas and behaviour.

The borderline between the tendencies, however, is hard to draw, as the concept of heresy, which naturally depends on the contemporary attitudes of the church, underwent considerable changes during the papal reform around the middle of the eleventh century and was controversial between supporters and opponents of the reform. These points were less important for basic theological principles than those raised again by the learned Berengar of Tours (*c*.1000–88) in his doctrine of the sacrament. But the link between Church attitudes and the concept of heresy was at its most manifest in the response to those radical supporters of Church reform, later collectively known as *Pataria*, who after 1057 took action, sometimes with violence, against the simoniacal and generally also married higher clergy of the Lombard metropolis of Milan, and not long afterwards in other Lombardy towns as well. In these battles they long found numerous followers among the laity, not least among the urban lower classes. The opponents of reform abused the Patarenes as heretics, but the Roman Curia supported them at least from the beginning of the 1060s. The knightly leader of the *Pataria* of Milan, Erlembald, even received St Peter's banner from Pope Alexander II around 1064. With the help of the *Pataria* the Gregorian papacy was able to enforce its religious and political aims in Milan even against King Henry IV. After the violent death of Erlembald (1075) Gregory VII declared him a martyr. Two years later the same pope used his influence in favour of a priest who had previously been sentenced and then burnt as a heretic by the bishop of Cambrai. To begin with he had been accused of dogmatic deviations, but had defended himself successfully. His condemnation only followed when he refused Holy Communion from the accusers, whom he thought to be all simoniacs. Gregory VII's subsequent judgement was the complete opposite: for him the true heretics were the clerical accusers.

[c] WANDERING PREACHERS AND HERETICS

The Gregorian papacy's early criticism of the opponents of reform was continued and partly intensified later by the wandering preachers and their supporters. After enforcing its main demands the papacy was once again more open to the interests of clerical office-holders. The bishops and other prelates suspected heretical ideas in the 'true poor of Christ' (*veri pauperes Christi*) all the more as they also deviated in their way of life from current norms, and in this, and in their sharp reproaches against the secularized clerics, found great resonance among the population. In close contact with the theologically uneducated people, the wandering preachers, who in general were clerics or monks themselves, were dependent on great simplifications of theological ideas. Thus their teaching struck a chord among their supporters which made it easy to brand these thoughts as heterodox. On the whole, however, only a few heretics and founders of sects are known from the first half of the twelfth century. Most of them were active in France; there were only a very few in the west of the German empire.

In this tradition of poverty and criticism of the church is to be numbered Arnold of Brescia (d. 1155). In his northern Italian home town, the then provost of a foundation for canons came into conflict with his bishop when he supported the demand of the urban population, probably still influenced by the *Pataria*, for the reform of the local clergy. A complaint made on these grounds to Pope Innocent II forced him to flee. He went to Paris, and there became a pupil of Abelard. The opposition of Bernard of Clairvaux, who in 1140 had enforced the condemnation of Abelard's teaching, forced Arnold, who wanted to continue Abelard's school, to flee again. He was welcomed in Zürich. After a reconciliation with the papal Curia he went to Rome. There he took part in the rebellion of the Roman commune, which had begun with the renewal of the Senate in 1144, against the papal lord of the city and friend of Bernard of Clairvaux, Pope Eugenius III. In these controversies Arnold's support for the reform of the Church in head and members created an explosive political effect. He reproached the popes with having failed in their true task as pastors, and maintained that they had therefore lost their authority; and they were just as little entitled to the secular lordship of the city of Rome. He called the college of cardinals a den of thieves. Arnold was captured and killed with the support of Frederick I during his first Italian campaign; his corpse was burnt and the ashes scattered over the Tiber to wipe out all memory of him. In spite of this a sect formed out of his circle of supporters, who, under the name 'Arnoldists', were mentioned in the first anti-heretic law of 1184.

In the third quarter of the twelfth century Ugo Spero from Piacenza also founded a sect. Ugo's anticlerical attitude, which was an important motive for his dogmatic deductions, had a concrete political background in a court case which he had had against the monastery of Santa Giulia in Brescia over important rights of toll. This consul, judge, rich landowner, and merchant, trained as a jurist at Bologna, as a judge of the imperial court during the 1160s stood in close contact with Barbarossa's court when the latter himself was proceeding against the papacy of Alexander III.

[d] THE CATHARS

These sects were quite narrowly regional, and their founders were, probably without exception, unconnected with each other. But from the 1140s onwards, there arose, in areas of ancient Western European culture, a heresy which took only a few years to spread across France and the west of the German empire: the Cathars ('the pure'). In their way of life the leaders of this sect, whose members also called themselves 'Christ's poor', were like the wandering preachers and the members of the Western European poverty movement. However, they had from the first a dualistic system of belief in which they differed strongly from Catholic dogma. Their beliefs, in basic form, were established in Bulgaria two hundred years before, when the priest Bogumil found his first followers. The spread of this sect in western Europe was furthered by the persecution of the Bogomils in the Byzantine empire. In their mission they simultaneously erected the basic structure of a Church organization of their own: they had bishops of their own, and chosen people, and also trained religious teachers. Even within the leading group there were women, who on the whole were represented in large numbers in the heretical anti-Church. It quickly gained many followers from all classes of the population: nobles, clerics, monks and nuns, peasants, and not least, weavers. They had different names in different countries: in Germany 'Cathars', in France 'texerant ab usu texendi', i.e. weavers, and in Italy they were usually called 'Patareni' in connection with the originally orthodox *Pataria*.

The initially diffuse dogma of the Cathar Church, which at an early stage founded numerous bishoprics particularly in the south of France, was altered and sharpened from the late 1160s according to a radical dualistic philosophy. With this dogmatization the importance of the religious life for the masses of believers retreated into the background. The 'perfect ones' relieved from their religious duties the other believers, who could not or did not wish to follow the strict ascetic norms. It was possible to unburden one's conscience by rich donations. The Cathar Church, which demanded the entire property of the 'perfect ones' when entering, gradually thus became a wealthy church. Particularly in the south of France, the Cathars early received political support from the high nobility. There Counts Raymond of Toulouse (1194–1222) and Raymond-Roger of Foix (1188–1223) were their most important protectors. In this way they were also pulled into political controversies. Other nobles of Provence hoped by supporting the Cathars to improve the basis of their power at the expense of the Catholic churches and monasteries.

The persecutions which reached their height in the south of France between 1209 and 1229 in close connection with territorial and political interests did not, however, lead to a complete eradication of Catharism, but at least they brought its expansion to a standstill, and finally isolated it. In northern Italy the Cathars were favoured even after 1229 by city communes and by the nobility, who also mainly lived in the towns. The papal Inquisition gained only a few successes against the resistance of the cities and the early city lordships. Pavia, Piacenza, Lodi, and Brescia were looked on as safe places of refuge by the persecuted heretics of the Languedoc. In the first half of the thirteenth century under the pressure of persecution the institutional Cathar Church brought itself closer to a 'middle-class religion'. After this the social level of the Cathars fell, and their Church organization decayed after the late thirteenth century even in Italy.

[*e*] THE WALDENSIANS AND OTHER COMMUNITIES CLOSE TO HERESY

While the Cathars from their first arrival in western Europe appeared as an organized anti-Church, the Waldensians, later often mentioned with them, were still completely coloured by the personality of their founder, the Lyons merchant Peter Waldo (d. before 1218). Because of the social position of their founder they showed great similarity to the Speronists, who at the turn of the thirteenth century were almost completely accepted into the community of the Waldensians, as probably were the Arnoldists. In their social and religious motivation they are best compared with the *Humiliati*, with whom they had a lot in common in their relationship to the Catholic hierarchy and to Innocent III. The *Humiliati* ('the humble ones'), who were based mainly in the north Italian cities and were possibly connected with the *Pataria* movement, led their evangelical life, which they spent mainly in weaving, within their families and other fixed social forms. They rejected the usury and oath-swearing common in the everyday life of the Italian communes. At the third Lateran council of 1179 their request for permission to preach in public was rejected. As they did not give way to this prohibition, they were included as heretics in the anti-heretic legislation of Pope Lucius III and Frederick I in 1184. Pope Innocent III at the beginning of his pontificate successfully reincorporated a part of the *Humiliati* into the Church. In 1201 he granted the *Humiliati* who were living communally a fixed status in which they received the rank of an order, separated into clerics and lay people. During their Sunday assemblies they were even allowed to preach, with certain restrictions.

Around the middle of the 1170s Peter Waldo, a rich merchant from the Rhône valley metropolis of Lyons, was moved to change his life radically by hearing the *chanson* of St Alexius—which describes, according to the fifth-century legend, the withdrawal from the world and voluntary acceptance of poverty of a patrician Roman. He had himself instructed in the Bible, which he himself could not read in the Latin version then available; he then renounced his property in favour of the poor, left his family, and together with some companions worked as a poor preacher. In their sermons they opposed the Cathars and their church, which meanwhile had become rich, but at the same time they joined them in criticism of the Catholic clergy. They hoped to be able to overcome the resistance from the local clergy which this created by asking Pope Alexander III at the Lateran council of 1179 for permission to preach. As the theologically untrained laymen could not defend themselves against the cleverly phrased trick questions of the theologians, they gained only mockery and scorn. In spite of the prohibition then pronounced, they resumed their lay sermons, in which they addressed Christians and heretics in the streets and squares of towns and villages. They taught their listeners Holy Writ in their native language, and called for repentance and conversion. Following this, in the heresy edict of 1184 they were declared heretical in close connection with the *Humiliati*, as 'the Poor of Lyons', although Waldo and his followers had hitherto been orthodox. Out of the opposition to the Church hierarchy that this brought about, dogmatic deviations later developed. These were inflamed mainly by the different position of the laity, and not least among them by the position of women, who also preached. In spite of this, the distinction between them and the Cathars in matters of belief remained. The Waldensians and Cathars were most widespread in the south of France and northern Italy, i.e. in urbanized areas.

Even during the founder's lifetime the Waldensian movement split into the Poor of Lombardy, who on their side had taken in numbers of *Humiliati*, and the Poor of Lyons. The main issue in this division, which also affected the German Waldensians, seems to have been whether all wandering preachers should renounce all property and earnings from manual work, and only live off begging, or whether, like the *Humiliati*, they could also earn their living in 'working communities'. Further, the Poor of Lombardy held the opinion that their supporters could dissolve marriages only in exceptional cases and with mutual consent. As with the north Italian *Humiliati*, Pope Innocent III in the first decade of the thirteenth century managed to extract individual groups out of the Waldensian movement.

After the Waldensian groups leaning towards orthodoxy had split off, the remaining communities, which had now expanded into Germany and eastern central Europe, were subjected all the more to persecution and inquisition. In the process the supra-regional organization of the Waldensian communities remained underdeveloped in comparison with the Cathars; none the less a clear tendency towards ecclesiastical institutionalization can be discerned. Women were more and more rejected as ecclesiastical office-holders. From the later thirteenth century the Waldensians were made up mainly of craftsmen and members of the lower classes, and so they increasingly lost contact with the urban ruling classes. They were only able to survive as splinter groups in remote areas.

The Béguines and Beghards are also to be included with the poverty and penitence movement of the Middle Ages in its many and various manifestations. Among them too the number of women, the Béguines, was much higher right from the start than that of the men. The area of origin of the Béguines, whose name is etymologically unexplained, is believed to be in the bishopric of Liège and the duchy of Brabant. By the beginning of the thirteenth century, they had spread to France, and into other regions of the German empire. They were also active in Italy under the name of *Bizzoche*. Through the mediation of Jacques de Vitry in 1216 Pope Honorius III gave them oral permission to live together under the vow of poverty and chastity. Their settlements were mainly in larger towns, where, as in rural settlements, the presence of Béguines and Beghards living alone can also be established. They often dedicated themselves to the care of the sick in hospitals and leper colonies. Otherwise, contrasting with the laity in their grey clothes, they earned their living by manual work, generally in the textile crafts, or by begging. In the thirteenth century many members of the rural nobility and the urban upper classes belonged to them. Pastoral care was often taken over by the mendicant orders, with which their convents were closely connected in many towns. In spite of this, again and again they fell under suspicion of heresy.

6

The Papacy, the Church,
and Monasticism

---

[a] THE PAPACY AND THE OFFICIAL CHURCH

In the more than two centuries under consideration here, the Roman Church expanded very widely. At the same time it radically changed its evaluation of itself, its inner structure, its effectiveness, and its position in the world. The strongest motor of change was the desire of the reforming papacy to push back the influence of the laity on the Church in general and on individual churches and monasteries in particular. This led to the fight against the investiture of clerics by laymen, and struck at the heart of the relationship between ecclesiastical and secular authority, clergy and laity. Given the close ties between the Church and secular government—as laid down in late antiquity, deepened throughout western Europe in Carolingian times, and strengthened in the following period—a new ordering of this relationship was bound to affect the whole of political and social life. With this was bound up the struggle for clerical celibacy, as married priests, in the opinion of the reformers, offended against the neat separation of clergy and laity; they necessarily constituted an embarrassment to the special position and the pre-eminence of priests.

On the other hand, alongside the noblemen, the kings, who until then possessed a spiritual status through their anointment and consecration, were demoted to mere laymen. By undermining the sacral character of kingship, the pattern for which had been set in the ancient Roman empire and which had been expressed in exemplary fashion by the priest-kings of the Old Testament, the Church reformers also attacked the kingship's independent claims to spiritual legitimation and function. The fundamental conflict did not just concern the hard and varied politico-religious controversies over the assignment of clerical and secular power, for which the phrase 'investiture conflict' is only shorthand. It was rather about a stricter limitation of the concept of the Church to functionaries of the official Church and holders of the priestly office, who were thereby distanced from the masses of lay believers. The introduction of the rood-screen, which in many churches from the late twelfth century marked the choir reserved for priests and monks and screened them from the rest of the church, is only a symptom of this. In the churches of the mendicant orders, who built their churches according to their ideal of poverty and preaching, the screen was significantly not adopted.

The change can be seen most clearly at the top of the official Church, in the papacy. Shortly before the middle of the eleventh century it was still in the hands of rival Roman noble families, whose rule of the Roman see was only decisively pushed back by the intervention of the Emperor Henry III (1046). Less than three decades later the former monk Hildebrand, Pope Gregory VII, from a non-noble family, in his twenty-seven guiding principles—the *Dictatus Papae* of *c.*1075— demanded the right to depose the emperor. Soon afterwards (1076), the same pope, who in the same source had declared the pope to be 'unquestionably holy', exercised this right against King Henry IV, the son of Henry III. Pope Gregory VII at times retained his own mercenary army, which as the *militia sancti Petri* was to be completely at his disposal for the aims of the papal see. A short time later the papacy succeeded in mobilizing the military potential of Western Europe for the Crusades. At the beginning of the thirteenth century the highly educated Pope Innocent III, of comital family, who had studied theology at Paris and law at Bologna, demanded 'the fullness of power' (*plenitudo potestatis*) over the whole earth for the successor of Peter and the vicar of Christ. Though this primarily referred to spiritual power, nevertheless the holders of worldly power, among whom Innocent III as lord of the patrimony of St Peter counted himself, should also be subject to the papal power of instruction. In his role as *arbiter mundi* (judge of the world), this spiritual monarch also intervened decisively in the struggle over the German throne. His successor of the same name had the Emperor Frederick II deposed at the Council of Lyons on 17 July 1245. In the final stage of the fight against the last Staufen the papal Curia came more and more under French influence, and with this the decline in the universal position of the papacy became obvious.

The pope's claim to the leading role in the world was based on the centralism of an institutional Church. This had aimed at the enforcement of papal primacy since the very beginning of the reformed papacy under Leo IX (1048–54). The necessity of strengthening the papal supremacy over against the patriarchs, the archbishops, and the bishops derived from the wish for reform; for the struggle against simony and married priests (Nicolaiteans), which the reformers considered unavoidable for the freedom of the Church and the salvation of the souls of all believers, could only be carried on with the expectation of success against the numerous regional oppositions if it could be based on effective papal powers and a strong papacy. For the first time in the long history of the Church, canon law, the study of ecclesiastical rights, was furthered by the popes and their close counsellors. This development, beginning with the reformed papacy, reached its first climax in the private work of Master Gratian, who, a member of an order of hermits—the Camaldulensians—finished his critical collection of the canons (*Concordantia Discordantium Canonum*) in a monastery in Bologna around 1140, i.e. at about the time of the enactment of the Assizes of Ariano by King Roger II. As the *Decretum Gratiani* it became the most important basis of official Church law. About two decades later, in Alexander III (1159–81) a great promoter of Church law ascended the papal throne, even if he might not, as was previously thought, have worked as a legal scholar in Bologna and himself have written important theological works. From then on, for a long while it was predominantly lawyers who reached the highest Church office.

With the legal formalization of the Church, and especially with the enforcement of papal supremacy, there was bound up a tendency towards unification within the Roman Church. It expressed itself in radical form as early as 1054 in the behaviour of the papal legates, and especially of Humbert of Silva Candida, towards the Patriarch Michael Cerularius of Constantinople. The confrontation, partly brought about by the personalities of the two negotiators, played a significant part in bringing about the schism between the Western and Eastern Churches. The attempts of the reformed papacy to suppress the traditional Ambrosian ritual in the province of Milan, which based on this its independence towards Rome, and the Mozarabic liturgy in the Iberian peninsula, are also significant. After the pushing back of lay investiture, and especially from the time of Innocent IV (1243–54), the popes often made use of the right to appoint and depose bishops, which Gregory VII in the *Dictatus Papae* reserved solely to the popes, in such a way that they even circumvented the cathedral chapters' right of election. An effective method of enforcing papal aims on regional powers and office-holders proved to be the institution of legates, which the popes from the middle of the eleventh century used to an extent previously unknown, and which they once again expanded in their fight against the Staufen in the second quarter of the thirteenth century. The mendicant orders, the Franciscans and Dominicans, which came into existence in the first decades of the thirteenth century, were a further support for the universal position of the papacy. The Inquisition, formalized as an established and permanent institution by Innocent IV in 1252, and in which, contrasting with earlier instructions, torture of the accused was permitted, was also run centrally by the papal Curia.

The rise of the papacy from dependence on the Roman nobility to the climax of its effectiveness in the thirteenth century was accompanied by the development of new institutions which have remained influential in the Roman Church until today. One such is the college of cardinals, which during the second half of the eleventh century was given firmer organization. In the papal election decree of the reform council of 1059 it had had assigned to it very important powers in papal elections, which in this way were to a great extent withdrawn from the influence of the German king and the Romans. The third Lateran council in 1179 decided that a majority of two-thirds in the college of cardinals is necessary for a valid papal election, a regulation essentially still valid today. From the second quarter of the twelfth century the development of the administrative organization, which had existed since the beginning of the reforming papacy, became more marked at

the papal court, which, simply because of its frequent absences
from the city of Rome, had to release itself from its earlier
anchoring in the city. As a result of its increasing prestige
and centralization, the papacy acquired many new duties, in
particular in the judicial field, which led to an expansion and
greater differentiation of the Curia.

The enforcement of the papal claim to leadership in the
Church and in the world, and the expansion of Church bur-
eaucracy, led to a great increase in the financial demands on
the papacy and the Roman Curia. They tried to meet this
need in many ways. The subjection of various lordships meant
that tribute could be exacted, and after the enfeoffment of the
Normans (1059) it could be imposed, at least for a time, on
other rulers as well. From the middle of the twelfth century, the
popes obliged other countries—especially Sweden and Norway—to pay Peter's Pence. To this were added payments from
protected churches and monasteries exempted from the power
of the bishops, the number of which rose considerably after
about 1100. Already Leo IX had demanded voluntary payments from the patriarchs, archbishops, bishops, and abbots,
which mainly had to be paid when visiting the papal court;
Innocent III organized these into an established taxation
system. From the beginning of the thirteenth century bishops
and abbots had to pay high dues on their appointment or
confirmation by the pope, to which the holders of other clerical
offices were also obliged by the middle of the same century.
Over and above these, the petitioners and receivers of benefices
had to pay a mass of duties and fees. From the Third Crusade
onwards the Roman Curia raised a special crusading tax from
the upper clergy, which in the course of the thirteenth century
was demanded more and more often. The fiscalism of the popes
and the Roman Curia promoted a similar attitude among the
higher clergy. Since the time of the investiture conflict this had
attracted sharp criticism, which was directed against the greed
of the papal court, but also against the rich official Church in
general.

[*b*] THE REFORMING PAPACY AND
CLUNIAC MONASTICISM

The course of development towards a rich and powerful official
Church can be traced back to the monasticism of Cluny—

though admittedly this was only one conditioning factor among others. The monasticism of this Burgundian reform centre had a prolonged influence on the reforming papacy. The monastery had from the time of its foundation been under the direct control of the apostolic see. For the first time in the history of Benedictine monasticism, Cluny organized numerous monasteries, priories, and churches into a hierarchical association controlled by the mother monastery, and thereby as far as possible withdrew them from subjection to the dioceses and from the involvement of lay powers. Many supporters of the reform papacy were very close to the various branches of the Cluniac reform, and even some popes, several of whom had been monks in monasteries of Cluniac type. Outstanding examples are the cardinal bishop Humbert of Silva Candida already mentioned; Hugo Candidus, from the monastery of Remiremont in the Vosges; Frederick, a member of the ducal house of Lorraine, who as abbot of Monte Cassino was elected pope (Stephen IX, 1057-8), and his successors Pope Nicholas II (1058-61) and Hildebrand (Gregory VII, 1073-85). The latter already under the pontificate of his predecessor Alexander II (1061-73) had exerted a decisive influence on papal policies. After the short pontificate of Victor III (1086-7), who had been made abbot of Monte Cassino by Stephen IX, Odo, the former monk and prior of Cluny, followed as Urban II (1088-99). The climax of Cluniac monasticism coincided to a great extent with the period of the reforming papacy (down to 1130) and with the rule of Abbot Hugh (1049-1109). At this time the Cluniacs once again expanded considerably beyond their existing area of influence, radiating from the Burgundian centre to the west of central France and the Rhône country, and especially into north-eastern and south-western France and northern Italy, with a few ramifications into England and northern Spain.

With no close ties to Cluny, attempts at Cluniac reform in Germany only became effective from the end of the 1060s. Up to then the monastic reform of Gorze and St Maximin (Trier), which was closely connected with imperial rule, had been predominant. The Cluniac monasteries exploited their generally huge landed property in traditional ways without the monks' doing any physical work, contrary to the wording of the Benedictine rule. The income from landed property, which at the turn of the eleventh and twelfth centuries was in most cases already paid in the form of money, and the valuable donations of noblemen and kings allowed the monks an almost extravagant life-style. They concentrated on the liturgy, performed with great splendour, in which the commemoration of the (noble) dead was much in evidence. With their form of religious life they addressed the noble ruling classes, from which almost without exception the members of the monasteries originated. An outward sign of Cluniac monasticism at the close of its golden age was the architecture of the third basilica of Cluny, begun in 1088, which, with its vast dimensions (187 × 77 metres), became by far the largest church in western Christendom. Although the convent is supposed to have trebled to *c.*200 monks within a few decades, these completely exceptional dimensions represent primarily the claims to power of the *monarchia monachorum* (monarchy of the monks) of Cluny.

[c] HERMITS AND HERMITS' ORDERS

Even during the building of this basilica (1088–1130) the Cluniac monastic ideal was vehemently disputed. Already before this period forms of religious communal life were practised which clearly differed from Cluny and Gorze, and which lay outside Benedictine monasticism. One such alternative was the eremitic life. The earliest attempts occurred in central Italy with the hermit communities of Camaldoli, Fonte Avellana, and Vallombrosa in the first half of the eleventh century. This movement acquired an outstanding leader in Peter Damian (1006/7–72), who rose to be cardinal bishop of Ostia under Pope Stephen IX. Only from the middle of the eleventh century did these hermit centres succeed in developing wider associations of monasteries. But among these, Vallombrosa, whose monks did not stop short of militant action against opponents of the Gregorian Church reform during the investiture contest, alone managed to win a monastic foothold in the north, beyond central Italy. On the whole the reform movements had passed their high point by the middle of the twelfth century.

The eremitical movement did not spread to France until towards the end of the eleventh century. There too it was strongly influenced by the south Italian–Byzantine model. The secular priest Bruno of Cologne (*c.*1030–1101) was in close contact with the south Italian hermits. After his career as head of philosophical and theological studies at the cathedral school of Reims, Bruno, who despised his episcopal city as a new Babylon, led the life of a hermit. From 1084 onwards he stayed for several years in a small community of hermits in the valley of the Grande Chartreuse (Dauphiné). After that, he was called to the Curia by his pupil, Pope Urban II. However, the pope allowed him to seek solitude again in southern Italy only a year later. Out of the hermit community of Grande Chartreuse in the following decades sprang the germ of the Carthusian order, whose main area of influence, to begin with, was in south-east France. Only in the fourteenth century were many Carthusian houses founded in the German empire.

[d] THE CISTERCIANS

The Cistercian order, on the other hand, made its first settlement in Germany only a quarter of a century after the foundation of Cîteaux in 1098. Robert of Molesme (d. 1111), the founder of the order, had turned away from traditional Benedictine monasticism even before 1075, when he founded the abbey of Molesme in Burgundy with a group of hermits. He left Molesme with a group of companions when the monastery no longer met his ideals, and around 1098 founded a new house in a remote place at Cîteaux, not far from Cluny. Further important abbeys were founded later by his followers, especially after the entry of Bernard of Fontaines into Cîteaux (1112): La Ferté 1113, Pontigny 1114, Morimond and Clairvaux 1115. Bernard became abbot of the new foundation of Clairvaux, and won a large number of young noblemen for the new form of monastic life. In 1119 Pope Calixtus II (1119–24) confirmed the existing constitution; furthermore he granted the Cistercians authority to rule themselves independently.

The Cistercians, with their stronger emphasis on solitude and the ideal of poverty in the Benedictine rule, stood right from the beginning in conscious opposition to the monasticism of Cluny. In contrast to the Cluniacs the Cistercian order at least at first renounced proprietary churches, income from rents and rights of lordships, tithes, and peasant servitude. Rather the monks themselves did physical work; in this they were helped by lay brothers (*conversi*) and especially by paid labourers, who soon took over the main burden of manual labour. Thus instead of the old monastic landed property, they ran an economy of their own, at first directed towards self-sufficiency, and which in general was won from the forest and wilderness by clearance and other measures. Every newly-founded monastery under its own elected abbot received far-reaching independence and was integrated into the order by annual assemblies of all abbots, and further by the right of visitation of the 'general abbots'. The order rapidly spread from its Burgundian homeland into all parts of Latin Christendom. By about 1130 there were already some 80 monasteries. By Bernard of Clairvaux's death (1153), the order had grown to about 350 monasteries; in the last decade of his life his pupil Eugenius III (1145–53), a brother of the order, held the highest office in the Church. The number had risen by 1200 to about 500 monasteries, by the middle of the thirteenth century to 650; but in the second half of that century only some 50 more were added. According to rough estimates the number of monks and lay brothers around the middle of the twelfth century was about 11,000; in the following century it probably doubled. Not included here are the numerous nunneries which from the end of the twelfth century until the middle of the thirteenth were incorporated into the Cistercian order, although the order approved of the affiliation of nunneries only for a few decades and restricted it again at the latest in 1228.

By this time the white monks, many of whose monasteries now controlled extensive landed property and were more closely connected with the cities and with urban markets, had fallen away in many respects from the original ideals of the order. The monks of this widespread order, with its comparatively centralized organization, grew during the twelfth century more and more into the role of assistants to the official church and papacy, so that a comparison with the Jesuits of the sixteenth and seventeenth centuries does not seem far-fetched. This can be seen in the rise of many Cistercians to bishoprics and the cardinalate, and not least in their great importance in the preparation and even the carrying through of the Crusades, as well as fighting heretics, and ultimately in the crusades against the heretics in southern France. The mendicant orders, which came into existence at the beginning of the thirteenth century and which, in strong contrast to the early Cistercians, were orientated towards the towns, played a part in the Cistercians' loss of function. In the long run the neglect of the cure of souls had a negative influence on the further development of the order. The abbey churches, kept simple in clear contrast to the churches of the Cluniacs, had room neither for bands of pilgrims nor for simple believers.

[*e*] WANDERING PREACHERS AS FOUNDERS OF
MONASTIC ORDERS

Right from the start the role of women was much more important in those orders which at the beginning of the twelfth century sprang from the activities of wandering charismatic preachers, who lived like hermits. These hermits became 'the wandering preachers from the forests'. They lived in complete poverty themselves, and in the penitential sermons which they delivered during their tours through town and country, generally outside churches and before many listeners, they demanded 'leaving the world, and, naked, following the naked Christ to the cross'. In this they exercised, from the end of the eleventh century, a previously unknown fascination on wide circles of the population, particularly in central and northern France and the Netherlands. Completely new was the echo they found among women. Their often sharp criticism of rich clerics, whom they measured by the ideal of *paupertas ecclesiae* (the poverty of the Church), increased the distrust, even hostility of many members of the established official Church towards these wandering preachers. Only those who fitted themselves and their followers into the official Church in the long run escaped being made heretics. For this it was necessary to obtain permission to preach, which was granted only in individual cases by bishops and popes, and to integrate the followers into monastic forms. The wandering preachers who thus integrated themselves into the official Church later often became the most effective opponents of heretical groups.

Life in poverty after the model of the gospels and wandering preaching (*vita apostolica*) were also the basis of the great successes Robert of Arbrissel (*c.*1060–1117)—previously a counsellor of the bishop of Rennes and then leader of a hermit community—had among the population in the west of France. In order to create a secure home for his companions and followers, he first founded the double monastery of Fontevrault on the Loire (1100/1), and then other similar monasteries. Shortly before his death he formed them into a congregation under the abbess of Fontevrault. Around the same time other orders came into existence in France founded by hermits and wandering preachers.

One exception was the order of Prémontré (in the diocese of Laon), which went back to the initiative of a nobleman from the lower Rhine, the imperial court chaplain and wandering preacher Norbert of Gennep (1120). At an early date the Premonstratensian order expanded, mainly in north-eastern France and in the Rhine country. In the course of the later twelfth century it founded settlements as far away as England and Ireland and northern Spain, as well as in the rest of central Europe. In Italy and southern France it remained restricted to a few monasteries. In the early phase double monasteries were usual in this order too, but around 1140 the nuns were settled separately in convents, often close to the men's monasteries, remaining under the spiritual leadership of the Premonstratensians. By the middle of the twelfth century in the diocese of Laon alone, 1,000 women are believed to have belonged to the Premonstratensian order, and in total as many as 10,000. From the late twelfth century (1198) those double monasteries which still existed were dissolved and no further nunneries incorporated into the order, which may have contributed to the simultaneous opening of the Cistercian order to nunneries.

[*f*] THE REGULAR CANONS

Unlike the Cluniacs and the Cistercians, the Premonstratensians saw themselves as a branch of reform in the tradition of canonical communities. For these regular canons, reform centres came into existence in the later eleventh century, mainly in Italy and France. The rules followed there, however, no longer met the demands which the reformers, more strongly influenced by the hermits, made of the canonical community at the beginning of the twelfth century concerning personal poverty and asceticism. In these efforts they came to rely on a rule attributed to the church father St Augustine. The 'Augustinian canons' were organized into numerous reforming groups and congregations. Until about 1125 many monasteries also had associated communities of canonesses, in the form of double monasteries, but later they were largely separated into independent convents. Within the stricter school the diversity among the Augustinian canons also showed itself in the varying emphasis on choir service (*vita contemplativa*) and the cure of souls (*vita apostolica*). But on the whole the regular canons and the Premonstratensians in the twelfth century became the most important pillars of pastoral care, which at the first Lateran Council of 1123 was put completely in the charge of the diocesan bishops concerned. Many of the houses of regular canons were sited on important routes and pilgrimage roads and on the outskirts of old cities, close to the rising centres of craft production and distribution; they often had hospitals attached to them. In the Church generally the regular canons won most importance between the third and sixth decades of the twelfth century. While the Gregorian reforming papacy of the previous decades was strongly marked by Benedictine monasticism with its centres at Cluny and Monte Cassino, now the regular canons gained greater influence at the papal Curia and in the college of cardinals. With the exception of the former Cluniac monk and later antipope Anacletus II (1130–8) and the former Cistercian monk Eugenius III (1145–53), all the popes between Honorius II (1124–30) and Adrian IV (1154–9) were regular canons.

An abundance of new orders and congregations replaced the relatively uniform Benedictine monasticism of the first period of Church reform under the Gregorian papacy. These were partly based on the Benedictine rule and partly on the supposed rule of St Augustine. The new impulses sprang out of a deepened religious feeling. This found a great echo among lay people, so that one can justifiably speak of the first religious mass movement in European history. In it women were more prominent than ever before. The traditional framework of the official Church proved to be insufficient. The wandering preachers, often opposed by local Church authorities, took over tasks of spiritual care in new forms, thus often exposing themselves to the suspicion, the reproach, or even the accusation of heresy. Following the ideal of poverty, the wandering preachers inspired many newly founded monasteries, orders, and congregations to increased pastoral concern, by which, however, they often came into conflict with the eremitic ideal. The great activity of lay people also showed itself in the legal integration of lay brothers and sisters (*conversi*) into monastic life.

[*g*] THE EARLY KNIGHTLY ORDERS

The new variety of religious and monastic ways of life was complemented about the same time by the rise of the first military orders. In these occurred a previously unimaginable symbiosis of two so far strictly separated ways of life: knighthood and monasticism. It only became possible in connection with the Crusades, but even then caused vehement criticism. The community of *milites Templi* (Templars), founded in the Temple of Solomon in Jerusalem in 1118/19 by Hugh de Payns (d. 1136), a nobleman from Champagne, at first also suffered because of this discrepancy. Besides poverty, celibacy, and obedience, the members bound themselves 'to armed battle against the enemies of the faith and peace, and to protect Christians'. To ward off criticism, about 1128-9 Bernard of Clairvaux composed his later widely distributed tract *De Laude Novae Militiae* ('In praise of the new knighthood') in the interest of the Temple knights, which his relative Hugh de Payns had requested of him. In this the already well-known Cistercian abbot, while strongly criticizing secular knighthood, justified this religious–military community, which was able to base its rules, finished in 1130, on his authority. Soon afterwards the heyday of the Templars set in, who concerned themselves with hospitals, founded many cells, and acquired rich property especially in France. In the second half of the twelfth century the Templars participated on a large scale in the credit business.

On to this new branch of the life of the monastic orders was grafted the history of the Hospitallers. This order arose out of a brotherhood founded shortly before 1080, originating from a monastery hospital in Jerusalem, which after the First Crusade established numerous branches and exemplary hospitals in Western Europe too. Besides care for the poor, pilgrims, and the sick, the Hospitallers from the end of the 1130s also took over military tasks. This assimilation to the Templar order was finalized and anchored in the Hospitaller statutes, drawn up before 1154. Other knightly and hospital orders subsequently followed these patterns. They contributed considerably to the Christianization of the knightly ideal, but also at the same time to the justification of war against the heathen and those of different faiths.

[*h*] THE MENDICANT ORDERS

Until towards the end of the twelfth century the history of monasticism continued roughly along the lines laid down before about 1130. New forms within the official Church, meanwhile hierarchically organized, were only forced through at the turn of the twelfth and thirteenth centuries, and partly against considerable resistance from within the Church. The official Roman Church was at the climax of its political position; at the same time it experienced the deepest breach in its credibility. Criticism and rejection grew out of a powerful lay movement of voluntary poverty and penitence, a substantial part of which disputed the claims to salvation of the Catholic Church on dogmatic grounds. The official church was freed from this real threat especially by the mendicant orders and the decisive co-operation with them of Pope Innocent III. In contrast to contemporary monasteries, the mendicant orders renounced, at least at the beginning, all or at least most possessions for their convents, so that their members really lived in poverty and were partly dependent on begging. Innocent made use of his unquestioned leadership to reintegrate into the Church part of the communities suspected or already accused of heresy, and, together with the mendicant orders of the Franciscans and Dominicans, to incorporate new forms of spiritual care and monastic life into the Church. The latter was a considerably bigger problem with the Franciscans than the Dominicans, because of the origins and attitudes of the founder.

Between 1216 and 1221—the year of its founder's death—the Dominican order expanded into France, Spain, Italy, Germany, and England, preferring the big industrial and trading cities. After Dominic's death the leadership of the order went to Jordan of Saxony (1222–37), who had studied at Paris; by 1230 it had houses in Scotland and Syria. Around 1300 it had more than 537 houses with *c.*15,000 members. With the foundation of a nunnery Dominic also considered the religious women's movement; in this too members of the urban upper classes played a prominent role. Other women's orders were influenced by this model and by that of the Cistercian nuns. The monastic model of St Dominic also affected the creation of lay brotherhoods, which finally gained an institutional framework in the Third Order of 'the Brothers and Sisters of the Penitence of St Dominic'.

Francis of Assisi was much closer in his social origin to the merchant Peter Waldo from Lyons, the initiator of the Waldensians soon to be accused of heresy, than to the founder of the Dominican order; he was the son of the rich cloth merchant Pietro Bernardone, and of Donna Pica, most probably of a noble family from Picardy. At the same time that Dominic and Diego first practised the new form of wandering preaching in Languedoc, Francis, at least twenty years old, decided (1206) to turn away radically from his former life, which promised him certain wealth and high social status in the urban upper class. In his decision to leave the world and to lead a life of poverty, penitence, and solitude, Francis was not alone of his class, even in central Italy. This no doubt also expressed an identity crisis among the merchant families, driven by ambitions for money and property. A life after the model of the gospel (*vivere secundum formam sancti evangelii*) at the same time was the ideal of many groups accused of heresy. Francis of

Assisi stood in this tradition and general atmosphere, which makes it easier to explain his effectiveness, but he and his companions put into practice this life of poverty to an almost extreme degree. Yet right from the beginning he put the movement he inspired under obedience to the official Church, and called upon his brothers to have respect for the priests.

As early as 1210 Innocent III granted Francis and his early followers a spoken acknowledgement of their rule, which, however, can hardly have contained more than a collection of Gospel texts. Up to his death in 1226 the 'Poverello' did very little to organize his followers—among whom, under the leadership of Clare of Assisi, the founder of the order of Poor Clares, were many women as well—into an established order. Soon after 1210 he handed the leadership of the Minorite order (the Franciscans) over to one of his first companions and led a restless life as pilgrim and missionary. The initiative towards a firmer organization came from the papal Curia, Ugolino of Ostia, later Pope Gregory IX (1227–41), being appointed the first cardinal protector of the order. In the *regula bullata*, decreed in 1223, internal and external mission was declared their main task; at the same time the poverty of both individuals and the community was laid down. In his will three years later Francis of Assisi again strongly emphasized the ideal of poverty and obliged the brothers to earn their living mainly by manual work; begging should remain an exception. In this respect too Francis took up older ideas of the ascetic value of manual labour, which the Cistercians had first stressed, in clear contrast to the aristocratic Benedictine life-style, but they themselves had taken it seriously only for a short time. In the case of the Franciscans too, it was only during the first decades that much manual labour outside the monastery was undertaken. Nevertheless, they thus assimilated themselves to the lives of the mass of the population, particularly in the industrial centres.

In spite of incomprehension and resistance from some ecclesiastical authorities, the Franciscans very quickly expanded even outside central Italy, the region where the accumulation of monasteries remained thickest. In 1217 France, Spain, Germany, and the Holy Land were integrated into the provinces of the order. According to a list of 1282 the order then had 1,271 convents. Around 1300 it had 30,000 members, i.e. more

than twice as many as the Dominicans. In the beginning the
order offered a place to anyone who obliged themselves to
follow Christ uncompromisingly. This openness was also influenced by the neglect of theological studies among the Franciscans at this time. In 1224, however, Francis himself, who
saw scholarly work as a temptation to human pride, agreed to
studies within the order. With the closer integration of the
order into the Church's pastoral work the importance of studies
grew among the Franciscans too.

The opening up of the order to the sciences then flourishing
was also favoured by the entry of great scholars into it. Among
them was the theologian and expert on Aristotle Alexander of
Hales (*c.*1185–1245), who became a Franciscan in 1236 when
a regent master of the theological faculty of Paris (from 1225),
and who thereby brought the Franciscans the first theological
chair at the university of Paris. At about the same time the
order also gained close personal contact with the other prominent educational centre of the period, Oxford University,
where natural philosophy was pursued particularly impress-
ively. There in 1224 the Englishman Robert Grosseteste (1175–
1253) became rector of the Franciscans and rose to be the first
chancellor of the university. The distinguished theologian and
natural philosopher Roger Bacon (1214–92), who as professor
of philosophy at Paris—and later at Oxford—entered the Franciscan order (1257), also called himself a disciple of Grosseteste.
His great knowledge of pagan, Arabic, Jewish, and Greek
philosophy supported his high esteem for mathematics among
the sciences.

Also a pupil of Alexander of Hales at Paris was the doctor's
son John Fidanza (1217–74), who around 1243 joined the
same order as his teacher under the name of Bonaventura.
He took a leading part in the mendicant controversy at the
university of Paris. This dispute lasted for two decades from
1252 and was conducted between the mendicant orders, which
claimed a right to posts as masters in the university, and the
'professorial party' which did not wish to allow them such
teaching positions. As early as 1255 the mendicants gained an
important success when Pope Alexander IV granted them
chairs at the university. While a professor at Paris only two
years later, Bonaventura was elected general of the Franciscan

order, which was then already racked by internal disputes. In this position he substantially influenced the constitution and organization of his order.

The opening up of the order to studies, which did not happen without criticism, was accompanied by an increasing clericalization. According to the Franciscan Salimbene de Adam (from Parma, 1221-*c.*1288), who wrote from about 1260, there were far more lay brothers than clerics in Tuscany during the 1240s. He said the acceptance of these uneducated lay brothers, who regarded the use of Latin as objectionable, was later forbidden almost completely. At the latest in the second phase of the order's development, which set in about 1230, members of the urban upper classes became dominant. This process did not erase the basic differences between them and the older monastic orders, whose members were mainly recruited from the nobility. It was, however, an important symptom of the assimilation of the Minorites into the models of urban society.

New conflicts sprang up within the order at this tendency to become 'bourgeois'. Already by the founder's death there were disputes between the 'lax party' around Elias of Cortona, who in 1239 was finally deposed as general of the order because of his noble-like life-style, and the zealots over the maintenance of the ideal of poverty. This ideal was circumvented even during the pontificate of Gregory IX, in such a way that the Minorites were allowed to do legal business through lay proxies. In 1245 Innocent IV replaced this legal construct by another, in which all the order's goods were taken over as property of the papal see.

The rising poverty dispute, which reached its climax towards the end of the thirteenth century, was mixed up with chiliastic ideas. Following the Calabrian Cistercian abbot Joachim of Fiore (*c.*1130-1202), whose teaching had been partly condemned at the Lateran Council of 1215, pseudo-Joachite writings in the first half of the thirteenth century announced the beginning of a new age of the world—the third. In this, the age of the Holy Spirit, the secularized and corrupt official Church was supposed to be replaced by a new ecclesiastical order led by the mendicants. These ideas could be interpreted so that in this last era the whole of the Church was to be led back to poverty in every respect, as was also declared in the manifestos of the Emperor Frederick II during the 1240s. In contrast to the Dominican order, which became one of the most important advocates of the Inquisition, the tense relationship with the official Church came through again and again in the Franciscan order.

The Dominicans and Franciscans were only the most successful orders within a broad and widely differentiated spectrum of poverty and penitence movements in the twelfth and thirteenth centuries; among the others were, especially, the important mendicant orders of the Augustinian hermits and the Carmelites. The former owed its existence to the efforts of the papacy to safeguard the centralism of the official Church by combining and integrating locally and regionally varying monastic initiatives. The order was created by Alexander IV in 1256 by uniting Italian communities of hermits. It also turned towards pastoral care, and for this purpose furthered the studies of its members. The Carmelites also go back to a hermit community, founded on Mount Carmel in Samaria in the twelfth century. From the second quarter of the thirteenth century its members in Europe were doing pastoral work, and in 1247 they received the status of an order. Besides these large mendicant orders, in the second and third quarters of the thirteenth century various others came into existence, mainly in Italy and France.

The mendicant orders played a considerable part in the survival of the papal hierarchical Church during the deep crisis of the twelfth and thirteenth centuries; but their far-reaching missionary work in North Africa, Syria, and Palestine—in the 1240s and 1250s they even advanced as far as Mongolia—was denied great success. But all the more effective were their efforts in pastoral care in the large cities and urbanized areas most affected by social change. There they strongly influenced the traditional forms of spiritual care, which had become insufficient, and generally added to and transformed them, lastingly affecting the religious life of the laity. They enabled the Church to adapt to progressive urban culture. In their backward orientation to the origins of Christianity, in which they could link up with predecessors in the eleventh and twelfth centuries, they were simultaneously innovators. This was nowhere more obvious than in the strong engagement of the

mendicant orders—first the Dominicans, then the Franciscans—in theology and philosophy. Theology continued to
be the mother of knowledge and the interpreter of the world.
This role it could only maintain by incorporating newly discovered ideas and new ways of thought.

7

Education and Learning

[a] THE ADOPTION OF CLASSICAL TRADITIONS IN THE
WEST

The important new approaches in learning, education, and art
in western Europe in the high Middle Ages were based on a
renewed and extensive appropriation of classical traditions,
especially of Greek philosophy and natural science and of
Roman law of late antiquity. This learning process was
initiated in Western Europe in the twelfth century, and the
same century gave it an established form which was decisive
for the following period. In this sense one can reasonably talk
of a 'renaissance', in the sense of a 'rebirth' of classical culture, in
the twelfth century. This period can thus be given an important
mediating role in world history between ancient and modern
times. In contrast to the previous resumptions of classical traditions in Carolingian times and at the turn of the tenth and
eleventh centuries, the renaissance of the twelfth century in
Western Europe began a continuity of scholarly thought, not
to be broken again, which gained a firm basis in the scholastic
method. Thus far this 'rebirth' was just as important for the
history of Europe as that 'Renaissance' on the threshold of
modern times which was first introduced and carried through
in Italy as a return to the antique for its own sake.

But in this connection it must be stressed that the 'renaissance' of the twelfth century, as Haskins called it [282], in the
central areas of philosophy and natural science was based on
the reception and assimilation of Muslim and Jewish scholars.
From the ninth century on, they had taken up the tradition of
Greek philosophy—especially Aristotle, who in the Latin West
had only partly been considered—and further developed it

independently, not least in medicine. The great Islamic text-books of natural science and medicine had been made accessible for the medical school of Salerno between 1070 and 1087 by the translations of Constantinus Africanus, most probably a baptized Jew. This was continued from the middle of the twelfth century by the school of translators in the Spanish city of Toledo. Among the scholars working there the Lombard Gerard of Cremona (1114-87) was outstanding, with translations of Arabic texts with which he opened up treatises of the Greeks—like Hippocrates, Archimedes, Galen, and Pseudo-Aristotle—to the Latin West.

Many texts on natural science of all kinds were translated from Arabic at the Sicilian court of the Emperor Frederick II as well. Other, smaller translation centres, as for example at Toulouse, expanded the range of knowledge. To this Adelard of Bath (c. 1070-1146), Abelard's contemporary, also contributed. After his schooling in northern France he travelled as far as Salerno, Sicily, and Antioch, and thus came into contact with ancient science obtained from Arab sources. Out of his efforts to study the Arabic world of knowledge (*Arabum studia scrutari*), grew editions and translations of several astronomical, astrological, and mathematical works from Arabic and Greek, among them a translation of Euclid. In the areas of Mediterranean culture with the liveliest contacts—in Spain, Sicily, and Provence—from the end of the eleventh century and even more from the middle of the twelfth, writings of Aristotle until then unknown in the Christian West were translated by Islamic, Jewish, and Christian scholars from Arabic, in general with the Arabic commentaries, and soon also from Greek, into Latin, the language of Western scholars. Now and then Hebrew exemplars were also used.

Thus at the beginning of the thirteenth century most of Aristotle's writings were known in Western Europe. But his works, and their generally Arabic commentaries, only began to have a greater effect in the course of the thirteenth century. It was considerably affected by the treatises of Islamic scholars influenced by Aristotle—particularly Avicenna, living in the Islamic East (c. 980-1037), Averroës (1126-92), who mostly worked in Cordoba, and not least the Jewish doctor and philosopher Maimonides (1135-1204). The writings on natural philosophy of Aristotle and his Arabic and Jewish commentators contained teachings which were partly incompatible with the Christian faith. Therefore as early as 1210 a Parisian synod forbade the reading of these Aristotelian writings. Such prohibitions were repeated during the following decades. In spite of this in 1255 the study of the same works was made compulsory for the whole of the arts faculty at the university of Paris. Basing themselves on Aristotle and especially on Averroës, Parisian philosophers—like Siger of Brabant, removed from his teaching post in 1276—soon advocated a rational philosophy and propounded theses which obviously contradicted Christian dogma. They were condemned in 1270 and again in 1277 at councils in Paris, without this being able to call a halt to such thoughts, especially among students of medicine and law.

Meanwhile the reception of Aristotelian philosophy in the Latin West had influenced current theological and philosophical traditions in various ways. To point out only the most important representatives in different subjects: the Franciscan Bonaventura from central Italy, whose historical theology was still strongly influenced by Augustine; the Dominican Albertus Magnus (c.1200–80), from a Swabian knightly family, who combined Aristotelianism with Platonism, especially Neoplatonism; finally, Thomas Aquinas (c.1225–74), the son of a south Italian count, fellow Dominican and disciple of Albertus, who integrated Aristotle's works into his own independent philosophical system.

Alongside the acquisition of Greek philosophy and natural science, especially medicine, in their Islamic- or Jewish-mediated forms, there also began at the turn of the eleventh and twelfth centuries the reception of late-antique Roman law. Scholarly study of these legal traditions was at first restricted to Bologna. There the teacher Irnerius (d. after 1125) created the basis of a law school with his commentaries and elucidations on the *Corpus Iuris Civilis*, which had been compiled around the middle of the sixth century under the Emperor Justinian, and which became known again in the Latin West towards the end of the eleventh century. The dialectical methods developed for use on Justinian's laws were later also applied to Church law and other types of law as well. Besides the science of civil law, Bologna from the middle of the twelfth century became the most important centre for canon law. Out of these legal studies, Bologna developed into the most important university of Europe after Paris. By the turn of the twelfth and thirteenth centuries, about 1,000 students from many West European countries studied there.

[*b*] HIGHER SCHOOLS AND UNIVERSITIES

In the first half of the thirteenth century the new organizational form of academic teaching, the university, developed out of societies of teachers and students, and expanded rapidly particularly in Italy and France but also in Spain and England. Besides the schools of Paris, Bologna, and Oxford, the medical schools of Salerno and Montpellier, already known earlier, gained university status too. During this period in Italy alone, Reggio, Vicenza, Arezzo, Padua, Vercelli, and Piacenza were added; in 1224 the Emperor Frederick II founded the first 'state university' for his kingdom of Sicily, in Naples. The universities, coming into existence almost exclusively in the larger cities, were the tip of a development which from the second half of the eleventh century grew out of the hitherto predominant monastery and cathedral schools. A first step was the loss of importance of the monastery schools to the urban cathedral schools. Already at the end of the eleventh and the beginning of the twelfth century there were students from England, Italy, and even Hungary at the cathedral schools of Laon, following the lessons of Anselm of Laon (d. 1117)—a pupil of the Benedictine monk and later archbishop, Anselm of Canterbury (d. 1109), at Bec in northern France, and of William of Champeaux (d. 1122). With their enlightening and deepening of the theology of the Church Fathers, as regards terminology and dialectic, these teachers were among the founders of early scholasticism.

In spite of his sharp criticism of his teachers, Abelard (1079–1142) also stood in this tradition. His followers celebrated him, for example, as 'the Socrates of the Gauls, the illustrious Plato of the West, our Aristotle . . . a prince in the world of learning'. Today, with some justification, he is called the first European intellectual. As a young man his teaching outside Paris had already made him appreciated, even before he became in 1114 the best known teacher at the cathedral school of Notre Dame. His love-affair with his young pupil Héloïse led to personal tragedy. In spite of hostility and condemnation he soon exercised his great power of attraction as a teacher once again, even in remote places. Towards the end of his life he taught again on the Mont-Sainte-Geneviève near Paris for a few years, thus contributing significantly to the rise of Paris as the greatest place of study in France and as the centre of philosophical and theological studies in Europe. In his lectures, and especially in his work *Sic et Non* ('So and Not So'), in which with exemplary system he contrasted the contradictory statements of authorities, Abelard decisively influenced further development towards high scholasticism.

From this time on dialectic won a higher rank among the traditional liberal arts, the level of which on the whole had risen considerably during the tenth and eleventh centuries; it penetrated all subjects as a way of teaching and thinking. This development prepared the ground for the reception of all of Aristotle's writings. Influenced by this, almost at the same time medicine grew out of the framework of the liberal arts into an independent science, for which they, however, remained necessary. The improvement of logic was also an essential precondition for the rise of schools of glossators and thus of the higher law schools. Dialectic and the enrichment of natural science gave the study of theology its most important new impulses.

On the whole, work with classical natural philosophy promoted the reputation of the *Quadrivium* (arithmetic, geometry, music, and astronomy) within the liberal arts, of which the *Trivium* (grammar, rhetoric, and logic) constituted the traditional foundation. Thierry of Chartres (d. *c.* 1155) was already convinced that the beginning of the universe could only be sufficiently explained by knowledge gained through the *Quadrivium*. As mentioned, in the twelfth and thirteenth centuries in these areas astonishing progress in knowledge of natural science and great technical progress were achieved, not least by experimental methods. The general striving for the acquisition of long-hidden traditions, made considerably easier by the conditions of the time, was the basis of powerful new approaches which up to then had been unknown in the West. Therein lies a lasting achievement. It was favoured by a freer development of the tension between reason and faith. It was based on an attitude formulated, in a way which still today deserves respect, by the eminent grammarian and sometime chancellor (1119–26) of the school of Chartres, Bernard—probably a brother of the Thierry mentioned above: 'We are dwarfs sitting on the shoulders of giants. We see more and further than they, not because our eyes are sharper or our bodies taller, but because they lift us into the air and make us bigger by their own gigantic size' [272: 54].

[c] RELIGIOUS, POLITICAL, AND SOCIAL CONNECTIONS

The renaissance of learning in the twelfth century and its first efflorescence in the following century were therefore the result of the combination of many factors. The reception of ancient knowledge in the Latin West only became possible because favourable conditions had been created for it, mainly in Italy and France, and because a fertile ground existed and had been nurtured. One of these conditions was the astonishing mobility of teachers and pupils, by which the exchange of ideas was made considerably faster and deeper. The school of Toledo is another example of this. Young scholars from England and France, from Dalmatia and Brabant, from Sicily and northern Italy hurried to this centre of communication between East and West. The numerous personal contacts and experiences created by travel in and through the Byzantine empire and the lands of Arabic culture can hardly be overestimated for Western European intellectual history. With the accessibility of new works, which now for the first time became known through translations directly from Greek into Latin, and with the expansion of the schools, the demand for quickly produced and cheap copies grew, and so by the thirteenth century professional scribes in major university towns made their living. Besides the increased use of simpler styles of writing (cursives), this increased demand also favoured the spread of paper as a cheaper writing material. The earliest paper-mill in Western Europe has been identified in twelfth-century Spain, in a place then still under Islamic rule. In the following century such places of production, which in the Arabic world were to be found from the eighth century, were already functioning in Christian Spain and Italy (1276). France followed around the middle, and Germany only at the end, of the fourteenth century (*c.*1390).

No further proof is needed that the gigantic growth of the towns which occurred in Western Europe from the middle of the eleventh century, and first in the Mediterranean areas, furthered the exchange of ideas and teaching in public—in the market-place. Accordingly towns now rose to be the leading school centres and to contain the first universities. In the corporative unions which now arose in manifold forms in the cities of Western Europe, the towns provided a model for the new associations of masters and students which first came into existence in the big school centres, and out of which grew the most important organizational forms of the universities. In the same nexus of power and society, which in this combination was unique in a world historical perspective, the scene was set for the acquisition and prosecution of new ideas and theories.

The balance between Church and world, between religion and state had again been called into question in the 'investiture struggle'. The predominance of one side or the other in most West European countries long remained undecided. The means of control at the disposal of the powers, pressing one another hard, were mostly quite rudimentary until the last quarter of the thirteenth century. Values often remained disputed even in essential matters. This was true for example for the term 'heretic' in the controversy between Frederick II and the papacy, so that the imperial persecuter of heretics was himself branded a heretic by the popes. It was only at the end of our period that the official Church hierarchy seems to have imposed lasting limitations on the permissible area for philosophical and theological dispute. For this the condemnations of Roger Bacon and Siger of Brabant around the middle of the 1270s will serve as evidence.

The expansion and intensification of schooling was furthered not least by the increased demand for literate specialists and intellectuals in establishing and exercising power, in the fields of law and administration—among these not least financial administration—particularly of the larger territories and cities, and in the provision of legal security for economic life and the increasingly complicated property relations. It is significant for these mutually dependent processes that from the beginning of the twelfth century some Western rulers were themselves educated in literature or at least deeply interested, gathering scholars, also as specialists, at their courts and deliberately furthering education and training. The Anglo-Norman king Henry I (1100–35), to whom an anecdote attributed the saying 'an uneducated king is a crowned ass' (*rex illiteratus—asinus coronatus*), could be mentioned, and his successor Henry II; the French king Louis VII, who himself was a pupil at the Parisian cathedral school; the Norman Sicilian ruler Roger II, who had the Arab Idrisi (d. 1166) produce a description and a map of the world, and who advised and supported him in the necessary research. The Staufen rulers can also be included here: Frederick II in this respect excelled all contemporary secular rulers in Europe. His son Manfred continued the tradition. The demand for legally trained specialists also shows in increasing legislation, and in the accumulation of legal codifications for countries and—especially in imperial Italy—also for cities, so that the latest research on the period from 1231 (Constitutions of Melfi) to 1281 speaks of a virtual 'wave of codification' in Latin Europe.

In the maritime trading city of Pisa the work of long years of collecting and systematizing the urban customs, including the complicated trade and maritime laws, was finished in 1160 and fixed in a two-part law-book, the *Constitutum Usus*. After this in the cities of imperial Italy the books of statutes multiply. The great importance of the legal life of these cities can be seen in the often large share which trained jurists, among them eminent scholars, played in the counsels of the consulates in the second half of the twelfth century. Legal experts were also necessary in the rule of the *Podestà*, which from the last quarter of the twelfth century became normal in many cities of imperial Italy; successful *Podestà* in the end held these offices in several towns, even professionally. In the twelfth century the jurists themselves created a profession of their own at Bologna.

In imperial Italy the same is true for notaries, who at the beginning of the thirteenth century also organized themselves into *societates*. Their legal knowledge was laid down in the framework of the liberal arts; from the beginning of the thirteenth century they were often prepared for their profession in notarial schools of their own. At the beginning of the twelfth century in Bologna a new genre of letter-writing literature came into existence, which, derived from rhetoric, was at first mainly directed towards the daily practice of writing letters and documents. Within a short time this literature developed in northern Italy; in France it was further developed independently towards the end of the twelfth century, while in Germany it found only a few individual imitators. This regional spread is on the whole a reflection of the spread of literacy among the laity. The erotic and frivolous contents of some of the model letters were most probably aimed at these customers.

8

Social Change

The far-reaching geographical mobility which marked the people of Western Europe between the eleventh and thirteenth centuries stood in close correlation to the dissolution, or at least loosening, of older personal and seigneurial ties. Together with the opening up of new political and economic opportunities, a high degree of social mobility came about: i.e. a great capacity for change in the social status of individuals, families, institutionalized associations, and other groups. At the same time new forms of common living and social classification arose. In the process co-operative unions, out of which there developed numerous brotherhoods, communities, communes, and other corporations, became more effective than ever before in European history; there are no parallels in other cultures. These unions were carried along by the idea of brotherhood anchored in Christianity, particularly in the New Testament. Thus they were also connected with the deepening religiousness of the period from the eleventh century on in Western Europe, which also expressed itself in the lay religious movements mentioned above. Admittedly these complex processes need not only be linked with Christianization. Like the religious deepening itself, they stood in an indissoluble connection with the seigneurial, economic, and cultural changes in the same period. Thus the changing power relationships offered new possibilities of action to the co-operative entities, which could also be supported by traditional lords in their own interests.

Under the influence of the progressive division of labour, as well as of growing new fields of activity, the social structure was differentiated to an extent previously unknown. Cases in point are the creation of new professions and corporations among the lay 'intellectuals' (masters in the schools and universities, jurists, notaries, doctors, etc.), particularly in the urban areas; from the middle of the twelfth century professional poets and troubadours, who in general were turned towards court life, can also be counted. Affecting the broad classes of the population, professional specialization was closely connected with urbanization; it flourished best in bigger cities, particularly in the trade and export centres which now developed. Profession became an important criterion of social status and thus reduced the old fixation with origins. But status according to birth was certainly not thereby abolished; rather it was defended and emphasized by the supporters and interpreters of the traditional order.

With the growth of the towns and of their legal independence, town-dwellers more and more detached themselves from the rest of the population. They distinguished themselves from the nobility and the peasantry. But it must be stated, however, that these distinctions did not lead to strict dividing lines; rather there was much overlapping between nobility, peasantry, and townspeople.

[*b*] THE CLERICS

Crossing-points were left open even in the boundaries between these large lay groups and the clerics. Thus many clerics, even when they already had an ecclesiastical benefice, only took minor orders, which allowed them to return to lay status. Numerous students contented themselves with the tonsure—i.e. they renounced ordination, which up to the eleventh century was necessary for the status of a cleric—and so obtained the numerous legal privileges of clerics. The term 'cleric' thus won the meaning of 'educated person', as still in the English word 'clerk', meaning scribe and secretary. The 'semi-religious', like the Béguines and Beghards, had an in-between position difficult to define. In their ways of life the clerics differed from each other as never before.

How far the social composition of clerics changed within Latin Christendom is hard to answer, because of the state of the sources and of research. It can, though, be taken as secure that the position of clerics in the official Church hierarchy presented a true reflection of the social structure at the time, and that it therefore also reacted to the changes taking place. Accordingly, in the old urbanized areas, clerics of citizen origin rose even to episcopal office. Here as in other countries, education opened new possibilities to clerics of lower social origin. According to a decree of Pope Alexander III, of 1179, a teacher to give free lessons to poor scholars should be employed at every episcopal see. In comparison with the older clerical communities and the hierarchy of the official Church, over which the holders of secular power often had much influence even after the investiture struggle, social origin was of far smaller importance in the mendicant orders. The Franciscan Salimbene de Adam, from Parma, however, started his chronicle, begun in 1261, with a detailed description of his urban middle-class family whose reputation and influence filled him with obvious pride.

Although the *oratores*, as the clerics were called in the older social doctrine, formed a professional group, the belief that there was a unified mentality among clerics in the period after the middle of the twelfth century is even less demonstrable than for the previous centuries. Given the diversity of social origins, of education and of forms of religious life, of offices and other areas of action, and given the often severe controversies among clerics, it is more to be expected among the nobility, townspeople, or peasants than among clerics.

[c] NOBLES AND KNIGHTS

The nobility in the countries of the Latin West—and it was really only at home in this culture—was not at all a uniform, clearly distinguishable social class. The separation of nobles from freemen and serfs, from peasants and townspeople only occurred in the course of our period, without having come to an end everywhere by the end of the thirteenth century. The distance between non-noble urban citizens and the nobles in the old urban regions of Italy and southern France, where

numerous nobles, even counts, lived in cities and had citizenship, was considerably smaller than in west and central Europe,
where cities had only started to develop from the eleventh or
twelfth century onwards. In the cities of imperial Italy even
contemporaries in the thirteenth century found it difficult to
distinguish between those urban dwellers who called themselves, or were called, noble from the other great men of the
city, so that they put these groups together as 'magnates'.

Such vagueness about the concept of nobility was not least a
consequence of the great spread of noble titles since the eleventh
century, to the very numerous groups of non-noble warriors
of free or even unfree origin. The noble title became almost
inflationary, a process which could only partly be restrained
by setting a lower limit. This extension was so closely tied up
with the predominant impulses and tendencies of our period
that it could be hindered only partly or not at all by legislation
against it which aimed at preserving the traditional order.
Interference of that sort could only hope for success when imposed by powerful rulers such as Frederick II at the climax of
his power in the Sicilian kingdom. Among the conditioning
factors for the integration of new groups into the noble élite,
the following should be emphasized: in connection with the
population increase, the expansion and development of new
settlement areas, the conquest of new as well as the expansion
and consolidation of existing dominions, and not least, the
crusading movement. Here, there arose numerous new possibilities for rising into more independent positions of power,
or service, tied up with important military and administrative
responsibilities. The strong rise in the number of castles and
castle-like fortifications, which began in many countries of the
Latin west from around the middle of the eleventh century and
which then continued in varying intensity, is evidence for this.
The consequences of the change in power on the structure of the
old ruling classes in the urban areas was described shortly after
the middle of the twelfth century by the noble German bishop
Otto of Freising when looking at the cities of Lombardy. In
order to gain enough power to suppress their neighbours these
cities had admitted even young people of lower origin or some
sorts of craftsmen to the belt of knighthood and to higher titles,
even those whom other peoples excluded like the plague from

more honourable and free positions. In Poland in the thirteenth century—to mention only one further example—even dependent peasants were made knights, and in general they went on living a peasant's life.

Various rulers from the middle of the twelfth century at least now and then attempted to cover their increased need of military force by recruiting bands of mercenaries. The Emperor Frederick I was probably the first in recruiting the so-called Brabançons (1166/7), and the English and French kings also turned to this method. The use of such groups, who did not shrink from pillage and other deeds of violence, remained limited, however, mainly because they mostly fought on foot. The Third Lateran Council of 1179 issued a general prohibition against them, which then was not even kept by the kings of England and France. On the whole mounted forces were the core of the armies. These riders supplied their equipment themselves, a long-standing tradition. For this they relied, in very varied ways, on their own estates and—at least in the areas of the former Carolingian empire and England—on their fees or their service tenures. This supplying of one's own equipment, and the associated incorporation into the law of service and into feudalism, which assured the independent rights of the fee-holder as well as duties, had already in Carolingian times been an essential precondition of nobility. Under these conditions service as a fighting horseman favoured a position similar to nobility, if not admission into the wider circles of the aristocracy.

These processes meshed with the new religiously and politically motivated upgrading of war and military science before and in connection with the crusading movement. After early attempts in the tenth century to elevate the warrior's profession by placing it in the Church's scale of values, the higher estimation of the warrior in the service of the Church was consolidated from the middle of the eleventh century on. Thus Pope Leo IX raised as martyrs all those who fell in the military campaign against the Normans (1053) led by himself. The same pope only a short time later was considered a saint; besides his fight against simony, his 'pious' war was mentioned as a principal justification for this, even though some reproached him with having gone into battle himself. The pope's behaviour and

the judgement on it of his contemporaries and future generations have to be seen against the background of the Peace
of God movement, which began at the turn of the tenth and
eleventh centuries, first in the south of France, and which soon
spread into other parts of France and as far as northern Italy.
This had already begun a re-evaluation of war, determined by
ecclesiastical aims, and a religious justification of the warrior
as far as he fought to maintain God's peace (*pax Dei*). Subsequently this was deepened and established in canon law.

In close connection with the promotion of the crusading
idea by the reformed papacy was Gregory VII's call for ritual
honours for the leader of the *Pataria*, fallen in battle in 1075—
the knight Erlembald. The same applied to the Roman prefect
Cencius, who at first wanted to become a monk, but who, after
Gregory had forbidden this, was slain in the summer of 1077
in Rome 'as an indefatigable knight of St Peter in the fight
against the schismatics' [compare 151: 198]. Cencius and
Erlembald became the great exemplars of ecclesiastical knighthood. In 1095—i.e. right at the time of the call for the crusade—
Pope Urban ordered a solemn translation of Erlembald's
remains. In his crusade sermon at the Council of Clermont the
same pope formulated the legitimation of the militant knight,
through participation in the crusade summoned by the highest
Church authority: 'Now let those become knights who before
were robbers (*nunc fiant milites, qui dudum extiterunt raptores*) [see
148]. Bernard of Clairvaux went on from there in his 'In Praise
of the New Knighthood'.

The Peace of God movement, and the Crusades, which were
strongly influenced by it, conferred a new, elevated religious
ethos on the warrior. This went beyond qualities derived from
family status. Rather it referred primarily to the attitude and
behaviour of the warrior in his profession, and thereby also to
his individual abilities and conduct. But this 'chivalric ideal',
unrestricted to begin with, also addressed the old nobility, who,
while consolidating their territorial power around castles and
also religious centres, now based their prestige more on their
family seat, on their descent in the male line, on their lineage.
In spite of opposing tendencies on the part of the traditional
nobility, the knightly ideal fortified by religion established common ground among the knights, who differed greatly in power

and social status and who felt obliged by this general ethic, or were unable to escape from it. In this way the rise of hitherto non-noble knights into the nobility was made easier. This important process, which promoted the reorganization of the élite, can be demonstrated in the change of meaning of the terms *miles* and *militia*, which first occurred in France from the middle of the eleventh century. There from this time onwards noblemen were also called *milites*. At the same time, in terms like *ordo equester*, a feeling of unity in the sense of a knightly order becomes conceivable. Knighthood in France in the first half of the twelfth century thus became a common symbol of aristocracy, so that even simple knights were counted among the *nobiles* and high noblemen among the *militia*. Knightly tournaments, which were more frequently held from the end of the eleventh century, were the showplaces of this community. It did not remove the real differences of status, but just covered them up. Even acceptance into knighthood by formal acts, like dubbing or the grant of the belt of knighthood, did not remove the differences of birth, power, and social position within the knightly order, which themselves varied from place to place.

In the course of the thirteenth century in the kingdoms of Aragon and Sicily, and then later in France, there were increasing efforts to make the grant of knighthood dependent on birth, i.e. to restrict it to the sons of knights. Thus the Emperor Frederick II decreed in the Constitutions of Melfi of 1231 that nobody should obtain knightly honours who did not originate from a knightly family. But the emperor kept for himself the right to allow exceptions in his own interests. Almost at the same time, and partly as a consequence of the consolidation of the power structure, the different levels within the nobility gained clearer outlines, so that the knight became restricted to the lower nobility.

The courts of the kings, of the high nobility, and of the clergy formed the most important foci of knightly life. For the majority of knights, who had to rely on service and enfeoffment, life at the still usually itinerating courts was one way to secure their existence, offering them the best possibility of rising. In this milieu the narratives of heroic legends were passed on, reaching back to the campaigns of Charlemagne. The threads of tradition were fixed in writing in poetic form in the *chansons de geste* from the end of the eleventh century. The changes in feudal society in twelfth-century France also had an effect on them; the epics of the Crusades came to join them. From the beginning of the same century a new literary genre began in the troubadour lyrics, which developed first in southern France under the initiative of William IX, count of Poitiers and duke of Aquitaine (d. 1127). In this courtly lyric the nobility of bravery won a higher place, service and *aventure* as the life-style of courtly knights were elevated, and courtly love, *Minne*, still lacking in the *chansons de geste*, was stylized into a 'principle of social order'.

This world of ideas, in which the social differences among knights were harmonized, was also taken up by the courtly romance. The legendary world of King Arthur, his court and his knights, was first taken up and developed in France from the middle of the twelfth century (Chrétien de Troyes, d. before 1190). The heroic epics, and the completely different courtly poetry, quickly spread into all the countries of west and central Europe. However, the various vernacular versions generally transformed their spiritual content. Under the cover of knightly models in the poetry there lurked a multitude of sometimes contradictory values and life-styles.

[d] PEASANTS, SERFS, AND SLAVES

The opposition of knighthood and peasantry was one of the characteristics of courtly poetry. The similarity in life-style between many knights and numerous peasants did not contradict this. In reality a broad area of contact remained, with many crossing-points between peasants and knights. Peasants were still called out for military duties, or took up weapons themselves in feuds, so that they were not completely unused to the bearing of arms. On the other hand, many knights became 'countrified' for economic reasons. But on the whole the changes in agriculture, where improved cultivation methods with the increase of grain-growing demanded greater personal attention from the peasant, as well as changes in warfare, promoted greater specialization of peasants and knights.

In contrast to those who had been able to shake off their servile status through qualified service and had passed over into feudal law, the peasants and the rest of the rural population remained bound in various forms of personal dependence. These forms, however, lost a considerable part of their importance from the eleventh century on, so that the legal status of free or unfree in its differing forms was generally of less importance for the social position of the rural population. In its place the framework of economy and lordship now became decisive for the social structure. As these factors showed an even wider range of variation than the legal levels of bondage which had been predominant before, social differentiation within the rural peasant population increased in our period.

In spite of great regional differences in preconditions and in results, it can generally be stated that the older type of lordship in formerly Carolingian areas, which formed the living-space of each group of serfs (*familia*), was pushed back or superseded between the eleventh and the late thirteenth century by new, territorially orientated forms of power. Whenever the lords did not succeed in getting these rights into their own hands, they had to accept that others with judicial powers or lay advocacies, the lords of castles and local territories, would exercise powers of compulsion up to the point of raising taxes, with burdensome economic results on the members of the *familia*. The peasants felt burdens which contradicted their traditions and their common laws to be particularly irksome.

In this way the traditional forms of organization, the *Villikationsverfassung*, of the larger estates were undermined, in so far as they still existed as extended self-sufficient units with the peasant lands assigned to each of them. Independent estates run with a large number of dependent serfs, and which demanded much compulsory labour from the peasants who otherwise worked independently, already before the middle of the eleventh century seem to have been of less importance in imperial Italy and southern France than in many areas of central and western Europe. These differences supposedly were influenced by the greater development of the market and thereby of the exchange of goods, in which the old urbanized areas of the south contrasted with other European regions. The advance of rural and urban markets and the further development of a money economy certainly had an effect on the decline of the manorial economy directed towards self-sufficiency.

The manorial lords themselves had an interest in substituting recurring or single payments for compulsory labour services when it came to reducing or dissolving these self-sufficient units. The serfs were thus able to shake off a major characteristic of their unfreedom, and could then pursue other possibilities of earning their living with the freedom of movement thus gained. But also other consequences of serfdom—like restriction of marriage to other members of the *familia*—lost their attractiveness for the lords if they could receive compensation, or were able to force through more profitable rights, instead. New gains, higher and often more easily obtainable, were promised particularly by market dues, various monopoly obligations (mills, ovens, wine purchase, etc.), and the various taxes from the inhabitants of larger villages and towns. Furthermore those lords who wanted to enforce a rule as free from competition as possible, over villages or over urban settlements, were anxious to free the inhabitants from manorial ties and duties to other lords: in this respect they were therefore prepared to meet the interests of the serfs.

These changes of status, resulting from very different causes, were carried out under various legal forms. The liberation of individuals and also of groups of serfs was undertaken, as before in preceding centuries. Yet to secure their legal position the freed people had to enter into protective relationships, from which, under unfavourable conditions, new personal dependencies could result. Far more often the serfs were only granted freedom from certain obligations; thus they could later be regarded as unfree without being very different from the legally free population. More characteristic of our period, especially from the twelfth century onwards, however, were those acts of liberation, and self-liberation, for the inhabitants of one or more settlements, be they villages, towns, or other privileged places. This development stood in close connection with the promotion of village and rural communes, as well as urban ones.

In many parts of France this process was expressed in the *chartes de franchises* for *villeneuves*, *bourgs*, and *sauvetés* (from Latin *salvitas* = security), granted more often from about 1100 on-wards. In imperial Italy the privileges for castle, village, and rural communities offered certain parallels to this. At about the same time in France the charters of liberty from particular servile duties began, and also the liberation of serfs of a whole region, several villages, or a town. Thus in 1147 King Louis VII abolished the death duty for the inhabitants of the city and bishopric of Orléans. His successor, Philip II, in 1180 then freed all the royal serfs in the same town belonging to the crown domain and within a circle of five miles. Similar collective liberations are found more often around the middle of the thirteenth century in imperial Italy, where the differences be-tween unfree peasants and 'free' tenant farmers had been lev-elled out from the tenth and eleventh century onwards. The best-known example of collective liberation was that granted by the city of Bologna in 1256/7, when it freed 6,000 serfs in its dominion in return for a very high sum in compensation in favour of the almost 400 lords. The freed people thereby lost their claims on their property, and the city commune on its part extended its rights of taxation to the former serfs.

The reduction or complete abolition of serfdom could there-fore be of advantage to the lords. For such legal actions the serfs often had to accept considerable disadvantages and services in return. By numerous compromises, and enforced freedoms, the border between freedom and unfreedom became more blurred. But perhaps against this background some indications of a new value for unfreedom are to be seen. Linking up with a tradition which had been transmitted to the Middle Ages from Augustine and Gregory the Great mainly by Isidore of Seville (d. 636), the influential expert on ecclesiastical law Bishop Burchard of Worms (d. 1025), and the equally important Bishop Ivo of Chartres (d. 1116) had interpreted serfdom (*servitus*) as a con-sequence of original sin. God had installed some as serfs and others as masters so that the possibilities of wickedness on the part of the serfs should be restrained by the power of the masters. Unfreedom was thus given a religious legitimation. Bishop Adalbero of Laon, Burchard's contemporary, however, traced back the differences between nobility (*nobiles*) and war-riors (*bellatores*) on the one hand, and serfs (*servi*) on the other, not to divine law (*lex divina*) but to man-made law (*lex humana*).

In this context it is noteworthy that the reforming orders of the Cistercians and Premonstratensians in their early statutes from the first half of the twelfth century expressly renounced unfree people, which ruling, however, they soon either repealed or did not observe.

In their original aims these reform centres contrasted strongly with the older Cluniac monasticism. In the middle of the twelfth century Peter the Venerable (d. 1156), the abbot of Cluny and himself one of the greatest landlords of the time, reacted to such critical voices in a revealing treatise. In this he first justifies monasteries' exercise of power over unfree peasants by a complaint against secular lords: 'It is known to everyone how secular lords rule over *rustici, servi et ancillae*. That is to say, they are not content with the normal servitude (*servitus*) due to them. Rather they mercilessly confuse things with people, and people with things. Accordingly they not only demand the usual dues, but plunder their goods three or four times a year or as often as they like. They torture them with countless obligatory services and load them down with heavy and un-bearable burdens. By this they generally force them to leave their own soil and to flee to foreign parts. And, what is even worse, they do not hesitate to sell these people for worthless money: that is, those people whom Christ redeemed with a price so precious, that is to say with his own blood. Monks, however, when they dispose of these people, do not own them in the same way, but completely differently. They only require the legal and obligatory services of the peasants to maintain their own lives, they do not torture them with tributes, they do not demand anything unbearable from them. When the peasants are in need, they support them with their own means. They do not treat the serfs like *servi* and *ancillae* but like brothers and sisters; and they only take from them fair services, ap-propriate to their capacity' [12: 189, col. 146].

In his defence of the power of monasteries over peasants and serfs the abbot of Cluny alleged a Christian understanding of power and servitude. In doing so he avoided arguing from the theological interpretation of serfdom, which the opposition's arguments had made untenable. The strengthened awareness of Christ's redemption, which was kindled and supported by the religious reform movements from the end of the eleventh century, overwhelmed and drove out the older arguments based on original sin and on mere single events in the Old Testament. In this light the Creation could be the foundation of arguments for the equality and liberty of human beings. Thus the clerical forgers of an alleged diploma of King Henry I of France of about the middle of the twelfth century justified the legal equality they wished monastic serfs and free men to have, on the grounds that the Creation and the belief in one religion had made people equal, and that at the Creation no person was put over another. Man ought not to have dominance over his fellow men, but only over other living beings and wild animals. About 100 years later the commune of Bologna in the collective liberation mentioned above also referred to the freedom of all people given by God.

The existence of pagan slaves was only indirectly affected by this Christian discussion. In western and central Europe, that is to say with the exception of the Mediterranean areas, slavery by the middle of the eleventh century had survived only in areas of warfare against the pagan Slavs, where even later, up to about the middle of the twelfth century, slaves were still taken for long-distance trade into the Mediterranean. In the Christian cities on the Mediterranean Sea slavery experienced something like a renaissance from the Crusades onwards. Slavery there increased to a great extent. At the same time, though, slaves were kept for housework and in individual cases for manufacturing. On the great estates of southern Italy and Sicily in the thirteenth century far more slaves were apparently used than in the previous two centuries. A similar development can be assumed for the same period in the countries of the Iberian peninsula. In both regions slaves had to live their lives in the cities too, under very varied conditions.

[*e*] TOWN-DWELLERS AND CITIZENS

As has already been indicated, in this phase when urbanization in many respects reached new lands for the first time since late antiquity, it is particularly difficult to sum up under one generally valid head the diversity of urban experience. The boundary between urban and rural settlements in many cases remained fluid. A way out seems to be to restrict ourselves to towns that were the seats of bishops. But even these settlements show very great variety in their economic, social, and seigneurial setting when it comes to comparing west and central Europe. This is easily shown by the enormous differences between for example Ratzeburg in Holstein, which was again raised to a bishopric in 1154, and the Lombard metropolis of Milan.

Equally questionable are attempts to classify city-dwellers as of one kind with citizens, or even with the bourgeoisie. Against this is the fact that the rights of citizenship in many urban settlements, especially in newly settled areas, only began to develop during the twelfth and thirteenth centuries. Besides that, even in fully developed towns not all inhabitants had citizen rights. The clerical inhabitants were in general without citizen rights, and particularly in episcopal towns they comprised a significant part of the population. The same was true of the Jews, who were already excluded from the Christian community by their religion; in many bigger towns the Jews constituted a community of their own. By far the largest part of the urban population without rights of citizenship was made up of those inhabitants who, through lacking economic power, did not or could not acquire them. Often citizenship was expressly made dependent on ownership of land or a house in the town. Citizenship, which was therefore not unusually held by only a minority of urban dwellers, was itself a precondition of political activity in the municipality. In this, only a more or less small circle of persons or families played decisive roles.

In many Mediterranean cities, such as those of Catalonia, southern France, Italy, and Dalmatia, the urban nobility, who generally owned extensive property and rights in their cities and their surrounding districts, especially belonged to this closer urban ruling class. In many German and also in French towns, on the other hand, ministerials were of very similar importance—and this although far into the twelfth century and often even into the thirteenth, they were bound by servile ties and were thus legally regarded as unfree. Besides the ministerials, much of the urban population in these areas was unfree in various ways without this causing their status as citizens to be questioned. On the whole, however, there was a tendency on the part of lords of towns to reduce or even eliminate the ties of lordship possessed by other lords over the inhabitants, which could also be in the interests of the towns themselves. On the other hand the citizens also tried, often successfully, to reduce or eliminate the effect of such dependency, but by no means in all cases did they thereby seek to abolish their legal status, as it could offer serfs considerable political and economic advantages. In the European context it must be stressed that neither noble nor servile status stood in fundamental opposition to the urban way of life. In the origin and nature of towns, the various attendant circumstances are much more important.

Even more varied than the social and legal position of urban dwellers were their fields of economic action. These reached from agricultural work through craft and industrial production and trade, to knightly and noble, or noble-like, life-styles. They were often hard to distinguish from one another, which furthered social mobility within the urban population. Nor is this in opposition to the highly developed division of labour in the towns, which also offered possibilities of rising.

Against this background the question of a uniform consciousness for the citizens, or even the 'bourgeoisie', does not need an answer. It is inconceivable. On the other hand a community feeling can be discerned among the inhabitants of individual towns, though it should not be overestimated, and was held only by part of the inhabitants. In connection with the creation of communities this became of high political importance. It was most clearly expressed in urban historical writing, which developed earliest in the cities of imperial Italy: i.e. in that area, full of traditions, in which the *civitates* were politically more important than any other cities during the high Middle Ages, and in which at the same time lay written culture reached its highest level in Western Europe.

An example of this is the Pisan Hugo Etherianus, who, as a layman, had had a theological education in France. During his stay at the imperial court in Constantinople he engaged in theological discussions, which were reported by Barbarossa's emissaries in Austria. His fellow citizen Burgundio of Pisa (*c.*1110–93) was well acquainted with the Greek language and culture. Besides his work as judge and ambassador for his home town, he mainly appears as an eminent translator of Greek works of theology, philosophy, medicine, and law. At the same time, in the same maritime trading city, Bernardo Maragone (*c*.1110–after 1188) was working as a jurist. The *Annales Pisani* came from his pen, a history of Pisa beginning with the year 1000 and reaching as far as Maragone's time. Around the middle of the twelfth century the consuls of Genoa, the Ligurian competitor of Pisa, declared the annals written by their fellow citizen, consul, commander-in-chief, and ambassador Caffaro the official city history. Around the same time similar city histories came into being in Milan and Lodi. In Germany comparable urban histories only developed, after sporadic beginnings in Cologne towards the end of the thirteenth century, during the course of the following century.

9

Typology and Transmission of Sources

The result of the development of civilization during the period treated here was the transmission of an increasing quantity of historical evidence reaching new levels of quality. This is true not only for written sources passed on to posterity, but also for more material remains. An important factor in this was the great increase in building. Beside the renovation of older churches and other ecclesiastical and monastic buildings, this was demonstrated by the establishment of a great many new buildings of this kind as the consequence of a spiritual and religious revival, of extended pastoral activity, particularly reflected in parish churches, and generally of reinforced regional development and the growth of settlements. The advance of stone as a building material called into being much better prospects for preservation or at least the chance of scientific reconstruction. Stone was also the raw material for works of art (for example, sculpture), and this, in many German states, from the eleventh century, caused more radical changes than in most of the former Roman, particularly Mediterranean, cultural regions. More than ever before, people were able to create artefacts giving an insight into kinds of thought and behaviour in the ways of life of laymen. Due to their sacred function and the more permanent ownership of great institutions like churches and monasteries, however, most of these objects had better chances of surviving than they would have had as the property of laymen. The spread of metal as raw material in the industrial production of objects, both for the everyday needs of the broader population and as the work of artists, contributed to the increase in historical evidence. Certainly many of these things and other remains have so far been only partially evaluated by historical research, for the study of the archaeology of the Middle Ages is in a most unsatisfactory state in most German regions.

Written source material in Germany in the high Middle Ages was, with few exceptions, still written by clerics, by priests and monks. The exceptions only begin at the turn of the thirteenth century. The effects of this dominating role were further strengthened by the fact that churches and monasteries were especially well suited to keeping writings over longer periods in their libraries and archives. In this respect they differed considerably from aristocratic families and even kings and emperors, who in Germany and imperial Italy did not have a fixed residence. Admittedly secular powers could fall back on nearby monasteries and churches to preserve important documents. The same is true for communes, which in general in the twelfth century at the earliest established lasting organizations and could thus develop the beginnings of archives. Written legal titles were anyway of higher importance for the smaller churches and monasteries than for secular powers. While nobles, dukes, and kings and ultimately also the larger city communes could use military power to enforce their legal claims, the former were much more dependent on securing legal title to possessions granted or enfeoffed to them against challenge by means of written evidence. Because of that, in conflicts they shrank even less from altering or forging charters. Instead of the sword, the clerics used the pen. But the higher clerics, especially bishops and imperial abbots, had at their command both swords and pens.

The clerical writers generally gave special attention to the history of their own monasteries, churches, and bishoprics, so that often they only noted local or regional events. Some authors, however, did include general Church history and also paid attention to imperial history. For this the sharp controversies of the investiture dispute and also the lasting conflicts between empire and papacy in the Staufen period offered a new impetus. This can be seen for example in the 'annual diaries' of the monk Lampert, who was opposed to the Emperor Henry IV, but came from the otherwise pro-imperial monastery of Hersfeld; from the time of the climax in the struggles against Henry IV (1969), his work departed more and more from the given framework of monastic annals. After all, numerous monasteries and churches in the area of the German empire, particularly in pro-imperial regions, were politically and constitutionally closely connected with the kingship. Several of these authors were close to the ruler's family, or belonged to the inner circle of the royal or imperial court. One of these was Bishop Otto of Freising (after 1111–58), who has been mentioned often before. As the son of the Babenberg Margrave Leopold III and Agnes, the daughter of the Emperor Henry IV, he was closely related to the Staufen rulers Conrad III, his half-brother, and to Frederick Barbarossa. This former Cistercian abbot of Morimond (1133–8), drawing on Augustine, wrote probably the most important work on the philosophy of history of the Middle Ages in his world chronicle (*Chronica sive historia de duabus civitatibus*). This bishop wise in the ways of the world wrote the best presentation of the history of the early Staufen period in his account of Frederick Barbarossa's deeds (*Gesta Frederici*), for which he used documents from the imperial chancery.

Among the narrative sources, the surviving biographies (in the form of the traditional *Vita*) show the preferences of the clerics most clearly. For example, the biography of Archbishop Anno of Cologne (1056–75) deserves special attention. This *Vita* was compiled after his death by a monk of the monastery of Siegburg, which Anno himself had founded around 1070 as a reform centre, with the aim of furthering the archbishop's canonization. Connected with this, and with the writings of Lampert of Hersfeld, is the *Annolied*, a poem in Middle High German praising this hero, probably written around 1080. The biography of Bishop Benno of Osnabrück (1068–88) is also dedicated to the founder of a monastery. The author, a monk in the newly founded monastery of Iburg, does not, however, try to turn his hero into a saint. Thus this imperial bishop and supporter of the Salian monarchy, to which Benno owed his rise from relatively humble social origins to a bishopric, strikes us all the more vividly as a representative of the imperial episcopate. At about the same time, directly after the death of Henry IV (1106), the *Vita* of this emperor was written by an anonymous supporter, adding to the brief series of biographies of rulers. The author was perhaps Bishop Erlung of Würzburg, who was the emperor's last chancellor.

From the second half of the eleventh century the written tradition discussed single noble families. At first this happened in the histories of monasteries and abbeys founded by nobles, which, so to speak, wanted to raise a written memorial to their founders. In the course of the twelfth and thirteenth centuries these beginnings of the history of eminent founding families were further developed. In Germany this happened first with the Welfs from 1125 onwards, when this high noble family in the person of Duke Henry the Black for the first time gained decisive influence in the election of the king. In imperial Italy the monk Donizo of the monastery of St Appolonio at Canossa, founded by the Margravine Matilda of Tuscany near the family castle of her line, shortly after the death of this most powerful helper of the Gregorian papacy (d. 1115) finished a description of her life. It mainly deals with the high nobility, but beyond that it offers a history of her family, which, since the marriage in 1054 of Matilda's widowed mother the Margravine Beatrice with Duke Godfrey of Lorraine, had exerted great influence in imperial politics.

The charter tradition for the German parts of the empire is accessible almost without a gap in numerous local and regional editions and *Regesta*, even if these are of rather varying quality. Among them the royal and imperial charters are of special importance. Unfortunately they are still not completely edited in the *Diplomata* section of the *Monumenta Germaniae Historica*, particularly for the period after Barbarossa's reign. This seriously hinders research on the reigns of Frederick II and his sons. From the investiture dispute onwards, papal documents for German recipients increased, which is also a sign of the increased political influence of the papacy.

The difference between written culture in the empire north of the Alps on the one hand, where the tradition, particularly in the north and east, began very modestly only in the twelfth century, and imperial Italy on the other hand, was also expressed in notarial documents. These can be found in the south-west German area, for example, only in single cases from the end of the thirteenth century onwards. For the maritime trading city of Genoa, however, 4,500 notarial instruments survive from the second half of the twelfth century; but these are only a fraction of the documents actually produced in the city. According to reliable estimates, in Genoa towards the end of the twelfth century about 20,000 notarial instruments were made out each year. Only the *Schreinsurkunden* of Cologne, which record part of the property transactions in the urban parishes of the city from about the middle of the twelfth century, offer some kind of parallel in the German empire. They increased tremendously from the beginning of the thirteenth century, when they were also collected in *Schreinsbücher*.

Charters and notices of gift are more widespread, and more of them remain in Germany. They mostly come from the southeast German/Bavarian area. The legal transactions recorded in them are generally grants by noblemen and also by persons of lower rank, and other agreements, between churches or monasteries and individuals from their own manorial dependencies (*familiae*). In contrast to most diplomas and the charters of clerical and secular lords, in these sources the middle and sometimes even lower social groups also come into our view. On the whole this material has not yet received sufficient attention.

New information, mostly for larger clerical manors, and about the peasant and sometimes also the urban population, is promised from the estate surveys and rentals. To a great extent they come from clerical lordships. The surveys of the imperial abbey of Werden should be mentioned, as well as that of the old Benedictine monastery of St Maximin outside Trier and the early thirteenth century rental of the archbishops of Trier. From the turn of the twelfth and thirteenth centuries secular lords also had their rights and incomes put down in writing in a similar way. The earliest example is the legal records of the counts of Falkenstein, which came into being between 1164 and 1170. About a generation later there followed the first version of the *Landbuch* of the dukes of Bavaria, and similar rentals for the Babenberg duke of Lower Austria and Styria These sources are a product of the developing administration of the rising territorial lordships.

Comparable individual documents from around the German royal court are also preserved from the twelfth and thirteenth centuries. The best-known ones are the royal *Tafelgüterverzeichnis*, the composition of which has been dated to around the middle of the twelfth century by the latest research, and the so-called 'imperial tax list' (*Reichssteuerliste*) of 1241-2. These lists, however, are certainly not the products of systematic administration. Rather they were compiled for specific occasions, i.e. without any long-term aim. The differences between them and for example the Anglo-Norman Domesday Book, from the late eleventh century, are obvious. They are rooted in the completely different basis of power and forms of administration in the two kingdoms. In 1066, the same year in which the Norman Duke William won the battle of Hastings and began the conquest of the Anglo-Saxon kingdom, the then sixteen-year-old King Henry IV, who had only just come of age, stood before the ruins of an imperial policy which had severely impaired the power and prestige of the Salian monarchy during a nearly ten-year regency.

II
GERMANY FROM THE MIDDLE OF THE ELEVENTH TO THE MIDDLE OF THE TWELFTH CENTURY: TRADITION AND CHANGE

Imperial Rule from Henry III
to Barbarossa (1056–1152)

At the news of Henry III's death, Humbert, cardinal bishop of Silva Candida, is said to have added to his mourning the almost programmatic request that God might have mercy and install princes who knew how to rule themselves and all their subjects: 'since from this our little king we can, alas, receive no lordly assistance' [332: i. 13].

The cardinal, a Lorrainer who came to Rome with Bishop Bruno of Toul (Pope Leo IX), was well able to judge the importance of the break caused by the death of the emperor at the age of only 39 (5 October 1056). The reformed papacy, to which the monk Humbert amongst others owed his advancement at the papal court, had only been able to stand its ground against the power of the noble families of Rome with the strong protection of the Salian emperor. The battle was not yet by any means decided. Church reform, supported by the emperor and furthered mainly by immigrants from the parts of the empire north of the Alps, or at least by non-Romans, had not yet made itself at home in Rome. German imperial bishops—among them especially Leo IX—had helped the efforts at Church reform to achieve a breakthrough at the papal court, which in turn strengthened the authority of the emperor. The Salian imperial Church policy, which was intended to push back the power of the aristocracy but which depended largely on aristocratic clergymen, had thereby taken over the papacy itself. The reformed papacy was dependent on the emperor. In vain had Leo IX tried to secure and enlarge the imperial–papal power base towards the south by military action against the Normans. After the defeat at Civitate (1053), the pope was even taken prisoner by the Norman victors, who released him only shortly before his death. With Bishop Gebhard of Eichstätt, who adopted the name Victor II (March 1055–July 1057), Henry III had been able once again to put a German on to the papal throne. Significantly, Victor II remained bishop of Eichstätt.

With the death of the emperor, the imperial bishop and pope, who had only been in Rome for a short time, lost his most important support—as Humbert surely realized. This struck at the roots of the reformed papacy. At best a substitute could be found in Duke Godfrey of Lorraine ('the Bearded'), who against the emperor's wishes had married Beatrice, the widow of the margrave of Tuscany and the lady of important dominions on both sides of the Apennines.

In 1055 Henry III had led his last Italian campaign against the duke whose rule was thus anchored on both sides of the Alps and Apennines, and had—not least owing to the support of cities within the margrave's dominion—won some successes. For some time Duke Godfrey had had close connections with reforming circles at the papal court. Under Leo IX his brother Frederick had even risen to the post of head of the still admittedly modest papal chancery. During the Italian campaign, in which Henry III and Victor II had worked together in the mutual interests of empire and reformed papacy, Frederick had withdrawn to the monastery of Monte Cassino. As sheet anchors for papal reform on the death of the emperor (whom, as one of the pope's entourage, he had seen at close quarters in his court at Goslar), the Lorrainer cardinal bishop and head of the radical wing of Church reform could make no more obvious choice than the ducal brothers Godfrey and Frederick of Lorraine.

The dying emperor had entrusted the empire and his successor, still only six years old, to the protection of his pope. Victor II fulfilled this task. The pope helped the king, for whom Henry III in 1053 had obtained the agreement, though conditional, of the high nobility, to secure the right of succession to the kingship. For the emperor's widow Agnes, the daughter of the duke of Aquitaine and Poitou, the pope secured the position of regent. At the same time he ended the conflict with Godfrey, who was reinstated as duke of Lorraine and margrave of Tuscany. After this the pope returned to Italy, but died before he could set foot in Rome. With Victor II the reformed papacy ceased to be rooted in the Salian empire.

A month before the death of Victor II, Godfrey's brother Frederick, who had previously been created abbot of Monte Cassino by Humbert, was raised to the cardinalate. With no consultation of the 'little king', whose legal title *Patricius* gave him the right of first voice, which Henry III had exercised several times, this cardinal was elected as Victor II's successor and consecrated as Pope Stephen IX. The reformers were forced to act quickly to prevent the election of a Roman noble. They sent a legation to the German royal court to seek subsequent agreement to the papal election. Before they reached it, Stephen IX died, after ruling for only eight months (August 1057–March 1058). Under him the monk Hildebrand, who had meanwhile risen to the rank of archdeacon, made his first contacts with the *Pataria* of Milan. Stephen IX not only designated as his successor as abbot of Monte Cassino Desiderius, who in 1086 under the name Victor III succeeded Pope Gregory VII, but the Lorrainer pope also designated his successor on St Peter's chair. In the Burgundian Bishop Gerard of Florence, who became Pope Nicholas II (1058–61), a confidant of Duke Godfrey once more took over the Reformed Church. The electors, assembled in Siena and led by five cardinal bishops, had possibly obtained the agreement of the German court even before the election. Political security in this was all the more necessary as immediately after Stephen IX's death in Rome the noble Tusculani party had already imposed a pope of their own in the person of Benedict X. Only at the beginning of 1059 was Nicholas II able to expel this nobles' pope from Rome, with massive military support from Duke Godfrey.

These events and political connections found their expression in the papal election decree of the Lateran council of 1059, expressly aimed at maintaining the freedom of the church (*libertas ecclesiae*). In this the decisive role in the election of the successors of St Peter was assigned to the college of cardinals, the members of which originally had only liturgical and charitable functions in the churches of the city of Rome. In close connection with the then unusual form of Nicholas II's own election, the seven cardinal bishops were awarded the right of proposal before the twenty-eight cardinal priests and deacons. If electoral freedom was endangered in the city they received even greater powers, so that an election outside Rome could practically be decided amongst themselves. The rights of the king were only acknowledged in a no doubt deliberately vague formula. But it was unequivocally stated that the right reserved to the king was dependent on papal grant, so that it could be withheld or withdrawn from any of Henry IV's successors. The main thrust of the papal election decree, however, was not aimed at the distant German king, but against the much closer Roman nobility, who threatened the reformed papacy directly and immediately. Thus the papal election decree can be interpreted as an emergency measure by the reformed papacy, which could not expect any help from its legitimate protector, the still infant German king.

Considering these circumstances, the view that the prohibition of 'lay investiture' at this synod, pronounced only in one sentence, was especially directed against the king's right of investiture, and thus undermined the legal basis of lordship over the imperial Church, becomes less convincing. The .prohibition read: 'No cleric or priest is allowed to receive a church from laypeople in any way, neither for nothing nor for money' [17: i. 547, no. 384]. This is not only directed against simony, which the Emperor Henry III had also opposed, but against the investiture of clerics by laypeople altogether. Meanwhile it has become questionable whether this clause can be interpreted as, so to speak, a short version of the opinions of Humbert of Silva Candida as he formulated them in the work he wrote in 1057–8 (Libri Tres adversus Simoniacos). In it the cardinal bishop, doubtless influential at the papal court, had disputed the right of the king, whom he put on the same level as the laity, to grant the ring and staff, the episcopal insignia. However, this work obviously remained without any wider resonance; therefore it cannot be ruled out that in the 1059 prohibition of lay investiture the king was not counted among the laity, and that in it only lesser churches were meant.

At any rate it must be stated that in the political conflicts between empire and papacy over the next decades, the prohibition of lay investiture only played a subordinate role. The general prohibition of investiture, which then was clearly directed against the German king or emperor just as against all other kings, was not announced by Pope Gregory VII until 1078, when the first peak of his conflict with Henry IV had already passed. In this respect also the Lateran synod of 1059 was not the signal for the conflict of principle between the reformed papacy and the German kings' rule of the imperial churches. But nevertheless the decisions made there show that the reformers primarily pursued the interests of the papacy, without taking into too much consideration the special legal claims of the Salian monarchy, for them, in practice, far away.

Only a few months later the papal court drew further political conclusions from this situation. The enfeoffment of the Norman princes in August 1059 marks another stage in the reformed papacy's growing independence of the royal court. By granting fiefs to the Normans Nicholas II passed over the emperor's legal claims in southern Italy and Sicily. The pope accordingly even bound his Norman vassals to support him in case of conflict with the German king and emperor. The Normans and Duke Godfrey of Lorraine and Tuscany also supported the election to the papacy of Bishop Anselm of Lucca, from a Milanese noble family, who took the name Alexander II (1061-73). A few weeks later, influential circles at the German court, in co-operation with Roman and northern Italian nobles as well as the imperial bishops, opposed him by installing Bishop Cadalus of Parma as a pope of their own (Honorius II, d. 1071/2). The reversal of the original positions seemed to be complete. However, it only lasted until 1064, when the royal court, led by Archbishop Anno of Cologne, abandoned the antipope Honorius in favour of Alexander II. In March of the following year, with the knighting of Henry IV, the independent government of the now fourteen-year-old Salian began.

During the regency the weaknesses of Salian imperial government, hidden, though sometimes only with difficulty, during the reign of Henry III by the personal authority of the emperor, became clearly evident in other ways as well. One of them was the fact that there were no generally accepted rules for the guardianship. After the death of Pope Victor II the empress relied on the advice of various high nobles and clerics. These usually tried to use their influence at court to advance their own interests.

In politics the most effective personalities among the imperial bishops were the Archbishops Anno II of Cologne (1056-75) and Adalbert of Hamburg-Bremen (1043-72). Already under Henry III they had both had close connections with the Salian monarchy. Anno, who came from an unimportant Swabian noble family and who was invested by Henry III, at first concentrated successfully on extending the rights of the Cologne see. He also tried from very early on to promote his relatives and friends, and especially to gain influential positions for them in the imperial church. In 1059 he succeeded in getting his nephew Burchard into the bishopric of Halberstadt. The next stage of imperial politics finally provided him with the justification for taking power over the royal child himself, and thus for decisively determining imperial policy. The occasion for this was when the emperor's widow Agnes took the veil after the installation of the antipope Honorius II and thereby in effect resigned the regency. Only a few months later, in April 1062, Anno abducted the king from the island of Kaiserswerth and took him to Cologne, at the same time taking possession of the imperial insignia.

With these hostages Anno, for a while undisputed, determined imperial policy, for which events in northern Italy now became more important. In the following year he managed to impose his brother Werner as archbishop of Magdeburg, although a high nobleman had already been elected to the office. Only a little later, however, he had to accept Archbishop Adalbert of Hamburg-Bremen as an equal partner at the royal court. Like the archbishop of Cologne, Adalbert had also been successful as a territorial politician, who did not shy away from conflict with the duke of Saxony. In contrast to Anno, Adalbert's political interests were mainly directed towards the north and east. There the archbishop, who came from a Thuringian comital family, pursued great missionary plans reaching as far as Finland, Iceland, and Greenland. Adalbert combined this, and his missionary work among the neighbouring heathen tribes, with the aim of gaining the status of a patriarchate for his bishopric. In this way he hoped to thwart the Danish king's plan to install his own archbishopric which would cover the whole of his kingdom. These diverging interests further sharpened the competition between the two archbishops at the royal court.

The court's lack of authority and power of enforcement during the minority, above all, shifted the balance of power between the kingship and the high nobility further to the disadvantage of the former, and thereby hastened a development which even Henry III had only with difficulty been able to restrain. The quick reconciliation with Duke Godfrey of Lorraine and Tuscany shortly after the emperor's death already pointed to changes in the basic situation. While Henry III had for years administered the duchies of Bavaria, Swabia, and Carinthia himself, his widow, soon after the death of the previous holder, still in the year 1057, enfeoffed the Burgundian noble Rudolf of Rheinfelden with Swabia. At the same time he was entrusted with the administration of the kingdom of Burgundy, which since 1032 had been united with the empire in the person of the emperor; in this *regnum Arelatense*, however, the kingship was very weak. The new duke of Swabia and rector of Burgundy simultaneously tied himself closely to the Salian royal family by marrying one of the emperor's daughters. After the early death of this Salian lady in 1060, Rudolf married the sister of the same Bertha of Savoy and Turin to whom Henry III in 1055 had betrothed his son and successor.

If in this case the tie of the new duke to the Salian ruling family seemed to be secure, the same was not the case when it came to the grant of the duchy of Bavaria, which the first Salians had effectively treated as crown land and which Henry III had finally entrusted to his wife. In 1061 Agnes appointed the high Saxon noble Otto of Northeim as her successor.

In the same year the royal court entrusted the Swabian noble Berthold of Zähringen with the duchy of Carinthia, where, however, he had as little success as his recent predecessors. More important for future developments was the assignment as early as 1059 of the duchy of Saxony to Ordulf, the son of the previous duke, Bernard, of the Billung family. Under Ordulf the conflict with Adalbert of Hamburg-Bremen came to a head. Through his marriage with a daughter of the Norwegian king, Ordulf obtained close personal contacts with the northern kingdom. Furthermore Harald, the king of Norway, was married to a sister of Yaroslav prince of Kiev, thereby reinforcing close connections with Scandinavia; Yaroslav's other sisters were the wives of the king of France, the king of Hungary, and the duke of Poland.

The range of the political activities of the German high nobility becomes even clearer with Duke Godfrey of Lorraine and Tuscany. The king, who in 1065 had just come of age, enlarged Godfrey's dominion with the duchy of Lower Lorraine which Godfrey demanded as his inheritance so that his power reached as far as the estuary of the Rhine in the north, and in the south to the borders of the Patrimony of St Peter. The noble family of the Welfs also had close contacts with northern Italy through the marriage of one of their daughters with Margrave Albert Azzo II of Este. After the extinction of the Welf house with the death of Welf III in 1055, Welf IV, the son of this margrave and of the Welf lady Chuniza, became the founder of the younger Welf line, which later became of great importance in the history of the empire.

The young king, however, even after coming of age, was prevented from setting out on the announced journey to Rome, and thus from boosting his reputation by obtaining the emperorship. To begin with, Archbishop Adalbert used his influence to postpone the Italian expedition, on which his competitor Anno might have gained an advantage through his office as arch-chancellor of Italy. But the rescheduled Italian journey did not happen in 1067 either, because Godfrey of Lorraine and Tuscany had forestalled the king with an ultimately unsuccessful military campaign against the Normans.

In 1065 the royal power base was even further eroded by grants of imperial land and monasteries. Characteristically the archbishops of Cologne and Hamburg-Bremen attempted to secure the lion's share for themselves. Anno saw to it that the royal grant of the imperial monasteries of Malmédy and Kornelimünster went to his archbishopric. About the same time Adalbert had himself granted the imperial demesne in Duisburg, as well as the old imperial monasteries of Lorsch and Corvey. In the same year the Salian family monastery at Limburg was granted to the bishop of Speyer. But through these annexations Adalbert aroused the resistance of other nobles, so that, against Henry IV's wishes, he had to flee the royal court. This loss of power by the archbishop worked particularly to the advantage of the duke of Saxony, while it encouraged an uprising by the heathen Obodrites. Directly after Adalbert's fall, Anno succeeded in having his nephew Conrad elected and invested archbishop of Trier. But this action met with resistance in the city of Trier. The burgrave of Trier ambushed Conrad and his attendants at Bitburg on his journey to Trier and held him prisoner, and a little later the burgrave's men threw him down a cliff and murdered him. The event demonstrates how far Salian kingship had lost its authority by the beginning of Henry IV's independent reign.

As there was no duchy directly available for the king himself, and control over the imperial churches and monasteries had been rendered considerably more difficult, he was all the more dependent for strengthening his position on building up a power base independent of the nobility and higher clergy. To begin with, Henry IV concentrated his efforts on the duchy of Saxony, the original home of his Ottonian predecessors. In this former crown land in the mean time a great part of the imperial estates had come into other hands. One exception was the relatively thinly settled Harz area with Goslar as its centre, where Henry III had created a favourable basis for an exclusive area of imperial lordship, with the imperial palace and the closely associated, richly endowed monastery of SS Simon and Jude. In addition, here in the Rammelsberg silver mines was by far the richest source of finance in the German empire.

In this restricted area, and in the neighbouring region of east Saxony, in 1067—i.e. about a year after the conquest of the Anglo-Saxon kingdom by the Norman Duke William—Henry IV began a castle policy which, in its ruthlessness and determination, many contemporaries regarded as unprecedented. Within a few years he had built a close-meshed net of castles in the east of the old Saxon tribal region, secured them with garrisons, and handed control of them to men who were mostly strangers to the region, especially Swabians, who in most cases were of low or even unfree origin. From the castles, these war-hardened administrators, completely dependent on the king—in general probably ministerials—worked at regaining the royal possessions and rights, genuine or merely alleged. The investigation of these claims is said to have been based on the testimony of witnesses; thus they used similar methods to those of the Norman conquerors in England. When the decision went in favour of the king—and according to the Saxons concerned this often happened arbitrarily—the existing owners had to offer various payments in kind, money, and also labour. Peasant labour was anyway used to build the castles and to attend to their upkeep.

To his adversaries in the opposition which grew out of this policy, Henry personally offered further opportunities to attack him when in 1069 he initiated a divorce from his wife Bertha, and only gave up the plan when the papal legate, Peter Damian, sharply protested. It seems that a year later the king used a mere excuse to proceed in court against the Bavarian Duke Otto of Northeim, in claiming that he had tried to overthrow and murder the king. Sentencing Otto and taking him prisoner in 1071 enabled Henry to take power over the large allodial possessions and fiefs which the duke held in the royal sphere of influence in the Harz area. The duchy of Bavaria, which was also taken away from Otto of Northeim, Henry granted to Welf IV. This son of the margrave of Este repudiated his wife, one of Otto's daughters, directly after the condemnation of his father-in-law, and soon after married a noble widow from England (a daughter of the duke of Flanders). The general sentiment in Saxony against Henry IV worsened when the king, after Duke Ordulf of Saxony's death, kept prisoner his son Magnus who had taken part in Otto of Northeim's feud, and thus further delayed the succession to the ducal office.

As a result of these occurrences an open uprising developed in east Saxony in the summer of 1073. In this the leading roles were taken by relatives of Anno of Cologne—Bishop Burchard of Halberstadt and Archbishop Werner of Magdeburg—by the bishop of Hildesheim, the duke's son Hermann Billung, and also by Otto of Northeim, after he had been released from prison. Henry IV did not accept the demands of the Saxons, who in particular wanted him to give up his territorial policy. He could only escape the threat posed by the superior forces of the rebels who besieged him in the Harzburg by fleeing to the south. He finally found security and active support with the citizens of Worms, in the middle of the old Salian family lands. The king's flight from the Harzburg into the urban 'castle' of Worms—from the centre of the Ottonian crown lands to the Salian family territories—clearly shows the constrained position of the Salian kingdom at the outset of the struggle between empire and papacy which began at the same time. Meanwhile the southern German dukes, Welf of Bavaria and Rudolf of Rheinfelden, who supported him, had alienated themselves from the king. Among the high nobility Henry IV could only rely on the support of Duke Godfrey 'the Hunchback' of Lorraine and Tuscany. After his father's death in 1069 Godfrey had taken over his large inheritance on both sides of the Alps and had secured it by marrying Matilda, the daughter of Beatrice of Tuscany-Canossa.

In these unfavourable circumstances Henry IV was obliged by the Peace of Gerstungen in 1074 to promise the Saxons to raze the royal castles—an undertaking which he made no haste to carry out. After the defensive positions of the Harzburg had been pulled down, peasants from the area looted the castle and the church and did not even shrink from violating the graves of members of the royal family there. Because of this obvious injustice to the king, Henry received wider support against other rebels. He now demanded the unconditional surrender of the Saxons, and of the Thuringians who had joined them mainly because of a tithe decision made against them in favour of the archbishop of Mainz. The royal army defeated the Saxon and Thuringian troops, who were heavily reinforced by peasants, near Homburg an der Unstrut on 9 June 1075. By the end of October in the same year Henry IV had enforced the unconditional surrender of his enemies: the leaders of the Saxon and Thuringian rebels were arrested, their possessions confiscated; and thus the king's castle policy, which he immediately resumed, gained great opportunities for development. At Christmas 1075 in Goslar Henry IV even managed to oblige the dukes to swear an oath to recognize his one-and-a-half-year-old son Conrad as his successor to the throne.

Only a few months after the victory over the Saxons and Thuringians and only a few weeks after the success in settling the succession to the throne, Pope Gregory VII during the synod of February 1076 deprived the king of the government of Germany and Italy, freed all Christians from their oaths sworn to him, and excommunicated him. The pope, who clothed this legal act in the form of a solemn prayer to Peter, the prince of the apostles, thus exercised the right to dethrone the emperor, as had been formulated—doubtless under the influence of Gregory VII—in the *Dictatus Papae*. This practical dethroning of the king by the pope, which had never happened before, was the first climax of an escalation which led from alienation between monarchy and reformed papacy to sharp and fundamental disputes between the two powers.

The conflict had come alight over the appointment to the archiepiscopal see in the Lombard metropolis of Milan. The conflict between the *Pataria*, supported by the reformed papacy, and the royal party, in this, the biggest city in imperial Italy, exerted a decisive influence on its course. But events in Saxony already mentioned affected it too. In 1071 Archbishop Wido of Milan (1045–71), who since the beginning of the *Pataria* had been the centre of the attacks of this religious–political movement, had resigned his office and had sent back to Henry IV the ring and staff, the symbols of his authority. The king immediately invested the Milanese cleric Godfrey (1071–5), also a noble. The *Pataria*, led by the knight Erlembald, took strong measures against Godfrey, who was excommunicated by Pope Alexander II. Ignoring the investiture rights of the German king, they raised their own archbishop in the priest Atto, who was supported by the pope. Only shortly before his death, at the Lenten synod of 1073 Pope Alexander excommunicated some of Henry IV's councillors for simony, which should have been taken as a sharp warning to the king.

Under the impact of the rebellion of the Saxons, who had also protested against the king's councillors, Henry in the late summer of 1073 reacted in conciliatory style to the reproaches of the papacy. Following this Gregory VII, who had meanwhile been raised as successor of St Peter, again without considering the royal right of consent, now on his part changed his tone. In the spring of 1074 the royal councillors were absolved from excommunication by a papal legation, but the plan of a reform synod in Germany pursued by the same legates foundered, mainly on the resistance of the imperial bishops. These objected to the growing centralism of the papacy, which had already proceeded several times against high clerics on the grounds of simony and had forced them to justify themselves at the papal court. The representatives of the German bishops, who at an assembly in Strasbourg at Christmas 1074 had openly voiced their independence of the papacy, were deposed by Gregory VII at the Lenten synod of 1075. At the same time the pope again threatened the royal councillors with excommunication. The pope's measures against various German bishops, among them Archbishop Liemar of Bremen (1072–1101), could be at least partly mitigated by personal appearances before the pope.

While the conflict between the papacy and the German imperial Church to some extent cooled down, that between Henry IV and Gregory VII gained new impetus by the king's intervention in imperial Italy. In Milan the fighting had come to such a point that the Patarene leader Erlembald himself exercised a quasi-dictatorial government in the city and the country around it; finally he was murdered shortly after Easter 1075. Strengthened by his successes against the Saxons and Thuringians, Henry IV tried to take advantage of the favourable situation. In agreement with the adversaries of the *Pataria* he invested the Milanese cleric Tedald as archbishop of Milan, who as a member of the royal chapel had close contacts with the royal court. He thus dropped Archbishop Godfrey, whom he had himself installed but who had not been able to make headway against the *Pataria* and its archbishop, Atto. Furthermore, in areas of close territorial interest to the papacy—Fermo and Spoleto—Henry had other bishops deposed.

At the beginning of December 1075 Gregory VII protested sharply against these measures, by threatening the Salian more or less openly with excommunication. Following this, at an imperial gathering in Worms on 24 January 1076 the German episcopate, led by Archbishop Siegfried of Mainz, reacted with an open breach. The bishops refused obedience to Gregory VII, whom they accused of morally objectionable conduct. Soon afterwards they were followed in this by the bishops of Lombardy. Henry IV also condemned the pope, whom he insulted as a 'false monk'. In a letter to the Romans he called upon them to rebel against Gregory and to elect a successor acceptable to him. He based his authority over the papacy on his office as *Patricius*, which had been bestowed on him by the Romans. In a manifesto destined for publication in Germany, which partly differed from the letter to the Romans, Henry once again stressed the sacral character of kingship: the king is the Lord's anointed, who is not to be judged except by God alone unless he apostatizes from the faith. Gregory VII took up this challenge and, as mentioned above, at the Lenten synod of 1076 declared Henry IV deposed and excommunicated.

[*b*] FROM CANOSSA TO THE POWER STRUGGLE
BETWEEN HENRY IV AND HENRY V

This period, embracing almost three decades, with its initial and final events—the penitential journey of the king deposed by the pope, and the emperor's loss of power, deprived of it by his own son—represents the downfall of the Salian monarchy and of the Western Roman Empire. Precisely during this period the high nobility in Germany, in co-operation with the reformed papacy, drew decisive and long-lasting advantage from the monarchy's loss of power and authority. On the other hand, the position of the imperial Churches in Germany and even more in northern Italy was in general badly affected by the severe disputes between empire and papacy, which mainly concentrated on the bishoprics and thus on the episcopal cities. The power struggles over the appointments to bishoprics often led to schisms lasting years. They often seriously hindered episcopal government at its centre—the episcopal city. In the power vacuum caused by this, the developing city communes found favourable conditions for expansion.

Already in the months after his excommunication by Gregory VII, whom Henry IV on his side had publicly excommunicated at synods, the king was forced to realize that his support against the pope was fading even among the imperial bishops. The Salian lost his most important supporter among the secular princes when Duke Godfrey of Lorraine was murdered in February 1076. Godfrey's widow Matilda, after the death of her mother Beatrice (April 1076), became the sole successor to the margraviate of Tuscany and to the further complex of lordships in imperial Italy. For a long time the

margravine had had close connections with the reformed papacy. Soon afterwards the rebellions in Saxony started again.
An assembly of princes at Tribur in October 1076 forced the
king to revoke the deposition of Gregory VII made at Worms.
The emperor had to promise obedience to the pope and had to
agree to dismiss his excommunicated councillors and to renounce the support of the city of Worms. The princes made
further recognition of Henry IV dependent on his obtaining
absolution from the papal excommunication by February 1077.
They agreed with Gregory VII that the pope would make a
decision in person on the conflict between the princes and the
king in Augsburg at the beginning of February. Henry's bitter
opponents were determined to elect a new king.

Henry IV forestalled these plans by setting off for Italy
around Christmas with his family and a small household, in
spite of the hard winter. When Gregory learned of the king's
expedition to Italy he broke off his journey to Germany and
went to Canossa, the family castle of the Margravine Matilda,
and put himself under the protection of the most powerful high
noble in imperial Italy. On 28 January 1077, after lengthy
negotiations in which Matilda and Abbot Hugh of Cluny,
Henry IV's godfather, also took part, and after three days of
royal penance in public, the pope received the king back into
the Church. At the same time Gregory VII acknowledged the
Salian as king once more. Henry IV for his part nevertheless
had to declare on oath his agreement to the planned papal
arbitration and had to grant Gregory a safe conduct to it.

It was one of Henry IV's achievements by his penitence
at Canossa to cut the ground from under the papal court of
arbitration. With the king's absolution his princely opponents
lost their religious-political justification and, not least, a part
of their adherents. A more severe and lasting consequence,
however, was the loss which the sacral legitimation of the kingship, the immediacy of his office of ruler to God, which Henry
had so strongly stressed only shortly before, had suffered at
Canossa. Through the act of penitence, which Henry performed
towards the pope like a lay person, the foundations of royal
precedence over the high nobility, and at the same time of
royal lordship over the imperial Church, were infringed and
even called in question.

The tactical advantage Henry IV gained at Canossa certainly disturbed the actions of the anti-royal German princes,
but it did not stop them. The number of these decided enemies
of the Salians, however, remained restricted. Probably not
more than a dozen of them—including the three southern
German dukes Rudolf, Welf IV, and Berthold, also Otto of
Northeim, and the archbishops of Mainz, Salzburg, and Magdeburg—held a new royal election at Forchheim in Franconia
in mid-March 1077. They raised Rudolf of Rheinfelden, the
Swabian duke and the king's brother-in-law, as the successor
of the Salian, in their opinion still dethroned. Rudolf had to
pledge himself in front of the princes and the papal legates
to appoint bishops only according to ecclesiastical law, and
to renounce hereditary kingship in favour of an unrestricted
princely right of election. In contrast to the hitherto current
practice of designation and the bloodright which it
strengthened, to which as recently as Christmas 1075 Henry
IV had bound the dukes, the kingdom was thus to be regarded
as an office, whose holder should be appointed by the princes
on the grounds of his personal suitability, in the name of the
people and in a free election. Instead of the election of a new
pope, as Henry IV had planned only a year previously, the
first anti-king in German history had been elected with the
agreement of many bishops and with the approval of the papal
legates.

In spite of some military successes gained by the anti-king's
party in 1078 and again at the beginning of 1080, the ensuing
war between the two kings brought no decision. The circle
of Rudolf's supporters remained restricted to those who had
elected him. In 1079 Henry IV enfeoffed Frederick, of the Staufen family, with the duchy of Swabia, and he also bound him
to the Salian dynasty by marriage to his only daughter Agnes.
In Swabia, however, the Staufen first had to succeed against
Berthold, Rudolf's son, who had been installed by the other
side. At first Gregory VII remained neutral in this struggle for
the throne, which added to the antagonism of the parties and
interest groups within the empire on other levels. No doubt he
was strengthened in this attitude by the powerful support given
to the Salian in imperial Italy, especially by the episcopate.

Only after Henry IV's defeat near Flarchheim on the Unstrut (27 January 1080) did Gregory VII at the following Lenten synod renew the excommunication and deposition of the emperor, again in the form of a solemn prayer. To King Rudolf's supporters he even granted remission of all sins, thereby drawing near to the crusading idea. In his Easter sermon the pope even prophesied death or destruction to Henry IV should he not have repented by 1 August. Gregory VII would have been supported in his confidence by the fact that the Margravine Matilda of Tuscany-Canossa only shortly before this donated all her possessions on either side of the Alps to the Roman Church, protecting them at the same time from seizure by Henry IV.

Gregory VII's prophecy, which the pope had formulated in the consciousness of complete agreement with the will of God, was not fulfilled. In June 1080 the members of a synod in Brixen, mainly bishops from Lombardy, in agreement with the Salian king, who was present, decided to dethrone Gregory VII in legal form. At the same time they raised as pope Archbishop Wibert of Ravenna, whom Gregory had already removed from office in 1078 as the leader of the pope's opponents in imperial Italy. God's judgement against Henry IV, voiced by Gregory VII, turned against the pope when Rudolf of Rheinfelden died immediately after his victorious battle at the Elster in mid-October 1080. For Henry IV the way was open for the royal coronation expedition to Rome, planned a decade and a half before, where the decision between the emperor and the Gregorian papacy was to be reached.

The prospects of success for the expedition to Rome, for which Henry IV set out in March 1081 with an army consisting mainly of ministerials, seemed favourable. Margravine Matilda's freedom of action was much restricted after a military defeat she had suffered in October 1080 at the hands of supporters of Henry IV. Shortly before this Gregory VII had been reconciled with the Norman duke, Robert Guiscard, whom he had previously excommunicated in 1075, but this papal vassal primarily pursued his own plans for a military campaign against the Byzantine empire, on whose western extremity he secured important bases for himself at Durazzo and on the island of Corfu. In spite of these favourable circumstances,

Henry IV had to break off the siege of Rome in June 1081. A renewed attempt the following year did not succeed either, in spite of the king finding support particularly in the Tuscan cities of Pisa and Lucca. To the citizens of Pisa Henry IV even granted a charter confirming their right of participation in the succession to the office of margrave of Tuscany, of which he had deprived the Margravine Matilda, whom he had outlawed. On a further attempt at conquest in June 1083 Henry was at least able to take over the Leonine city with St Peter's, on the west bank of the Tiber, but without the Castel Sant'Angelo, the former tomb of the Emperor Hadrian.

Henry IV did not attain the main objective of his Italian expedition until March 1084, after three years of campaigning. Meanwhile he had made a pact with the Byzantine emperor, mainly directed against Robert Guiscard, and had also taken advantage of antagonism among the Normans. Favoured by political changes in the city of Rome, in which the money the Salian had been given by the Byzantine emperor probably played a role, Henry IV with Wibert of Ravenna, destined to become pope, now gained access to the city east of the Tiber. A council condemned Gregory VII, who had taken refuge in the Castel Sant'Angelo, for high treason, and excommunicated and dethroned him. Wibert was again elected pope in Rome and on Palm Sunday enthroned in controversial form in St Peter's church as Clement III. On Easter Monday the pope, dependent on Henry IV, carried out the emperor's coronation. Thus the Salian for his part made his imperial title dependent on the fate of the pope he had elevated.

Only when his papal lord was under the utmost threat did Robert Guiscard (d. 1085) decide to come with a large army to the assistance of Gregory, still besieged by the emperor in the Castel Sant'Angelo. The military supremacy of the Norman duke, who in the event of the emperor's victory could expect further interventions by Henry IV in his as yet by no means secure south Italian dominions, caused the Salian and his pope to leave Rome. The city was conquered by Guiscard's troops and Gregory VII freed. The Norman army, however, committed such devastation and atrocities that Gregory could not feel safe there without the protection of his liberators. He spent the last year of his life in Salerno. In the same year Clement III was even able to return to Rome for a long period. The 'holy Satan', as Gregory was called by the moderate reformer Cardinal Peter Damian, died in his Norman exile, in Salerno on 25 May 1085. His well-authenticated last words, 'I have loved justice and hated iniquity: therefore I die in exile', again show his deeply rooted belief that he had acted in accordance with God's will. Not until the Counter-Reformation (1606) was Gregory VII canonized. With the death of this pope who for more than a quarter of a century had exerted a decisive influence on the reformed papacy and during his pontificate had stamped it with his own image, the reform party entered into a period of crisis, also caused by splits within the college of cardinals. While the imperial pope Clement III found acceptance far beyond the area of Henry IV's power, it was not until a year after Gregory VII's death that the opposing side were able to choose a successor in the person of Abbot Desiderius of Monte Cassino (Victor III), who was consecrated in March 1087 under Norman protection. After his pontificate of only six months it again took six months until the reform party elected as its new pope, Urban II, the former prior of Cluny, Odo, who had been made a cardinal by Gregory VII. In spite of the successes Urban II achieved, mainly in France, with his compromise politics, he was not able to reside permanently in Rome until 1093. The consolidation of the reformed papacy, thereby instituted after more than a decade of external trouble as well as internal tension among the reformers, began in the same year as Henry IV's empire experienced its deepest decline so far.

Yet Henry IV's Italian campaign, from which he returned in summer 1084, had strengthened the emperor's position in Germany. Since August 1081, however, the anti-kingship had been renewed with the election of Count Hermann of Salm, from a once very influential Lorrainer noble family. This second German anti-king, who himself had only a modest power base, found right from the beginning far less support among the crucial German nobles and among the bishops than his predecessor. In the following years Hermann remained restricted to eastern Saxony with Goslar as his centre—i.e. approximately the former scene of Henry IV's castle policy; thus it was not

possible for him to take action in imperial Italy in favour of
Gregory VII and against the Salian. After the end of Henry
IV's Italian campaign the anti-king lost further support, especially among the Saxon episcopate. In 1088 he even had to
retreat from Saxony to his Lorraine homeland, where, still
in the same year, he was killed, probably during inheritance
disputes with his relatives. The German anti-kingship, supported by the papacy, had broken down. In this form it was
only renewed more than one-and-a-half centuries later, after
the deposition of the Emperor Frederick II.

Henry IV on the other hand already in 1087 had his son
Conrad, then thirteen, crowned in Aachen, and thus secured
the succession in his own family. The emperor also had success
with the renewal of lordship over the imperial Church after his
return from the Italian expedition. In spring 1085 an imperial
synod in Mainz, attended by about twenty archbishops and
bishops and many secular princes and other nobles, decided on
measures against the anti-imperial party. Fifteen archbishops
and bishops, all of them, however, in less important sees, were
excommunicated and dethroned as adversaries of the emperor.
In so far as this had not already happened, Henry IV in the
following years installed his supporters in these bishoprics, so
that schism ruled in many sees. At the same synod at Mainz
the bishops announced a Peace of God effective over the whole
empire. In Mainz for the first time the emperor took a direct
part in this politically important form of peacekeeping, which
for a few years had been occasionally used by his supporters,
and also by his Saxon opponents, but only with regional effect.
Thus the emperor participated via his bishops in the Peace of
God movement, which also found a strong echo among wide
circles of the population.

Also in Mainz the emperor had Duke Vratislav of Bohemia
made king of Bohemia and Poland (d. 1092), and with this
royal title, which was only of personal application, he
strengthened his ally's connections with imperial policy. Vratislav's support was of further value during the following years
when Henry IV was fighting in Saxony. In 1089 Henry
removed another source of conflict by granting the duchy of
Lower Lorraine to the margrave of Antwerp, Godfrey of
Bouillon, the nephew and adopted son of the Duke Godfrey

who had been murdered in 1076. Continuing former Salian policy Henry IV had until then kept this duchy and handed it over to his son Conrad, who meanwhile had been crowned king. The emperor, however, did not succeed in overcoming the opposition of the southern German dukes, Berthold of Rhein-felden (d. 1090), Berthold of Zähringen, and Welf IV, nor in coming to a compromise by negotiation. The danger emanating from this powerful group on the contrary increased, when in 1089 Urban II managed to arrange a marriage between Welf IV's seventeen-year-old son (Welf V) and the forty-three-year-old widow Matilda of Tuscany-Canossa. Created by political calculation, this link between the most important anti-imperial powers on either side of the Alps contributed considerably to the collapse of imperial power.

The emperor began the fight against this dangerous coalition right at the beginning of his Italian expedition in 1090. The military conflict in Italy against the margravine, however, to-wards the end of 1092 began to go against the emperor. At about the same time Matilda managed to persuade Henry IV's son—King Conrad, who then had begun the struggle for the rich inheritance of his grandmother Adelaide of Savoy-Turin (d. 1091) in north-west Italy—to desert the emperor. Matilda and Welf V supported the king's son so far that he was crowned king of Italy in Milan at the beginning of 1093. By this legal act the Salian acknowledged the existence of an imperial Italian kingdom independent of the German kingdom. About the same time the communes of Milan, Cremona, Piacenza, and Lodi made a pact directed against the emperor, which underlines the growing importance of the Italian towns in imperial polit-ics, and which can furthermore be called the first urban league in medieval history. These events forced the emperor to retreat to the region around Mantua, Verona, and Padua, where he had only very limited freedom of action. This general power-lessness of Henry IV, whose route to Germany remained barred by Duke Welf IV, lasted until the beginning of 1097. Mean-while Henry IV's second wife, Praxedis (a daughter of the grand duke of Kiev), whom the emperor had married in 1089 after the death of his first wife Bertha (d. 1087), had broken with her imperial husband with many accusations. King Con-rad (d. 1101) remained without great influence in imperial

Italy despite his close feudal ties with Pope Urban II, who had also arranged the wedding of this king with a daughter of Count Roger of Sicily, a papal vassal. Henry IV's return to Germany in spring 1097 only became possible after the emperor's settlement with Welf IV, to whom he granted the duchy of Bavaria anew in 1096. An important precondition for the Welf duke's going over to the powerless king had been his son's separation from the Margravine Matilda in 1095.

In the same year as the empire had to take such a severe blow to its authority, the reformed papacy under Urban II had proved its leading role in the Christian world more clearly than ever before by summoning a crusade, and by the start of this—in the full sense—auspicious holy war in the Holy Land. The participation of German knights in the crusade was small. The only member of the high nobility who took part was Godfrey of Bouillon, who as duke in Lower Lorraine had attained only very little influence. He supplied considerable means of his own for his large Lorraine contingent of vassals and knights, which he financed by the sale of his estates—including even his family castle. After the brutal capture of Jerusalem which led to the foundation of a kingdom under Godfrey and later under his brother Baldwin, Duke Welf IV (d. 1101), accompanied by other nobles from the Bavarian duchy, also set off for the crusade. However, he lost the greater part of his army in battles in Asia Minor. As in France, even before the start of the crusade as set by the pope at August 1096, members of lower social groups, who were especially severely hit by a famine, had gathered as a band of crusaders. They used the crusade atmosphere to blackmail the Jewish communities of several towns into paying them money. Pillaging and murdering, they caused the worst persecution of Jews yet in the Middle Ages.

The head of the Jewish community at Mainz even before the pogrom had turned for help to the emperor, who, however, in his unfortunate situation could only request their protection by letter. Soon after his return to Germany, still in 1097, Henry allowed those Jews who had been forcibly baptized by their persecutors to return to their faith. This measure, with which Henry IV underlined his position as protector of the Jews, was condemned even by his own pope as an unheard-of crime (*inauditum nefarium*). In the same year the Salian proceeded against Archbishop Ruthard of Mainz (1089–1109), since he had not given the Jews of Mainz, before the 1096 massacre with 600–700 people the largest and most respected Jewish community in Germany, sufficient protection against their persecutors. Furthermore, relatives of the archbishop and possibly even he himself were said to have enriched themselves with the property of murdered Jews. Ruthard withdrew from the proceedings begun against him, and went over to the opponents of the emperor in east Saxony and Thuringia. In the following years Henry IV used the city of Mainz as one of his most important bases in the middle Rhine area, where the centre of his remaining power already lay.

With further concessions to the Welfs, to whom in 1098 he promised the succession of the duke's eldest son, Welf V, to the duchy of Bavaria, Henry IV was finally able to overcome the enmity of this high noble family—also influential in southern Swabia—which had already lasted for a quarter of a century. At the same time he reached a settlement between the Staufen Duke Frederick and the Zähringer Berthold II. The Zähringer duke, after the death of his brother-in-law Berthold of Rheinfelden, had taken over his estates and rights in Swabia and Burgundy, and in 1092 had been chosen duke of Swabia by Henry IV's opponents. Retaining his ducal title, Berthold renounced the duchy of Swabia in favour of the Staufen Frederick—i.e. Henry IV's son-in-law. In return, the emperor enfeoffed him with the imperial estates in and around Zürich. A little later Berthold localized his ducal title on his family castle of Zähringen, which expressed his independence of the duchy of Swabia. After this great success Henry IV was even able in May 1098 to rearrange the succession to the throne. His deposed son Conrad, who exercised his kingship in Italy dependent on the papacy with even less success than Wibert (Clement III) exercised his papal authority dependent on the emperor, was replaced by Henry's second son, Henry V, then still under age; taking a special oath of allegiance to his father, Henry was elected king at an imperial court in Mainz, and at the beginning of the following year he was crowned at Aachen.

Henry IV's attempt to come to an agreement with Urban II's successor, Paschal II (1099–1118), did not succeed. Paschal, under whom the struggle between empire and papacy was further narrowed down to the investiture dispute, prevailed without difficulty against the imperial pope Clement III. Although the anti-papacy after his death was renewed several times by the opponents of the reformed papacy, the successors of Clement posed no serious threat to Paschal. In 1102 Paschal renewed the excommunication of the emperor. As an agreement with the reformed papacy seemed hopeless, in 1103 the excommunicated emperor pursued a plan to obtain absolution by means of a pilgrimage to Jerusalem. At a Reichstag in Mainz at the beginning of 1103 Henry IV in this connection announced an imperial Peace, confirmed on oath by the princes present, which, taking in the Jews, was to be valid for four years. However, in the following year all the successes so far achieved by the emperor were brought to nothing when his son of the same name started an uprising with the aim of deposing him.

[c] FROM HENRY V'S UPRISING TO THE SOLUTION
OF THE INVESTITURE DISPUTE

The emperor's son, crowned five years before and from whom Henry IV had demanded a special oath of allegiance, used the military expedition against Saxony planned by the emperor to leave the imperial court at Fritzlar secretly in December 1104. He went to Regensburg: a city in which at the beginning of the same year sensational events had taken place. There Count Sigehard of Burghausen, after a long siege of his lodgings by ministerials of various lords, had been murdered. He had made a decision against his ministerials which not only those directly affected had looked upon as an infringement of their legal status. The emperor, who had stayed in Regensburg for some time, had done nothing to protect the count, whom for other reasons he was said to hate. Still less had he called the culprits to account, including most probably inhabitants of the town. The noble relatives of the murdered man were among Henry V's first helpers after his desertion of the emperor. The emperor's son no doubt feared that the after-effects of the Regensburg events, which increased the mistrust and enmity the princes felt against the emperor—particularly the secular ones—might further diminish his prospects of succession to the throne. The renewed excommunication of Henry IV, who owed his imperial title to the failed, and now dead, anti-pope, had already made clear the threat that his son's candidacy for the succession might come to nothing because of co-operation between the papacy and the princes.

The rebellion against the father, however, seemed promising. Henry V quickly received the support of Paschal II, who absolved him from his oath to his father and freed him from excommunication. At the same time he gained the supporters of the pope for himself as well as those nobles and clerics who for quite some time had been working against his father in Saxony and Thuringia, led by Archbishop Ruthard of Mainz. With the help of the papal legate, who held out the prospect of generous treatment by the pope to previously excommunicated bishops, Henry V even drew on to his side many bishops invested by his father. Anyway, the king installed bishops in the same way as his father. The death of the Staufen Duke Frederick of Swabia in July 1105 was advantageous for the emperor's rebellious son. Frederick's sons, Frederick (II) and Conrad, were only fifteen and twelve years old at the time; they could not count as allies for their imperial grandfather. Henry V on the other hand a few months later arranged the marriage of his sister Agnes, the widow of the Staufen duke, to the Babenberg Margrave Luitpold of Austria. The pact between the Salian king and the Babenberger, thus strengthened, had a decisive effect on the conflict between father and son, as in autumn 1105 the Babenberger, immediately before an expected battle at the Regen, refused to give the emperor the military help he had promised. As well as Luitpold, the emperor lost the help of his brother-in-law, Duke Borivoi of Bohemia. Deserted by these hitherto closely allied dukes, the emperor had to flee the Upper Palatinate region before his son. He retreated to the Rhine, where he found refuge first in Mainz and then in Cologne.

Shortly before Christmas 1105 Henry V, under the pretence of reconciliation, kept his father prisoner in the castle of Böckelheim, on the Nahe, and later in the royal palace at Ingelheim. But even in this situation the emperor refused the public confession of sin demanded from him by the papal legate, with which he would have sealed his own deposition. At a Reichstag called by Henry V in Mainz, at which almost all the German princes were assembled (52 or more are mentioned), Archbishop Ruthard of Mainz at the beginning of January 1106 handed over the imperial insignia to the king with the agreement of the papal legates. The princes swore an oath of allegiance to Henry V. Supported by the papal legates and acknowledged by most German lords, Henry V's kingship in place of the deposed emperor seemed to be secure. Henry IV, however, did not accept the decision. After his flight from Ingelheim the emperor found help in the city of Cologne and in Lower Lorraine. In the following months he was even able to score some successes against his son.

Only the emperor's death, in Liège at the beginning of 1106, decided the struggle for the throne between father and son. Contrary to his last wish, Henry IV's body was not buried in the cathedral of Speyer, the building of which he had considerably furthered, but in an as yet unconsecrated side-chapel of the cathedral. Not until the fifth anniversary of his death—7 August 1111—did Henry V have his father transferred to Speyer cathedral and buried next to the grave of Henry III. He had obtained Paschal II's agreement for this a few months previously, but only after taking the pope prisoner to force from him the right of investiture and his own coronation as emperor.

Henry V's hope of removing the by now roughly thirty-year-old open conflict between empire and papacy by deposing his father was not fulfilled, though the actual political dispute between the two powers had been ended at least for the time being through a community of interest between the king and Paschal II. At the same time the papal legates even during the struggle between the two Salians facilitated the return to the papal Church of many excommunicated clerics who, since the death of Clement III, lacked an 'imperial' pope of their own. Where there were still schisms between imperial and papal bishops, signs of lasting solutions could be seen. At the synod of Guastalla—a possession of the Margravine Matilda on the Po—the pope left in their offices all bishops and clerics who had been installed during the split in the Church, as long as they were not simoniacs and had not committed other crimes. At the same synod Paschal held fast to the unrestricted prohibition of investiture by laymen. The prohibition thus renewed also affected the Salian king, who previously, like Henry IV, had appointed many bishops.

In the period which followed, the dispute between the reformed papacy and the Salian monarchy concentrated on lay investiture, which up to then had played rather a subordinate role in the far deeper conflict between empire and papacy, between the spiritual and the temporal sword. Only now did the investiture dispute in the restricted sense begin for the empire. For the government of the king of the Romans, *rex Romanorum* as Henry V now had himself called more often, it was of far greater importance than for any other kingdom, especially as regards the German regions of the empire, as nowhere else did the bishops and the abbots of the greater monasteries, as a result of royal or imperial grants, control such important rights and properties as in Germany. When under Henry V a workable compromise was reached concerning investiture, at the Concordat of Worms, the result for the dispute over the limits of competence of the secular and spiritual power was only a partial solution, though admittedly an important one. The fundamental question concerning the relationship of papacy and empire, of spiritual and secular power, of Church and State, had not thereby been answered. It went on causing controversies far beyond the twelfth century, and has remained an open problem in many regions and states up to the present time. In this connection the reign of the last Salian, which lasted only a little over one and a half decades, is worthy of special note.

When the investiture dispute between the king of the Romans and the head of the Roman Church once again led to sharp disagreements, at the latest from Henry V's Roman campaign of 1111, compromises had long been reached between the papacy and the other most important kingdoms in the West, France and England. Already in the last years of the eleventh century Bishop Ivo of Chartres, who was scholastically educated and trained in theology and Church law, had created the conceptual basis for the removal of the cause of dispute, by sharply distinguishing between the *spiritualia* and the *temporalia*. In line with this he forbade laymen to grant the office of bishop

as a sacramental act, while allowing the king the right to grant
the temporalities. In 1098 for the first time the French king
Philip I adapted to this distinction. From then onwards he only
demanded the oath of allegiance from the bishops, elected with
his agreement—renouncing the investiture by ring and staff,
and the homage which was otherwise normal in the act of
enfeoffment. After that the cleric was installed in his estates
and lordships, which, however, for most French bishops were
considerably smaller than for the German ones. In spring 1107
Paschal II made a pact, obviously directed against the Salian
king, with Philip I and with his son Louis VI; Philip had
previously been repeatedly excommunicated because of his—
according to Church opinion—adulterous relationships. The
pact was to have a lasting effect in the generally good relations
between the French kingdom and the papacy.

In August of the same year, at the 'Concordat of London',
the Anglo-Norman King Henry I and Archbishop Anselm of
Canterbury came to an understanding on the investiture question, to which Paschal II also agreed. According to this the
election of holders of clerical offices should take place in the
presence of the king or his representative, who thereby secured
his influence on the outcome of the election. The king renounced investiture with ring and staff, the symbols of the
spiritual office. In return he was granted that the elected bishop
should do homage for the temporalities before his consecration.
The retention of homage—as well as the oath of allegiance—
was in open contradiction to the demands the reformed papacy
had made earlier on. Apart from that, the legal formula for the
granting of the temporalities remained open.

Henry V's delegation, led by the archbishop of Trier, which
negotiated with Paschal II at Châlons-sur-Marne in May
1107—i.e. only shortly after the pope's agreement with the
French king—insisted on the traditional procedure: the agreement of the emperor had to be asked before the election of a
cleric could be announced. The cleric then goes to the emperor,
who invests him with ring and staff and receives from him
homage and fealty for the *regalia*. By *regalia* was meant towns,
castles, bridges, tolls, and other imperial rights, in other words
all the temporal possessions of a given church. The pope
objected sharply to this demand of the emperor, which in

principle held fast to the system of private churchrights (*Eiggenkirchen*). In a treatise about the investiture of bishops handed over to the Roman Curia in 1109 the standpoint of the German royal court was repeatedly and thoroughly explained.

The opposing viewpoints concerning the investiture question, however, for the time being remained without important political consequences. After his engagement to Matilda, the then eight-year-old daughter of the Anglo-Norman king, and the crowning of his bride which followed in June 1110, in August Henry V began his Roman expedition, which had been announced some time previously. As a consequence of the now strengthened Salian kingship, many bishops and noblemen took part in it. In recruiting his relatively large following, Henry was able to use the enormous sum of 10,000 silver marks which he had received as dowry from the English king.

Henry found further support in imperial Italy, where several times he took successful action against hostile cities. In particular he succeeded in forcing the Margravine Matilda, whose power base had been considerably reduced, mainly by the bigger cities, to take up a neutral position. The loss of this high noblewoman, who up to then had been closely allied with the reformed papacy, narrowed down Paschal II's room for action at least as severely as the pope's small prospect of obtaining any effective support from his Norman vassals in south Italy and Sicily.

In this situation—awaiting the Salian, who insisted on his unrestricted right of investiture, and his successful royal army—Paschal made an agreement with the royal negotiators on 4 February in the church of Santa Maria in Turri, close to St Peter's, which contained a radical solution of the investiture dispute. By taking up older conceptions within the church, and possibly under the influence of the contemporary poverty movement—which had repeatedly been condemned as heresy—the former monk and present pope promised that, for the complete renunciation of the investiture of all churches in the empire, the king and future emperor should be given back all properties and rights which had formerly belonged to the kingdom or empire. The churches, even the cathedrals and big abbeys, should only keep tithes, and those estates which had been or would be in future given to them by other, non-royal donors. This regulation, however, was not to hold for the Roman bishop and the patrimony of St Peter.

The fulfilment of this contract, also accepted by Henry V, would have overturned the imperial constitution, grown up over centuries, and would have anticipated the secularizations of the Reformation and the French Revolution. Vast estates and huge lordships in towns and in the country, extending to whole counties and margraviates, would have been the king's to rule. The mainly aristocratic bishops and abbots would have been stripped of their power, and some possibly even impoverished; new possibilities would have been opened up for the papal centralization of the Church's structure. Not least, the secular aristocracy, which almost without exception held Church estates in feudal tenure, would have lost a great part of its power. On the other hand the empire would have had to renounce its current foundation along with lordship over the imperial Church, and build up a completely new power structure, for which it as yet lacked the institutional and organizational preconditions. On the whole, empire and papacy could have derived the greatest profit from the contract, but only at great risk.

Only eight days later, when it was made public on 12 February 1111 in St Peter's, the contract proved to be Utopian. From the moment it was read out it provoked very bitter resistance from the imperial bishops and nobles assembled there. They even condemned the pope's proceedings as heresy. The resulting tumult and sharp disputes even prevented the emperor's coronation, set for that very day. Henry V finally had the pope and the cardinals who were there taken prisoner, along with further clerics. A few days later the king withdrew from the Leonine city with his army and the prisoners. Abandoned by the Normans and the Margravine Matilda, on 11 April 1111 at Ponte Mammolo near Rome the captured pope entered into a new contract with Henry, in which he conceded to the king the long-disputed right of investiture with ring and staff before the consecration of a bishop or abbot. The pope performed the coronation of the emperor, also promised, in St Peter's on the following Thursday (14 April). The emperor, crowned by the captured pope, quickly set out on his return journey. Still in May 1111 he gained another success of lasting importance when the Margravine Matilda granted the hereditary succession in all her allodial lands to the Salian, who was related to her, thereby withdrawing her earlier donation to the papacy.

The extorted contract of Ponte Mammolo soon proved a fictitious solution. As early as March 1112 a Lateran synod, attended mainly by Italian clerics, renewed the ban on lay investiture. At a synod in September 1112 in his Burgundian see Archbishop Guy of Vienne excommunicated the emperor, acting so to speak on behalf of the pope, who had had to promise not to act against the emperor. After a break of only half a decade the configuration within the empire seemed to return to what it had been since the 1070s, i.e. for about forty years.

Still in the year 1112, in the duchy of Saxony and soon in Thuringia too, an aristocratic opposition to the Salian formed. The Saxon Duke Lothar of Supplingenburg was one of its leaders. In autumn 1106 Henry had installed Lothar who was now fighting against him and who had already fought against Henry IV, as duke of Saxony, rejecting the demands of other high nobles. In 1112 Archbishop Adalbert of Mainz (1111–37), of the comital family of Saarbrücken, also joined this anti-imperial group. The emperor had invested his former chancellor and ablest counsellor, who during the negotiations with Paschal II had very effectively represented the emperor's interests, only in August 1111. The conflict between Adalbert and the emperor, who in the mean time had himself exploited the archbishopric, vacant since 1109, was chiefly motivated by territorial politics. It resulted on the one hand from Henry V's policy of placing castles and ministerials along the middle Rhine, which he pursued more intensively from 1111, and on the other from the interests of the archbishopric of Mainz and of the counts of Saarbrücken. Towards the end of 1112 the emperor, who was unscrupulous in these matters, succeeded in taking the archbishop prisoner in Saxony. He stayed in prison for three years, probably in the imperial castle of Trifels, where other noble prisoners of the emperor were also kept. Only a rebellion, organized by the noble burgraves of Mainz and the clerics of the city, forced the emperor towards the end of 1115 to release Adalbert. He immediately rejoined the emperor's opponents, who had meanwhile become more numerous.

At first the emperor had succeeded in breaking up the noble opposition in Saxony. Duke Lothar even had to submit to the emperor at a Reichstag in Mainz in early 1114. But again in summer 1114, under the leadership of Archbishop Frederick of Cologne (1100–31), a new rebellion started on the lower Rhine, in Lower Lorraine and Westphalia. The city of Cologne, allied with its archbishop in the fighting which soon began, assumed a key military position. Then, at the beginning of the year in which the emperor was forced to release the archbishop of Mainz, the Saxon rebels led by Duke Lothar inflicted a decisive defeat on the imperial army in a battle at the Welfesholz on the river Saale on 11 February 1115. Henceforward the emperor retained only slight influence in Saxony. After further opposition successes in autumn 1115 a papal legate was able to announce the excommunication of the emperor once more, in Goslar itself, the old centre of Salian power. Besides the archbishops of Mainz, Cologne, Magdeburg, and Salzburg, further bishops invested by Henry, who were absolved from excommunication by the pope or his legates, broke away from the emperor. Thus the extorted success at Ponte Mammolo had only briefly been able to cover up the fragility of traditional imperial power over the Church. The conflict with the papacy it had brought on further strengthened the position of the German princes as against the monarchy, and set narrower limits to the Salian's field of action in Germany.

But meanwhile the death of the Margravine Matilda (25 July 1115) opened up to the emperor the prospect of considerable allodial and imperial estates and important lordships in imperial Italy. Mainly for this reason, in spring 1116 Henry V with a small following set off on his second journey to Italy. He was in fact able to dispose of Matilda's inheritance without difficulty, and found support from several north Italian cities. At the same time the emperor made contact with the jurists who had been working at the margravine's court. Irnerius, the most important representative of the law school of Bologna, resided for a while in the entourage of the emperor, whom he served in the imperial court together with Ubaldus of Carpineti, another prominent jurist. In spite of these successes the negotiations with Paschal II, who demanded from the emperor the revocation of the 'wicked privilege' (*privilegium*) of 1111, led to no results. When Gelasius II (1118–19), Paschal's successor, also declined the emperor's demands, Henry, supported by the Roman nobility and advised by Irnerius, raised an anti-pope in the person of Archbishop Maurice of Braga, who on his enthronement in March 1118 took the name of Gregory VIII. Protected by his Norman vassals, Gelasius II thereupon renewed the excommunication of the emperor.

This gave fresh impetus to the opposition in Germany. There the emperor's representatives, his Staufen nephews Duke Frederick II of Swabia and his brother Conrad, who was mainly active in Franconia, and Godfrey, the count palatine of Lorraine, were unable after the military successes of the archbishop of Mainz and Duke Lothar to prevent an assembly of princes in Würzburg from being planned, at which the emperor should be called to account or, should he not appear, be deposed. Henry was able to avert this danger on his return to Germany in autumn 1118. The negotiations between emperor and pope were resumed at the beginning of Calixtus II's pontificate (1119–24); he was the former Archbishop Guy of Vienne, who in February 1119 in a questionable election at the monastery of Cluny had been elected the successor of Gelasius II, who had died there. Under the influence of Abbot Pons of Cluny and William of Champeaux, the founder of the school of St Victor in Paris, Henry V now even agreed to renounce investiture with ring and staff, as long as the service of the imperial Church to the emperor was not thereby diminished. The completion of the already formulated agreement fell through, however, at Mouzon, near Reims, because of Calixtus II's intention to deny the emperor the right to invest the bishops and abbots with the *regalia*.

When the emperor refused, he was again put under the papal ban, but the political implications of his excommunication remained slight. In 1119 and 1120 Henry was even able to regain influence on the lower Rhine and in Saxony. In contrast to Henry IV's times the Welfs, with their important positions in Bavaria and Swabia, remained on the emperor's side. After the death of Welf V in 1120 his brother Henry the Black obtained the duchy of Bavaria. In 1121 his daughter Judith married

Duke Frederick II of Swabia, the emperor's eldest nephew. When in the same year Henry V, having secured his rear, besieged the city of Mainz, and Archbishop Adalbert with his primarily Saxon allies came to the assistance of his city, to which in 1118 he had granted generous privileges, the princes intervened. A commission of 24 lords, which was made up of equal numbers of members of both parties, prepared a peace, which was agreed in autumn 1121 at a Reichstag in Würzburg. In this the princes also pledged themselves to bring about an agreement on the investiture question between emperor and pope, safeguarding the rights of the empire.

The negotiations between the papal legates, the emperor, and the princes began on 8 September 1122 in Worms. Resulting from these lengthy negotiations, a compromise was announced between emperor and pope on 23 September on the *Laubwiese* outside Worms. In a charter addressed to the 'catholic Church', Henry V with the agreement and advice of the lay lords renounced investiture with ring and staff and granted all churches in the kingdom and the empire canonical and free election. He obliged himself to give back to the pope all alienated possessions and *regalia* or to work for their recovery. The same should apply to the possessions of all other churches and the princes. In the charter, which was made out in the name of Calixtus II for the Emperor Henry V—i.e. not expressly for his successors too—the pope grants the emperor the right that the elections of bishops and abbots in Germany should be held in the presence of the emperor. In case of division within the electoral college the emperor, after hearing the advice and judgement of the relevant archbishop and suffragans, should support the 'wiser party' (*sanior pars*). The elected but not yet consecrated bishop then receives from the emperor the *regalia*, symbolized by the sceptre: i.e. the lay possessions and rights of the church or abbey (*temporalia*). For this the invested cleric has to perform the service owed to the emperor. In the *regnum Teutonicum* the consecration of the cleric is therefore only performed after the investiture. However, in the other kingdoms, Burgundy and Italy, the granting of the sceptre should follow the election and consecration of the cleric within six months, with the same consequences.

The vague formulation of the bishops' and abbots' duties towards the emperor left open the possibility that, in connection with the regalian investiture, he might also demand an oath of allegiance and homage from the clerics, and bind them to himself by feudal law, like the Anglo-Norman king, Henry V's father-in-law. That was how Henry V's successors actually tried to play the game. This way they would be able at least partly to recoup the loss of the substance of their power over the Church, sealed in the Worms concordat, by means of feudal law—as Henry V had no doubt intended.

Even after the peace treaty with the papacy Henry V could not reduce, let alone break, the resistance in Saxony led by Duke Lothar. On the contrary, the course of the following years showed that the anti-Salian forces in Saxony, which for half a century had taken advantage of the controversies between kingdom and papacy, could succeed even without this support. The emperor also failed in his plan to support his Anglo-Norman father-in-law in his disputes with the French king. Under the banner of St Denis in 1124 the French king and his influential adviser Abbot Suger of St Denis were able to raise an army so strong that Henry V had to break off the campaign against France. As the son of the English King Henry I had died in 1120, the Empress Matilda, the only surviving child, had a promising right of succession to the English crown. The Salian's actions of this kind and his hopes of widening his power apparently nourished rumours during the famine years 1124 and 1125 that the emperor, following his father-in-law's advice, wanted to introduce a general imperial tax. That such an attempt was in complete opposition to the constitutional situation within the German empire was clearly demonstrated during the settlement of the succession to the throne which followed the death of the childless emperor in May 1125.

[*d*] ELECTORAL MONARCHY UNDER LOTHAR III AND CONRAD III

Lothar III's government of the empire, just like that of Conrad III, his opponent of many years' standing and his successor, was essentially determined by its starting-point. It was the result of a more or less strongly developed coalition of interests between the less powerful princes and the papacy. For different reasons papacy and princes both aimed at a kingship they could influence. The elimination of the prerogatives of blood, i.e. birthright, strengthened the electoral rights of the princes, newly laid down in 1078, and thus also the opportunities for papal influence on the succession to the throne. This did not only mean that the king thus elected was dependent on the support of the electing princes and also of the papacy; it also meant that the king had to succeed against the power of candidates favoured by birthright who had been passed over. The discontinuity thus introduced into the succession to the throne prevented a gradual accumulation of power in the royal family and an increasing distance between the royal dynasty and the other princes. Lothar III only reached agreement with his Staufen opponents after nine years of his twelve-year reign. Under Conrad III the conflict with the Welfs continued all his reign, nearly one and a half decades. All the more were Lothar III and Conrad III forced to fall back on kinship ties to strengthen their rule. The inadequacies in the institutional effectiveness of the monarchy had to be met by personal relationships, and these were dependent on biographical chance.

The monarchy's links with the papacy, which Henry V had at times tried to dominate by force, though with little success, under Lothar III reached a closeness previously unknown. Because of his weakness the king-emperor was dependent on cooperation with the papacy, which could also give him powerful backing with the imperial churches. On the other hand the papal schism of 1130-8, brought about not least by rivalries among leading Roman noble families, forced the pope to rely on protectors: in the case of Anacletus II on Roger II, of Innocent II on Lothar III. Therefore Innocent on his part was interested in a stronger presence of the Supplingenburg emperor in Italy—especially in military action against Roger II, as long as the political and legal claims of the papacy were not thereby impaired. Within these limitations, under Innocent II and Lothar III there was an apparent flowering of cooperation between empire and papacy, the two universal powers of the West, which reached its climax during the second Italian campaign of Lothar III and his Welf son-in-law Henry the Proud, which advanced far into the Italian south. For these reasons it was just as important for the same pope to set a counterweight against the power concentration of the Welfs thus furthered, through the election of the former anti-king, the Staufen Conrad, after the end of the schism and Lothar's death. But that then meant that the Staufen anti-king remained too weak to offer effective help to Innocent II against the Norman king Roger.

In 1142 it became possible to bridge the differences between the Staufen king and the Welfs by means of favourable personal connections, when Gertrude, the widow of Henry the Proud and mother of Henry the Lion, married Conrad's half-brother, the Babenberger Henry II. At a Reichstag in Frankfurt in May 1142 Conrad enfeoffed Henry the Lion, who was still under age, with the duchy of Saxony. At the beginning of 1143 he granted the duchy of Bavaria to his Babenberger half-brother, the husband of Henry the Lion's mother. But this compromise, secured by family politics, was doomed to fail after Gertrude's death in April 1143.

Shortly before his death Henry V had tried to influence the succession to the throne in favour of his eldest nephew, Duke Frederick II of Swabia, by giving him the Salian family property, which had become closely bound up with the imperial estate during the long period of Salian kingship. As well as Duke Frederick II and his brother Conrad, the Babenberg Margrave Leopold III of Austria came into consideration for election as king by family right, as the husband of the emperor's daughter Agnes. Soon after Henry V's burial at Speyer in early June 1125, a long-standing opponent of the emperor as well as of the Staufen, Archbishop Adalbert I of Mainz, gained decisive influence over the election process. He also succeeded in getting into his possession the imperial insignia kept in the castle of Trifels, thanks to the emperor's widow Matilda, who soon afterwards returned to England. At the election assembly in August 1125, in his city of Mainz, and in the presence of a papal legate, by clever tactics he forced his long-standing ally Duke Lothar of Saxony on the electoral committee, which consisted of representatives of the great German tribes (Franks and Lorrainers, Swabians, Saxons, and Bavarians).

The then fifty-year-old Lothar also recommended himself to

the princes because he did not have a male heir, so that their legal rights in the next vacancy on the throne would again be unrestricted. Lothar's only daughter, Gertrude, at the time of the election was promised to the son of the Bavarian duke, the Welf Henry the Proud, almost like a payment in return for a vote. With this quid pro quo for Welf support, Lothar, who incidentally had another ally in his half-brother Duke Simon of Upper Lorraine, created a decisive counterweight to the family and political ties between the Welfs and the Staufen— Duke Frederick II had already for some years been married to Judith, the sister of Henry the Proud. Isolating the Staufen among the southern German nobility, Lothar III gained another success when he granted the county of Upper Burgundy (around Besançon) to the Zähringer Duke Conrad in 1127.

When in 1127 the Staufen brothers succeeded in standing their ground in the war against Lothar III for the imperial estates in Franconia, the Swabian and Franconian princes proclaimed as king in December 1127 the Staufen Conrad, who had himself called duke of Franconia. Conrad, excommunicated by Archbishop Adalbert and soon afterwards by Pope Honorius II as well, and who thus unlike the anti-kings under Henry IV stood in opposition to the papacy right from the beginning, went to imperial Italy in the following year. There, in June 1128 in Monza, he was crowned king of Italy by the archbishop of Milan, who himself was opposed to the Roman Curia. By his association with the commune of Milan, Conrad fell into the politics of the Lombard communes, already grouped around the two most powerful, Milan and Cremona. But above all Conrad did not manage to gain control over the Matildine lands, to which he, as the nephew of Henry V, had hereditary claims. In 1130 he returned to Germany.

There the prospects of enforcing his kingship had meanwhile sunk even lower. By a pact with his Welf son-in-law, who had succeeded to the duchy of Bavaria in 1126 after his father's death, Lothar had succeeded in narrowing the Staufen power base. About the same time that the Staufen anti-monarchy was proving unpromising, in Rome there arose a papal schism. This came about, without any influence from the German court, after the death of Honorius II as a consequence of rivalries between the Roman noble families of the Frangipani and the

Pierleoni, who in the previous decades had been an important factor for the papacy. The majority of the college of cardinals in February 1130 decided for Cardinal Peter Pierleoni, who took the name Anacletus II. Shortly before, a powerful minority had chosen the cardinal deacon Gregory of St Angelo, who also belonged to a Roman noble family, the Papareschi. The latter—Innocent II—was first supported by the Frangipani, but then dropped. He soon had to give way to Anacletus and leave Rome. In France and England Innocent II, who leant strongly towards the new orders of the Cistercians and the Premonstratensians, won influential supporters. Both rivals turned to Lothar III, who, together with the majority of German bishops, in October 1130 decided for Innocent II.

In the late summer of 1132 with only a small army, to which mainly the Saxon bishops had contributed contingents, Lothar III set out for Rome. The emperor did not succeed in driving Anacletus out of the city. As the Pierleoni pope held the Leonine city with St Peter's, which had by now become the principal church, the coronation of the emperor had to be performed in the Lateran basilica, on 4 June 1133. Contrary to the emperor's expectations, Innocent II was not compliant over investitures, in which Lothar aimed at improving on the Concordat of Worms. Purposefully Innocent also made use of his opportunities in granting the Matildine lands. He invested the emperor, who unlike the Staufen had no hereditary claims, with the margravine's allods only for his lifetime in return for an annual tribute of 100 pounds of silver, with the further obligation that the castellans and administrators would swear an oath of allegiance to the pope. In the event of Matilda's properties being handed on to Lothar's son-in-law Henry the Proud and his wife Gertrude, the Welf would be obliged to do homage and swear fealty to the pope. The enfeoffment was apparently only carried out on Lothar III's second Italian campaign, when Henry the Proud also held the margraviate of Tuscany. This arrangement was interpreted by the Roman Curia as the emperor taking on an enfeoffment. In a painting in the Lateran it was even presupposed that Lothar III had received his imperial crown as a fief from the pope. The service of *strator* and marshal (leading the horse and holding the stirrup), which

Lothar had rendered to the pope at their first meeting in Liège in March 1131, was also mobilized for this interpretation.

After he had come back from Italy (August 1133) the emperor, in co-operation with his Welf son-in-law, in autumn 1134 achieved important military successes against the Staufen brothers, who had now opposed Lothar's imperial government for nine years. In March 1135 a reconciliation took place between Duke Frederick II and the emperor, possibly mediated by the papal legate, who at this time was permanently at the imperial court. Frederick was only obliged to participate in the planned Italian campaign. The anti-king Conrad experienced similar treatment in autumn 1135. Duke Conrad even took part in the Italian campaign of 1136 as imperial standard-bearer, while his brother made a large contingent available.

The main aim of the Italian campaign was to fight the Norman king Roger II, granted his royal title by his papal protégé Anacletus II. In this aim the interests of Lothar III, Innocent II, and the Byzantine Emperor John II Comnenus (1118–43) met, although the contacts between the two empires, dating from 1135, did not lead to mutual assistance in this campaign. During his long stay in northern Italy, Lothar III tried with some success to make his imperial lordship mean something as against the larger communes. This revealed the differences of political interest between emperor and pope, which became even clearer in the military campaign which the Bavarian Duke Henry the Proud undertook through Tuscany as far as Monte Cassino, Capua, and Benevento. At the same time Lothar III advanced with the rest of the army as far as Apulia, where in the early summer of 1137 he was even able to take Bari, then the most important town on the south-eastern coast of Italy. After the union of the two armies before Bari, Lothar was also successful against Melfi and Salerno. Opposition in the German army to a continuation of the war against Roger II, who had retreated to Sicily, finally forced the emperor to return. Already before they set off, an open dispute arose between emperor and pope concerning the overlordship of Apulia. To secure the conquered land against Roger II they finally agreed on a joint enfeoffment of the duke of Apulia they had installed. However, he had only small prospects of long-term success against the Norman king.

Lothar III obtained no great advantage from this costly war against Roger II. The emperor died on his way back to Germany, in December 1137. But also for Innocent II this imperial Italian campaign proved to be without effect in the long run. Though the death of Anacletus II in January 1138 freed him of his most dangerous rival, in 1139 he finally had to accept Roger II's conditions. During the same campaign of 1136-7, Innocent had had sufficient experience of the dangers to papal policy of the concentration of power in the hands of the Welf duke of Bavaria. Besides the Matildine lands, Henry the Proud in 1137 had taken over the margraviate of Tuscany. Shortly before his death Lothar had also made over to his Welf son-in-law the duchy of Saxony and had given him the imperial insignia. With his large dominions and exploitable claims in Germany and imperial Italy, the Welf double duke excelled every other princely power in the empire.

Fears of Welf supremacy united the interests of the papacy and the German princes. In the presence of the papal legate Cardinal Dietwin, Archbishop Adalbero of Trier, who in October 1137 appointed permanent papal legate for the German empire raised to the kingship in a questionable election at Koblenz in March 1138 the former opponent of Lothar III, the Staufen Duke Conrad. The subsequent coronation at Aachen was performed by Cardinal Dietwin. The Staufen was an attractive candidate for the princes and the pope not least because his own power base was small compared to that of other secular princes. His failure as anti-king was only a few years past. His titular duchy in Franconia was only weakly anchored. He could, however, fall back on the Staufen family lands and could reckon with the help of his brother Duke Frederick of Swabia, who after the death of his Welf wife Judith around 1131-2 had married Agnes, the daughter of Count Frederick of Saarbrücken. Other allies were Conrad's half-brothers, the Babenberg margraves Leopold IV and Henry Jasomirgott. The margraviate of Austria then still belonged to the duchy of Bavaria, so for that reason too the Babenbergers would oppose a strong Welf duke.

Henry the Proud quickly acknowledged Conrad's election; he even handed over to him the imperial insignia. He did, however, demand enfeoffment with the duchy of Saxony, which his father-in-law Lothar had possessed and had handed over to him. But the Staufen king refused this, and in July 1138 granted the duchy of Saxony to the Ascanian Albert the Bear, margrave of the Saxon Nordmark and opponent in territorial politics of the Saxon duke. At the same time Conrad III deprived the Welf of his duchy of Bavaria by process of feudal law and imposed the imperial ban on him. In 1139 the king granted the duchy of Bavaria, now formally untenanted, to his half-brother Leopold IV, the Babenberg margrave of the Bavarian Ostmark. Both measures were acts of political desperation, in which Conrad III supplied less powerful opponents of the Welfs with legal titles. In this crisis he especially favoured his relatives. In the same year, 1139, Conrad III granted the duchy of Lower Lorraine to his brother-in-law Godfrey of Louvain. Two years later he also handed over the palatine county of the Rhine to his other brother-in-law, Hermann of Stahleck.

In this hopeless situation, the early death of Henry the Proud in October 1139, at the age of 35, brought unexpected opportunities for the Staufen monarchy. In Saxony, though, the Ascanian duke remained unsuccessful against the emperor's widow Richenza (of the Northeim family) and her grandson Henry the Lion, only ten years old. The Babenberg duke of Bavaria, Leopold IV, now had to take up the struggle against Welf VI, the brother of Henry the Proud and uncle of Henry the Lion, who could rely on the large Welf family domains in the Bavarian–Swabian border region. Some stability only developed when Conrad III managed to defeat the Welf before Weinsberg (near Heilbronn) towards the end of the year 1140.

For Conrad III a way out of the confrontation seemed to appear when in 1141 the widow Richenza and the Babenberg Leopold IV died. At a Reichstag in Frankfurt in May 1142 the king granted the young Henry the Lion the duchy of Saxony, in which Albert the Bear had not been able to establish his rule. At first Conrad III kept Bavaria himself, without making any new disposals in it. Already before that the king had arranged the marriage of Gertrude—Henry the Proud's widow, Lothar III's daughter and mother of Henry the Lion—with the Babenberg Henry II Jasomirgott, the brother of Leopold IV. Conrad did not enfeoff Henry II, his half-brother, with the duchy of Bavaria until January 1143. This inter-family settlement between the Welfs and Babenbergers, however, collapsed only three months later, when Henry II's wife died in childbed.

Welf VI had in any case not agreed to the arrangement of the Frankfurt Reichstag. He remained Conrad III's most important opponent. In his struggle against the Staufen, Welf found political and financial support from the Norman King Roger II and from King Geza II of Hungary (1141–62). At the same time close contacts already existed between the German royal court and the Byzantine emperor. The planned pact between the two empires, directed against Roger II, was to have been strengthened by the marriage of the emperor's son with a sister of the queen, Bertha of Sulzbach, but as the emperor John II Comnenus died in April 1143, further preparations for the pact and marriage had to be postponed. This clearly shows the widening of the controversy between the Welfs and the Staufen into the European field. Here again Italy played a central role, where the Welfs as successors of Henry the Proud still had claims to assert to the Matildine lands and the margraviate of Tuscany. Probably as early as 1138 Conrad III had made the German noble Ulrich of Attems margrave of Tuscany, but he remained almost completely without influence. The long-planned coronation journey failed, mainly because of the weakness of imperial power in Germany.

The situation of the papacy, which after the military defeat of Innocent II had had to acknowledge Roger II's kingship, worsened in 1143 when a revolt against papal power broke out in the city of Rome, and the communal senate created a city government of its own after the ancient model. In the next year the brother of the former Pope Anacletus II, Jordan Pierleoni, assumed the leadership under the title of *patricius*. Pope Lucius II (1144–5) thereupon began negotiations again with Roger II, who, however, only forced him to make concessions to his kingship. The appeals for support directed to Conrad III also remained unanswered. The next pope, Eugenius III (1145–53), a former Cistercian abbot from Pisa and a confidant of Bernard of Clairvaux, also repeated them in vain in 1145. The pope again called for help in 1146, with an offer to crown the Staufen emperor. In the same year the pope put into effect his promise to canonize Henry II, the last ruler of the Ottonian family. At about the same time negotiations between Conrad and the Byzantine emperor Manuel I Comnenus (1143–80) led to a treaty, and at the beginning of 1146 to the marriage, planned earlier, of Conrad's sister-in-law with the emperor. In the same year, 1145–6, Welf VI entered into formal agreements with King Geza II of Hungary and Roger II, with opposing political aims.

Thus the political constellation was created which determined the course of the Second Crusade. The intensity of the relations between the opponents in Germany and the leading European powers was unprecedented in the history of the German empire. This knotty conflict between the Staufen and the Welfs coloured Conrad III's rule until the end of the reign of the first Staufen king. This far-reaching connection was itself influenced by the political and religious universal movement of the second crusade. In contrast to the First Crusade, which was wholly directed towards the Holy Land, the Second Crusade split up into several distinct aims. They included the Spanish *reconquista*, and also the forcible conversion of the pagans in the east of the German empire, geographically the sphere of interest of the Welf duke of Saxony, Henry the Lion.

The crusade had been triggered off by the fall of the county of Edessa, its capital of the same name having been conquered at Christmas 1144 by the atabeg of Mosul and Aleppo. Towards the end of the year 1145 Eugenius III called the French king to the crusade. Because of Eugenius's precarious situation, dependent on the help of the Staufen king because of the controversy with the Roman senate, the pope had not intended Conrad III to participate in the crusade. Thus from spring 1146 Bernard of Clairvaux in numerous sermons in the name of the pope recruited for the crusade only in France. When the Cistercian monk Rudolf preached the crusade in the Rhineland without permission, calling in his sermons not only for revenge against the Muslims but also for the eradication of the Jews in German towns—thus instigating numerous pogroms, particularly in the episcopal towns—Bernard of Clairvaux went to Germany himself. There he energetically preached against misuse of the call to crusade, for which he now himself made propaganda according to his own aims in a number of sermons.

At a diet in Frankfurt in November 1146, against the wishes
of the pope, who simultaneously set off from Viterbo to France,
he asked the German king to participate personally in the
crusade. After some resistance, Conrad III finally gave way.
The king used this plan, which found great resonance among
the German princes too, to put through the election as king
and his successor of his son Henry, then only ten years old, at a
Reichstag in Frankfurt in March 1147. Now for the first time
since Henry IV's death the succession seemed secure. At the
same time a general Peace for the empire was decreed, which
also bound his Welf opponents for the period of the crusade.
The general Peace seemed to be secured all the more as Welf
VI, who had originally intended to join the French crusader
army, participated under the leadership of Conrad III. With
them was also the nephew of both Conrad and Welf, Duke
Frederick, who after the death of his father of the same name
had succeeded him in the duchy of Swabia. In the dispute
between his uncles the future king Frederick I Barbarossa by
no means took a definitely pro-royal position.

They set off for the crusade in May 1147. In the autumn of
the same year the German crusader army reached Byzantium
before the French. With Conrad III, Welf VI also survived the
severe defeat of a part of the army on 25 October 1147 near
Dorylaeum. The king, Welf VI, and their nephew Frederick of
Swabia first returned to Constantinople. After a long stay at the
imperial court they arrived in Acre in April 1148, on Byzantine
ships. The decimated crusader armies undertook a politically
completely senseless military expedition against the kingdom
of Damascus. The siege of the capital of this king, who alone of
the Muslim rulers would have been prepared for an agreement
with the crusader states, had to be broken off without success.
After this catastrophic end to the crusade, Conrad III on the
way back in October 1148 made an agreement with Manuel I
Comnenus in Thessalonica. In this the Staufen obliged himself
to undertake a military campaign against Roger II with the
financial and military aid of his imperial son-in-law, and to
transfer parts of the Norman dominions to the Byzantine
empire after the conquest. These lands in southern Italy were
formally to be regarded as the empress's dowry. The marriage
between the Babenberg duke of Bavaria, Henry II Jasomirgott,

and Theodora, a niece of Manuel I, served to secure this pact, in which the Italian merchant cities of Venice and Pisa were also to be included. On top of this, a marriage between Conrad III's son, King Henry, and a Byzantine princess was planned. Military and political action against Roger II had meanwhile become more urgent for the Byzantine emperor as the Norman king in autumn 1147 conquered Byzantine Corfu, and during his pillaging raids into the empire destroyed the centres of the Byzantine silk industry at Thebes and Corinth.

Welf VI had not taken part in the campaign against Damascus. He had already left the Holy Land and had gone to Roger II's court. There concrete measures by the Welf against King Conrad were planned to prevent the Staufen's advance against Roger. Directly after his return from Italy in March 1149 Welf began action against the king, who only returned to Germany in May 1149. Roger, who meanwhile had lost his position in Corfu to the Byzantines, in the autumn of the same year made a treaty against Byzantium with Louis VII of France at a meeting in Calabria, which the Capetian had visited during his return from the Holy Land. According to this a new crusade was to take place, which, almost in anticipation of 1204, should first be directed towards Byzantium. The Hungarian king Geza was projected as a partner. Both kings tried to win the pope over to this plan. Eugenius III, however, after long wavering, refused to join the pact. Before the pope had committed himself in this direction, the leaders of the anti-papal Romans again tried to make contact with Conrad III. Around summer 1149 they approached the king with a request for support against the Roman Curia and the Norman king. In return they offered him the grant of the imperial crown by the senate, according to the ancient Roman tradition.

The struggle against the Staufen royal house, which Welf VI took up already before Conrad III returned, was at first restricted to Swabia. Henry the Lion, who shortly before the beginning of the crusade had again brought up his claims to the duchy of Bavaria, did not directly take part in these conflicts. Probably soon after the end of the crusade against the Wends, in which apparently Duke Conrad of Zähringen was the only south German prince to have taken part, the duke of Saxony had married Clementia, the Zähringer's daughter, and had thereby strengthened the Welf party among the southern German princes. It was not until the end of 1151 that the military action in Saxony between Henry the Lion and Albert the Bear, the ally of Conrad III, began. At about the same time Conrad III and Welf VI made a peace treaty through the mediation of Dukes Frederick of Swabia and Conrad of Zähringen. It was advantageous for the southern German Welf since it largely ignored the fact that in February 1150 Welf VI had had to accept a severe defeat at Flochberg (near Nördlingen) from King Henry, who died a few months later. Nevertheless this peace weakened the unity of the Welfs.

In this situation Eugenius III's call in summer 1151 to Conrad III to come to Rome to be crowned emperor and to help the pope against the rebellious Romans became realistic. At a Reichstag in Würzburg on 15 September 1151 the coronation expedition and the military campaign against Roger II were decided. The departure date was fixed as 9 September 1152. The long delay until the beginning of the campaign was supposedly meant to allow time for co-ordination with the Byzantine emperor. But the death of Conrad III on 15 February 1152 intervened. The prospect of direct succession to the throne within the narrow royal family had already been diminished by the death of King Henry, Conrad III's eldest son. Knowing that his other son Frederick, only about eight years old, had no chance of succeeding, Conrad shortly before his death designated as heir his nephew, the Swabian Duke Frederick, nephew of Welf VI and cousin of Henry the Lion.

With Frederick Barbarossa, who was to rule for almost four decades, a new phase of imperial policy emerged, as it seems from the effectiveness of this reign. The far-reaching changes in the imperial constitution which had taken place in the century between the beginning of Henry IV's reign and the death of the first Staufen king continued to provide a framework, but alterations were made to it, and, taking in new factors, it took a new form which fixed essential characteristics for German history down to the present. Let us now try to bring home the basic elements and evolution of the power structure which became visible in the long period between the middle of the eleventh and the middle of the twelfth century, against the backdrop of imperial rule just discussed.

The Power Structure and its Evolution

In this survey of the events of imperial rule both constant factors and changes in the power structure within the German empire have been mentioned. They will now be clarified in outline and their mutual effects described. In this the study of the interaction of kingship, nobility, and Church seems to claim priority. In the history of institutions this complex and significant relationship can best be expressed in the formation of allods, territorial political expansion, and feudalism. This raises the question of the part played by independent and—at least as far as formal law is concerned—derived forms of lordship. The varied forms taken by the triad of kingship, aristocracy, and Church found expression in the enforcement of the Peace of God and the various regional Peaces. The change became most apparent in the communes, which in this period gained considerable political weight in the larger German cities. Besides religious, political, and military factors, social change also had a strong influence; its effects on constitutional history will be emphasized in the following sections.

[a] NOBILITY AND MONARCHY, CHURCHES AND
MONASTERIES

The Ottonians and early Salians had to a great extent been able to bring under their control the appointment of bishops and abbots in the German parts of the empire—in clear contrast to Burgundy and imperial Italy. But in general, to fill the leading positions they had had to fall back on the nobility, against whose power the Ottonian–Salian imperial Church system was mainly directed. The royal chapel was to serve to reorientate the noble clerics towards ecclesiastical and royal interests. Along with their investiture policies went the kings' efforts to expand the power of the churches and monasteries, and especially of the bishops, and to strengthen them legally with numerous privileges of immunity and protection. The powers of the holders of immunities, particularly in judicial rights, became increasingly similar to those of the high nobility, and accordingly from the beginning of the eleventh century whole counties were granted to bishoprics. Immunity rights thus often covered a far wider area than the narrower manorial lordship, in the form of territorial immunities. Such closed regions of lordship were concentrated mainly on episcopal towns and their environs, where the influence of other—i.e. noble— powers was to be completely excluded. On such legal titles was based the episcopal rule of towns in Germany. At the same time the kings also tried to control the appointment of lay advocates as executors of the jurisdiction and to curtail their activity in favour of the ecclesiastical holders of immunities.

The foundation of the monarchy's power was essentially the shared right to use the imperial churches and monasteries, and not least the service dues of the clerical officials and their institutions. Among these were military and court duties, work in the chancery, and the shouldering of political and diplomatic tasks in the interests of imperial policies. There were also hospitality duties for the itinerant royal court, which only in this way could secure the effectiveness of the monarchy over such a large area. Henry IV's reign joins up with Ottonian and Salian imperial Church policies.

From his coming of age to the climax of his conflict with Gregory VII, Henry IV more than his predecessors seems to have installed clerics of lower origin. Benno, from a Swabian ministerial family, who was made bishop of Osnabrück by Henry IV in 1068, was extremely versatile. Already under Henry III Benno had been working as a teacher in chapter and cathedral schools, among others that of St Simon and St Jude in Goslar, and had been accepted into the court chapel. After that he took over various high administrative offices in the dioceses of Hildesheim and Cologne. Furthermore he stood out as the 'architect' of imperial palaces and churches, an activity which he kept up as bishop. Archbishop Liemar of

Hamburg-Bremen, whom Henry IV in 1072 appointed successor to the high noble Adalbert, came from a Bavarian family
of imperial ministerials. When members of the clergy and the
people of Cologne went to the king's court in Goslar after
Archbishop Anno's death at Christmas 1075, 'the king', as
Lampert of Hersfeld reports, 'suggested a certain Hildolf, a
canon from Goslar' and a court chaplain. Henry IV 'emphatically pressed them to elect him. But they resisted him with
all their might, arguing that he was a tiny little man (*homo
statura pusillus*) with a repulsive face, and of low origin (*genere
obscurus*). He could show neither physical nor spiritual advantages which would make him worthy of such high office.
The indignation over this procedure caused such hatred against
him at the royal court that, as soon as he showed himself in
public, everyone plagued him with insulting calls and mocking
songs like an ancient monster, and threw stones and mud at
him.' Henry IV, in spite of great resistance, is said to have
insisted on the election, to 'install a successor whose compliance
he could misuse at his will for everything he wished' [3: xiii.
342 f.]. To enforce his intention the king himself moved to
Cologne. During his short period in office (1076–8) Hildolf was
in fact one of Henry's closest advisers and helpers.

In the following decades Henry IV's influence on episcopal
sees decreased considerably, particularly because in many cases
his opponents set up anti-royal bishops against the royal candidates. At first the circumstances of Henry V's reign were
more favourable for the continuation of the traditional Church
policy, but finally he too had to consider conditions in the
dioceses and monasteries when filling bishoprics and abbacies.
The legal framework laid down in the Concordat of Worms still
left the king with some influence over the election procedure in
the German regions, but on the whole the position of the chapters of cathedrals and big monasteries was strengthened. But
these were ruled by single nobles or noble families. A further
step towards the secular nobility sharing in the rule of the
imperial churches was taken when Duke Henry the Lion after
the crusade against the Wends claimed the right to invest the
bishops to be established at Oldenburg, Ratzeburg, and Mecklenburg, and in the case of Ratzeburg in 1150 even managed
to enforce it. Thus the Welf duke in this distant part of his

duchy for the first time in the German empire broke the royal monopoly on the investiture of bishops.

More important in the long run was the fact established by the Worms concordat that the Ottonian and Salian rule of the imperial Church, hitherto based on the *Eigenkirchen* system, should from now on be remoulded according to feudal law. The remarks of the Bavarian regular canon Gerhoch of Reichersberg in 1128-9 show that from the point of view of contemporary radical Church reformers, a further danger of secularization threatened the upper clergy. Since the Worms concordat 'the bishops, abbots, and abbesses ... after their election were forced to come to the royal court to receive the *regalia*, for which they have to swear homage and fealty'. With the grant of the *regalia* and the homage the clerics were obliged 'to give the empire tribute and service'. The consequence of this, passionately criticized by Gerhoch, consisted in their 'again on their side granting imperial Church property to dukes, nobles, and also ministerials, and receiving homage in return, being tied to the world, and instead of holding spiritual office in poverty and dedicating themselves to it, surrendering to secular life, appearing like princes, under certain circumstances even doing military service, but in any case giving out the property of the Church to warriors, because imperial law seems to demand this' [359: 428 ff.].

With the integration of German bishops, abbots, and abbesses into the feudal system, they obtained a constitutional position which up to then had been reserved for the secular nobility. The area of feudal law in Germany after the investiture dispute was considerably widened to the large group of clerical lords. They were legally ranked among the nobility, and thus they reached a new degree of secularization. The feudal dependence of churchmen on the king came about, we may remember, in other kingdoms too. This is particularly true of the Anglo-Norman realm. At the time of Frederick I the same situation can be demonstrated for some bishops and abbots of imperial Italy and Burgundy; but only in Germany did clerical principalities develop on this basis. The peculiarity of the German development can best be explained by the fact that the imperial churches and greater monasteries, as a result of Ottonian and Salian policy towards the Church, had been granted larger and more important rights and lands than in other parts of Europe. Equally decisive for them was the fact that at the end of the investiture struggle, because of the weakening of the kingship which had occurred in the mean time, they gained great freedom of action *vis-à-vis* the monarchy, and that particularly the bishops, at least in the older settlement areas, had a sufficient power base to stand their ground against noble competitors, in spite of many crises.

For the same reasons there remained a community of interest between the monarchy and the imperial churches after the Worms concordat. Obviously the existing difference between clerical and secular princes also remained important afterwards: in the succession to clerical posts not hereditary right but electoral law applied. This basic situation, even after Henry V, offered the kings plenty of opportunities to claim the traditional service dues of the imperial churches and monasteries, or to reactivate them. The course and result of the investiture conflict thus did not cause a collapse of imperial Church power, but only its transformation.

From the end of the sixties Henry IV invested imperial churches with important new rights, but with few exceptions only if they had previously been, or still were, in the hands of his opponents. The exceptions were relatively few bishoprics, like Speyer, Hildesheim, and Osnabrück, which at the time of the grant stood in a specially close relationship to the monarch. Under Henry IV the privileges of imperial ministerials increased. Henry IV's successors also restricted themselves generally to the confirmation of earlier privileges, and granted more documents limiting the rights of lay advocates, to the advantage of churches and monasteries and against the interests of the nobility.

Continuity is also to be seen in demands made on imperial churches and abbeys for service dues; and in the long term is expressed also in the places on the royal itinerary. Henry II, besides his imperial palaces, had increasingly used the episcopal cities. From 1073 onwards—i.e. after the failure of Henry IV's castle policy in Saxony—the bishops' towns became still more prominent in the imperial itinerary. Henry V used almost nowhere else, but under Conrad III the imperial palaces regained in importance, a process which reveals the growing distance between the monarchy and the imperial bishops, partly evened out by greater recourse to the king's own direct power base. The imperial palaces which became more important were generally accompanied by developed urban settlements, so that they were more easily able to offer a susbtitute for the episcopal cities. The latter, however, continued to play a large part as residences for the kings and emperors.

Even greater than the monarchy's loss of power to the older imperial bishoprics and abbeys was that to the monasteries and churches which were newly founded in large numbers, particularly from the second half of the eleventh century. Up to the middle of the eleventh century the kings—though obviously with increasing difficulty—had almost without exception succeeded in incorporating the monasteries and convents founded by the aristocracy into the imperial Church system by means of grants of immunity and protection, and thus had effectively restricted the development of aristocratic *Eigenkirchen*. After the death of Henry III the nobility and the bishops increasingly tried to exclude the king's share of rights over the new foundations by avoiding handing them over to the king where possible. They now preferred to obtain papal protection privileges. In contrast to royal protection and immunity, only small losses to the lords resulted from papal protection. Noble and episcopal founders of monasteries could thus retain greater influence on their new foundations. Though the nobles in general had to declare their formal renunciation of lordship over *Eigenkirchen*, in its place they were granted the hereditary office of lay advocate by the papacy itself, especially from the pontificate of Urban II.

This pact between the papacy and German dynasts often went against the interests of the numerous new foundations, as often enough without the monarchy they had no backing against their founders and hereditary lay advocates. Thus it becomes comprehensible that even under Paschal II the royal grant of the rights of ban for the lay advocate is mentioned, in some cases even in papal charters. As the king's grant of the ban gave the lay advocate the right to his function, the monarchy thus obtained some chance of controlling the lay advocates. For this reason during Henry V's reign many newly founded or reformed monasteries tried to gain contact with the kings. In this they often fell back on to a constitutional model which had been agreed just before the climax of the struggle between kingship and papacy for a Black Forest monastery, later a reform centre, in the so-called Hirsau formulary (1075). Henry V endeavoured to expand this framework in individual cases and further to limit the rights of the lay advocates. Several monasteries at that time acquired such legal titles by forgery, which, however, according to their legal understanding was quite legitimate and not 'fraud' in the modern sense.

These new approaches under Henry V on the whole came too late for the monarchy, particularly as the last Salian was hindered by his conflict with the papacy. The noble lay advocates, not the emperor, won the fight for rule over the newly founded or reformed monasteries. Although the lay right to the possession of churches, under the pressure of the reforming papacy, had been eliminated in theory and also reduced in practice, it was replaced by new forms of power which admitted the continued influence of the nobility in the affairs of churches and monasteries. By far the most effective legal title was now the office of lay advocate, held by a noble. During the twelfth and thirteenth centuries this office became one of the most important components in the development of the principalities.

In spite of manifold sources of irritation between monasteries and their noble hereditary patrons, the relationship was often of advantage to the clerical institutions. With their ties to the neighbouring aristocracy, limited as far as possible, they found a promoter of their material existence in a period when the kingship had to accept considerable losses in its religious and political position. For the same reason it was generally not in a position to exercise effective protection over the monasteries and canonical foundations, which had become numerous. Thus the monarchy could not keep pace with the increase in ecclesiastical and religious activities, as expressed in the new foundations.

Alongside the nobility, a number of bishops also tried to acquire influence over newly founded monasteries by pushing back other powers, and to use them as bases for territorial politics. It was probably the archbishops of Mainz at the turn of the twelfth century who carried out this policy most consistently. Like the popes, they had monasteries made over to them, copying the model of papal liberties (*libertas Romana*) with an archiepiscopal liberty (*libertas Moguntina*). In contrast to the papacy, which in Germany lacked a sufficient power base to fill out its nominal supremacy over the clerical institutions given to it by exercising actual functions of lordship, the archbishops endeavoured to keep up their position as the lords of churches and to unite the clerical and secular powers in their own hands by eliminating the lay advocates and other lay lords. The archbishops of Cologne behaved similarly towards the monasteries belonging to the Siegburg reform, founded by Archbishop Anno.

[b] ALLODS, FEES, AND TERRITORIAL POLITICS

The core of independent rule lay in the allodial character of the property and lordship rights of the noble family. This was also the basis for noble lordship over land, which the latest research sees as the direct effect of rule over the household. Hence the nobility needed no legitimation from the monarchy to exercise the power over land and people anchored in the old manorial lordship. It owned it due to its own rights. Only the ecclesiastical lords were dependent, at least formally, on devolved rights. Complexes that were still interconnected in the older type of landlordship, like power over vassals and serfs, judicial rights, lay advocacies, and power over the land, from the high Middle Ages tended to separate themselves from one another and were exercised by different holders, who often were in competition with one another. They could, however, also remain united in one hand. In Germany this change developed markedly from the middle of the eleventh century. As will be seen, this basic transformation was closely connected with economic and social changes. But it was influenced not least by territorial politics, which from that period were carried on by various holders of power with increasing intensity.

The effects of territorial politics on the transformation of the power structure were especially great in Germany, as the nobility in most areas of the country owned extensive allodial property. Allod in the narrower sense meant 'property fully owned', in a more general sense 'property not held as a fief'. It thus referred to everything that was controlled without restriction. What exactly was looked upon as an allod or a fief depended mainly on the power balance between the monarchy and the nobility. In the German areas of the empire this fact already long before the mid eleventh century promoted the allodial establishment of noble power. While in England the Norman conqueror was able to suppress the allodial basis of the nobility, and eliminate it formally and legally in the Salisbury oath of 1086, in Germany the disputes of the investiture contest even strengthened the allodial character of noble power.

The predominance of the allod directly affected the formation of feudalism. The powerful nobles succeeded in expanding their hereditary claims even to the high office of duke, and further to secure them by their power. The most spectacular testimony for this is the Welf family in the duchy of Bavaria, and, from Henry the Proud, also in the duchy of Saxony. This happened at the same time as hereditary right to the succession to the throne was diminished. The kings lacked the power base for an active feudal policy. In contrast to the Anglo-Norman kings, and also to the Capetians, they were not in a position to develop feudalism into an instrument against the noble allodial lords and imperial vassals. Nor did they succeed in winning greater influence over the tenants of the great imperial vassals. Lothar III in 1136 decreed a law of fiefs, but this was restricted to imperial Italy. The centrifugal character of feudalism in the German empire also indicates the dangers for the effectiveness of imperial power over the Church which in the long run resulted from the incorporation of imperial churches and monasteries into feudal law.

This framework explains the high priority given to the royal territorial policy. The first attempts at this can be seen under Henry III. They centred on the region of the Upper Palatinate and the Bavarian Nordgau district, as well as especially on Saxony, on the Harz with its centre at Goslar. The imperial castle and ministerial policy under Henry III in Franconia, with its centres of gravity around Nuremberg and Forchheim, was directed against the bishopric of Bamberg, which had been founded, and endowed with a lot of imperial property, by Henry II. Significantly, the imperial ministerial Otnant, still supported by Henry III, had his privileges in the Nordgau

curtailed during the minority of Henry IV—especially his right
of clearance (*ius extirpandi*), granted to him by Henry III. This
limitation of the ministerials was described from the point of
view of the church of Bamberg by the master of the cathedral
school, Meinhard, as 'an escape from the furnace in which that
hound of Hell had tantalized them for so long' [352: 53]. But
together with other ministerials, Otnant was able to keep important royal positions in the Nordgau even afterwards.

A few years after his coming of age, Henry IV continued this
territorial policy, predominantly in eastern Saxony, which was
then also called *coquina imperatoris* ('the emperor's kitchen')—
i.e. a kind of fertile ground for the emperor. Lampert of Hersfeld
stresses the low origins of the strangers installed there by Henry
IV [3: xiii. 176, 180, 182, 384]. Most of them in fact came from
Swabia, many of them apparently of ministerial origin. Henry
IV's systematic castle policy finally failed, as we have seen,
through the resistance of the Saxon dukes and further political
events in the empire connected with it.

As a consequence of ducal opposition and of his conflict with
the papacy, Henry IV had to fall back for his Italian campaign
of 1081-4 mainly on the military support of the imperial ministerials. During his last stay in Italy the emperor even raised a
ministerial (*regni Teutonici famulus*) called Werner as margrave
of Ancona and duke of Spoleto, when around 1093-4 his own
position in Italy had become extremely precarious. It was on
Werner's initiative that in 1105 an antipope was installed,
admittedly without success. Werner himself married the heiress
of an Italian comital family, and so strengthened his position.
His successors retained these imperial offices until the end of
the 1160s.

Henry V's difficult early years hardly offered him any opportunity to resume the imperial ministerial policy. After this
phase, in which at least until his father's death he was dependent on the support of the princes, he again followed a
systematic castle and ministerial policy in the footsteps of his
predecessors. He concentrated his efforts on the middle and
lower Rhineland, the Palatinate, and once again on Saxony.
Under the same king—the earliest evidence is from 1077
onwards, under Henry IV—imperial ministerials were several
times named as requesting or witnessing royal charters: clear

proof of their established position in the imperial government, and of the social rise inseparable from it. Now in Germany too, individual ministerials were used for tasks previously reserved for high nobles. An excellent example of this is Heinrich Haupt, from the imperial ministerial family of Pappenheim, which became famous in Staufen times. Henry V installed him as burgrave of Meissen, against the margrave of Meissen and the archbishop of Magdeburg. As in the organization of the imperial lands around Goslar under Henry IV, the imperial ministerials under his son in some places exercised in the king's name jurisdiction hitherto reserved for the nobility—as in the imperial vicariates of Aachen and Zürich. At least for the regions of his intensive territorial policy, Henry V thereby contained the danger that nobles might gradually gain control over imperial property by means of rights of 'higher jurisdiction', which dealt with serious crimes up to murder and major theft, over imperial serfs.

One consequence of the change of dynasty in 1125 was that Lothar III could not continue the Salian territorial policy. In his efforts along the same lines he was largely restricted to his limited sphere of influence in his duchy, Saxony and Thuringia, where his intimate counsellors and permanent followers usually came from. Conrad III on the other hand could have recourse to the late Salian heartland, but with the exception of Saxony. His ministerial policy mainly aimed at the Egerland, at the middle Rhine area, and at the lower Moselle country, but especially at Franconia, with centres at Nuremberg and Rothenburg ob der Tauber. This brought into the foreground those regions in which Conrad III had been active in his position as duke of Franconia and as part-heir of the Salian family property.

His brother Frederick II as duke of Swabia pursued a similar policy in Swabia and Alsace, on the whole with more success, though he had a head start through the extensive family property there. His half-brother Otto of Freising characterized his castle policy with the words: 'Duke Frederick always pulled a castle after him at the tail of his horse' [3: xvii. 152 f.]. He garrisoned the newly built castles with ministerials and lower nobles, who extended them into castleries. How important these castles were to the duke is shown by the fact that for the purchase of two castles he used a precious golden reliquary cross from Byzantium, which he had acquired through his Welf wife Judith—and this even though he valued the relic as 'a pledge of God's help, granting victory' in his numerous military undertakings [see 147: iii. 10]. Apparently the possession of castles seemed more reliable than the prospect of God's help thus obtained.

For the Staufen too, control over monasteries was an essential part of territorial policy. The Staufen dukes of Swabia at an early stage founded monasteries in the region of their estates, which they mainly acquired by marriage. After Duke Frederick I had built a castle at Staufen, which gave its name to this noble family, he transformed his castle on the mountain of Lorch into a Benedictine monastery (consecrated between 1097 and 1102), which became the family burial place. He also founded an abbey at Schlettstadt, which was part of the large dowry in Alsace of his mother Hildegard of Bar-Mousson. In around 1100 he acquired the lay advocacy of the important imperial monastery of Weissenburg in Alsace, which was very well endowed. Other monasteries in Alsace and Franconia were added, and in the second quarter of the twelfth century several Cistercian and Premonstratensian monasteries. Frederick III built on the foundations of the territorial policy of the Staufen dukes in Swabia. After his election as king, Barbarossa used this to strengthen the power base of the monarchy, and in doing so he fell back on what his predecessor and uncle Conrad III had achieved as duke and king.

In general, the consolidation of power in territorial forms which started around the middle of the eleventh century strengthened the allodial element in the imperial constitution in favour of the nobility and the imperial churches. After the failure of the castle and ministerial policy of Henry IV in eastern Saxony, the territorial efforts of the monarchy were also largely restricted to family properties as a starting-point; and during the controversies of the investiture struggle, lasting decades, these had anyway been almost completely ineffective. Especially under the elected kings Lothar III and Conrad III, the monarchy was thus pushed back on to its core of family lands, and found itself in a similar position to its noble competitors. For the kings, the nobles, and the imperial churches which were making themselves independent, the best opportunities were to be found in the thinly settled areas. The penetration of lordship into these regions occurred in many forms and by various methods. It was not restricted to castles and monasteries, but also included the exploitation of the land in the widest sense: i.e. forest clearance, building and promoting settlements, even founding towns, and the various political and economic activities inseparable from these.

Because their effectiveness was restricted to quite small regions, the territorial policies of the monarchy were hardly adapted to secure royal influence over large areas, such as had been possible in the Ottonian and early Salian period on the basis of control of the imperial Church. Consequently the question of how far the kingship could acquire a substitute by participation in the Peace of God movement in its various forms was a question of great moment for the balance of power between the monarchy and the princes.

[c] THE PEACE OF GOD AND THE PUBLIC PEACE (*LANDFRIEDE*)

Henry III had taken up the idea of the Peace of God, which sounded a great echo in the population and constituted the first political–religious mass movement of the Middle Ages; but he had integrated it into his method of ruling, coloured by a priestly kingship, by means of regionally restricted orders, without taking over the whole procedure of the Peace of God. After the emperor's death the Salian royal court could not continue this tradition. The occasional Peaces decreed by Henry IV from 1068 onwards (1068, 1074) remained restricted to Saxony. The integration of the bishops into the traditional imperial Church structure for several decades prevented the imperial bishops from setting up the Peace of God themselves after the model of the southern French bishops. Only at the beginning of the eighties, when Henry IV was on his Italian campaign, did individual bishops in the west of the empire begin to take up this peace movement. The Peace of God obliged those who swore to observe it to protect clerics and others in need of protection, especially the poor, widows, and orphans, as well as churches and Church property in general. It also forbade feuds at certain times, for example on Sundays and holy days, and during Advent and Lent. Breach of the Peace was primarily subject to spiritual and corporal punishments.

The first peace decree of this type on German soil, thus using a new kind of law, was enacted in the diocese of Liège in 1082. For this even a new law court was installed. Henry IV is supposed to have sent his agreement to this peace from Italy, according to dubious sources. But the same source also reports the participation of the count of Namur in the arrangement of the Liège Peace of God. In the next year (1083) a similar 'holy peace' was confirmed by oath in the bishopric of Cologne. It said that when executing the punishment imposed, not only counts, officials, and other powerful individuals, but also the wider population—the whole of the people—should take part. The supporters of the pope and opponents of Henry IV in the following year installed a Peace of God at Goslar, in the expressly mentioned presence of the anti-king Hermann of Salm. As the Peace of Goslar was not restricted within diocesan boundaries, it shows clear signs of the transition from the Peace of God to the public peace. This peace, pledged with the participation of the anti-king, was soon followed in 1085 by the Peace of God enacted at a synod at Mainz called by Henry IV and his pope, Clement III. In spite of the emperor's personal presence, the enactment was carried out by the bishops loyal to him.

In the following years the initiative in the Peace of God movement again slipped out of the hands of the Salian monarchy. Instead, significantly, it went over to its high noble opponents. Under the leadership of Welf IV and Berthold II of Zähringen and with the participation of numerous Swabian nobles, an oath of peace was sworn in 1093 at Ulm, first until Easter 1094 and then for two more years. This was to be valid for all of Swabia. Duke Welf arranged the extension of the peace to Bavaria; it was apparently pledged in Alsace, and in Franconia too. The peace movement had finally grown out of its ecclesiastical framework. If in Ulm the anti-Salian Bishop Gebhard of Constance, simultaneously papal legate, had had great influence, the initiative in this south German peace of 1093-4 came from the secular princes, who wanted it to strengthen the anti-Salian front. The Peace of God movement in Germany thus turned into the public peace (*Landfriede*), in which secular penalties prevailed. The Peace of God in the older style, however, was still sometimes proclaimed even later.

The emperor regained contact with this form of keeping the peace only when in 1103, at a Reichstag in Mainz, he announced his plan for a pilgrimage to Jerusalem. Just as the proclamation of the First Crusade at Clermont-Ferrand in 1095 was accompanied by a declaration of the Peace of God, the emperor now ordered a peace for the whole empire, to last four years. The emperor himself promised on oath to observe the peace, and demanded that all other lords pledge themselves to it as well. With this first empire-wide public peace (*Reichslandfrieden*), Henry IV integrated into imperial government the idea of public peace, which itself had emerged from the Peace of God. He thereby gained a weapon against the nobility's unlimited right of blood-feud. To enforce the imperial public peace, though, he was dependent on the participation of the nobility.

With the Peace of Mainz Henry contributed to the fact that peace edicts in Germany in the twelfth century 'were primarily the responsibility of the emperor and the empire' [420: 173]. He thus prevented the nobility and the bishops from putting into practice this idea 'of state' on their own. His son and successor, Henry V, repeated such imperial public peaces in 1119, 1122, and 1125. Lothar III tried to use this instrument right after his election, almost programmatically, but had very little success with it. Shortly before setting off on his Italian campaign in 1135, he proclaimed an imperial public peace to last ten years. In 1147 Conrad III used the forthcoming crusade to enforce an imperial public peace. It was broken by his main opponent of the time, Welf VI, even before the king's return, without Conrad being able to call him to account for it. In spite of such failures, the imperial public peaces gave new substance to the monarchy, and also opened up real possibilities for empire-wide policies.

[*d*] THE RISE OF THE COMMUNES

Within the framework of the investiture conflict the rise of town, village, and rural communes was substantially furthered. This was most obvious in the larger episcopal towns in the old settlement areas. During the disputes, which lasted decades, they gained greatly in importance. Their role as fortifications and military bases of incomparable value stands out from Lampert of Hersfeld's words about Worms. Towards the end of 1073 Henry IV had taken refuge there and received active support from the residents, among them also the Jews: 'The king thus controlled a very strongly fortified city. From then on it was his main residence in war, the bulwark of his kingdom. No matter how the situation was to develop, it offered him a very secure refuge, as it had numerous inhabitants and was invincible because of the strength of its walls. It was very prosperous because of the fertility of the surrounding lands, and well supplied with everything that was necessary for warfare' [3: xiii. 208 f.]. A few weeks later, at the beginning of 1074, the king compensated the people of Worms together with the Jews living in the town with important customs exemptions, and so tied them to his interests for the future.

Still in 1074 the citizens of Cologne looked for protection to Henry IV in their revolt against Archbishop Anno. When Henry IV was deposed by his son they readily accepted him into their town, which they had fortified more strongly, while their archbishop and lord stood on Henry V's side. It was said that the people of Cologne even imposed a war tax to finance their defence works. At about the same time the citizens of Mainz also supported the emperor, who often stayed in the metropolis on the middle Rhine, particularly during the expulsion of Archbishop Ruthard between 1098 and 1105, and who ruled the city directly at this time. In 1105 some town office-holders together with the ministerials and other citizens asked the emperor in a letter to help them against the archbishop and the other supporters of Henry V. They also told him that they had already allied themselves (*coniurare*) with a large number of people from the Rhine country, so that now an army of 20,000 knights and infantry were gathered near the city of Mainz. 'If God gives us victory, then we shall all be secure, you upon your throne and we in our place.'

The close bond between the emperor and the citizens of Mainz, however, was dependent on the situation. At the latest between 1118 and 1122 they also took military action outside the city for their anti-Salian Archbishop Adalbert I against

Henry V. In return the same archbishop at about the same time granted them valuable special privileges. In 1114 the citizens of Cologne, together with their equally anti-Salian archbishop, joined a large opposition group on the lower Rhine against the emperor and fought against his army outside their city walls, with the support of archers, which before then are only known in England. But five years later, in contrast to the attitude of the inhabitants of Mainz at that time, they accepted the emperor, excommunicated anew by the pope, into the town against the will of their archbishop. Also the citizens of Worms did not by any means always support the Salian monarchy. Although in 1112 Henry V granted them an extension of their customary privileges of 1074, and two years later also granted them important partial exemptions from servile dues, they turned against the emperor in 1124, relying at least partly on Duke Frederick II of Swabia.

The Salians and their successors were no more concerned to fight for the interests of the citizens than the latter were to pursue a basically pro-royal policy. The townspeople were in any case far from uniform in their attitudes and reactions—as the contrasting political positions of Cologne and Mainz around 1119 showed. Rather their actions were influenced just as much as those of their opponents and partners by regional and local power relationships. Also they did not by any means always stand in direct opposition to their episcopal lords, with whom they often enough fought for mutual interests outside the city walls. But it remains true that the numerous controversies between the traditional holders of power in many cases not only shook the bishops' urban lordships and weakened the overall position of the monarchy, especially towards the episcopal towns. In the competition between the traditional powers the urban ruling groups were forced to look for partners, in the interests of the other urban dwellers too. These partners on their part were dependent on the military and economic support of the cities, or expected advantages from them, so that they were prepared to give the citizens help in return. The urban ruling groups were for this reason almost forced into greater political independence. From this basic situation there followed impulses in the urban population towards giving co-operative forms a firmer organization, and thereby for a corporative anchoring of political decision-making. Possibilities for improvement in the economic, social, and legal position of the urban population also resulted from it.

The ministerials were best placed among the citizens to perform the growing political and military tasks. They had already been used by the lords of the cities for military service as well as administrative tasks, and thus had at their disposal the necessary experience and politically important connections. Many of them also had landed property and fees outside the episcopal towns. Furthermore they often participated in trade, or exploited it via the administration of lucrative lordship rights such as markets, mints, and customs. An example of the far-flung activities of a town-dwelling ministerial at the turn of the eleventh and twelfth centuries is provided by Wignand of Mainz. Around 1092 he financed the erection of buildings at the Black Forest monastery and reform centre of Hirsau. Even greater were his contributions to the monastery of Comburg near Schwäbisch Hall, a daughter of Hirsau, which had earlier been made over to the archbishop of Mainz. Other properties which Wignand had received in hereditary right from his episcopal lord eventually went to the monastery of St Alban outside the city of Mainz.

The sort of opportunities to influence the balance of power in a town which could under favourable circumstances flow from such a position are shown in the career of the Trier ministerial Ludwig, of the von der Brücke family, whose home was in the *Barbarathermen*, close to the Roman bridge. Ludwig had been at the head of the episcopal ministerials from 1107; from 1115 he held the office of chamberlain, from the beginning of the 1120s also that of city prefect. He pushed Archbishop Godfrey (1124–7) out of his position in the cathedral and wanted him to be restricted to his clerical office. 'For the bishop's meals Ludwig allowed daily', as the Trier sources report, 'one sester of wine and two sesters of beer, while he himself dined like a great prince with a considerable following ... and he ruled all the country in every respect' [14: viii. 250]. When after a two-year vacancy of the see (1129–31) part of the cathedral chapter elected as archbishop Albero (Adalbero, 1131–52), a member of the Metz cathedral chapter. Ludwig in 1132 organized a conspiracy (*coniuratio*) and proceeded violently against the electors and their supporters. Sometimes one of his allies was William, count palatine of the Rhine and lay advocate of the archdiocese. Lothar III in 1131 named Ludwig as the leader of the people of Trier (*primorem Trevirorum*) and gave him and other distinguished citizens of the town (*meliores*), who were to be chosen by Ludwig, responsibility for widening the river valley of the Sauer [19: viii, Lothar III, 36]. Although Ludwig later had to recognize Archbishop Adalbero, he was able to maintain his position in the city of Trier until his death (*c*.1141). After the end of the personal predominance of the episcopal ministerial, the people of Trier, during heavy warfare between Archbishop Adalbero and the count of Namur, carried out the construction of their city walls almost independently and also participated in military action against the count outside the city. Only a few years later, possibly as early as 1147, they possessed their own city seal. In 1149 they used this seal, which is probably the oldest town seal in Europe, for a charter given by them, which, besides fixing the toll for the merchants of Trier in Cologne, contained a general agreement between the people of Trier and Cologne. This agreement in writing can be designated with good reason as the first known contract between German municipalities. While further evidence for such agreements in Germany is not found until the 1220s, similar agreements between towns in northern Italy had already been concluded since the end of the eleventh century. By the middle of the twelfth century, besides Trier, both the other Rhenish cities, Cologne and Mainz, had at their disposal municipal seals, among the earliest in Europe. In their design and symbolic meaning they maintained a link with the sacral, ecclesiastical traditions and functions of their *civitates*, and they played no small role in legitimizing these municipal corporations [no. 379].

In spite of the far-reaching political independence of the larger episcopal towns and of the evidence of seals just mentioned, the communal organization of the German towns before the middle of the twelfth century, and in many cases far later, is hard to grasp. Here apparently, in clear contrast to the cities of imperial Italy and southern France, some ruling groups of corporative type going back to older forms of organization long remained influential. The colleges of lay judges (*scabini*,

Schöffen) apparently formed an important link; they took over legal and administrative tasks in the city by order of the lord. But, with few exceptions, they are only known in the towns along the Rhine, Maas, and Moselle from the second half of the eleventh century. In Cologne from about 1130 they even had the archaizing title *senatores*. Even around the middle of the twelfth century it is hard to decide how far the lay judges were representatives of the lords or a committee of the independent town commune. The combination of both competences was not by any means excluded, as is suggested by the political co-operation of city dwellers and city lords for which there is convincing evidence. The ministerials living in the city apparently played a major role in these *Schöffen* colleges in many towns.

The growing independence of the *Schöffen* colleges as organs of urban administration was favoured and accompanied by the liberation of city dwellers from the demands of other powers, and by the development of urban legal districts. The earlier privileges, which in the first quarter of the twelfth century were granted to all the inhabitants of German towns, are also relevant to this. The removal of the towns from the power of other rulers was an important precondition for the development of a separate system of urban law. In many cases parts of older market laws, filled out with merchants' laws, were brought together and turned into city laws, which in some cases—as in Strasbourg—were already fixed in writing in the first half of the twelfth century. In contrast to the market laws, which referred to a place, the merchant laws referred primarily to a group of individuals, but they soon came to refer to a place as well. Both merchant and market law were directed towards the special needs of trade, and of groups participating in the exchange of goods. Thus, both constituted special rights within an otherwise overwhelmingly agrarian environment. More rational forms of arbitration in disputes and in criminal jurisdiction formed part of this, whereby especially the ordeal and the duel were relegated.

Groups of individuals, mainly merchants, had early aspired to such privileges, and sometimes succeeded in obtaining them, from the early eleventh century onwards. In the northern

French–Flemish, Netherlandish, and lower German areas—as incidentally also in England—from this time on, merchant guilds became active; but their existence can be proved only in a few cities. The role of these brotherhoods in the creation of the city communes is hard to evaluate. They could quite well act in the general interests of the city-dwellers, and also add to the development of urban community feeling. In all known cases, however, they remained an association of individuals which united only a relatively small part of the urban population, so that not even all the merchants in the towns concerned were part of it.

To the circle of the co-operatives which brought together at least part of the urban population, there also belonged the brotherhoods, craftsmen's associations, and guilds of other traders and artisans. The first certain evidence in Germany does not go back beyond the early twelfth century. Just like the guilds, which did not only represent the economic interests of their members, the craft associations tried to provide wider help for their members, so that they were also concerned in cases of death, illness, or accident. This mutual support soon expressed itself in religious and social forms too, up to communal church services, wakes, meals, and drinking sessions. Such all-embracing aims are a reflection of the needs and aspirations of a society in which social provision and care were borne only to a very limited extent by the traditional holders of power. This gave these associations of individuals, orientated towards family, friends, religion, and also towards trade, an extensive field of activity which also might include some of the functions of power. They were not only co-operative creations; they could also be put to use by the town government for the control of markets, or for the supply of the court. The latter was the case with the chamber personnel, who were mentioned in the city laws of Strasbourg in 1131–2. Minting and money-changing were entrusted to the guilds of moneyers and money-changers; in several German cities they were probably in existence before the middle of the twelfth century.

As an expression of the co-operative elements in urban society, the guilds, craftsmen's associations, and other brotherhoods, and also other communities and co-operatives, represented a fertile soil for the development of the city communes as political bodies and also helped to consolidate them. They were not, however, the germ of the city communes, as was often assumed in older works. The role of the oath-fellowship (*Schwureinung*; Latin *coniuratio*) in the origins of the city communes is also disputed. It must be pointed out that for the whole area of south-west Germany proof for such fellowships is lacking. In contrast to earlier interpretations, the rising of the citizens of Cologne against Archbishop Anno in 1074 is no longer regarded as having a direct effect on the creation of the city commune. Even the 'union for freedom' (*coniuratio pro libertate*) according to more recent interpretations falls away as an essential support for the theory of the *Schwureinung* as the necessary basis for the city commune, as this event can well be understood as a pact between the episcopal lord of the city and the citizens of Cologne from the year 1114 when both partners, together with others, stood together against the emperor.

3

The Basis and Development
of the Economy

[a] POPULATION GROWTH AND THE SUPPLY
SITUATION

The rough estimate that the population in western central Europe multiplied by about three between the beginning of the eleventh and the end of the thirteenth century can hardly be made more precise in chronological terms. There are hints at a relatively continuous increase, at least in the old settlement areas, though with a faster increase in the twelfth century. Thus for the Moselle country, which in the valleys had long been densely settled, for the eleventh century there was an increase in places mentioned in charters from 350 to 590. The number increased again in the course of the twelfth century to 990. In the period dealt with here the number of rural settlements most probably doubled, which allows us, albeit with some methodological reservations, to assume an equally high population growth. Most of these new settlements were established in the higher areas of the Eifel and Hunsrück, often at heights of 400 to 600 metres, at which intensive agriculture was very risky because of its high dependence on the weather.

Part of the population growth was taken up by immigration into urban settlements, especially the larger episcopal cities. The frequent extensions of town walls point to this, even if they mainly resulted from military needs. The area protected by the walls of Cologne for example was increased from 122 to 203 hectares by the new wall of 1106. The population probably reached more than 20,000 in the twelfth century, and the commune created an even bigger ring of wall from 1180 onwards, which nearly doubled the walled area, to 403 hectares. Growth rates in the smaller cities, and in the even more numerous market towns, difficult to distinguish from villages in one direction and from urban settlements in the other, are less well attested. The growing urban population was especially dependent on increasing agricultural production.

Towards the end of the eleventh century there were increasing signs that agriculture could no longer supply the increased need for food. The lack of food was no longer simply caused by bad harvests, but rather by the long-term disproportion between agricultural production and population growth. Thus in 1090 the monk Bernold, who lived in various monasteries in the Black Forest, wrote from personal experience: 'A great famine has again afflicted many areas, although no great crop failure had preceded it.' For 1094 the same author mentions a great mortality in Bavaria, and in other regions too. He states, no doubt with exaggeration, that in the certainly large city of Regensburg alone, 8,500 people died in twelve weeks [14: v. 450, 459]. The catastrophe of 1094, also recounted in other contemporary sources, continued in the following years. The annals of Liège for 1095 laconically say 'The famine, already long, worsened' [14: iv. 29]. And still from the Maas area, Sigebert of Gembloux testified in the same year: 'This year, for many suffering from hunger, has been very bad, and also for the poor. The latter on their part pushed the rich hard by theft and arson' [14: vi. 367]. In some areas the famine continued into the first years of the twelfth century. In order to stop it, Count Charles of Flanders (1119–27) is supposed to have ordered that one-third of the arable land be sown with broad beans and peas. According to a contemporary opinion this step was meant to supply the poorer part of the population with food quickly during famines. The cultivation of these kinds of vegetables, which put nitrogen back into the soil, was especially suitable because their fast growth and early ripening bridged the time until the next harvest, or alleviated foreseeable bad harvests.

This is the period in which the Crusades struck a chord among wide circles of the population. It was expressly reported that the crusade preachers in France in 1095 found it especially easy to persuade the inhabitants to leave home because of political struggles, hunger, and heavy mortality. This was the

background both to the dreadful persecution of Jewish communities in Lorraine and other German areas, and to the ra-
pacious behaviour of some crusader bands on the way to the
Holy Land.

An exceptional number of more than local famines can also
be observed in the period leading up to the Second Crusade.
From 1139, in southern Holland, in Flanders, and in neighbouring regions, famines accompanied by epidemics occurred,
which in 1144 spread to England, the western Rhineland, and
the upper Maas region. In the following year they spread even
further, and stayed as widespread and severe until 1147, when
the crusaders set out. The famines and epidemics apparently
then influenced the anti-Jewish pogroms of 1146 in Germany.
Once again many people of low or servile origin participated
in the crusade; some wanted to get to know other countries;
some went, as contemporary sources stress, because of want,
and hoped to alleviate their poverty. Others thought they
would escape their duties towards their masters, which means
they had decided to leave their homelands for ever. After a
brief improvement, famines again occurred in 1149 and 1150
in several parts of Germany. In 1151 they developed into a
terrible catastrophe, with great mortality of men and beasts
all over Germany, and also in eastern France and Lorraine.
Afterwards, apparently, the food supply situation returned to
normal, and remained so with few exceptions throughout the
reign of Frederick Barbarossa.

When the famines were accompanied by warfare, the pres-
sures to escape want and seek alleviation far away were
increased. This combination is found for instance in the Moselle
area between 1140 and 1146, during the bitter fighting between
Archbishop Adalbero of Trier and Count Henry of Namur-
Luxemburg. The consequences for the population of such con-
tests are described in exemplary fashion by a source from Trier:
'Thus the miserable people are driven from the soil of their
fathers, and live and die as refugees, tortured from all sides.
Those who stayed did no work, so great was their need to hide
from the enemy. The cattle were driven off and the land around
devastated; the peasants bemoaned the times, because even
the young animals were stolen. Farming ceased in all ... the
country. And while the enemy caused this evil, God did little

against it, as the animals that were driven away for fear of the enemy were attacked at night by wolves . . .' [14: viii. 241].

In desperate situations like this, rumours, or even reports, of a foreign 'paradise' were the more readily believed. Thus the messengers whom Count Adolf II of Holstein in 1143 sent to all his western and southern neighbours—Flanders and Holland, Frisia and Westphalia—met a great response. They called everyone suffering from lack of land to come with their families to Wagria, a country which the count controlled, and in which at about that time he founded the trading settlement of Lübeck which he secured with a castle. 'Whereupon a huge number from various peoples set out with family and possessions, and came to Count Adolf of Wagria to take possession of the land he had promised them' [3: xix. 210]. Many a tale about Hungary by those returning from the Second Crusade might have had a similar effect. A widespread view of this country is given by Otto of Freising, a participant in the crusade: 'Fields stretch into the vast plain, watered by streams and large rivers and rich in forests full of game of all kinds. The country is gracious in its natural beauty. It is rich through the fertility of its fields, so that it appears as beautiful as God's paradise, or Egypt (*ut tamquam paradisus Dei vel Egyptus spectabilis esse videtur*)' [3: xvii. 192–5]. Probably these attractive prospects followed the first settlers from the Maas and Moselle country in connection with the Second Crusade, and created the beginnings of German settlement in the Hungarian district of Transylvania.

[b] AGRICULTURAL EXPLOITATION AND THE BEGINNINGS OF URBANIZATION

The severe crisis in food supplies of the late eleventh and early twelfth century, which was expressed in long famines followed by epidemics, apparently provided the impetus to cultivate permanently for grain production areas which had not previously been cultivated, or not intensively. At the same time there are increasing hints of settlement activity in eastern areas by settlers from areas further away. But the settlement of the east only began in earnest after the middle of the twelfth century, when hunger had ruled again for several years in many old settlement areas.

The character of the sources and the state of research, which cannot yet have recourse to much archaeological data, unfortunately make it difficult to give a more precise description of the extent of colonizing activity. The optimistic view of earlier research, that statements about the chronology of settlement could be made by allocating particular types of place-name to certain periods, has long been dampened. Thus extensive groups of place-names ending in *-rode*, *-rade* or *-reuth* (etc.) [from *roden*, 'to clear'] can quite often be shown to have existed from the Carolingian period. These place-names by themselves are therefore not enough to date forest clearance in the high Middle Ages. Place-names ending in *-hagen* are rather an exception in this respect. They certainly date from after the middle of the eleventh century, and therefore from the narrower high medieval period of clearance. The stem *Hag* (scrub, wood, grove) itself points to the clearing activities of the settlers. These place-names are concentrated on the middle Weser area and its neighbours to the east.

The forest-clearing activities of the Cistercians began in Germany only in the second quarter of the twelfth century. Among the first houses were Kamp on the lower Rhine (1122), and Ebrach and Walkenried (1127), founded from Morimond. From the beginning of the 1130s the settlements of the order in Germany increased, for example Himmerod near Trier, Otterberg in the Palatinate, Pairis in Alsace, and Salem on Lake Constance. The order was restricted to the old settlement areas until the middle of the twelfth century. With their systematic clearings the Cistercians took up activities which had earlier been furthered by other lords. In contrast to the Cistercians, who at first did most of the clearing themselves with their monks, lay brothers, and paid labourers, most of the other patrons of forest clearance used peasants for this generally arduous and unrewarding work. Cistercians and—though to a lesser extent—Premonstratensians were also active in other fields of rural development, such as drainage.

The local peasants might simply enlarge existing fields, or good opportunities might be taken to clear new ground in the vicinity of older settlements. One such older settlement was

Eschershausen, where the bishop of Hildesheim used immigrant peasants for clearing work by 1114 at the latest, and promised their rights to them in writing in that year. According to this the peasants remained free of taxes and tithes as long as they were occupied with cutting down trees and removing the roots and other obstacles. During this time they were only able to work the ground with a hoe. This freedom remained valid for the first six years in which they could plough their fields. Only in the seventh year did the payments of tax and tithes begin, with small sums at first, rising to the final dues in the tenth year. The immigrants had considerably fewer rights in the use of the forests for pannage for pigs than the bishop's serfs who had already been living in Eschershausen for a long time. If they did not have a pig for fattening—and this was obviously not rare—they could perhaps still acquire a pig by taking over the animals and rights of someone else. The peasants owned the land they had cleared in hereditary right. They kept freedom of movement, but had to pay a duty when they sold their property. They were obliged to pay a death duty, being comparable in this respect to the episcopal serfs [3: xxxi. 178–85, no. 71].

It seems that those settlers recruited in large numbers in Franconia at the beginning of the twelfth century by Count Wiprecht of Groitzsch moved a huge distance from their original home. They were intended to clear a large area in the diocese of Merseburg for him. The annals of the monastery of Pegau, which Wiprecht founded in the same diocese in 1091, report in 1104 that the count ordered the outside colonists to clear the forest completely, and they would then own the land in hereditary right. This measure was apparently successful. With the help of the immigrants Wiprecht was soon able to found numerous villages between the rivers Mulde and Wiera (a tributary of the Pleisse). The peasants tried to secure their legal rights, hard-won by their own labour, by calling the properties and places after their own names, thus imitating the noble landowners. In the middle of the clearance area Wiprecht founded a small monastery, to which the tithes of the peasants were made over [3: xxxi. 164–7, no. 65].

A contract the archbishop of Hamburg-Bremen made with people from Holland in 1106 for the draining of the Weser marshes sheds another flood of light on the forms of agricultural development and the conditions of life of the peasant population which carried out the work of colonization. According to this a small group of Dutchmen turned to the archbishop with a request to let them have some uncultivated, swampy land in the diocese of Bremen for cultivation (*ad excolendam*). Among the leaders of the settlers, who originated from the diocese of Utrecht, was a priest. The church the settlers were to build was made over to him for life. He was to be maintained by the tithes fixed for the church and by cultivating the landed endowment of the church (one *Hufe*). These settlers were also granted the right of hereditary succession, but with no mention of taxes or even death duties. They were only obliged to pay measured, precisely fixed tributes of one-tenth or one-eleventh of their yield. Furthermore they received far-reaching rights of self-government [3: xxxi. 168–73, no. 67]. The Dutchmen, who had long been familiar with draining marshes in their homeland 200 kilometres away, expected a large number of their countrymen to take this opportunity. The experience of long-lasting famines in their home country in previous years must no doubt have played a part in this.

Increased internal colonization and the first attempts at eastward settlement were expressions of an economic change which simultaneously affected the traditional lordships in the old settlement areas. The strongest influence for change was the growing market orientation of agriculture. This was especially noticeable at an early stage in the specialized wine-growing trade. Thus for instance the wine-growers in the market town of Wasserbillig on the Moselle before the 1140s offered prolonged resistance to their manorial lord, the abbot of St Maximin outside the gates of Trier. Because of this he described them as stubborn and rebellious serfs. Besides the confirmation of their right to inherit, the wine-growers also compelled the fixing of their dues and payments—although not of their labour services [see 435: 37 f.]. In the second half of the eleventh century the lordship of the old Benedictine nunnery of Kitzingen on the Main was much influenced by the money economy, market relations, and also industry, although its organization still to a large extent drew on traditional forms ('villication'). Part of the manorial complex was a market in Kitzingen, and a ferry close to the nunnery, which was especially profitable [3: xxxi.

138–43, no. 55]. From the beginning of the twelfth century in many areas, for example the Moselle region, a decrease in demesne farming—the core of the old 'villication' system—can be observed; this led to a lessening of service dues.

The greater concentration of agriculture on the market did not only develop through the growth of the episcopal towns, but also through the transformation of many market towns into larger urban settlements, and through the rise of new markets. Thus Schaffhausen on the upper Rhine, where a high noble's mint is known from the year 1045, had by 1111 an annual fair and a ferry. Around the middle of the twelfth century it had at least 112 tenements, nine beer- and two wine-shops, as well as bakers and butchers. The palace town of Goslar took the last steps to becoming an urban centre between 1100 and 1140; the core had already been fortified in 1073 with a wood and earth rampart. A stone wall was begun in the middle of the twelfth century by the citizens, which extended the settlement, from 1131 on always called a city (*civitas*), to 84 hectares.

Among the market foundations was that of Radolfzell at Lake Constance, under the abbot of Reichenau in 1100. The most famous example is the foundation of the market of Freiburg im Breisgau by Duke Conrad of Zähringen in 1120. Merchants called together from all around were required to found and develop a market settlement at a virtually uninhabited place, on the basis of a sworn agreement at the duke's will. The duke promised those attending the market peace, security, and if necessary compensation for stolen goods out of his own pocket. Each merchant was allocated a plot at a fixed annual rent, on which he could build his own house. Besides freedom from toll each citizen was assured of unrestricted right of inheritance, as well as use of pasture, streams, and forests. The citizens received the right to elect their judge (*advocatus*) and their priest. Disputes should be settled according to the customs and rights of all merchants, particularly those of Cologne [386]. The market-place, which to begin with was only secured by ditches and palisades, quickly developed into an urban settlement.

However, such a straightforward development as that hardly ever occurred. The little town founded by the castle of Logne south of Liège by Abbot Wibald of Stablo in 1138, where the market-place was laid out as a rectangle 330 by 60 feet, re-mained considerably more modest. The abbot, who was prominent in imperial politics, created the basis for the settlement by transferring another one; the desired immigrants were to own their building plots with gardens in hereditary right without payment. The abbot was mainly interested in the market dues, and made concessions on the personal legal position of abbey people who settled there [see 435: 29].

[c] MONEY, TRADE, AND INDUSTRY

The fact that minting rights from the tenth century onwards were essentially exercised only by the ecclesiastical and later also by the lay nobility, was a consequence of Germany's centrifugal constitutional development. By keeping at least part of the proceeds—i.e. the difference between the value of the metal and the nominal value of the coins—they gained an additional source of income. The kings could participate in the minting profits of the ecclesiastical lords, who were in a great majority, by means of imperial control of the Church. The most important mints from the middle of the eleventh century were to be found almost entirely in the episcopal towns in the old settlement areas. But from the tenth century on they were also founded in what were at first still agricultural settlements, in connection with new markets. Such new foundations appeared in large numbers in the area of Saxony, and thus in the heartland of Ottonian–Salian imperial power. Until the beginning of our period, however, the Rhine still marked the border between the more highly developed money economy of the Schelde, Maas, Moselle, and Rhine countries, including Flanders, on the one hand, and the neighbouring areas to the east as far as the Elbe on the other.

The backwardness of the money economy in north-western Germany further decreased from the middle of the eleventh century. Up to the beginning of the Staufen period, minting places with considerable output developed between the Ems and the Elbe. Among them were not only episcopal towns, like Magdeburg, Merseburg, Bremen, and Hildesheim, but also larger markets like Goslar, Bardowick, Jever, and Brunswick. Further to the west, trading centres like Soest and Dortmund sprang up. In the Rhineland the monetary predominance of the old episcopal towns remained. As well as these, Duisburg, and Zürich further south, gained importance. Not many new minting places were founded in southern Germany, where the mint of Regensburg remained dominant. With the exception of Regensburg and Goslar the most important mints in the German empire were situated in the Rhenish episcopal cities of Cologne, Mainz, Worms, and Speyer. The Maas and Schelde areas with Flanders on the one hand, and the lower Rhineland on the other (Cologne, Aachen, Maastricht, Liège, Deventer, Huy, Namur, Brussels), made up an outstandingly dense monetary zone, with an accumulation of smaller and larger mints.

In this way the west–east axis mentioned previously in the north-west European area was further strengthened. It now offered a favourable starting-point for trade into areas east of the Elbe as far as Russia. Numerous finds of German coins dating from the tenth century onwards in the north and east show that this trade was in existence by the eleventh century. Around the middle of the eleventh century Saxon and probably also Frisian merchants traded with the Slavs on the other side of the Elbe despite warfare, which in 1066 led to the destruction of the important trading centres of Schleswig and Hamburg. They mainly exchanged furs, especially the valuable marten, mostly from Prussia, against woollen cloths from the West. Even in distant Novgorod around 1100 Flemish cloth from Ypres was so well known and valued that it was demanded as the price of entry into the merchant guild.

One consequence of the lasting controversies and recurrent wars between Christians and pagan Slavs was that both sides enslaved their prisoners. Up to the end of the eleventh century pagan slaves were traded to the Mediterranean slave markets, partly by Jewish traders, or taken directly to the courts of the caliphs in Muslim Spain. This large-scale slave-trade seems to have gone on until the middle of the twelfth century.

Otherwise, trade in the countries beyond the Elbe and in the Baltic area does not seem to have increased until the second half of the twelfth century. The trade of the Danube area, which had its main centre at Regensburg, had already spread to the east, south-east, and south. The old north–south trade route along the Rhine and over the passes of the Alps, where it reached the monetarily much more highly developed Italian economy, still constituted the fundamental backbone of long-distance trade in the German empire. West–east trade became more important only in the middle of the twelfth century.

As a consequence of the close connection of mints and markets in Germany—in contrast to imperial Italy, where the mints remained restricted to a few episcopal cities—the regional differences in minting were reflected in the development of the markets. The number of markets rose from 40 to 90 in the tenth century. In the course of the eleventh century it increased to 140, and reached 250 in the following century. Only one-third of the 15 most important markets, namely Magdeburg, Dortmund, Goslar, Würzburg, and Bamberg, did not have an old tradition going back to Roman times. It was no doubt the Rhine cities of Cologne and Mainz and the south-east German trading centre of Regensburg which were of the greatest economic importance. No less than one-third of the towns are situated on the Rhine: as well as Cologne and Mainz, also Constance, Basle, and Worms. Metz and Trier on the Moselle can also be added to the group of the most important markets.

In the area on the right bank of the Rhine, fairs with a wide catchment area were only established from the eleventh century onwards, the markets on the left bank serving as a model in this respect too. Cologne once again had a special position. At the beginning of the twelfth century three annual fairs took place there. According to the *Vita Annonis*, people from all the Rhenish towns, and also from 'overseas' and countries further away, participated in the Easter fair [14: xi. 518]. From the turn of the eleventh century Cologne was already an important meeting-point of the far-flung trade of the Jews.

Shipping routes remained predominant for larger amounts of goods. Traffic in the old settlement areas was accordingly concentrated mainly on the Rhine and its tributaries, and also on the Danube. How costly overland transport of heavy materials was can be seen in the collection of material for the building of the monastery of St Trond, north-west of Liège, around the third quarter of the eleventh century. The stone for the pillars was transported from Worms to Cologne by ship. There it was loaded on to wagons, together with other stone.

It was then carted by road with draught animals. The populace also took part by helping to drag the wagons along with ropes. Without using any bridges the stone was finally taken to St Trond via the Maas. It seems little was done to improve the country roads. The Life of the technically gifted Bishop Benno of Osnabrück emphasizes as one of his remarkable achievements that around 1070 he had had solid roads constructed through impassable swamps [3: xxii. 396 f.]. He had also been successful in securing the foundations of the Salian cathedral at Speyer against being undermined by the Rhine.

New bridges were not erected in large numbers in Germany until the late eleventh century. These are distinguished by technical progress, which led from floating bridges to those with pillars, and from wood to stone [see 445: 274]. In a charter of 1133 Bishop Embricho of Würzburg praised the master mason of the cathedral Enzelin, a layman, who had supervised the construction of the bridge over the Main. At about the same time (1135) the people of Regensburg began a stone bridge which spanned the Danube on sixteen arches. The construction of this bridge considerably influenced the change of route for traffic from northern France into the Danube lands, from the Worms-Wimpfen-Passau route increasingly via Würzburg-Nuremberg-Regensburg. It is therefore not surprising that Bishop Reginbert of Passau in 1143, shortly before the Regensburg bridge was finished, stated that for the sake of his soul nothing was more desirable than 'to build a bridge over the Inn at Passau' [457: 216f.].

The biggest boost to trade in Germany was the expansion of industrial activity. One can see from the customs duties and privileges of around the turn of the eleventh and twelfth centuries, such as the Koblenz 'customs roll' (which was, however, probably composed later), that the largest part of the goods traded was raw material for industrial production, as well as finished products of industry, especially the metal industry. Thus merchants from the Maas towns of Liège and Huy bought copper in Cologne. But they also travelled on from Cologne via Dortmund to Saxony, and there, most likely in Goslar, they also bought this metal. Copper was transported down the Rhine from the upper Rhine area as far as Koblenz and beyond. But also merchants from the Maas region—Huy, Liège, Dinant, and Namur are mentioned as places of origin—traded up the Rhine with finished products of the metal industry, like cooking-pots and frying-pans.

As well as the metal industry of the Maas region, that of Cologne also reached a higher level of development in this period. Swords from Cologne, for example, are mentioned in the city laws of Strasbourg of 1131-2. Cologne is the most likely source for the swords which were sold in larger numbers around 1100 in Koblenz. The harnesses made in Mainz, which were traded as far as England, also enjoyed a high reputation at the time.

In Cologne, however, the textile industry was of even greater importance. Significantly, specialization occurred earliest here. This process had already gone far by the middle of the twelfth century, when the blanket weavers of Cologne founded a guild of their own, and the veil and scarf weavers in the linen industry had their own organizations. While the cloths of Cologne were of inferior quality to those of Flanders and were therefore aimed at poorer buyers, the cloths of Regensburg already in the first half of the twelfth century enjoyed a special reputation as luxury goods. Abbot Peter the Venerable of Cluny in his revision of the statutes of his order expressly forbade the monks scarlet and 'Barchent' cloths from Regensburg. It is, however, hardly likely that these precious clothing fabrics, also including silk and furs, were actually produced in Regensburg. They were more likely imported goods from the east and south, not least from Byzantium, which the long-distance merchants of Regensburg might also have obtained via Kiev. Even before 1135 'Roman' merchants—probably mainly Italians—were living in the street called *inter Latinos* (later Walengasse) in Regensburg.

Textile production now became a literary topic too. According to the poem 'Dispute between Sheep and Flax', written around 1070 in Trier, the Rhineland and Swabia were then known for the production of naturally-coloured, black, or red fabrics. According to the same source the cloths from Flanders, 'which suit the gentleman', and which were produced in green, grey, and deep blue, were of even higher quality. The superiority of Flemish products over those of the other countries north of the Alps may be explained by technical innovations, which came about here first in the middle of the eleventh century, as supposedly also in the county of Champagne.

The vertical loom, a typical women's tool, which was sometimes still used in the *Gynaecea* (workhouses for women with craft occupations) of the large manors in the eleventh century, had already been pushed out by the horizontal foot-loom. This instrument, already long in use, was now considerably improved. With skilled operation by two people, not only cloths of 15-20 metres in length, but also wider fabrics of more even quality could be produced. The fulling mill also added to the improvement of quality, and achieved higher productivity as well. The steps of the process were distributed among several specialists and demanded a high level of organization, for which the cities offered the best conditions. Another essential precondition for success was co-operation between the craft specialists—the weavers, fullers, and dyers—and the long-distance merchants, and thus the co-ordination of industry and trade.

Thus trade was no longer restricted to luxury goods and other requirements of the courts, but now also included articles required for daily use for a wide population range in the old settlement areas. The traders therefore became more and more orientated towards the towns, and also settled in towns and markets. The towns at the same time became the most important centres of industrial production. The latter provided a decisive impulse for the expansion, both quantitative and qualitative, of trade, because of its need of raw materials and the need to export the end-products. At the same time the outlines of larger industrial areas could be seen in Germany, in which the metal industry in the Maas area and cloth manufacture in Flanders, which was partly French, reached an especially high standard.

[*d*] THE BEGINNINGS OF NEW ECONOMIC FORMS

There are many signs that Germany underwent profound economic changes between the middle of the eleventh and the twelfth centuries. An acceleration of developments, generally already under way, seems to have occurred, especially around the turn of the twelfth century. Population growth in the old settlement areas caused longer famine periods, which compelled increased mobility and the examination of new ways of life, sometimes far away. The settlement movement connected with this led to the expansion and concentration of village as well as urban settlements, and to the expansion of the agriculturally exploited area in the old settlement regions, and also in the areas further away in the east. In both places a greater independence of peasant agriculture was tied up with this. Through these factors, and through greater orientation towards the market, the traditional organizational forms of agricultural production were loosened even further, if not replaced.

The money economy in most areas reached a level which made it possible to include in the market process objects of daily use for the wider population. This promoted the division of labour, which was especially to be found in the urban and rural markets. For the first time, not only were settlements endowed with market rights, but also market settlements of urban character were founded. The division of labour showed itself in the expansion and differentiation of industry in the country and especially in urban settlements. At the same time the beginnings of regional concentration on certain industrial products increased. By integrating industrial products destined for the needs of more of the population, and by supplying industry with raw materials, the goods traded were expanded in quantity and improved in quality. The centres of government receded as destinations of long-distance trade in favour of the markets and, especially, the bigger cities. The holders of power did their utmost to improve roads and the prospects for trade, in the interests of their financial income from trade and market dues. Added to this was a regional expansion of trade. This was favoured in the north in the long run by the gradually increasing density of settlement between the Rhine and the Elbe. The borders to the pagan Slavonic east, however, long remained effective. The exchange of goods with the Mediterranean area was still more or less limited to a thin stream. Also for the trade with the west a stronger impulse was lacking.

Thus by the middle of the twelfth century numerous new beginnings in economic life, particularly in the more highly developed old settlement areas, had appeared in outline, but they were not yet able to develop more strongly. The large economic gap between this and the Mediterranean area, especially imperial Italy, hardly decreased; it might even have increased further, as the new impulses there were simultaneously more direct and more effective.

4

The Church, Piety, and Education

[a] MONASTIC AND CHURCH REFORM

From the end of the eleventh century the various non-noble classes of the population in Germany constantly increased in importance, not only in politics, the economy, and trade. The transformation of religious and ecclesiastical ways of life stood in close correlation to these processes. The new forms of piety, which on the whole contained a more profound Christianity, can most clearly be grasped in the transformation of monastic and other ecclesiastical communities.

According to the testimony of the priest Bernold of Constance (d. 1100), the son of a priest and educated in Church law, and who lived for some time in the reformed monastery of St Blasien in the Black Forest, the communal religious life within the *regnum Teutonicum* among clerics and monks, and also among lay people, had undergone a huge upswing in the last decades of the eleventh century—i.e. in a period of severe religious and political controversy. According to him, laymen in large numbers renounced secular life and joined the various ecclesiastical communities in serving capacities, without becoming clerics or monks themselves. Apparently in general this was within the framework of the institution of lay brotherhood, later to become firmly established. Among them were numerous women, as Bernold emphasizes—even some of peasant origin. The model for this piety, mainly found among the village and peasant population, was the common life of the early Church, the *primitiva ecclesia*. However, this return to the origins of Christianity, which called in question the traditional forms and norms, met with some disapproval, as Bernold also reports [14: v. 452 f.].

Such new approaches occurred in various forms in Germany, as in other areas of Western Europe. An important innovation showed itself towards the end of the sixties and the beginning of the seventies, i.e. in a period when the opposition of German higher nobles and imperial bishops to the monarchy of Henry IV began to take shape. In this political context, the reformed monasticism of Cluniac type, as developed in an especially strict form in the north Italian monastery of Fruttuaria, was introduced into two monasteries in the middle of the empire by two great lords. With the exception of the border areas of Lorraine, far away from the king, where Cluniac influence had been effective since long before the middle of the eleventh century, with considerable consequences for the reformed papacy, monasticism on the model of Gorze had hitherto been predominant in the German empire. In contrast to Cluniac monasticism, which aimed at far-reaching independence of secular powers, the Gorze reform had been furthered by the Ottonians and early Salians in the context of their lordship of the imperial Church.

Against this background it is all the more striking that Archbishop Anno of Cologne about 1070 installed monks from Fruttuaria in the territorially and politically very important monastery of Siegburg, which he founded, and thus drove out the monks from the monastery of St Maximin in Trier. Anno soon saw to the expansion of this reform in other monasteries he controlled. In 1072 the Swabian Duke Rudolf of Rheinfelden, later the anti-king, introduced the customs of Fruttuaria into the Black Forest monastery of St Blasien, which was important for securing his power. The acceptance of the monastic customs of Fruttuaria in Siegburg and St Blasien, which then became models for a large number of other monasteries, cannot, however, be interpreted as 'an attack on the imperial church system', despite the political entanglements. It was rather an expression of the increasing independence of the imperial princes, which had become clearer during the previous decades. That stricter rules of Cluniac type were now taken up in the middle of the empire had to do with changed religious ideas within the ruling class, without such ideas necessarily being connected with anti-royal attitudes. An opposite example is provided by the historian and monk Lampert of Hersfeld, who criticized the 'new' monasticism and at the same time was sharply opposed to Henry IV.

Besides Siegburg and St Blasien, the hitherto unimportant monastery of Hirsau under Abbot William, who originated from St Emmeram in Regensburg, became a centre for the spread of Cluniac-type monasticism. The customs of Cluny were introduced to Hirsau directly from the mother-house in 1079, when the political confrontation between the Salian monarchy and the anti-king Rudolf of Rheinfelden, who was supported by the papal party, had come to a climax. In the following years, the monks of the monastery of Hirsau, newly founded around the middle of the eleventh century, agitated even in 'public' sermons against the supporters of the Salian kingship. These activities, incompatible with the habits of traditional monasticism, met with sharp criticism from the imperial monasteries of Hersfeld and Lorsch, by whom they were insulted as schismatics and heretics, as deviants and hypocrites.

Up to the middle of the twelfth century, when Cluniac monasticism had already for several decades passed the peak of its influence, nearly 200 monasteries in the German empire, mostly founded by bishops or dynasts, were influenced by the so-called 'neo-Cluniac' reform centres of Siegburg (39), St Blasien (36), and Hirsau (114). Hidden behind these numbers is a religious renewal which mainly concerned the interrelated lay and clerical ruling groups. The reform which came into existence at the beginning of the tenth century at Cluny in Burgundy was at the peak of its religious and political importance when, with considerable modifications, it spread to Germany. It seems that a preference for nobles gradually prevailed, also in the Hirsau-type monasteries, which to begin with seem to have accepted non-nobles in their convents.

In contrast to the monasticism of Cluny, which in its long development had often deviated from the norms of the Benedictine rule, Cistercian monasticism, which had come into existence at the turn of the twelfth century, likewise in Burgundy, attempted a radical return to the ideals of Benedictine monasticism. With isolation from the world, and the simple life-style of the monks, it aspired to a return to the ideal of poverty, connected with the demand of physical work for the monks. In Germany, however, it only spread from the 1130s, when the original approach to reform, especially in respect of manual labour for the monks, was already being relaxed. Although the Cistercians were also directed towards the nobility, and right from the beginning most monks came from the nobility, the order remained open to other social groups. This, however, in the course of time mainly happened within the framework of lay brotherhood.

While the different Benedictine reforms which came into existence outside the German imperial area reached Germany relatively late, and the more extreme forms of eremitism were not generally influential there, the reform of the secular canons took root early. The first centres came into existence in the last quarter of the eleventh century in Rottenbuch in the diocese of Freising (1079) and at Marbach in Alsace (*c.*1090). On the model of the early Church and the stricter forms of the so-called Augustinian rule, making greater demands for poverty, manual work, fasting, and nightly prayers, Richard of Springiersbach (d. 1158), the son of a ministerial of the count palatine, developed even before 1119 a new monastic model within the regular canonical reform in the monastery which his mother founded on the middle Moselle. However, the monastic congregation which Richard founded during the next decades, and which included several nunneries, remained restricted to a narrow region on the Moselle and middle Rhine.

More important was the effect of this model on the Salzburg and probably also on the Halberstadt canonical reforms, which, on the initiative of their respective bishops, dedicated themselves especially to pastoral work. The rule developed at Springiersbach influenced not least the forms of religious life at Prémontré, the place of origin of the Premonstratensian order, founded *c.*1120 by Norbert of Gennep (d. 1134). Norbert, a member of a noble family from the lower Rhine, had previously made a promising career as a canon of Xanten and a member of Henry V's court chapel. Yet he turned away from it, and from 1115 worked for some years as a wandering preacher in France and Germany. Like most other wandering preachers of the time, he struck a chord among women, many of whom joined his following. In these activities Norbert encountered resistance from the Church hierarchy, so that he was accused of illegal preaching at a synod in Fritzlar. Although following this in 1118 he received permission for wandering preaching from Pope Gelasius II, it was not renewed in the following year. Norbert failed in his plan to lead the reform of a house of canons in Laon with which the bishop of Laon had entrusted him, because of the resistance of the canons to his strict demands. Only now did he found his own community in the deserted area of Prémontré, close to Laon. A nunnery was affiliated with it. After that, Norbert periodically resumed his wandering preaching, though without a permanent following, before in 1126 he rose to be archbishop of Magdeburg.

Between 1120 and 1126 Norbert, despite considerable resistance from the German bishops, founded nine new settlements in the dioceses of Laon, Soissons, Cambrai, Liège, Münster, Mainz, and Metz. He linked up the new foundations in a monastic association, which was subordinated to him and the monks of Prémontré, including property rights. The Premonstratensian monasteries, however, only received a more firm institutional framework under Norbert's successor Hugh of Fosses (1128–61), on the model of Cistercian organization. By the middle of the twelfth century nearly one hundred and fifty Premonstratensian monasteries had been founded in the German empire. Including the Augustinian canons, who were close to the Premonstratensians, and the associated nunneries, the number of these reformed monasteries in Germany then grew to about 300, most of them new foundations. About 40 of the *c.*150 houses of canons of this type were situated in or very close to cities. Many of them included a hospital, which underlines their concern with the important centres on communications networks, and thus with the needs of the urban population.

The many new beginnings which are observable in Germany from the last quarter of the eleventh century onwards not only gave the religious, ecclesiastical renewal an institutionally established framework; they also incorporated new attitudes and activities which went even beyond the Church's framework. The return to the ideals of the early Church should be pointed out, the revaluation of voluntary poverty, of manual labour, and not least of pastoral care. But it must also be stressed that traditional patterns of behaviour remained important, and in many cases decisive, alongside these new approaches, and often disguised them. Such differences and contrasts for example are shown in the mid-twelfth-century exchange of letters between the abbesses of two nunneries, Tenxwind of Andernach and Hildegard of Bingen. Tenxwind, a ministerial's daughter and *magistra* of an Augustinian nunnery, the sister and confidante of Richard of Springiersbach, strongly criticized the magnificent liturgy and particularly the rigorous exclusion of non-noble women in Hildegard's convent, by referring to the New Testament and conditions in the early Church. The noble Benedictine Hildegard defended her measures with proofs from the Old Testament and by referring to the saving function of noble power, thus upholding the traditional type of 'noble saint'. Fundamental to these contradictory views of the world, growing from different religious and social roots, were almost opposite ideas of God: for Tenxwind, who grew up in the *pauperes Christi* movement, the *pauper Christus* (the poor Christ) is the model; for Hildegard it is the ruler of the world, the *rex potentissimus* and *fortissimus et nobilissimus Deus*, to whom one owes awe and honour.

[b] PASTORAL WORK AND MISSIONS

There was no unity over the forms of spiritual care either. The dispute between the Gregorian monks of Hirsau, who in the 1080s addressed the wider public in their sermons, and the pro-Salian monks of Lorsch and Hersfeld has already been mentioned, and likewise the conflict between the wandering preacher Norbert of Gennep and the official clergy in the second decade of the following century. In Germany also, the dispute about the canonical way of life of clerics, especially concerning simony and celibacy, was fought out with great ferocity. In the year 1075, when the conflict between the *Pataria* and their opponents reached its climax in Lombardy, and Gregory VII at the Lenten synod once again insisted on the prohibition of simony and priestly marriage, Bishop Altmann of Passau was so severely threatened by the opponents of celibacy among his diocesan clergy that he feared for his life. In the diocese of Constance in the same year, 3,600 clerics assembled at a synod expressly repudiated the papal celibacy order, which met with particular resistance from the lower clergy. At the same time the pro-Salian monk and historian Sigebert of Gembloux (*c.*1030–1112) deplored the severe attacks against priests of incontinent life: 'They are jeered at in public; when they show themselves they are violently insulted; they are pointed out with fingers, and maltreated. Some have been made to lose their goods and property; they have fled, as they do not want to live like paupers and beggars where they were once held in high respect. Others have been mutilated . . .' [15: ii. 438].

Since radical Church reformers condemned simony and Nicolaitism as heresy, after these papal measures clerical office-holders who offended against them were considered excommunicate. Hence they were no longer able to administer valid sacraments. Contrary to this, however, it had long been dogmatically undisputed that even priests living unworthily could administer valid sacraments. These opposing viewpoints gave the parties the opportunity to accuse their respective opponents of heresy.

Thus in autumn 1130 the canon Gerhoch, who after his entry into the reform centre of Rottenbuch had been active as a pastor in the market and trading town of Cham in the Upper Palatinate, was accused in Regensburg of heresy for denying the validity of sacraments administered by simoniacal or married clergy. His teaching, which questioned the whole ecclesiastical prebendary system by widening the meaning of simony, was condemned as heretical by the clergy of Regensburg. Gerhoch only managed a narrow escape from his sentence through being protected by Bishop Kuno of Regensburg (1126–32), who had earlier been a monk of Siegburg, by Archbishop Conrad of Salzburg (1106–47), the greatest promoter of the regular canonical life in southern Germany, and also by the papal legate, Archbishop Walter of Ravenna (1118–44). The archbishop of Ravenna had previously been a canon of the cathedral of his home town of Regensburg, and, as abbot of Santa Maria in Porto in Ravenna, had been the leader of one of the most important centres of the regular canons. Furthermore he had been in close contact with the circle of the female hermit Herluca of Epfach (on the Lech), a disciple of William of Hirsau. The canon of Rottenbuch and active pastor thus had to be protected by important representatives of radical pastoral reform against condemnation as a heretic by traditionalist clergy. Although some of these reformers already held leading posts in Germany in the second quarter of the twelfth century, their aims, coloured by the poverty ideal, continued to be disputed.

The ecclesiastical renewal produced not only significant impulses towards a more intensive spiritual life, but also towards the conversion of the pagans. The missionary activities of Bishop Otto of Bamberg (1102–39) gained fundamental importance in Pomerania, which during the 1120s had been conquered by the Polish duke. At about the same time the Bremen canon Vicelin, who had studied in France and had been consecrated priest by Norbert of Xanten, resuscitated the mission to the Elbe Slavs in Wagria. For this he created an important centre in the Augustinian foundation of Neumünster. In the following decades Vicelin's missionary work suffered many set-backs and failures, mainly as a result of the close ties between the mission and the political conquest of the pagan Slavs. Although mass baptism occurred in connection with the crusade against the Wends in 1147, this proved to be an illusory success, as an attack by the Slav Prince Niklot destroyed all attempts at conversion and colonization.

The 1147 crusade against the Wends brought a new accent into the pagan mission. Although conversion and conquest had always been closely bound up together, forcible conversion was now for the first time legitimated by the Church in this secondary theatre of the Second Crusade. The Cistercian Abbot Bernard of Clairvaux, who opposed the persecution of Jews by the crusaders, forbade the participants in this German crusade to make peace with the pagan Slavs in return for payment of money or tribute—as apparently had been customary. Supported by the theory of the just war against violent opponents, the Cistercian abbot in his recruiting letter calls for either the complete destruction of the pagans or their complete conversion. The slogan 'death or baptism' deriving from this was probably not carried out with grim determination except by those crusaders who had no political interests of their own in the country to be conquered. The Saxon princes and knights went on making compromises with the pagan enemy in their own interests. The religious motive, however, served them as legitimation of their conquering policies; as Henry the Lion's chancery put it in 1163: 'As heavenly grace has granted success to our campaign, we have been able to triumph over the Slav hordes in such a way that we have led the obedience of the humble to eternal life by baptism, and the defiance of the proud to eternal death by spilling their blood' [20: 86f., no. 53].

[c] HERETICS

After the foundation of Prémontré, Norbert of Xanten, who himself had come into conflict with Church officials a few years before as a wandering priest, preached successfully at the beginning of the twenties against the so-called Tanchelmists in Antwerp, and against heretics in Cologne and Cambrai. The Tanchelmists were the followers of the alleged monk Tanchelm, who in 1115 had been murdered by a priest. During his wandering preaching in Antwerp, Flanders, Zeeland, and Brabant, a priest called Everwacher and a smith called Manasse had been by his side. Tanchelm originally belonged to the circle of those religious and political reformers who opposed secularized and unworthy priests. His opponent in the diocese of Utrecht accused him of disregard for the priesthood, the pope, the bishops, and the clergy. It was probably just a consequence of his severe criticism of the official Church that he was also accused of refusing the sacraments and rejecting tithes. Tanchelm won many followers. Thousands are said to have followed him on his journeys, among them many women. It was said that he received rich donations from his followers, who held even his bath-water sacred. He regarded himself, his opponents said, as God or God's son. It is an open question how far these accusations were justified.

Tanchelm was one of those wandering preachers who were active in Western Europe from the end of the eleventh century. Because of their harsh criticism of the rich official Church they were often accused of heresy by their opponents. Such charges could be corroborated all the more easily when the wandering preachers struck a great echo from the theologically untrained

population, whose spiritual care had so far been generally neglected. Their teachings thereby ended up in the swamp of sim-
plified popular religion. In the second decade of the twelfth
century a canon called Ellenhard was similarly active in the
episcopal city of Utrecht. Discontented with the secular life as
a canon of Utrecht cathedral, Ellenhard had entered the house
of regular canons at Springiersbach in order to emulate the life
of the *pauper Christus* as one of the *pauperes Christi*. As he was
physically unable to cope with the strict demands, he returned
to Utrecht. There, among the simple clerics and layfolk, he
gained many followers with his interpretation of the Scriptures,
which his opponents condemned as heretical.

There were concrete grounds for the opposition of the official
Church to the wandering preachers when, as often happened,
they called on the faithful to refuse to make offerings, especially
tithes for the rich clerics. In 1074 in southern Germany the
peasants apparently preferred to burn the tithes of their fields
than to give them to the clerics. To change the opinion of
unwilling tithe-payers, around 1100 the poet Amarcius, from
the middle Rhine, offered the priests the following argument:
'Miserable man, why do you doubt your duty to pay a small
debt? God only demands a little, though he could demand
much, as he created the field which you work with your bent
ploughshare. From him comes the art of ploughing; he gave
you oxen; he sent you the rain and the mild west wind ... And
as everything is God's and you have only the liberty to plough
the field with the work of your hands, for which you are allowed
to take the tithe, you ought to leave the rest to Christ. But he
in his charity and generosity leaves you nine parts, so that you
give the tenth all the more willingly . . .' [19: vi. 172].

On the whole the heretical movements, or those suspected
of heresy, which generally felt bound to the rigorous ideal of
poverty, in the area of the German empire were concentrated
on the lower Rhine and Maas–Schelde region. In these areas
at that time particularly far-reaching economic and social
changes were taking place. There too the first traces of the
Cathars in Germany are to be found. They are first evidenced
in the city of Cologne in 1143. They called themselves 'the poor
of Christ'. They did not differ from previous heretics growing
out of the poverty movement in their life-style, so much as in

their fixed dogmas and their independent Church organization. In the same year Cathars were burnt in Cologne and Bonn. Soon afterwards they were also discovered in the bishopric of Liège.

[d] SCHOOLS AND LEARNING

In view of the unsatisfactory state of research into education and learning, only a few reliable statements can be made. Compared with the progress made in the neighbouring countries of France and Italy at the same time, development in Germany went in rather traditional ways. This backwardness had several causes. Among them is the fact that the German cathedral schools did not manage to open themselves up to a larger circle of people beyond the canons of the cathedral, and thus they did not develop into urban schools such as came into existence from around 1100 in France and—on a different basis—in Italy. The cathedral school of Bamberg is an example of this: with no considerable change or external influence, it remained a 'school of the imperial Church system'.

From the eleventh century onwards monastery schools generally lost importance in other European countries too, as under the influence of the reformers they concentrated on an internal monastic theology. This is even more true of the reformed monasteries than of the old imperial ones, which retained the early form and content of their instruction. It was clearly different with the regular canons, who were often in any case topographically closer to urban life. Although within the monasteries and canonical houses there was awareness of some writings of French theologians and philosophers, their characteristic dialectical methods remained without more profound influence, or even met with open rejection. Typical of this are the Benedictine theologian Rupert of Deutz (d. 1129-30), and Gerhoch of Reichersberg (d. 1169), the Augustinian canon often mentioned already—two contrasting leading figures of German spiritual life in the first half of the twelfth century.

The fact that numerous German clerics of the late eleventh century spent a long time studying in France—mainly in the

Île-de-France and Normandy—is only in apparent contradiction to these findings. It was now apparently advantageous even for high nobles to gain 'extra qualifications' for their careers by studying in the famous schools of France. Examples of this are the later archbishops of Cologne Rainald of Dassel (1159–67) and Philip of Heinsberg (1167–91), Archbishop Eberhard of Salzburg (1147–54), Bishop Gebhard of Würzburg (1122–7), his successor Embricho (1127–46), who had also studied at Italian schools and even had some knowledge of Greek, the Babenberger Otto, who after his studies first became a Cistercian monk and then bishop of Freising, and also Vicelin (1149–54), the non-noble missionary and bishop of Oldenburg.

The education of Archbishop Adalbert II of Mainz (1138–41) of the comital family of Saarbrücken, decided by his uncle and predecessor Adalbert I (1109–37), is known in more detail. At first he studied at the cathedral school of Hildesheim; he was then sent to Reims, where he studied numerous ancient pagan writers and also some Roman law. After that followed a longer period of studies in Paris, where he mainly deepened his knowledge of rhetoric, grammar, and logic. In connection with a pilgrimage to St Gilles, Adalbert went for a short time to Montpellier, to the famous university with its emphasis on natural science and especially medicine. But the main point is that in Germany noble origin remained decisive for promotion to a bishopric, and scholarly qualifications, no matter how high, in contrast to France were by no means sufficient for such positions of ecclesiastical and secular leadership.

5

Groups and Communities
in Transformation

As Hildegard of Bingen's comment in the mid twelfth century hinted, the legitimation of noble rule according to doctrines of salvation remained widespread in Germany. The noble Benedictine nun relied in this respect on a tradition reaching back to the early Middle Ages, which was primarily transmitted by Isidore of Seville (d. 636). According to this, servitude (*servitus*) was a consequence of original sin, or of Noah's curse on his son Ham, to mention only some attempts at explanation. This bipartite principle of interpretation emphasized the qualitative differences between freemen and serfs, between rulers and ruled, between nobles and non-nobles. This division was modified in the course of the twelfth century to a tripartite pattern, as taken up by Honorius of Autun (d. after 1130), who probably originated from England and finally worked at Regensburg: based on the three sons of Noah, he divided society into free = nobles (*liberi de Sem*), warriors (*milites de Japhet*), and unfree (*servi de Cham*). Apparently the learned theologian thus found it easier to apply the religious meaning to the actual social conditions of his time, in that the border between the free and the unfree had long lost its importance.

Besides this tradition, in which power and serfdom were derived from divine institution and thus secured for all time, at the beginning of the eleventh century at the latest interpretations such as that of Bishop Adalbero of Laon arose, which saw the differences between *nobiles* and *servi* as the consequence of human law. From such points of view are derived the beginnings of a functional 'doctrine of rank'. In this the mutual ordering of the 'ranks' (*ordines*) is emphasized, so that the evaluating, hierarchical system was pushed into the background or even eliminated. This functional interpretation also offered a framework for an interpretation according to professional groups into which new professions could be integrated. Gerhoch of Reichersberg, who was familiar with urban life, opposed the prejudice against merchants widely held by clerical authors: if the trader's profession 'is carried on without lies and fraud, it is not wrong in itself'. This author even assigned the merchants an independent position among laypeople in the circle of kings, princes, dukes, lawyers, *milites*, and peasants. By considering merchants and also craftsmen as professional groups of their own, placed between nobles and lords on the one hand and peasants on the other, theory, as it were, caught up with the social changes that had meanwhile taken place.

The traditional learned models of *ordo* reacted only very hesitantly, if at all, to changes in the social surroundings: they did not aim to describe social conditions, but to interpret them. This reflects in particular the attitude of the higher clergy, which generally originated from the nobility. But from the silence of the sources it must not be believed that such interpretations were accepted by all groups and classes. The criticism which the ministerial's daughter Tenxwind of Andernach made of the noblewoman Hildegard of Bingen should be recalled in this context. The lives of both women contradicted the traditional 'doctrine of rank', which in general said nothing about women. That the social status of women began to improve from the end of the eleventh century onwards can perhaps been seen most clearly in the increasing veneration of Mary.

Therefore one can by no means deduce, as often used to be attempted, a stability of social conditions from the 'doctrine of rank', which, following traditional patterns, tried to achieve an interpretation valid universally and for all time. Nor can the doctrine be taken as proof for a strict division between lords and serfs, or between those who fight, those who pray, and those who work, and just as little for any internal homogeneity within these schematic entities. In any case the Jews confront

us with a social group which remained altogether unconsidered
in the Christian doctrines of rank.

[*b*] THE NOBILITY, WARRIORS, AND KNIGHTS

A profound change in the nobility in Germany is signalled by
the fact that from the eleventh century onwards nobles were
more and more often mentioned in the sources by the name of
a castle, as well as by their first name and perhaps a title. Noble
families called after castles in Swabia, for example, were those
of Calw, of Nellenburg, the Staufen, and also the Habsburgs.
Thus the group of higher nobles first changed from having one
name to having two names in the course of the eleventh century,
which makes it considerably easier for us to assign individuals
to families and clans. In the first phase, the identity of the
'residence' often varied, until finally the main castle won
through as the name. This process indicates that now the castle
began to be established as the centre and a characteristic of
the noble family. At the same time it is symptomatic of the
territorialization of lordship. Characteristically, it was the
mountain-top castles in the hands of influential dynasties and
dominating larger regions that were now built in stone, instead
of wood, which had formerly been common. Thus they
became both longer-lasting and more representative.

At the same time the nobility's image of itself changed. With
the orientation towards single centres of lordship, an increasing
vertical consciousness—i.e. a sense of successive generations—
in the noble family came into existence. They based their claim
to power on service, and thus also on the property and position
of their ancestors, among whom, according to the law of inheritance, the male line played the larger role. The extension
of the hereditary principle to fiefs, which the more powerful
nobles were the earliest to enforce, stood in direct causal connection with the change of consciousness of the high nobility.
But the great wave of noble foundations of churches and monasteries, which can be observed in Germany from the second
half of the eleventh century, was equally important in this. At
about the same time that the nobility began to be named after
their castles, they founded their family monasteries which in
general served as the family burial-place. As the castle was the

power centre of noble rule, the family monastery, often nearby, was the spiritual and religious centre. In connection with the various monastic chronicles, the first written versions of the history of individual noble families were created. The disputes of the investiture struggle did not eliminate the complex symbiosis of the nobility and the clergy, who themselves mainly originated from noble families, but only put it on to a new footing.

In contrast to this tendency of the nobility to arrange itself in families and generations, it also has to be borne in mind that the long-lasting heavy fighting during the period here dealt with loosened the inner structure of the nobility in Germany. Political conditions favoured the rapid rise, and also the quick descent, of individual nobles and families. The Staufen for example experienced a quick rise. By clever marriage politics, and contacts with the monarchy strengthened by family ties, and not least by a persistent territorial policy, they rose from a relatively modest position around the middle of the eleventh century, when they were still restricted to a small area in Swabia, firstly to possession of the Swabian ducal title (1079). Only one generation later, after the death of the last Salian, they intervened in the sucession to the throne. Barely one and a half decades later they founded a ruling dynasty which considerably influenced the history of Europe for more than one hundred years.

On a different level, this dynamic can also be seen in the career of Wiprecht of Groitzsch, whom we have already met as a colonizer and the founder of his family monastery of Pegau. Wiprecht, who came from a free family, certainly did not originally belong among the leading families of Saxony. According to the annals of Pegau, Wiprecht's grandfather created a dominion in the eastern Altmark by force of arms, which he left to his son of the same name. This elder Wiprecht married a woman from an otherwise unknown comital family; he probably died young. The son was handed over to Margrave Udo II of Stade to be educated and trained. When he had grown up, the margrave enfeoffed him with the castle of Tangermünde, which was situated close to the estate Wiprecht had inherited from his father. For unknown reasons the margrave soon removed him from the Nordmark and gave him as a substitute the castellanship of Groitzsch (between the Pleisse and the Elster), where Wiprecht failed to win through against the resistance of many other nobles. So between about 1075 and 1080 he went to the court of the Bohemian Duke Vratislav. In 1075–6 Vratislav had been enfeoffed by Henry IV with the marks of Lower Lusatia and Meissen, in opposition to the east Saxon families of the Brunones and the Wettins, and from him Wiprecht hoped to gain support for the reconquest of Groitzsch. Wiprecht quickly gained great influence at the court of the pro-Salian Bohemian duke. After returning from Henry IV's Italian campaign he married a daughter of Vratislav, whom the emperor had made a king. He thereby acquired extensive property, particularly in the district of Bautzen. With this backing he succeeded in recovering his rights over Groitzsch by force. His extensive settlement policy belongs to this period. Still during Henry IV's reign, Wiprecht finally rose into the circle of imperial princes. He strengthened his position under Henry V. From 1112 onwards, however, he followed an anti-imperial policy and in the following year he became the emperor's prisoner in the castle of Trifels. The emperor reprieved him from the death sentence in return for cession of all his properties. Only in 1116, together with two other Saxon nobles, was he released from imprisonment in exchange for the imperial ministerial Heinrich Haupt. He subsequently seems to have regained all his rights. In 1123 the emperor, by-passing the Wettins, even enfeoffed him with the margraviate of Meissen, where, however, he was unsuccessful.

The dynamic which these examples demonstrate worked across a large spectrum of the nobility. It included a small but open circle of noble families with, at least at times, great influence on imperial politics, and which, closely related to the royal family, formed a leading group within it. This group grew considerably closer to the monarchy as a consequence of the investiture struggle and the advance of electoral rights in the succession to the throne. The bottom of the spectrum reached as far as an open and wide zone of noble free persons, and even down to the leading group of the unfree, the ministerials.

This openness of the nobility even towards the unfree, and the lack of strata within the élite, are expressed in the text of a Peace of God which can be dated only vaguely to the end of the eleventh century [17: i. 608f.; no. 426]. Concerning breach of the peace and refusal to undertake military action against peace-breakers, the rules differentiated between the following groups: noblemen (*nobiles*), among whom 'the princes of the land' (*principes terrae*) are singled out; the 'free or ministerials' (*liber aut ministerialis*); the serfs (*lito aut servus*). Regulations for litigation concerning breach of the peace, however, differentiated only between the free (*ingenuus aut liber*) on the one hand, and the unfree (*servus, tam lito quam ministerialis*) on the other. As far as court procedure was concerned, i.e. in the narrower legal sense, the border between freedom and unfreedom remained valid. From the point of view of lordship, however, the legally free were segregated into princes, nobles, and other free individuals. In this respect the ministerials, who in court were treated as unfree, were regarded like the 'ordinary' free. Alongside these categories, when discussing penalties for defamation the same source differentiates according to profession, between *miles* and *rusticus*, i.e. between warrior and peasant; in this the legal status of free or unfree was unimportant. It was left open whether this *miles* was a noble or a ministerial, or whether he belonged to a further group; what mattered was that he was at least predominantly active as a warrior.

In the second half of the eleventh century, and even later, peasants and townsmen still participated in warfare. Thus the members of the Saxon noble opposition enlisted groups of peasants for war service as well as their vassals and servants. When in 1075 Henry IV advanced towards Saxony, great optimism about the chances of victory spread among his troops—as Lampert of Hersfeld reports—'as the royal feudal levy, consisting of experienced warriors, was not expecting any special difficulty in battle with the opposing army, which was more suitable for ploughing fields than for warfare, and which had been forced to be there by the Saxon dukes' [3: xiii. 286 f.]. According to the same source Duke Otto of Northeim, who around 1070 had devastated the royal estates with his vassals and ministerials, allocated one part of his booty to peasants who had lost their land through the fighting, and called upon them to help him with their prayers, as they were unsuitable for warfare [3: xiii. 128 f.]. The same author also denied merchants any military ability. In spite of this he could not but mention the participation of peasants and merchants in the numerous wars.

It is in any case certain that experience and skill in military matters, and thus lengthy service as a warrior, were essential for membership of the *milites*, not just social origin and even less legal status. In this respect therefore social status was determined by function, which explains the assimilation of *liber* and *ministerialis*. Thus it was not at all impossible for *rustici* to rise to be *milites*. Frederick I's public peace of the year 1152 shows that such a rise was not rare. In this, only those were granted the status of knight (*miles*), which was connected with the privilege of judicial duel, who could prove that they had long been legal knights by origin [19: x. 1. 43, no. 25]. Therefore there were also knights (*milites*) who did not fulfil these criteria of birth status, but who acted as knights and furthermore were regarded as knights. A prohibition in the same public peace shows that peasants also carried the knightly weapons, lance and sword. Therefore in fact the border between knight and peasant around the middle of the twelfth century was still open, even if Barbarossa's public peace deliberately tried to achieve a stricter segregation.

Doubtless already before the middle of the twelfth century ministerials in Germany, that is to say, unfree men, were regarded as knights, and therefore distinguished themselves from peasants and townsmen, from the mass of the population. They were thus associated with the noble *milites*, but in no way became equal in rank with them. It is hard to estimate how far the knightly ideal up to the middle of the twelfth century, promoted in Germany by the idea of crusade, succeeded in bridging the gap between ministerials and the nobility. Such a sense of community in any case seems to have developed in Germany later than in France. The first knightly tournament in Germany is evidenced in the year 1127, outside Würzburg: it was arranged by the Staufen Dukes Frederick and Conrad, as a kind of demonstration against King Lothar III.

[*c*] FREEDOM AND UNFREEDOM IN TOWN AND
COUNTRY

The openness and mobility which are to be observed in the nobility with its gradations and movement, which reached as far down as the ministerials, were inseparably connected with mobility in the unfree population. Around the middle of the eleventh century the proportion of the unfree in the whole population in the old settlement areas of Germany was probably up to 90 per cent. This proportion hardly changed at all in the following hundred years. What did change fundamentally was the form and meaning of freedom, which became much more variable. As the manifold privileges within serfdom were called 'freedoms' (*libertates*) in contemporary sources, and as the legal distinction between free and unfree were of little importance for social status anyway, it is all the more justified to take the categories of freedom and unfreedom as the basis when describing the legally unfree population. Thus it becomes comprehensible that towards the end of the eleventh century a free woman gave herself and her three daughters over to the monastery of St Emmeram in Regensburg on condition that she and her successors should on paying an annual rent receive the status of 'free serfdom' (*libera servitus*) [29: 329f., no. 684].

Not only did these forms of dependence vary greatly within the group of serfs of the *familia*; the economic field of action and the manorial situation of the serfs did too. Many lived on dependent peasant plots on the manors. They worked these lands to a great extent independently for generally fixed rents and limited compulsory labour services which they had to do to maintain the lord's demesne. With the retreat of demesne farming, which seems to have occurred increasingly from around 1100, the number of peasant tenements increased, the demesne being divided among them. At the same time the need for compulsory labour services decreased; they were commuted for money payments. They were usually also burdened with a death duty—the best beast or piece of clothing. As they held their tenements almost without exception as heritable fees, there was the danger that in case of marriage with a member of another *familia*, the inherited land and the children of such a marriage would be lost to the lord. Consequently such a marriage could only be undertaken with the lord's permission.

Others lived in or around the manors, or at the lord's residence in castles, and in towns and markets. In contrast to the peasants with land, who were bound to the soil, these serfs enjoyed greater freedom of movement in so far as they were not bound to a place by certain services—for example servants or maids at the lord's court. This large group of serfs was even more differentiated within itself than the landed peasants. Apart from the servants and maids, probably mostly unmarried, who were obliged to perform unlimited daily work at the lord's residence, this group also included those with skilled tasks in the lord's household, such as craftsmen, merchants, holders of administrative posts within the lordship, and ministerials entrusted with military and administrative tasks. For these services they received various material rewards, in the form of service fees from their lords. Depending on the status of the serf and the political and economic position of the lord, these servile fees, also called *beneficia*, could consist of agricultural land, peasant tenements, castles, larger areas of forest clearance, payments in kind or cash incomes from the manorial estate, of market dues, or other rights over land and people. While the prohibition of marriage with partners from other *familiae* was valid for this group, as for all serfs, the death duty was often remitted from the beginning of the twelfth century, at least for imperial ministerials, who held the top position among serfs. It generally was no longer applied to servants or maids, who anyway had no possessions and who were obliged to do unlimited menial services.

In contrast to these groups of serfs, who were bound to their lords for the economic basis of their existence and by their service dues, there were other serfs who were only loosely connected with their clerical or lay *pater familias*. These had their own economic basis independent of their lord, though often only a small one. For them there were new possibilities in the growing and developing towns and markets, as day labourers, craftsmen, or tradesmen, and also in colonizing new areas. The ties of these serfs were essentially based only on a relationship of personal protection, for which they had to pay an annual head-tax. Beyond that they might be obliged to pay to redeem labour services. To this group also belonged freedmen, who after the legal act of liberation were still dependent on a protective relationship. Depending on conditions fixed at liberation, their payments could be increased annually. The death duty for these serfs, who because of the head-tax were also reckoned among rent-payers, was not generally obligatory.

The various rights of the *familiae* subordinated to the different lords—the household laws—were almost always a matter of custom until the beginning of the eleventh century. Only from this time on were they increasingly fixed in writing. Members of the *familia* were given a share in drafting these codes as they increased in number from the beginning of the twelfth century, at least to the extent that, asked about their legal status, they gave information or, as witnesses, even their agreement. They could also force their masters to compromise in cases of disagreement. The abbot of St Maximin at Trier around the middle of the eleventh century came to an agreement with his serfs from the Moselle village of Wasserbillig, who, as it was put on this occasion, had persistently refused the demands of the monastery and had shown themselves rebellious and almost uncontrollable. The agreement, it was emphasized, was not unbearable for the serfs and not disadvantageous for the monastery.

The numerous wars and the sharp religious and political disputes in the following period further weakened the position of the competing lords towards their serfs, especially as at the same time new opportunities opened up for the serfs in the army, in administration, in agriculture, and in forest clearance as well as in trade and industry. There was a danger in the old settlement areas too that serfs might go over to the *familia* of another master with more favourable conditions. Thus the monk Ortlieb of the Swabian monastery of Zwiefalten on the Danube, writing around 1135, reports that from the foundation *c*.1090 of this reformed monastery of the order of Hirsau, many serfs bought their freedom from their former masters because of the heavy and manifold burdens of serfdom, and had become members of the *familia* of the monastery, in which they could lead a quiet life. They now lived as peasants, vine-growers, bakers, shoe-makers, smiths, and also as merchants and in other professions [31: 44–9].

An insight into the possibilities of rising within the manorial system, and the changes of attitude and behaviour connected with them, is given by the continuator of the monastic chronicle of St Gallen in the middle of the eleventh century. The abbot, so it says, did not sufficiently supervise the serfs who had to administer the monastery lands. The manorial reeves exploited this liberty to their own advantage. They had begun carrying polished shields and weapons. They had learnt to sound the horn, unlike the other village inhabitants. They had kept dogs and trained them for hunting. To begin with they had only hunted hares, but then wolves, and finally even bears and wild boars. The dependent office-holders had thus, on the economic basis of their servile fees, exercised 'élite' noble ways of life, neglecting their duties [3: xxxi. 132–5, no. 53].

From the middle of the eleventh century the ministerials had even better chances of rising, as the example of the imperial ministerials has already shown. Such were the ministerials of the imperial bishoprics, the great monasteries, and also those of the more powerful nobles as well as the imperial ministerials. Because of their military duties the ministerials were to a great extent at liberty. In the late Salian period they had succeeded in getting rid of various other characteristics of unfreedom. Their legal tie to their lord easily became dependent on the grant of a servile fee. The ministerial law code of the chapter of Bamberg cathedral, written down in 1061/2, states that a ministerial who had not been enfeoffed with a servile fee by the bishop of Bamberg was allowed to serve a different master of his own free choice but not to enter into a feudal relationship with him. This was supposed to prevent the ministerial thus liberated from detaching himself completely from his master and in this way reaching a noble position [3: xxxii. 120–3, no. 31]. Accordingly, the chronicle of the monastery of Ebersheim in Alsace, in the middle of the twelfth century, characterizes the ministerials of the *familia* of the Bishop of Strasbourg as so noble and skilled in warfare that they were comparable only to free and noble people [14: xxiii. 433]. In addition, some contemporary sources of the same monastic provenance count these ministerials as individuals whose ancestors had obliged themselves to free service through a feudal relationship with the church. According to these records, with only a small fief, all they had to render was a limited, restricted war service, a service which encouraged their assimilation into the chivalrous life of the nobility. Because of the central role of the episcopal towns above all, one must assume that among the ministerials living in these cities (*civitates*) or at least performing their most important activities there, were several who, in their own judgement or perhaps in fact, were of noble origin and therefore claimed a position equal to the nobility. In any case, their family relationships, their financial resources, their military capabilities, and their far-reaching political experience corroborated their leading position, which they evidently exercised in many towns, chiefly in long settled lands either in established or developing towns but also in the formation of municipalities. However, ministerials with less opportunity to exercise power must not be ignored, nor the tendency of ecclesiastical or secular lords to emphasize the alleged or actual lack of free descent and the servile ties and obligations of the ministerials, in order to integrate them firmly into the *familia*. The Ebersheim Chronicler argued against these trends, partly using the legend of imperial and Roman descent. According to this, Julius Caesar assigned the ministerials to the noble *militia* with the rank of lords (*domini*) and defenders (*defensores*) in the service of princes, so that they were not abused as serfs (*servi*) or bondsmen (*famuli*) [no. 311].

From the middle of the eleventh century another class, growing in numbers, lived within the *familia*, both in urban and rural settlements, whose position can be contrasted with that of other serfs: the rent-paying tenants (*Zensualen*). In the chronicle of Eberheimsmünster they are ranked immediately after the ministerials, and described as 'obliged to pay money, obedient, very respected, and content with their legal position'. Although they had their own legal status within the *familia*, considerable social differences are to be found amongst them. Moreover, the *Zensualen* could at the same time hold the legal status of ministerials, as was often agreed when they took on their status. The social spectrum of the *Zensualen* extended from high nobles, who, often under favourable conditions, became 'payers of tax to an altar' (*Altarzinser*) [no. 311], down to serfs. These serfs, just to discharge their *servitium cottidianum*, service obligations unlimited in theory, had to undertake the obligation of paying a tax, without changing their basic, long-term, legal position.

As the rich south German sources testify, up to the middle of the twelfth century it was overwhelmingly women who became *Zensualen*, though the proportion of women had been rising slowly over the previous century. This fact might be explained by the lower 'labour value' of women. For this reason manorial lords were more readily prepared to free female serfs for a money payment. In addition, very personal reasons played a role in many transfers of women into the rent-paying group by their former masters. Thus around 1120 a man, with the agreement of his wife and sons, handed over to St Emmeram in Regensburg the daughter whom he had had by a concubine [28: 352f., no. 755]. Not least did many formerly free women transfer themselves in order to safeguard their endangered legal position or their property rights. This motive is clearly stated at the end of the eleventh century in the self-transfer of Willerad, a Frisian and the widow of a freeman from Mainz-Kastel. She transferred herself and her daughter to the monastery of St George on the grounds that in this way she would receive protection against the relatives of her late husband who were trying to take her inheritance by force. Besides a modest head-tax of two pence she obliged herself and her successors to pay a death duty. Among her property was a house with a small *familia*, so she herself therefore owned several serfs [3: xxxii. 156-9, no. 41].

The protective relationship, however, by no means always proved to be a guarantee against deterioration in status. Apparently additional burdens were often imposed on *Zensualen*, or they were even treated like serfs by lay advocates or by ministerials of churches and monasteries. Thus the descendants of a free woman, who around 1100 made herself and her successors rent-paying tenants of the monastery of St Emmeram, had been made to do unjust services only a generation later. After this had been cancelled by the abbot with the help of the bishop of Regensburg, the following generation also met the same fate, so that it again became necessary to restore their freedom and legal status (*libertas et iusticia*) [28: 417 f., no. 864].

The latest research has rightly emphasized the great importance of these rent-payers for social change in the urban population. This has been shown by the example of several Flemish towns, and especially of Regensburg, as far as the history of their origins was bound up with clerical institutions. Liberty of movement and freedom from servile duties, i.e. the typical advantages of *Zensuale* status, gave the urban population the necessary freedom of action for trade and industry. But it will need further research to discover how far this legal status was widespread in the towns, and particularly how *Zensuale* status was distinguished from other forms of serfdom.

The local lords aspired as far as possible to eliminate the rights of others over the inhabitants, and thus to diminish the personal dependency of the latter. Thus the count of Namur in the mid eleventh century declared to the inhabitants of the *villa* of Dinant that all immigrants taking permanent residence there should be his property. The bishop of Liège, on the other hand, in 1066 granted to the manorial lords that unfree people, even after they had settled in the episcopal *villa* of Huy, should continue to do service to them. But the onus of proof of the immigrants' servile status lay on the manorial lords. Furthermore, they were not allowed to trouble their serfs living in Huy with non-customary servile dues; so the bishop made the realization of the lords' demands considerably more difficult.

Liberation from the burdens of serfdom was not from the beginning connected with the legal status of the urban citizens, but was the product of a long and not at all straightforward development. In the first comprehensive privilege of a medieval emperor for the inhabitants of a German town, Henry V in 1111 freed the inhabitants of the episcopal city of Speyer, closely connected politically with the Salians, 'from that worthless and wicked rule, namely from that burden which is usually called *buteil*, by which the whole city was ruined because of great poverty' [see 419: 21 f.]. This burden, which is certainly exaggerated here, applied to all those inhabitants who had married members of outside *familiae* without the permission of their manorial lords. The masters demanded from them a considerable part of their inheritance—up to two-thirds—at the expense of the heirs. In the charter of 1111, though, which he made out three years later in similar form to the neighbouring city of Worms, the emperor granted full inheritance rights to the city dwellers [3: xxxii. 178-83, no. 48]. Therefore in both cases no formal liberation from serfdom of the city inhabitants was decreed, but only a reduction, albeit considerable, in the resulting burden on the right of inheritance.

Undiminished right of inheritance was also allowed in the first foundation privilege for a German market settlement of urban character, the charter of the duke of Zähringen for Freiburg in 1120. In a similar way it was also established in the rights of new settlers in the early twelfth century. The undiminished right of inheritance widened the economic basis for the family in the modern sense, that is to say with the loosening of dependencies in the *familia* the peasant and urban family first became possible. Thus the emperor Henry V in his charter for the inhabitants of Worms expressly declared that the marriages of citizens should be valid even if the partners came from two different *familiae*, and that the bailiff or lord should not be allowed to separate them. Only eighty years before, the first Salian emperor had granted the abbot of his family monastery of Limburg the right to dissolve such marriages at will.

The continued existence of servile forms of dependence in German towns and pre-urban settlements in the eleventh and twelfth centuries was much greater than earlier research was prepared to accept. In the decisive phase of urbanization in Germany the ruling stratum in the towns was made up of the leading servile group, the ministerials. As well as them, legally free merchants were similarly active. This once again expressed the close connection between town and country. In both environments social differentiation was only partly touched by the various personal legal statuses. Servile links were not always disadvantageous; they could provide important advantages. More important for social position were the various economic and seigneurial fields of activity. Many factors contributed to reduce the negative consequences of serfdom. Among them was the change of religious values, as most clearly expressed in the poverty movement from the end of the eleventh century, and

its social consequences, because it was in close correlation with
changes in the manorial and economic fields.

[*d*] THE JEWS AS AN ALIEN MINORITY

The basic concepts of the Christian community are reflected in
the history of the Jews, who as a religious minority found no
place in traditional Christian theories about social ranks. Like
no other group the Jews in Germany, as generally in western
continental Europe, were concentrated in the towns. Definite
written proofs of Jewish settlements in the German imperial
area up to the end of the eleventh century refer almost without
exception to episcopal cities on the more important trade
routes—the Rhine, Main, Moselle, Danube, Elbe, Vltava,
and Saale. As well as Prague, Magdeburg, Merseburg, Regensburg, Mainz, Cologne, Speyer, Worms, Bamberg, and
Metz, Trier can also be mentioned. Not until the first half of
the twelfth century are Jewish settlements found in other urban
centres. The immigration of Jews, which in Germany really
only began in the tenth century, seems to have been mainly
from the south (Italy) and the west (France): therefore from
Latin lands with a more developed urban culture.

The large contribution of the Jews towards urbanization in
Germany was recognized by contemporary rulers. Thus Bishop
Rüdiger of Speyer in his privilege of 1084 for those Jews who
wished to settle in Speyer especially emphasized that he hoped
to increase the reputation of his place of residence, which he
wanted to transform from a village into a town (*urbem facere*), by
settling Jews there. Besides many individual rights the bishop
granted to the Jewish community the best law that Jews had
in any town in the German empire [374: i. 266f.].

The common religion of the Jews suggested establishing
themselves as far as possible in closed settlements within the
cities, where they could attend to their intense religious–
political communal life undisturbed. The Jewish settlements
were usually in the city centre, on the main street, at the
market, or close to the cathedral precinct or the castle. This
situation was not just the consequence of the religious position
and the economic activities of the Jews, but also of their need
for the lords' protection. Until the great persecutions of 1096

the Jews were mainly active in trade, particularly of luxury goods from the Orient or slaves from the border areas in the east, but also in finance: a Jew from Mainz perhaps lent a large sum of money to Henry IV before 1096 and received the treasure of the empress Agnes, the emperor's mother, as a security [518]. Their trade connections reached as far as the Mediterranean area, i.e. into the centre of gravity of world trade. In the eleventh century they even reached as far as Russia, where the Jews of Regensburg worked alongside those of Prague and probably also with Jews from Mainz. At the latest from the tenth century they had been pushed out of Mediterranean trade by growing competition, especially from the Italian sea-borne trading cities, while in Germany in the eleventh and twelfth centuries they formed the prototype of the merchant, as teachers and pioneers of long-distance trade. Accordingly in 1074 in his customs privilege for the inhabitants of Worms, which was a reward for support in a severe crisis, Henry IV granted the Jews and other inhabitants of Worms (*Judei et coeteri Wormatienses*) freedom from toll [3: xxxii. 132–5, no. 33].

At the end of the eighties and the beginning of the nineties Henry IV granted comprehensive protection charters to the Jewish communities in the Salian episcopal towns of Speyer and Worms. After the model of Ludwig the Pious's privileges for individual Jews, these granted protection to life and property, and also to the practice of religion. They were also permitted to trade in pagan slaves, but were forbidden to buy Christian ones. On the other hand, pagan slaves were not permitted to be taken away from them by baptism. They were expressly allowed to employ male and female Christians as paid labourers or servants and nursemaids. In cases of dispute amongst themselves they were permitted to exercise their own law, so that the independent, religiously based legal tradition anchored in the Talmud was guaranteed a wide sphere of operation within the Jewish community. The Jews in the larger German cities already at that time had developed a community structure.

The events of 1096, already mentioned several times, which in several towns led to the first large pogroms in German history, occurred under extraordinary circumstances. As had already happened in France, now in Metz, Speyer, Worms, Mainz, Cologne, and Trier, vicious mobs, which had preceded or followed the crusaders and who were also joined by towns-people, threatened the Jews on the pretext that they had to be punished as enemies of Christ. The unorganized hordes which committed the murderous acts against the Jews were certainly not only made fanatical by the crusading atmosphere, but also set in motion by a famine which had already lasted for a long while. These extreme conditions of religious psychology and economic existence affecting wide circles of the population finally coincided with a severe crisis in the traditional power structure. On the one hand the authority of the emperor and the bishops—the most important protectors of the Jewish mi-nority—was very deeply shaken as a consequence of the in-vestiture struggle; on the other hand, the developing town communities as yet had no very firm organization to keep peace and justice effectively.

When the first news of the persecution of the Jews by un-organized crusader mobs reached Germany in the spring of 1096, the episcopal lords and many members of the urban ruling groups in most German towns took measures to protect the Jews. Among the leaders of one such crusader horde was Peter the Hermit, an eloquent wandering preacher from Picardy, usually encrusted with filth, who rode through the country on a donkey; among his followers was the knight Wal-ter, who became especially known under the significant name 'penniless' ('sans avoir'). To begin with, Peter only demanded money and provisions for the journey from the Jews of Trier. A contemporary Hebrew source testifies that the anti-Jewish atmosphere of the crusaders also spilled over to the citizens of Trier. Up to that time the citizens are said never to have spoken of doing any harm to the Jewish community. Now the citizens had become envious, as in many places persecution of the Jews had already taken place, but in their city the Jews had re-mained unmolested. The Jews, who had already paid high sums to individual crusader bands, tried to forestall further violence from the citizens by giving them money. Finally Archbishop Egilbert of Trier was himself threatened by the crusaders, so that he called on the Jews who had taken refuge in his palace to avoid being murdered by undergoing baptism. When they refused, he had some Jews taken to the crusaders, who murdered them. Servants of the archbishop forcibly carried Jewish women and children to be baptized. Other women bravely resisted their persecutors and supported their husbands' faithfulness. In their distressed love Jewish men and women would kill their children and finally themselves (*kiddush ha-shem*). The following year virtually all of the surviving Jews who had been baptized returned to their old belief with the support of the emperor. Several years later, in the imperial public peace decreed in Mainz in 1103, Henry IV specifically required the special protection of the Jews. The emperor was exercising a duty which at the same time was intended to document his rights over the Jews.

In the long run the events of 1096 left deep traces in the consciousness and liturgical memory of the Jews. They also seem to have affected their position as a religious and social minority in the German towns considerably, although substantial Jewish communities came into existence after a few decades, even in places where there had been pogroms. The Jews were once again endangered by the preparations for the Second Crusade in 1146, especially in the Rhineland. Bernard of Clairvaux's interference, however, prevented greater persecutions. Now there are more reports of Jews being pushed into money-lending and pawnbroking; but they were still engaged in trade, in which, however, they increasingly came into competition with Christian merchants.

In their Christian surroundings the Jews were distinguished by a highly developed written culture with a long tradition of learning in which the essential components of Jewish, Arabic, Greek, and Latin education were incorporated. In some cases Christian scholars in Germany sought the advice of scholarly Jews, especially in the translation of Greek texts. Because of their close contacts with Arabic culture, individual Jews were highly regarded among Christians as chemists and doctors. Thus the Jew Joshua, from Trier, was held in high esteem as a doctor by Archbishop Bruno (d. 1124), who suffered a lengthy illness. According to the *Gesta Trevirorum*, Joshua, who was also distinguished for his perfect knowledge of chronology and Jewish literature and culture, went about in knightly clothes. Only after lengthy discussions with the archbishop about the Holy Scriptures and after many requests and demands did this scholarly Jew, who was willing to be assimilated, have himself baptized by Archbishop Bruno. Such conversions, among which that of Hermannus Judaeus, the later prior of the Premonstratensian monastery at Scheda (near Hamm), caused a great sensation, remained exceptions.

[e] FAMILIA AND FAMILY

The basic traits of the social history of the period of the investiture conflict can be ranged between the poles of the manorial *familia* on the one hand, and the family in the senses of the nuclear or small family, or large extended family, on the other. For the great mass of the population the decisive fact was that in this period the range of action of the *familia* was loosened more than ever before.

One important reason for this loosening derived from economic changes connected with the advance of the money economy and the market-orientated exchange of goods, as well as with population growth and the intensification and expansion of agriculture and industrial production, which overall increased the value of human labour. These factors caused the holders of power to grant favourable conditions to their dependants in order to secure their rents and services in the long run, even if to a diminished extent. By commutation of those traditional services and dues which the serfs no longer wished to perform because of other possibilities open to them, the manorial lords at least drew some short-term advantages. In one way or other many serfs, legally or in practice, gained greater opportunities of building up an independent economic existence without being restricted in access to their own labour by obligatory service dues. The freedom of movement granted to freedmen and *Zensualen*, which was also obtained by other serfs, left them the possibility of settling in towns under favourable conditions. In either place the right of inheritance gave further motivation for economic productivity in the interests of the narrower family, especially of their own children. With this the essential preconditions were achieved for the economic existence of the 'family', in the sense of the succession of generations. With the diminution of restrictions on marriage between partners of different *familiae* and thus of the lords' opportunities to intervene in such marriages, the nuclear family was also established for those who were still bound as serfs. Like the citizens of Worms and Speyer, the latter had detached themselves from their former masters in economic and seigneurial respects, and had been supported in this by those lords who were trying to eliminate other influences in their own spheres of interest.

In this course the most successful groups within the *familia* were generally those which stood close to the ruling class because of their functions in the army or administration. Outstanding among them were the ministerials, who were in the direct service of their masters, and who also exercised lordly, i.e. noble functions on their behalf. Under the influence of the numerous wars and political disputes, reinforced by the investiture struggle, personal ability in military service, as well as in the territorial politics closely connected with it, gained especial significance for social position. Under these circumstances servile ties were ousted in favour of whatever demands the serving-man was able to make for his services, so that a serf might become a vassal equal to a noble. The feudal lord might thus replace the manorial master. Thus the ministerial left the *familia* and could become the founder of a noble family, which admittedly was rare in the eleventh and early twelfth centuries.

The existence of both free and noble families was legally impregnable. In reality, however, there was a considerable range of variation in family relations between these two groups. The most important differentiating feature was the lordly qualification of the house, the local centre of the *familia* as well as of the family. In close connection with the development towards independence and regionalization among the high nobility of our period, a special family consciousness was being developed, which reached back far into previous generations along the line of the paternal ancestors, and which supported itself mainly by insistence on the right of inheritance of the property essential to lordship—even fees. Below the small group of high nobility and the more powerful families, in crises there often arose among those who were legally free a need to enter a contractual protective relationship, and thus to acquire ties which could partly be similar to dependence within the *familia*, or which might even be almost identical with it. But such dangers could also be overcome, or at least limited, by new co-operative arrangements, such as became politically important in the rising communes.

III

GERMANY
UNDER THE STAUFEN:
NEW FORMS AND
LIMITATIONS

I

Imperial Rule in the Staufen Period

[*a*] FROM THE ELECTION OF BARBAROSSA TO THE PEACE
OF VENICE (1177)

The situation at the beginning of Frederick I's reign was decisive in the long run. One advantage was that Barbarossa possessed a territorial power base in the duchy of Swabia which included the Staufen and Salian family estates. At least equally important were his family relationships. He was related by marriage to Duke Matthew I of Upper Lorraine (d. 1176) through his sister Bertha, and to the Landgrave Ludwig II of Thuringia (d. 1172) through his half-sister Judith. Furthermore he could link up with other kinship relations of the Staufen family, which had once supported Conrad III's kingship. Unlike that Staufen line, though, Frederick I also occupied a mediating position based on kinship between the Staufen and the Welfs.

In return for being favoured by his uncle Conrad III, who denied the succession to the throne to his son Frederick, still under age, the former Swabian duke had promised his cousin the succession to the duchy of Swabia. But this exchange of successions to the kingship and the Swabian duchy remained without much political importance until the king's son came of age. To secure the election for himself and to make his kingship a reality, Barbarossa above all had to win over the noble opponents of Conrad III. First among these were the Welfs, closely related to Barbarossa—his uncle Welf VI, and his cousin Henry the Lion, and also the duke of Zähringen, Berthold IV (d. 1186), the brother-in-law of the duke of Saxony. Only in this way could Barbarossa succeed in preventing the old conflict between the Staufen and the Welfs from spreading into European politics, as had happened under Conrad III with the anti-royal pacts of Welf VI.

In autumn 1152 at the latest Barbarossa granted his uncle Welf VI important Italian imperial offices and estates, some of which had previously been held by Welf's brother Henry the Proud: the duchy of Spoleto, the margraviate of Tuscany, the duchy of Sardinia, and especially the extensive Matildine lands. Barbarossa thus bound this influential noble to the royal policy, as Welf VI could only make good his legal claims in Italy with the help of the Staufen. In this way Welf VI simultaneously came into conflict with papal interests, as the popes claimed the overlordship of Matilda's estates, and had even succeeded in putting the claim into practice with Welf's brother. Only a short time after the election, Frederick made a written agreement with the Zähringer Berthold IV, in which he admitted his claims to upper Burgundy and Provence in return for support during the royal coronation expedition. There the Zähringer could put forward claims to an old legal title, which Lothar III had granted to his father without the latter having been able to enforce it. Already before the royal election Barbarossa had promised his cousin Henry the Lion the duchy of Bavaria, which he had long desired. Barbarossa thus violated the rights of another relative, the Babenberger Henry II Jasomirgott, who since his marriage to a niece of the Emperor Manuel I had had close political connections with the Byzantine court.

These agreements by Barbarossa contributed to the fact that the papal Curia was unable to exercise any considerable influence on the election of the king, thus differing fundamentally from the elections of 1125 and 1138. The attempt by Archbishop Henry of Mainz to raise as Conrad's successor Conrad's son Frederick, who was under age, was a failure. In his election announcement to Pope Eugenius III, therefore, Barbarossa could all the more convincingly stress the immediacy to God of his royal office, granted to him by election, and the equality of the secular and clerical powers.

At least to the beginning of the seventies the imperial policies of Frederick I were marked by close co-operation between the Staufen and his Welf cousin. First Barbarossa saw to an arrangement between Henry the Lion and the Babenberger

Henry II Jasomirgott. As early as 1154 the duchy of Bavaria was *de jure* given to the Welf by the emperor. In September 1156 it was finally made over to him as a second duchy, alongside Saxony. However, the margraviate of Austria was separated from the duchy of Bavaria and was given on favourable terms to the Babenberger as an independent duchy (*privilegium minus*).

Frederick I granted Henry II and his wife Theodora, the niece of the Byzantine emperor, the right of inheritance of the new duchy in the male and female lines. Furthermore, jurisdiction within the duchy was made dependent on the agreement of the duke. Equally significant was the limitation of the feudal duties of the Babenbergers towards the empire: the Austrian dukes now only had to participate in imperial expeditions into neighbouring areas. The duchy thus separated from the old tribal duchy of Bavaria received a legal framework which gave the Babenbergers in the south-eastern border region of the empire an advantage in comparison to the other princes in developing their rule over the country.

In connection with these negotiations Barbarossa in June 1152 married Beatrice (b. 1140/1144), the heiress of the free county of Burgundy. As Beatrice mainly had properties to which Berthold IV of Zähringen, the brother-in-law of Henry the Lion, had acquired rights in 1152, he was compensated by the emperor with the lay advocacies of the bishoprics of Geneva, Lausanne, and Sion and the right to invest these bishops himself. This pact was only another step by the Staufen in the continuing process of pushing the Zähringer out of their positions in Burgundy. The partnership between Barbarossa and his Welf cousin was to be seen not only on the coronation expedition of 1154–5 and on the emperor's second Italian campaign of 1158–62.

After the emperor's relations with Berthold had come to a head, Henry the Lion in 1162 divorced his Zähringer wife. In 1165 both Henry and Frederick simultaneously came to marriage agreements with the English king Henry II: the Welf secured for himself the marriage, consummated later, with Henry II's oldest daughter Matilda, while the emperor arranged the marriage of his son, then only one year old, with a sister of the future duchess.

Henry the Lion's support made it easier for the emperor in effect to push aside Welf's claims in imperial Italy when, after the favourable outcome of the second Italian campaign, Welf first had an opportunity to make them good. The death of Welf VI's son, Welf VII, who like so many others fell victim to the malaria epidemic in the imperial army before Rome in 1167, greatly reduced his interest in these rights, which would anyway be very hard to enforce. In 1173/4 he renounced them in favour of his imperial nephew, in return for a large payment.

Frederick I's relations with the Roman Curia turned out to be even more complex. They were at the centre of Barbarossa's imperial policies and were inseparably connected with his intense Italian interests. In the quarter-century between the beginning of his rule and the Peace of Venice with Pope Alexander III, Barbarossa spent more than ten years in imperial Italy. From the beginning of the second Italian campaign in 1158, a legate was almost continually active in imperial Italy on the emperor's behalf when he was not present himself.

In a treaty made at Constance in 1153, Barbarossa and Pope Eugenius III undertook to guard one another's interests and rights. The king promised the pope not to make peace with the Normans and the Romans without his consent, and not to grant any land in Italy to the 'king' of the Greeks. With the · latter promise Barbarossa carefully moved away from the undertaking his predecessor had given to the Byzantine emperor in 1148, without losing sight of the aim of this pact—opposition to the Norman king. Eugenius on his part promised to crown Frederick without further demands during his long-planned Italian campaign.

Frederick I also used the co-operation agreed in the Treaty of Constance to proceed against his opponents in the German episcopate. It proved useful during his coronation expedition, which he began in autumn 1154 and on which he was finally crowned emperor by Eugenius's successor Adrian IV in summer 1155. Barbarossa, however, had to forgo fighting the Norman king, for which Manuel I Comnenus had promised his support. This was a favourable opportunity to advance against the Norman kingdom of Sicily, as after the death of King Roger II (February 1154) his son William had to fight against an opposition which flared up again and again. The

German princes, however, refused to carry through this campaign of the two emperors in Italy in the heat of summer. Frederick also had to postpone the fight against the commune of Milan, which was opposing a pro-imperial coalition led by the communes of Cremona and Pavia.

The victory of the Sicilian king over Byzantine and rebelling Apulian troops at Brindisi caused the Roman Curia shortly afterwards to make a treaty with William I, at Benevento in June 1156. In this the king acknowledged the pope's overlordship, and committed himself to annual payments to the Roman Curia, which in return granted the Normans extensive powers over the Church in the kingdom. The tension between emperor and pope, heightened by these events, exploded in October 1157 at the court in Besançon. In a letter, Adrian IV had reminded the emperor that the pope had granted to him power over the empire and had granted further *beneficia*. Rainald of Dassel, then the imperial chancellor, knowingly translated this term as 'fiefs' and not as 'favours'. This interpretation by the chancellor, which in fact expressed the intentions of the pope and his legates, caused a sharp anti-papal reaction, at the time and also later, among the high nobility and the ecclesiastical lords. In June 1158, shortly before the emperor set off on his second Italian campaign, the Roman Curia had expressly to disavow this interpretation, and thereby to acknowledge that its view of papal supremacy, heightened under Lothar III, could not be enforced against Barbarossa.

The antagonism between empire and papacy intensified during Barbarossa's second Italian campaign. The Curia had previously brought about an agreement between the Norman king and the Byzantine emperor, who was a wealthy competitor of the Staufen, particularly in the area of Ancona and Ravenna. After his success against Milan, which the emperor finally conquered in September 1158, and the subsequent Diet of Roncaglia at which the emperor, with the co-operation of legal experts from Bologna, laid down a programme for centrally directed rule in imperial Italy, the imperial court proceeded ruthlessly against the territorial and political claims of the papacy in northern and central Italy. One such action was the take-over of the Matildine lands, whereby Welf VI's legal rights were only partly taken into account.

In the following period the papacy found close allies in the Lombard metropolis of Milan and its partners when, after the Diet of Roncaglia, the imperial court began to put its aims into practice by means of new methods of administration, not least at the expense of Milan. Milan rebelled again and soon found allies in the communes of Brescia and Piacenza. Adrian IV was soon on the side of the rebellious communes. After the death of the English pope, a papal schism broke out. From autumn 1159 the papacy was contested, after a tumultuous election, between the pro-imperial Cardinal Octavian, who originated from a noble family from the country around Rome, and the cardinal and jurist Roland, who was well known to be anti-imperial. Roland, Alexander III, openly joined the Milanese opposition group; his opponent, Victor IV, was supported by the imperial party. The conquest of Milan and its Lombard partners by the imperial army and its allies—among them Milan's competitors Cremona and Pavia, which played a considerable part in the subsequent destruction of Milan—narrowed the anti-imperial coalition's prospects of success.

The threat to the recently established imperial rule in Italy, however, increased only two years later when the Byzantine emperor Manuel I, with the help of large funds, managed to organize a new opposition group under the leadership of the trading republic of Venice and with the participation of the cities of Verona, Padua, and Vicenza. This 'league of Verona' widened in 1167, after the disaster in the imperial army before Rome, into the Lombard League. Besides the Byzantine emperor and the Norman king, Pope Alexander III also contributed to this arrangement.

In the mean time Frederick I had little success in opposing the threatening coalition between Alexander, the Norman king, the Byzantine emperor, and the anti-imperial forces in northern and central Italy. Negotiations with the French king, begun in summer 1162 over recognition of the pro-imperial pope, failed. On the contrary, in the same year Alexander III succeeded in arranging a reconciliation between the English and French kings. However, at the beginning of 1164 at the latest, Henry II came into conflict with Alexander because of his vigorous Church policies. By the following year, in May 1165, envoys of the English king at the Würzburg diet signed a proclamation, couched in an extremely hostile tone, against Alexander III and his supporters, among whom were numbered a few members of the German episcopate, in particular the archbishops of Mainz and Salzburg. At about the same time Barbarossa arranged for the canonization of Charlemagne by the imperial pope. In this way the imperial court propagated the idea that the Roman empire, refounded by Charlemagne, was held directly of God.

Frederick I, however, did not find the English king an effective ally, as he had to concentrate all his forces on the continual conflict with the king of France. The emperor sought a decisive battle in Italy, where Alexander III was under the protection of the Norman king. He accordingly set off for Italy in autumn 1166, on his fourth Italian campaign, with an army replenished by mercenary troops (Brabançons). After military successes against supporters of the Byzantine emperor in the region of Ancona, the imperial legates—Archbishops Christian of Mainz and Rainald of Cologne—towards the end of May 1167 succeeded in defeating the Romans crushingly near Tusculum. At the end of July the Leonine city was captured and the imperial pope, Paschal III, was enthroned in St Peter's. But the malaria epidemic which broke out at the beginning of August in the imperial army, and to which Rainald of Dassel fell victim, destroyed all the plans of the emperor, who had wanted to proceed against the Sicilian king. The city of Alessandria, founded in 1168 under the protection and with the help of the Lombard cities, became the symbol of the close community of interest between Alexander III and the league of north Italian cities which now consolidated itself. The emperor Manuel gave considerable financial support to the rebuilding of the city of Milan, destroyed in 1162. His far-reaching plans to establish supremacy over the important centres of northern Italy, however, were bogged down right from the start.

After this severe defeat in the battle against Alexander III, and the almost complete destruction of imperial supremacy in upper Italy, the co-operation between Barbarossa and Henry the Lion again proved useful for the imperial position in Germany. With the death of the emperor's cousin, the duchy of Swabia became vacant, and he raised his three-year-old son Frederick as successor. Around 1170 he gave the reversion of the Swabian duchy to his even younger son Conrad (born 1167, died 1191), who soon afterwards was given the name of his brother and predecessor Frederick, who had died. Thus in reality Barbarossa himself was in control of this duchy, in which lay the main bulk of the Staufen family estates. As the emperor had granted the county palatine of Lorraine, with its centres on the Moselle and the middle Rhine, to his half-brother Conrad in 1156, the imperial family now possessed a large sphere of direct influence stretching from the middle Rhine over what is now the Palatinate as far as southern Alsace, and embracing Swabia and Franconia. The close kinship ties with the duke of Upper Lorraine and the landgrave of Thuringia remained useful. In this way the imperial court could even now prevent Alexander III from gaining more supporters among the ecclesiastical princes in the German empire. In summer 1169 the emperor imposed the election and coronation of his three-year-old son Henry, and thereby secured the succession to the throne in the Staufen family.

In spite of that the papal schism represented a constant source of danger for the emperor's position in Germany. In imperial Italy it had undermined the foundations of imperial rule, even though the emperor and his pope still had considerable influence, particularly in central Italy. After 1167 Alexander III gained even more support in France and in the Anglo-Norman kingdom, where the murder of the archbishop of Canterbury, Thomas Becket (29 December 1170), weakened the position of the king. In Burgundy, Denmark, Poland, Bohemia, and Hungary the supporters of Alexander III pushed out the remaining partisans of the imperial pope.

In the following years imperial politics remained concentrated on solving the papal schism. The negotiations taken up with the French and English kings as well as with the Byzantine emperor, however, proved largely unsuccessful. The efforts for a settlement with Alexander III, who kept insisting on including the Lombard League in any peace with the emperor, failed. Once again the emperor had to seek a decision in Italy. His military activities during his fifth Italian campaign (1174–8), for which he had again recruited mercenaries, were first directed towards the destruction of the hated anti-imperial symbol, the papal–Lombard new foundation of Alessandria.

After he had had to give up the six-month siege of the city, the emperor, in spite of this obvious defeat, was able to make peace with the Lombard League in April 1175 at Montebello; here the tensions between the old rivals Milan and Cremona again came clearly into the open. But the peace, which had not yet been negotiated in detail, collapsed in the following months because of the emperor's demands for the destruction of Alessandria, and because of the new condition raised by the Lombard League, now under the leadership of Milan, that Pope Alexander III should be included in the peace. In the fighting which soon started again, the imperial army, to which Henry the Lion had denied his support, suffered a defeat near Legnano in May 1176. Using the weaknesses of the Lombard League, which Cremona publicly left after the battle of Legnano to join the imperial side in return for a large consideration, the emperor's representatives in negotiations at Anagni in November 1176 achieved a far-reaching settlement with Pope Alexander III. In this, Barbarossa went far to meet the papal demands, among other things renouncing the Matildine lands in favour of the pope.

Having thus split up the dangerous coalition between Alexander and the remaining cities in the league, the emperor was in a better position for further negotiations with the pope. Thus he was able to secure for himself the disposal of the Matildine lands and continuation in office for his episcopal partisans who had previously been deposed by Alexander. The peace was solemnly declared in Venice in July 1177. At the same time a truce was agreed with the Lombard League for six years, and with the Norman king for fifteen years.

[*b*] FROM THE CONFLICT WITH HENRY THE LION
TO THE THIRD CRUSADE

After the Peace of Venice the Emperor Manuel I tried to continue his anti-Staufen policy in imperial Italy despite his serious difficulties in the east of the Byzantine empire. He was supported by a few central Italian communes, but mainly by the leading noble family of the margraves of Montferrat, whose power base was chiefly in Piedmont. This coalition even succeeded in holding captive for a long period the imperial legate, Archbishop Christian of Mainz, who after the Peace of Venice had been active in the Patrimony of St Peter on behalf of Alexander III; but these partial successes became politically meaningless after the Emperor Manuel's death in 1180. In the peace negotiations begun with the Lombard League in spring 1183 the emperor was in a far better position than at the Peace of Montebello. In the Peace of Constance, of 25 June 1183, Frederick I had to grant the members of the Lombard League, with Milan at its head, extensive constitutional independence within the city walls and the city territory. But he retained important rights, which under favourable political conditions could make large financial profits possible. An integral part of the peace was a pact between the emperor and the Milanese group of cities, directed against Cremona. The emperor exploited this competition between the two large Lombard communes in his last Italian campaign (1184–6), thus strengthening his influence in Lombardy. After the peace treaties of Venice and Constance, the imperial court even recreated a relatively dense network of imperial administration in central and north-western Italy.

The Peace of Venice and the later successes of the emperor in the kingdom of Burgundy, where he had himself solemnly crowned king in 1178, gave him enough support to proceed against Henry the Lion. The Welf double duke was the last of the circle of powerful high nobles to whom Barbarossa had had to make large concessions to obtain his kingship. The claims of the Zähringer in Burgundy had long been pushed aside by the emperor. Welf VI, after selling his rights in imperial Italy, probably in 1178 but at the latest in 1179, even sold to the emperor extensive Swabian family estates between Lake Constance and the Lech, but reserving the use of much of them for his lifetime. With this purchase, which linked up the old Welf centre in the south-west with the Staufen sphere of influence, Barbarossa succeeded in outmanœuvring his cousin Henry the Lion. The duke had probably come to an agreement in 1175 with his uncle, Welf, who after the death of his only son led an extravagant life and also acted as a generous patron, but Henry had not paid the agreed sum.

The alienation between Frederick and Henry became obvious at the latest at the beginning of 1176, when at a meeting at Chiavenna Henry refused to give the emperor military support against the Lombard League. The duke, who was not feudally obliged to give such help, demanded in return the imperial lay advocacy of Goslar with its rich income from the silver mines of the Rammelsberg, which, however, the emperor was not prepared to sacrifice. At that point at the latest it became clear that the partnership between the cousins, which had lasted for decades, had given the Welf double duke a quasi-royal position, which he was strengthening especially in the north-east of the empire. This high position was bolstered by his marriage with the daughter of the English king, the marriage in 1166 of his daughter Gertrude with the son of Conrad III, the duke of Swabia, and Gertrude's second marriage to the son of the Danish king Valdemar (1131–82). Even in the east and at the court of the Byzantine emperor the Welf was highly respected, as became clear during his pilgrimage to the Holy Land in 1172.

The emperor used the negotiations with Alexander III at Anagni and Venice to proceed against the Welf. While the imperial court insisted at Venice that all bishops installed by Frederick I should be confirmed in their offices by Alexander III, those new investitures made under the influence of Henry in the archbishopric of Bremen and the diocese of Halberstadt should be re-examined. All grants by the prelates acting there as tools of the duke, and who had enfeoffed him with extensive Church estates, were declared invalid in the peace treaty.

In his proceedings against his cousin the emperor at first restricted himself to letting the complaints of the Welf's opponents in Saxony be decided by the courts, rather than attempting to mediate as he had done before. Among the accusers was Bishop Ulrich of Halberstadt, who had once been deposed by Henry. He was allied with the influential Archbishop Philip of Cologne, who claimed his nephew's Saxon inheritance, confiscated by the duke. On top of that there had long been sharp territorial conflicts in Westphalia between the chapter of Cologne and the Saxon duke. As Henry the Lion did not obey the summons to court in a trial according to local law, he was banned, that is to say subjected to temporary outlawry. Then in the late summer of 1179 the emperor started a trial in feudal law. His cousin again ignored the three summonses. The outcome of this political trial was that he was deprived of the two duchies and all imperial fiefs by sentence of the princes delivered in January 1180 at a court in Würzburg, and they were given to the emperor to dispose of.

At an imperial court at Gelnhausen in April 1180 the fees were regranted. The duchy of Saxony was split up and distributed to those powers which had been fighting the Welf duke for decades—to the archbishop of Cologne, who received the separated duchy of Westphalia, and Count Bernard of Anhalt, the youngest son of Albert the Bear who had died in 1170. Both thereby received legal claims which they yet had to make good against Henry the Lion. In the middle of September 1180 the duchy of Bavaria, which Henry the Lion had held since 1156 although his main activities had been concentrated on Saxony, was granted to the count palatine Otto of Wittelsbach, who particularly in the fifties and sixties had been an active supporter of Barbarossa's Italian policy. However, the Wittelsbach did not receive all the duchy of Bavaria in its full extent fixed in 1156. The duchy of Styria was separated from it and granted to the former margrave, Ottokar of Steyr.

Thus during Barbarossa's reign two more independent duchies were separated out of the duchy of Bavaria, which amounted to a wholesale splitting-up of this vast power block. Saxony included, in 1180 five dukes were active in the two duchies which Henry the Lion had personally united. The process of dissolving the original duchies, begun earlier, now increased, and was deliberately furthered by the emperor. In the Wittelsbachs Barbarossa raised a family which up to then had lagged behind the noble family of Andechs from a territorial-political point of view. After their ties of dependence on the duchy of Bavaria were dissolved, the Andechser were compensated with titles far outside the Bavarian duchy; from this time on they appeared as dukes of Dalmatia, Croatia, and Merano. In the following year, 1181, Frederick I was actually able to subjugate Henry the Lion, mainly with the help of the Saxon competitors of the former duke. Of his allodial possessions he kept only Brunswick and Lüneburg. He had to go into a long exile in England, to his father-in-law Henry II, from where, however, he returned in 1185.

In the late eighties Frederick I's policies generally went along previously determined lines. The negotiations with the Roman Curia, resumed before the peace with the Lombard League, led to no concrete results. The emperor's proposals aimed at narrowing the secular power of the pope in Italy. These plans, put into practice, would have amounted to a financial and economic dependence of the papacy on the empire. For the final cession of the Matildine lands, Barbarossa was prepared to grant the pope and the cardinals one-tenth each of the income of imperial Italy; the pope and the Curia would thereby have been tied to the financial policies of the Staufen. In negotiations at Verona (1184) the two powers only agreed on a joint campaign against heretics.

With the engagement of Henry VI to Constance (b. 1154), eleven years his senior, the daughter of Roger II and aunt of the contemporary Norman king William II (1166–89), a threatening situation arose for the Curia. The two dominant Italian powers, which had long been opposed to one another, to the papacy's advantage, entered into an agreement which went far beyond the truce of 1177. The Curia could clearly see the danger that the Staufen might inherit the kingdom of Sicily, which up to then had been feudally dependent on the papacy. Although it was still not completely impossible that there might be children from the marriage which took place in 1179 between King William and Joanna, the daughter of the English king Henry II, apparently in 1184 even the king himself no longer expected this.

Against this background it becomes comprehensible that in 1186, after the marriage of Henry VI and Constance, the emperor dropped all consideration for the papacy. His son occupied the whole of the Patrimony of St Peter. Significantly, this measure was closely connected with the political situation in the German empire, and especially with imperial rule of the Church, since Pope Urban III had disputed in principle the emperor's right to the *regalia* and *spolia* as hitherto practised. Not only that, but in the long-standing dispute over the archbishopric of Trier, the pope had consecrated the anti-Staufen candidate. This situation came further to a head when Archbishop Philip of Cologne in his anti-Staufen attitude, based in territorial politics, offered the starting-point for a far-reaching opposition to Frederick. Not only was this party joined by several ecclesiastical and secular lords in Germany: Archbishop Philip was also supported by Urban III, and made contact with the French king. At the same time there was the threat of the Danish king's joining the group. Frederick, however, managed to limit the danger by a pact with the French king, Philip II Augustus, in May 1187, so that Archbishop Philip of Cologne had to submit to the emperor in March 1188.

At the same court in Mainz Barbarossa, his second son Frederick duke of Swabia, and numerous bishops and secular nobles committed themselves to a crusade to the Holy Land. In October 1187 the Sultan Saladin, the supreme lord of Syria and Egypt, had conquered Jerusalem, after having defeated the Christian army near Hattin by the sea of Galilee. Like the English and French kings, who had already committed themselves to the crusade, Barbarossa still had to arrange important matters before the departure, fixed for spring 1189. He especially had to prevent Henry the Lion's interference during his absence. Barbarossa forced his cousin again to go into exile in England for three years. At the same time the emperor arranged the distribution of power within his own family. Henry VI, who had had some experience of ruling since 1186, was entrusted with the regency. The younger son Conrad, who had been the son-in-law of the king of Castile for a year, received the Staufen estates around Rothenburg. Otto, who a little later married the daughter of the powerful and extremely rich count of Blois-Champagne, was installed as count palatine of Burgundy, and was thus introduced into the family lands of the Empress Beatrice, who had died in 1184.

In May 1189 the crusader army set off from Regensburg under the leadership of the emperor, then aged about 66. According to contemporary reports, certainly exaggerated, it numbered 100,000 men. The passage through the Byzantine empire was difficult. The Byzantine emperor not unjustifiably regarded the Norman–Staufen alliance as a great danger, and had therefore renewed his pact with Saladin. Only after Frederick threatened to conquer the Byzantine empire did its emperor, by the Treaty of Adrianople of February 1190, decide to support the passage of the crusader army to Asia. After a victory at Iconium over one army, that of Saladin's son-in-law, and the crossing of the Taurus mountains, Barbarossa drowned in the River Salef on 10 June 1190. Many crusaders then left the army and journeyed back again. The rest, under the leadership of the emperor's son Frederick of Swabia, went on to Antioch, where the emperor's body was buried in the church of St Peter. His bones, which it was originally intended to take to Jerusalem, were finally buried in the cathedral of Tyre. The German army went on as far as Acre, where the siege was only ended successfully in July 1191 with the support of the contingents of the English and French kings, who had arrived shortly before. Duke Frederick of Swabia had already died of an epidemic in Acre in January 1191, so that the rest of the crusade was completely under the leadership of the rival kings of England and France. The emperor had died in great esteem on the crusade in fulfilment of the universal Christian mission. Henry VI, his royal son, educated, politically experienced and long appointed to the throne, inherited a government which, in spite of all concessions wrung from the emperor or deliberately granted by him, still offered a great deal of opportunity. Imperial rule was still strongly centred upon the figure of the emperor and thus dependent on him. By the claim to the kingdom of Sicily and the still unfinished crusade, the course of future imperial policy was at the same time being directed towards a comprehensive Mediterranean policy.

[c] HENRY VI: THE SPELL OF MEDITERRANEAN
POLITICS

Shortly after Frederick I had set off for the east, Henry the Lion broke the agreement and came back from his exile in England. This posed a threat which prevented the then twenty-four-year-old regent Henry VI from receiving the imperial crown. This had been assured to him in the so-called treaty of Strasbourg of April 1189 in return for handing back the papal lands, though reserving the imperial rights. Only one month after Henry the Lion's return to Saxony, King William of Sicily died childless, and so Constance, since 1186 Henry VI's wife, became heiress to the kingdom. Her right to the inheritance, however, was immediately disputed by an illegitimate grandson of King Roger II, Count Tancred of Lecce. Tancred found supporters, particularly in Sicily. He was supported by the pope as well as by the Byzantine emperor, and was crowned king with the agreement of the pope. Richard the Lionheart, the son of Henry II of England, also put forward claims in the Norman-Sicilian kingdom.

In July 1190 Henry VI made an agreement with Henry the Lion, granting him the estates around Lüneburg and Brunswick and also half the income of Lübeck, now an imperial city. Having secured his rear, Henry set off for Italy in January 1191. Although he achieved his imperial coronation, he failed in his main aim: to reconquer the kingdom of Sicily. Shortly after the emperor's defeat near Naples, Henry the Lion's son of the same name started a rebellion in Saxony. At the same time he spread the rumour that the emperor had died of plague outside Naples. The emperor's situation became even worse through the confusion in connection with the dispute over the bishopric of Liège. When the emperor did not manage to clear himself credibly of the suspicion of having had a part in the murder of the candidate from the family of the dukes of Brabant, the rebellion against Henry VI spread all over the German empire.

In this extremely threatening situation he received help from an unexpected quarter. At the end of 1192 King Richard of England, who had been shipwrecked and had passed through Austria in disguise, was taken prisoner by Duke Leopold of Austria, his enemy because of happenings in the Holy Land. In February 1193 Leopold handed the king over to the emperor. Henry VI only released his prisoner in 1194, after he had received the immense sum of 150,000 marks in silver as ransom from the Anglo-Norman kingdom, and Richard had received his kingdom as a fief from the emperor against an annual tribute of £5,000.

This money allowed the emperor in May 1194 to resume the Sicilian campaign abandoned fruitlessly in 1191. Before he set off he succeeded in making peace with Henry the Lion. In this connection Henry the Lion's son of the same name had been married to Agnes, a daughter of the count palatine Conrad of Staufen, in November 1193; two years later the Welf even became his father-in-law's successor in the palatine county of the Rhine. As on his first Italian campaign, Henry VI now again tried to play the old rivals Milan and Cremona off against one another by clever dealing, and thus to gain freedom of action for his Sicilian affairs. At the same time the imperial administration in central Italy was further developed and a close net put around the Patrimony of St Peter.

The conquest of Sicily at Christmas 1194 reached its climax with the emperor's coronation as *Rex Sicilie* in Palermo cathedral. Soon afterwards Henry VI continued the traditional anti-Byzantine policies of the Normans. He demanded the cession of the area between Dyrrhachium and Thessalonica, which William II had conquered in 1185 and then lost again. Furthermore he demanded a large sum of money and the participation of the Byzantine fleet in the planned crusade. Supported by the legal claims of his younger brother Philip (b. 1176/7), whom he had married to the daughter of the Byzantine emperor in April 1195, he now proceeded even more vigorously against the Eastern empire. The plan to conquer Constantinople, however, had to be put off because of consideration for the papacy, which justifiably saw a deadly threat to its political position in such an expansion of Staufen–Norman rule in the eastern Mediterranean.

At that time Henry VI still had to show consideration to the pope in order to gain agreement to his plan for a hereditary empire, which would have fundamentally altered the contemporary imperial constitution. The plan for a hereditary empire not only aimed at removing the German princes' right of election, but also at a permanent linkage of the Sicilian kingdom with the empire. This threatened the current situation of the papacy, which therefore refused its assent to the plan. Although at an imperial court in Würzburg in April 1196 Henry VI, during his last stay in Germany—for one year, 1195–6— succeeded in winning over the majority of the German secular and ecclesiastical princes to agree to this plan, in return for granting the heritability of imperial fiefs and renunciation of the right of *spolia*, a large group under the leadership of Archbishop Adolf of Cologne remained opposed to this fundamental change in the imperial constitution. Therefore Henry VI for the time being had to break off the negotiations in order to reach agreement with the pope.

Pope Celestine III was opposed to Henry VI both because of the emperor's independent Church policy in Sicily, and because of encroachments by the imperial administration in the Patrimony of St Peter. In the negotiations which began in November 1196 he demanded that these complaints be dealt with, and especially the recognition of papal suzerainty over Sicily. He refused agreement to the plan for a hereditary empire, and rejected the coronation of the emperor's son Frederick (b. December 1194), who at first was to be called Constantine but upon baptism received the names of his grandfathers, Frederick Roger. The pope maintained his refusal even when the emperor, while refusing the oath of fealty for Sicily, made him a far-reaching offer. We do not know its exact contents, but according to Henry VI neither his father Frederick nor any other predecessor had ever gone so far to meet papal demands. This 'best offer' most probably had a financial side. In all episcopal churches the pope and the cardinals would be entitled to the highest canonries. As the Curia's counterpart, the renunciation of all disputed property claims outside the Patrimony of St Peter was expected.

As a result of papal resistance, and also through the opposition of the German princes, Henry VI was forced to drop the hereditary empire plan for the time being. Nevertheless in December 1196 he at least succeeded in obtaining the election of his two-year-old son Frederick as king of the Romans by the princes. Up to his death on 28 September 1197 in Messina, the emperor concentrated on suppressing a revolt of Sicilian nobles and on preparations for a crusade. In the negotiations with the papacy this had always played a great part; it could have supported the further expansion of the Staufen empire in the Mediterranean area.

[*d*] THE STRUGGLE FOR THE THRONE BETWEEN
THE STAUFEN AND THE WELFS

The early death of Henry VI, who left only a three-year-old
son (b. 26 December 1194), gave the papacy the chance to free
itself from the threatening embrace of the Staufen. Innocent
III, Celestine's successor, made use of it. His first actions were
mainly concentrated on re-establishing and extending papal
power in central Italy.

In the course of 1198 the pope also proceeded against the
margraviate of Ancona, where the imperial ministerial Markward of Annweiler, from the Palatinate, was able to offer stiff
resistance. Besides Ancona, Markward from 1195 on also held
the duchy of Ravenna and Romagna as an imperial fief. Furthermore he had been installed by the emperor as count of the
Abruzzi and Molise, so that his districts formed a bridge between northern and southern Italy. As Constance, Henry VI's
widow and regent for her son Frederick, emphasized the independence of the Sicilian kingdom and fought the Staufen
partisans, Markward tried to maintain imperial rule in the
Sicilian kingdom as well as in his own districts, even after
the death of Constance (28 November 1198). This gained him
the bitter enmity of the pope, who after Constance's death had
taken over the regency for Frederick II as the supreme feudal
suzerain of Sicily. In spite of the support of German officials,
of Saracens, and of the city of Pisa, Markward in 1200 was
defeated near Monreale (south of Palermo). None the less, up
to his death in September 1202 he exercised decisive influence
in Sicily. In 1202 he even succeeded in getting the royal child
into his hands. Markward based his political actions on dir-
ections in the late emperor's will.

In Germany Philip, from 1196 duke of Swabia, at first
supported the succession to the throne of his nephew Frederick. But as this seemed a hopeless prospect he had himself
elected king in March 1198 in Thuringia by a large number of
princes. The reason for this lay in the activities of a group of
anti-Staufer princes led by Archbishop Adolf of Cologne and
financially supported by Richard I of England. Adolf of
Cologne, and at first the archbishop of Trier too, furthered the

election of Duke Berthold V of Zähringen as king of the Romans; but he was soon drawn over to the Staufen side in return for promises by Philip—and he received the lay advocacy of Schaffhausen.

Following this, Richard the Lionheart urged the election of a member of the Welf house. As Count Henry, the eldest son of Henry the Lion, was still on crusade together with many other German nobles, his younger brother Otto presented himself; as count of Poitou he was a vassal of the English king, but controlled only one-third of the family lands remaining to the Welfs around Brunswick and Lüneburg. Archbishop Adolf I of Cologne (d. 1220) had reservations about this Welf who had grown up at the English court because of Cologne's duchy of Westphalia, but these were pushed aside by the English king and also by pressure from the citizens of Cologne, who had been fostering trade connections with England for some time. In June 1198 Otto was elected king and in July of the same year was crowned in Aachen—i.e. in the right place—after having given the archbishop of Cologne security for his possessions and for the duchy of Westphalia. In the following period Otto was unable to improve his position against the Staufen Philip, whose main supporters were imperial ministerials and whose followers subsequently increased among the high nobility too. Otto's position became worse when in April 1199 Richard the Lionheart died, and his successor King John could not give the Welf any substantial help.

Philip was not crowned until September 1198, in the wrong place and by the wrong person—at Mainz, by the archbishop of Tarentaise. To stem English-Welf influence he could at least fall back on the imperial treasure, amassed by Henry VI in the castle of Trifels. At the same time he also relied on the renewal of the Staufen-Capetian treaty made in June 1198. His situation further improved when Philip II Augustus of France won military successes against the English king.

The political situation pushed the pope into the role of referee in the struggle for succession to the throne, in which the English and French kings each supported a different candidate. Innocent III based his claims to judicial competence on the superior dignity of the priesthood, represented by the pope, as against the kingship, and on the fact that with the coronation of

Charlemagne the empire was transferred by the papacy from the Greeks to the Franks (the theory of *translatio imperii*). About the turn of the year 1200 the pope in consistory supported the Welf ('*Deliberatio super facto imperii de tribus electis*' in the *Regestum super Negotio Imperii*) with the argument, among others, that Otto IV had been elected by those princes who were especially and principally called to do so—in other words those belonging to the smaller circle of electors, thus drawing the outlines of the later college of electors. Innocent's main argument against Frederick was that through him the kingdom of Sicily would be connected with the empire. An argument against the Staufen anyway, so he said, was his membership of a family of persecutors of the Church. With this the pope branded Frederick I, Henry VI, and also Philip, who had been excommunicated by Celestine III because of his activities as duke of Tuscany (1195/6). The pope was utterly opposed to succession in the Staufen family, for whose legal basis in the empire Henry VI had striven in vain, also in the interests of the *unio regni ad imperium*. By Philip, the husband of the Byzantine emperor's daughter, the crusade the pope summoned in August 1198 could have been directed towards the Staufen plans for the conquest of Byzantium—as Innocent hinted.

The pope's decision for the Welf, then considerably weaker in the German empire and dependent on papal help, had already been prepared. In summer 1198 Otto IV gave his agreement to the papal 'recuperations' in imperial Italy, and committed himself to support the papacy in the legal claims still outstanding, which to a considerable extent were still in the hands of Staufen imperial officials. As Otto in July 1201 at Neuss again assured the papal legate on oath, the Welf promised to enforce papal supremacy over the kingdom of Sicily, the guardianship and regency of which Constance, the emperor's widow, had handed to the pope shortly before her death. Otto entered into similar engagements for his policies towards the cities of imperial Italy and the French king.

The papal choice in favour of the Welf and the excommunication of the Staufen King Philip, however, could not substantially influence existing power relations in Germany. As well as many secular princes, numerous bishops backed the Staufen against the pope. In November 1204 Philip even succeeded in drawing Archbishop Adolf of Cologne to his side in return for considerable financial and political concessions, so that in January 1205 he was crowned 'properly' at Aachen. In these successes Philip was favoured by the defeat of the English King John by Philip II of France.

Now even the Roman Curia gave in. In August 1207 Philip of Swabia was absolved from excommunication, even after he had fought against the papal 'recuperation' policy in imperial Italy in 1204 and 1205, with an army led by the bishop of Worms. The negotiations already begun were continued in Rome with representatives of Philip and Otto. The disputed central Italian areas of Tuscany, Spoleto, and the margraviate of Ancona should be given as imperial fiefs to a nephew of the pope, who was to marry one of Philip's daughters. But they did not come to an agreement on Philip's imperial coronation, or on the other matters discussed, among them the free election of bishops and the renunciation of the right of *spolia*. In June 1208 King Philip was murdered at Bamberg by the Bavarian count palatine, Otto of Wittelsbach. The main motive of Wittelsbach, who himself was killed a year later, apparently lay in the fact that Philip's daughter, up to then engaged to him, was to be married to the pope's nephew.

After Philip's death the German princes quickly agreed on Otto IV, who in Frankfurt in November 1208 again had himself elected king. The endeavours of the French king to raise the duke of Brabant to the German throne in opposition to Otto IV, who was allied with the English king, were a failure. The Welf had to repeat his previous promises to Innocent III before he was crowned emperor in Rome in October 1209.

Directly after the coronation, however, Otto IV, advised by the Staufen ministerials, began once again to extend the imperial administration in central Italy at the expense of the Patrimony of St Peter. At the beginning of 1210 he even installed as duke of Spoleto Diepold, the imperial ministerial who with Markward of Annweiler and other Staufen administrators had resisted papal policies in central and southern Italy. After a campaign to northern Italy in spring 1210, Otto IV made it clear that he also intended to conquer the Sicilian kingdom, where the young Frederick II was having trouble with the barons. In autumn 1210 Innocent III answered this attempt, undertaken by Otto IV with an army consisting of German ministerials and Italian troops, with solemn excommunication, strengthened in spring 1211 with the release of all vassals from their vows of allegiance. In Germany meanwhile a princely opposition had formed with papal support, under the leadership of the archbishop of Mainz, the king of Bohemia, and the landgrave of Thuringia. This forced Otto, who after his successes in southern Italy was preparing to conquer Sicily, to return to Germany which he reached at the beginning of 1212. Only a little more than six months later he was followed by the Staufen Frederick, who already in April 1212 had begun negotiations with Innocent III.

Only shortly after his arrival in Germany, at a court in Frankfurt in December 1212, Frederick II with the support of the papal legate was elected king, and thereby attained a status which his father had procured for him about one and a half decades earlier. The coronation had to take place in Mainz, by the archbishop of Mainz, as the coronation place at Aachen was under the control of Otto IV, and the archbishop of Cologne was on the side of the Welf. As a consequence of the long disputes, which had increased during recent years, between the English King John, who continued—though with little effect—to support his Welf nephew, and King Philip II of France, Frederick II in November 1212 renewed the by now traditional treaty between the Staufen and the Capetians. This also brought him urgently needed financial support, 20,000 marks in silver. In the fight against the Welf in northern Germany, the Staufen at first gained no decisive successes. With the support of the Bohemian king he only managed to force Otto to retreat from Thuringia and to draw the margrave of Meissen on to his side. The Golden Bull of Eger has to be seen in this political context. In this solemn charter Frederick II in general repeated the concessions to the pope already made by Otto IV, but now with the express agreement of the princes: these concerned the expansion of the Patrimony of St Peter, the renunciation of the rights of *spolia* and *regalia*, free election of bishops and abbots, unrestricted right of appeal to the Curia, as well as the king's support in fighting heretics.

Only two months before, King John, who in 1209 had been excommunicated by the pope because of the occupation of the archbishopric of Canterbury and the confiscation of Church property, had submitted to Innocent III and received his kingdom back as a papal fief. In spite of this massive surrender, John could not be sure that Philip Augustus would not use the authorization to conquer the rest of the realm, i.e. England, granted to him only a few months previously by the pope. Thus, in close contact with Otto IV, he tried to attack the French king on the Continent. But the English army under John's leadership was defeated on the Loire. A little later, on 27 July 1214, Otto IV with the army of his allies (the counts of Flanders-Hainaut, Boulogne, and Holland) suffered a severe defeat at Bouvines, east of Lille, by the French king.

For the Emperor Otto, Bouvines meant the end of his influence on imperial history. In July 1215, after subjugating the Welf supporters in the Lorraine-lower Rhine area, Frederick II had himself crowned at Aachen, in the proper place. In the following month Otto had to flee from Cologne. Until Otto's death in 1218, Frederick always had the fear that the imperial bishops and the high nobility would come together around the Welfs in an anti-Staufen opposition. Against this background it becomes understandable that Frederick II followed a friendly overall policy towards the princes at this time. He promised Innocent III shortly before his death that after his anticipated coronation as emperor he would renounce the kingdom of Sicily in favour of his eldest son Henry, born in 1211, who had already been crowned king in 1212.

[e] THE IMPERIAL RULE OF FREDERICK II AND HENRY (VII)

Immediately after the death of Innocent III, Frederick tried to circumvent his promise to the pope by pushing forward the election of Henry as German king; after the extinction of the Zähringen family he had already made Henry duke of Swabia and *rector* of Burgundy. But this aim could only be arranged with the German episcopate, who were fully aware that these policies were against papal interests, in return for other concessions by Frederick. Directly after the election of Henry (VII) as *rex Romanorum*, on 26 April 1220 in the 'Treaty with the

Ecclesiastical Princes' Frederick announced the price paid to reach his goal. But in spite of the king's concessions towards the territorial politics of the higher clergy in this *Confoederatio cum principibus ecclesiasticis* [3: xxxii. 376–85, no. 95], the relationship of mutual interest between the German imperial Churches and the monarchy also manifested itself. On 22 November 1220 Frederick II, without making serious concessions to Pope Honorius III (1216–27), reached his next aim, coronation as emperor in Rome. He had only had to agree not to carry out the integration of the Sicilian kingdom into the Roman empire in constitutional law, in spite of the existing personal union. Further imperial decrees ordered in connection with the coronation meant no loss to the emperor; in close accord with late-antique Roman imperial law they were to have a statutory character, and therefore, at the instance of the Staufen emperor, were to be added to Justinian's *Corpus Iuris*. Among these were the heresy laws passed here, which were clearly formulated by the Roman Curia.

The flexibility of the Roman Curia towards Frederick, who within a few years had again achieved the threatening union of the Norman kingdom with the Roman empire, is only comprehensible against the background of the papal crusade policy. One of the primary aims of Innocent III had been to make real the papal claim to leadership, including the direction of the crusades. For this reason Innocent, at the Fourth Lateran Council, which with its 1,300 assembled prelates served primarily to prepare the crusade, completely left out of account Frederick's crusading oath which he had sworn that year. But only Austrian and Hungarian troops under Duke Leopold VI and King Andrew followed the call to the crusade in large numbers, and otherwise some from Frisia and the lower Rhine under the leadership of Oliver, master of the schools of Cologne cathedral—and only a few Frenchmen. The crusaders, who to begin with lacked a united leadership, were only able to undertake significant action before the Egyptian harbour town of Damietta, where papal legates tried to impose their leadership on the crusader army. The siege of the town was not successful until November 1219. In the unpromising situation of the crusade in 1218, Pope Honorius III called up Frederick II to help. In 1220 his participation became all the more urgent as meanwhile the Hungarian king as well as the Babenberger Leopold had set off for home. Tl❡ renewal of Frederick's crusader oath at his imperial coronation under the circumstances demanded a considerable service in return from the emperor.

After his coronation as emperor, Frederick II first concentrated fully on dealing with the almost chaotic conditions in his Sicilian kingdom. He merely sent 500 knights under the leadership of Duke Ludwig of Bavaria to Damietta. The crusader army, however, suffered a great blow when, after taking Damietta, they finally tried to conquer Egypt. In September 1221 the crusaders, stuck in the mud of the Nile, had to promise to leave Egypt and to observe an eight-year truce; in return they were allowed an unhindered withdrawal. In spite of the failure of the crusade and the harsh rule over the Church which Frederick II exercised in his hereditary lands, the pope at first allowed the emperor to postpone his departure for the crusade. In July 1225, however, in the treaty of San Germano Frederick II finally committed himself to the crusade. In this, contrary to Innocent III's aims and also to Honorius III's original intention, the emperor was given the sole leadership of the crusade. Against the high fine of 100,000 ounces of gold and the threat of excommunication, expressly agreed with the emperor's consent, Frederick had to promise to start the crusade in August 1227, come what may. In November 1225, directly after the treaty, the emperor began preparations by marrying Isabella, the fourteen-year-old daughter of John of Brienne, the king of Jerusalem. Immediately after the marriage, Frederick II contended with the contemporary king for his position, by now also bearing the title king of Jerusalem, which he was legally entitled to do.

In 1226 Frederick used the instrument of the crusade against the cities and lords of northern Italy too. He summoned them to come to a court in Cremona to prepare for the crusade and to renew imperial rule. Because of this many cities formed a new Lombard League under the leadership of Milan, the old rival of Cremona. The emperor could not break the resistance of these northern Italian cities by military means. He had to content himself with banning them for breach of the peace and disturbance of the crusade. Finally, through papal mediation, the Lombard cities did consent to put up a contingent of 400 knights for the crusade.

The emperor's crusade, already announced several times, seemed to begin favourably in August 1227, the date agreed with the pope, but at the beginning of the voyage the emperor fell so severely ill that he had to return. As he had not secured himself against this eventuality in the Treaty of San Germano, this breaking off of the crusade gave Gregory IX, the new pope, the legal basis for excommunicating the emperor on 29 September 1227, and also for taking the political instrument of the crusade out of the emperor's hands. In spite of that Frederick II took up the crusade again, starting from Brindisi in June 1228 with 1,000 knights and about 10,000 pilgrims, to the surprise of the pope, who had expressly forbidden him to do so. A successful crusade was the emperor's only hope of breaking the Roman Curia's resistance and thus of securing his rule in the empire and Sicily; and as king of Jerusalem it was his only hope of supporting his authority as universal ruler, whom contemporary eschatological notions expected to destroy Islam. Soon after his arrival in Acre in September 1228, Frederick resumed the negotiations with the Sultan al-Kamil, which he had begun from Italy. Thus in Jaffa on 18 February 1229 the emperor, who spoke fluent Arabic and was familiar with Islamic culture, succeeded in concluding a peace treaty for ten and a half years with the equally highly educated sultan.

The status quo was generally maintained, but Jerusalem with a few places between the city and the coast again came under the power of the king of Jerusalem, so that at least the most important part of Saladin's conquest of 1187 was recovered. The Dome of the Rock and the al-Aqsa mosque remained Islamic sanctuaries. No high prelate was prepared to crown the emperor. Thus on 18 March 1229 Frederick II crowned himself in the church of the Holy Sepulchre in Jerusalem, and thereby stressed that his kingship came directly from God. On this occasion he published a manifesto to Christendom 'in which he presented his success as a miracle of God and the heavenly hosts, and himself as a direct instrument of God'. 'On this "day of salvation" Frederick II formulated the idea of his "kingdom of David", and put it into reality; in Jerusalem he surrounded himself for the first time with the nimbus of directness to God' [544: 932]. This proclaims an imperial self-image which was generally accepted by contemporaries, against the background of widespread apocalyptic expectations, of which the imperial court was also well aware.

The emperor bolstered this increase of authority after his return by military successes against the papal army led, among others, by John of Brienne—the ex-king of Jerusalem and former father-in-law of Frederick—and against uprisings in Sicilian cities, and also by an advance into the papal state. These events forced the pope to make peace in July 1230 at San Germano, through the mediation of Hermann of Salza and some German princes, with the emperor who had previously been condemned as a 'disciple of Muhammad' and a 'persecutor of the Church'. In return for freeing the papal state, and granting free episcopal elections and the judicial and fiscal freedom of the clergy in the kingdom of Sicily, the pope lifted the excommunication of the emperor.

But this meant that Frederick again had his hands free for the fight against the rebellious north Italian communes, especially Milan, without the pope being able to lift a finger as an open ally of the Lombard League. In the following year the Constitutions of Melfi were decreed in the Sicilian kingdom, and for northern Italy a Reichstag in Ravenna was announced for November 1231. Because of the resistance of the Lombard League, however, the Reichstag did not lead to the desired success, so that in January 1232 the emperor again outlawed the rebellious cities. But at Ravenna important questions also arose concerning the German part of the empire, where the emperor had not set foot since leaving for the Italian campaign in 1220.

In the German empire after the election of Henry (VII), Archbishop Engelbert of Cologne, from the Rhineland noble family of the counts of Berg, had been entrusted with the regency for the not yet ten-year-old *rex Romanorum*. Archbishop Engelbert tried to create some stability in the political situation by instituting regional public peaces. But in his attempts to bring about closer relations with the English royal court, in line with Cologne tradition, and to bolster them by marriage projects between the Staufen king and the English royal family, he was certainly not following the emperor's intentions. After the war between the English and French kings broke out again in 1224, Frederick preferred to make a new pact with the Capetians.

Then there were the differences between the emperor in Sicily and the archiepiscopal regent concerning the treatment of King Valdemar of Denmark, who had been taken prisoner. Frederick endeavoured to force Valdemar to give back former imperial areas between the Elbe and the Baltic which Otto IV and also he himself (in 1214) had granted to the Danish king. Archbishop Engelbert himself fell victim to his own extensive family and territorial politics (1225). Instead of being wedded to one of the daughters of the English king, as urged by the archbishop, the *rex Romanorum*, who was still a minor, was married to the daughter of the Babenberg Duke Leopold of Austria in November 1225. As the successor of the murdered Engelbert of Cologne in the summer of the following year, Frederick II nominated as imperial regent and guardian of Henry (VII) Duke Ludwig of Bavaria.

In the Golden Bull of Rimini for the Teutonic Order, made out only shortly before in March 1226, Frederick also took action against the claim of the Danish king to the areas of Livonia, Estonia, Samogitia, and Semigallia, which were still to be converted. The imperial privilege of June 1226 for the city of Lübeck, which by now had fallen under Danish rule, was also directed against the same Danish king. The legal status of an imperial city which this granted, and which committed them to no more than small services to the emperor, could only be secured by the people of Lübeck afer their victory over King Valdemar in July 1227 near Bornhöved, in which they had military support from Hamburg. Since the disputes over succession to the throne the larger German cities, especially the episcopal ones, showed clear attempts at more independent policies. In the German parts of the empire this reached a new dimension in the league made around the middle of the twenties between the cities of Mainz, Worms, Speyer, Bingen, Frankfurt, Gelnhausen, and Friedberg. This, the first German league of cities, was forbidden in November 1226 at a court under the new imperial regent, Duke Ludwig of Bavaria, mainly following the wishes of the ecclesiastical princes who were lords of cities.

Under Duke Ludwig, who himself pursued an intensive territorial policy in his duchy directed equally against the ecclesiastical lords, it was on the whole no longer so easy for the ecclesiastical princes to get what they wanted as under the previous regency of the archbishop of Cologne. Now imperial ministerials, like the butlers Conrad and Eberhard of Winterstetten and the steward Eberhard of Waldburg, gained more influence at the royal court. The excommunication of the emperor by the pope in September 1227 probably played a role in this. In the following year, 1228, it came to an open split between the now eighteen-year-old king and the imperial regent. The military conflict in summer 1229 which developed out of this was successful for Henry, so that he himself took over rule. The policies of the young king, who amongst other things in summer 1230 recognized a league of cities mainly under the bishop of Liège (Liège, Huy, Dinant, St Trond, Fosses, Tongeren, and Maastricht), incited the opposition primarily of the ecclesiastical princes, who saw their rights of lordship infringed by the endeavours of the city communities towards independence, particularly in their Rhenish seats. At a court in Worms in January 1231, urged by the bishop of Liège, all unions, associations, sworn confederations, pacts, or similar things were declared illegal by a declaration of the princes, even if previously agreed by the king or the lords of the cities [3: xxxii. 418 f., 106].

At another court in Worms in April 1231, it was again mainly the ecclesiastical lords who put through the 'law in favour of princes' (*Statutum in favorem principum*) [17: ii. 418–20, no. 304], which was also valid for the secular princes. On most points it recapitulated the *confoederatio* of 1220. In view of the royal territorial policies which Henry (VII) had meanwhile reactivated, at least partly, and the clearly growing prestige of the emperor, the *statutum* was far more than a mere formal repetition. Significantly it was the bishops of Würzburg and Strasbourg, whose territories were in specially close contact with the imperial ministerials, who were the chief complainers against the king, and also against the cities. Frederick II's courts of spring 1232 led to a repetition and intensification of the anti-communal decisions of the court at Worms. Revoking all privileges to the contrary, in April 1232 the emperor cancelled the legal basis for any community representation, councils, mayoralties, or other governing organizations and official functions in German cities which had been installed without the consent of the relevant episcopal lord [3: xxxii. 428–33, no. 113]. Already in March 1232 Henry had offended against his own laws in confirming amongst other things a city council to the citizens of Worms. When, after being summoned several times by his imperial father, the king in April 1232 appeared at a court, which meanwhile had been transferred to Aquileia and then to Cividale, he had to commit himself on oath to obey the emperor's orders fully and to comply with the wishes of the princes. At the same time the emperor confirmed with a few changes the *Statutum in favorem principum*, wrested from the king in the previous year [3: xxxii. 434–9, no. 114].

Henry (VII) now had very little room for manœuvre. At the smallest offence against the decisions of Ravenna and Cividale the princes complained to the emperor and the pope against the king. In this situation he decided on an open split with his father. Since the outlawing of the rebellious cities, the emperor's battle against the Lombard League had intensified. In November 1234 the king opened negotiations with the federated cities, leading to a pact in the following month. Henry could count on the support of the French king Louis IX, with whom he had already been allied for some time, while Frederick was then in contact with the English court. This, and probably also the desire to counteract the increase of King Henry's followers in Germany—among them several imperial ministerials, cities, and his Babenberg brother-in-law Frederick of Austria—made Frederick II return north of the Alps in spring 1235, after almost 15 years of absence.

In the fight against his son, Frederick II was sure of the support of influential German princes who had already visited him on the other side of the Alps. Therefore he went to Germany without an army. There he appeared like a potentate from a different culture, as a contemporary description makes clear: 'He travelled as became the imperial majesty, in great splendour and glory, with many wagons laden with gold and silver, cambric, purple, precious stones, and valuable objects, with many camels and dromedaries. Many Saracens and Ethiopians skilled in various arts, with monkeys and leopards watched over his money and his treasures' [14: xxii. 348]. In Wimpfen in the Palatinate Henry was forced to submit to the emperor. At a court in Worms which followed, he was declared deposed and led into imprisonment—and at first he was held by his bitterest enemy, the count palatine of the Rhine, Otto of Wittelsbach. After seven years of imprisonment in the dungeons of the Sicilian kingdom the emperor's son supposedly took his own life. His followers were mostly pardoned.

During his stay at Worms, where his son was sentenced to life imprisonment, Frederick almost simultaneously celebrated his wedding to Isabella, the sister of Henry III of England, which had been prepared some months before. This marriage had come about by the pope's mediation. It disturbed the previous pact with the French king only briefly, although the emperor was able to strengthen his influence in the Burgundian area, especially as against the high nobility there; the English king had hoped for support from the emperor in his fight against the French king. At the same time also the old Welf–Staufen opposition was stilled; for decades this had had a decisive influence on the political relations of the Staufen imperial family with the Plantagenets and the Capetians. Otto, the grandson of Henry the Lion and nephew of Otto IV, at a court in Mainz in August 1235 was made a duke and *princeps* for his allodial estates of Lüneburg and Brunswick, which still remained with the Welfs. He had previously surrendered these estates to the emperor and received them back as an imperial fief [3: xxxii. 484–91, no. 120a].

With the advice and consent of the ecclesiastical and secular princes, Frederick II at the same court decreed a public peace for the German empire [3: xxxii. 462–85, no. 119]. In this imperial public peace, given at Mainz, which later kings and emperors adopted as a model, Frederick endeavoured to reactivate and secure jurisdictional rights, as well as those of coinage, toll, and escort which were important for trade and traffic and which were the only ones still remaining to the German monarchy. In this the emperor even urged the removal of those tolls and mints which had been installed without royal or imperial consent after the death of Henry VI. Following the organizational model of the Sicilian kingdom, Frederick introduced the institution of a royal justiciar, who was to exercise the royal judicial rights in the absence of the emperor. In contrast to its successful enforcement in the centralized 'bureaucratic state' of south Italy, this institution proved largely ineffective in the very different constitutional system of the German empire.

The public peace of Mainz of 1235 also served the emperor's far-reaching political aims, especially his fight against the rebellious northern Italian cities under the leadership of Milan, which had only been suspended during his son's rebellion. Thus Frederick made the princes swear on oath to participate in a campaign against the northern Italian enemies of the empire, fixed for spring 1236. But on this campaign, which started late, the emperor was accompanied almost solely by imperial ministerials from the Staufen family lands in Swabia and Alsace.

Some of the princes of the empire were tied up with other tasks in Germany which were also in the emperor's interests. This was especially true of the duke of Bavaria and the king of Bohemia. Together with the king of Hungary they had been entrusted on the emperor's departure with executing the imperial ban which Frederick in June 1236 had inflicted on the Babenberg Duke Frederick, the brother-in-law of Henry (VII). But their actions remained largely unsuccessful, so that at the beginning of 1237 Frederick II himself set off from Italy to Austria. He was denied great military success, but in Vienna, which he made an imperial city, he nevertheless managed to enforce the election of his nine-year-old son Conrad IV (from his marriage with Isabella, the queen of Jerusalem) by the imperial princes present without having asked the pope's consent. As formulated in the election decree, the *principes* took the place of the Roman senate and elected Conrad IV 'king of the Romans and the future emperor' [3: xxxii. 502–9, no. 124]. Once again a high ecclesiastical prince of the empire was appointed guardian and imperial regent, this time the archbishop of Mainz, Siegfried III of Eppstein (1230–49). The attempt to integrate the Babenberg duchies of Austria and Styria into the imperial administration failed. The emperor's clearly stated intention, in contrast to the events of 1180, not to distribute the duchies of the outlawed duke among those who had participated in subduing him, caused the king of Bohemia and the duke of Bavaria to ally with the Babenberger against the emperor, after Frederick II's departure for Italy in autumn 1237. This, and the further sharpening of the conflicts with the pope, even forced the emperor to cancel the outlawry of the Babenberger and to recognize him once again as duke of Austria and Styria. Only after duke Frederick's childless death in 1246 did both duchies come into the emperor's control. In the following years, under different governors, he tried to build up a strictly organized imperial administration on the Sicilian model, which, however, only partially succeeded.

[*f*] THE STRUGGLE FOR SUPREMACY BETWEEN EMPIRE AND PAPACY

In the mean time the situation in the empire, and especially the relationship between emperor and pope, had changed fundamentally. After his return to imperial Italy, Frederick II resumed the fight against the rebellious Lombards, whom he had repeatedly accused of heresy, a charge aimed especially at Milan. There meanwhile the papal legates had been working against the emperor. It came to an open breach between Pope Gregory IX, who again tried to send the emperor off on a crusade, and Frederick who gave absolute priority to the fight against the enemies of the empire in northern Italy. At the end of November 1237 near Cortenuova Frederick II defeated the Milanese and their allies, with the support of the confederated cities of Pavia, Cremona, Verona, Parma, Reggio, Modena, and Ferrara, the troops of Ezzelino da Romano (from 1238 the emperor's son-in-law), and 10,000 Saracens from the settlement of Lucera which Frederick had previously founded. He rejected a peace offer from the Milanese, and demanded unconditional surrender. Only in this way did it seem to him possible to enforce an intensive imperial administration on northern Italy, which was economically highly developed and therefore also politically extremely important.

Under the authoritative influence of Peter de Vinea, the emperor's chancery in a letter to the kings and princes of Europe stylized the struggle against the Lombard rebels into a fundamental dispute between legitimate royal or princely power, and the rebels. His call to send forces for the fight against Milan was answered by the kings of France, England, Castile, and Hungary and even by the emperor of Nicaea, John III Ducas Vatatzes, who later (1244) married one of Frederick II's illegitimate daughters. From Germany a large and well-armed contingent arrived in northern Italy in June 1238, and furthermore a troop of Saracens from the Sicilian kingdom. In spite of this the siege of Brescia, begun in July 1238, did not lead to the desired success and had to be broken off in September. Following this the opposition in northern Italy grew, and to it the pope now openly showed his support. The emperor on his part created another conflict with the pope when in October 1238 he married his illegitimate son Enzio to Adelasia, the heiress of the judicates of Torres and Gallura on the island of Sardinia. From the eighth century Sardinia had belonged to the area claimed by the papacy, which based this claim on the 'Donation of Constantine'.

The long-awaited second excommunication of the emperor on Palm Sunday, 20 March 1239, was justified by the pope with sixteen accusations. Eleven of them concerned the kingdom of Sicily alone, especially imperial policy towards the Church; others related to Frederick II's political position towards the papal city of Rome. In the vehement propaganda war which now began, the emperor tried to defend himself against the papal accusations by an appeal to a council. In July 1239 the accusations of the papal Curia reached a first climax in an open letter. In this the pope characterized the emperor as a forerunner of Antichrist, and imputed to him the remark 'the whole world has been deceived by three impostors, namely Jesus Christ, Moses, and Muhammad'. Furthermore the emperor was said to have called fools all those 'who believe that God could be born of a virgin', as 'nobody could be born whose begetting was not preceded by the union of man and woman'; also 'man ought not to believe anything other than what could be proved by the power and reason of nature' [538: i. 455].

More important than the emperor's replies to these accusations was the occupation in 1240 of the duchy of Spoleto, the margraviate of Ancona, and also southern Tuscany, thus of wide areas of the Patrimony of St Peter which had been separated from the imperial administration and placed under papal overlordship from the time of Innocent III. Furthermore the emperor had taken prisoner on their journey most of the foreign participants in a council called to Rome for May 1241 by Gregory IX. In August 1241 the emperor abstained from his planned attack on the city of Rome when he learnt of Gregory IX's death, as he first wanted to await the new election. When the emperor later released other influential cardinals, in June 1243, after a long, only briefly interrupted vacancy, the Genoese cardinal and great legal scholar Sinibaldo Fieschi was elected and enthroned as Innocent IV (1243–54).

In Germany the emperor's excommunication at first had little effect. Only in autumn 1241—after the acute danger of wide areas of central Europe being conquered by the Mongols had passed—did the archbishop of Cologne, Conrad of Hochstaden (1238–61), and the imperial regent Archbishop Siegfried of Mainz make a pact against the emperor. The decisive motive for this change of sides by the archbishop of Mainz was apparently territorial–political considerations, mainly concerning the imperial abbey of Lorsch assigned to him by Frederick II, which was in the sphere of interest of the pro-Staufen count palatine of the Rhine. The activities of the two archbishops mainly concentrated on the middle Rhine area, the '*vis maxima regni*', but they were at first without effect. The breakaway movement from the Staufen party, however, became stronger in 1244 when the recently initiated negotiations between the emperor and Pope Innocent IV broke down and the pope went via Genoa to Lyons, where he remained until Frederick II's death. There he called together a council for the year 1245.

Before this assembled, the pope again showed his willingness to absolve the emperor from excommunication. The renewed conquest of Jerusalem in 1244 by the Muslims and the hopeless situation in the Holy Land certainly gave a strong impetus to the papal readiness to negotiate. But it did not come to negotiations, if only because the emperor had further attacks carried out in the patrimony of St Peter and thereby flouted important conditions of the peace efforts, which had already failed because of attempts to include the rebellious Lombards.

In July 1245 at the Council of Lyons, which only a few bishops from the empire attended, the pope solemnly announced the deposition of Frederick II as emperor, German king, and king of the Sicilian *regnum* because of perjury, breach of the peace, sacrilege because of taking the prelates prisoner, and suspicion of heresy. This act included a summons to the German electors to elect a new *rex Romanorum*. The kings of France, England, and Castile, however, remained neutral in the following period. Only the king of Hungary was openly on the side of the pope.

The election of the Landgrave Henry Raspe of Thuringia in May 1246—he had been made imperial regent by the emperor in 1242—by the archbishops of Cologne and Mainz and with the consent of the archbishop of Trier, did not bring about any considerable change in the German empire. More important was the integration, admittedly only partial, of the duchies of Austria and Styria into the imperial administration. After Henry Raspe's death in February 1247, the three archbishops in October 1247 elected Count William of Holland as anti-king, who to begin with could only rely on his electors, some bishops, and the duke of Brabant; but soon he won over the city of Cologne.

Innocent IV, who had given the first anti-king considerable financial support (25,000 marks in silver), had the dispute fought primarily by ecclesiastical and religious means. Followers of the Staufen party among the episcopate he threatened with deposition, which, however, was carried out only in a few cases. The pope also gave his legates authority to dispense secular rulers from marriages, which in view of the great importance of marriage especially in territorial politics meant more than just a personal indulgence towards the secular princes. He had the clergy and the mendicant orders preach the crusade against the emperor, by promising everyone who participated in the military campaign against the Staufen the same favours—among them especially absolution of sins—as the participants in the crusade to the Holy Land received: i.e. in the crusade which the pope had preached at the Council of Lyons with little success, and for which Louis IX set off in 1248.

In a letter of July 1246 to the papal legate in Germany, Pope Innocent IV expressly ordered that preaching for the planned crusade in Palestine should take second place to that of the crusade against the emperor, but without making these recommendations public. As early as the beginning of 1246 the imperial chancery, in a circular letter to numerous Christian rulers, had pointed out the consequences of the papal measures: 'What then should you not fear . . . from such a priestly prince, when he who is not entitled to do so dares to depose Us, who by solemn election by the princes and with the consent of the whole Church . . . according to God's bidding are decorated with the imperial crown, and gloriously rule other noble kingdoms as well' [1: ii. 50, no. 46]. In the same letter the emperor also criticizes the life of the higher clergy, including the pope, a criticism also partly made by heretics: 'The enormous incomes with which they enrich themselves by exploiting many kingdoms truly make them mad.' Therefore it was his intention 'to lead the clerics of every kind, but especially the highest ones, to the condition in which they were in the early Church, imitating the Lord's humility in an apostolic way of life . . . For this you and all princes must use every endeavour to make them shed everything unnecessary and to serve God, content with moderate possessions.'

The activities of the papal party in the course of 1248 brought some successes in Germany and imperial Italy. Among them was the defeat of the imperial army in February 1248 at the siege of the city of Parma, which shortly before had broken with the emperor. It meant a great loss of prestige for the emperor that the siege camp which he erected and all too optimistically named 'Victoria' was destroyed in this, and that part of his treasure and his insignia were lost.

In autumn 1249 the new anti-king, William of Holland, made progress by conquering the imperial cities of Kaiserswerth, Dortmund, and Aachen, so that he could finally be crowned king in Aachen by the archbishop of Cologne. In his attempt to gain a further foothold on the middle Rhine during the next two years, however, he failed because of the resistance of the imperial cities of Boppard, Frankfurt, and Gelnhausen. In imperial Italy the loss of cities so far friendly towards the Staufen ('Ghibellines'), in which power was now taken over by parties opposed to the Staufen ('Guelfs'), continued after the defeat at Parma and the capture of Enzio. On the other hand the imperial troops successfully repelled the military advances of the papacy in the margraviate of Ancona, the duchy of Spoleto, and the Romagna. At the same time Frederick II turned the severe defeat of the French king on the crusade near Mansura in April 1250, during which Louis IX was taken prisoner, against the pope, who had had the crusade preached against the Staufen instead of against the pagans, and for this had used considerable sums raised from the Church. Now the pope was urged by the French royal family and Burgundian nobles to make peace with the emperor.

Frederick II's prospects in the fight against the pope were not bad. His sudden death on 13 December 1250 at Castel Fiorentino, not far from his favourite palace at Foggia in the Capitanata, fundamentally changed the political constellation in Europe. According to Matthew Paris, during his absolution by Archbishop Berard of Palermo, who undertook this despite the papal excommunication, he was dressed in the habit of a Cistercian. He was, however, buried in his splendid imperial robes in a sarcophagus made from porphyry, the imperial stone, in Palermo cathedral. When Frederick's grave was opened in 1782 his body was found wrapped in precious Arab robes made from red silk embroidered with mysterious Arabic patterns. On his left shoulder he wore a cross, in memory of his crusade in 1228-9.

[g] THE EMPIRE AFTER THE DEATH OF FREDERICK II

The term 'interregnum' can be misleading, as one cannot speak of the period between 1250 and 1272 as an 'interval between rulers' in the legal sense. In fact after Frederick's death the kingship in Germany remained in existence almost without interruption. This is also true for the period from 1256, when King William died, to 1273 when the Habsburg Count Rudolf was elected and crowned. In this period, the reign of Richard of Cornwall, who in 1257 had been elected by a princely party and who was finally crowned king in Aachen by the competent archbishop, that of Cologne, a legal *rex Romanorum* existed until Richard's death in April 1272. Admittedly he was not recognized by all the princes. In the same year, 1257, another group of princes elected Alfonso of Castile as *rex Romanorum*, who never set foot on German imperial soil and therefore was never crowned. Richard of Cornwall on the other hand spent almost four years in Germany. Both competitors were closely related to the Staufen: Alfonso of Castile was a grandson of Philip of Swabia; Richard of Cornwall was a nephew of Emperor Otto IV, brother of the English King Henry, and Frederick II's brother-in-law.

In his will Frederick II had provided that his eldest legitimate son Conrad IV should take over the kingdom of Sicily as well as the empire. In 1252 Conrad IV, who by hereditary right could also claim the kingdom of Jerusalem, went to Italy, where his younger half-brother Manfred (b. 1232) for the time being had taken over the regency of the kingdom of Sicily for him, but in May 1254 he died. He left a son, Conradin, only two years old. In 1258 Manfred had himself crowned king of Sicily, disregarding his nephew, who was a minor. From Sicily he intervened in imperial Italy. In this he linked up with institutions and political configurations from Frederick II's reign; he also gained influence in the patrimony of St Peter. The papacy's efforts to find an effective candidate of their own for the Sicilian throne led to success only in 1263, when Charles of Anjou, the brother of the king of France, declared his willingness to fight for the Staufen hereditary empire, acknowledging papal suzerainty. In 1266 he was crowned king of Sicily in St Peter's, Rome. In the same year he defeated Manfred in the battle of Benevento. Two years after the death of Manfred, Charles of Anjou, who also won influence in imperial Italy, defeated Conradin, the last Staufen candidate for the throne, whom he subsequently had executed.

In Germany Staufen rule had already come to an end one and a half decades earlier with the death of Conrad IV. A power vacuum appeared in the German kingdom, in which the imperial princes especially managed to extend their supremacy by exploiting the monarchy, which was effective only sometimes, in some places. In this way some of the essential characteristics of the late medieval empire were prefigured in these two decades.

A year and a half after Frederick's death—i.e. while Conrad was still in Germany—King William obtained recognition from the Ascanian margrave of Brandenburg, and from the duke of Saxony, who was from the same family, as well as that of the Rhenish archbishops on whose support he had previously been completely dependent. In this he had the advantage of having just married the daughter of the Welf Duke Otto of Brunswick, who was related by marriage to the Ascanians. With this recognition by the Ascanians, the legal position of the anti-king to a large extent corresponded to the interpretation predominant in north Germany, as formulated a few decades before by Eike of Repgow in the *Sachsenspiegel*. According to this, the three Rhenish archbishops, the count palatine of the Rhine, the duke of Saxony, and the margrave of Brandenburg had the right of electing the king before all other imperial princes. Favoured by Conrad's departure to imperial Italy and even more by the death of this Staufen rival, William soon obtained the consent of important towns (like Goslar, Nordhausen, Mühlhausen, Frankfurt, Gelnhausen, Speyer, Worms, Oppenheim, and Hagenau) as well as of other cities formerly friendly to the Staufen.

In July 1254, after Conrad's death, numerous cities, among them Mainz, Cologne, Worms, Speyer, Strasbourg, and Basle, joined together in a public peace treaty (*fedus sancte pacis*) [17: ii. 579–89, no. 428]. They were joined almost immediately by the three Rhenish archbishops, the bishops of Worms, Strasbourg, Metz, and Basle and also numerous nobles. It quickly spread, and in 1255 embraced about 70 towns in the Rhineland, Westphalia, and southern, central, and northern Germany, as well as numerous ecclesiastical and secular lords. King William recognized this heterogeneous public peace union in February 1255. The union, whose unity was considerably lessened by the great increase in its members, after William's death (28 January 1256) even exerted itself in maintaining imperial interests, in which admittedly only the towns were active.

In spite of the obligation of the members in the event of a double election not to support either candidate, the 'Rhenish League' could not prevent the double election of 1257. In January 1257, the archbishops of Cologne and Mainz and also the Wittelsbach count palatine of the Rhine elected Richard of Cornwall king; King Ottokar of Bohemia agreed to this election. The English prince had paid a considerable price for his election. The archbishops of Cologne and Mainz each received 8,000 marks in silver, the count palatine was promised an English princess with a dowry of 12,000 marks. At the election of King Alfonso on 1 April 1257, on the other hand, Archbishop Arnold of Trier (1242–59) was a leading participant; furthermore the duke of Saxony and the margrave of Brandenburg, and again—in spite of his previous vote in favour of Richard—the king of Bohemia were also involved. The double election of 1257 became decisive for the later history of electoral rights. In practice the right of royal election, in which originally all imperial princes participated, was narrowed down to the holders of the first votes, who thereby grew into the role of Electors.

While King Richard of Cornwall largely remained restricted in his field of action to the area left of the Rhine with its centre at Aachen, in the east a new power block was established under King Ottokar II, whose membership of the group of imperial princes was again expressed in his participation in the royal election. Ottokar himself was several times suggested as a candidate for the title of *rex Romanorum*. To this eminent role in the empire he was marked out by his close relationship with the Staufen as well as because of his successful territorial policy, which was connected with plans for expansion into the pagan Baltic area, supported by crusades into the regions of the Teutonic Order. The Bohemian king, born *c.* 1230, was the grandson of King Philip of Swabia. Furthermore he had married the widow of Henry (VII), Margaret (born *c.* 1210), two decades his senior, who after her husband's death had lived in a Dominican convent in Trier. Ottokar readily obtained the pope's dispensation for this marriage. He was thus able to secure for himself the Staufen duchy of Austria. In 1261 he also acquired the duchy of Styria. The possession of both duchies was legalized in 1262 by King Richard, with the enfeoffment of Ottokar. Four years later, King Richard also made the Bohemian king imperial vicar in the areas to the right of the Rhine. In 1269 the duchy of Carinthia with Krain devolved upon him.

This power base gave Ottokar II a good start in the royal election which became necessary after Richard of Cornwall's death in 1272. But the electors decided in favour of the far less powerful Count Rudolf of Habsburg. Although proposed by the Italian Ghibellines, another descendant of the Staufen—Frederick, born in 1257 of the marriage between the emperor's daughter Margaret and the Margrave Albert of Meissen—was excluded, especially as the pope had expressly forbidden his election. The other surviving Staufen from the male line of Frederick II, namely the three sons of Manfred of Sicily, had been thrown into prison by Charles of Anjou after the battle of Benevento. Enzio (1300) and Henry (1318) died there. Frederick escaped in the first years of the fourteenth century; he stayed for a while at various European courts, but eventually disappeared. He is supposed to have died in Egypt in 1312.

Under Rudolf of Habsburg the rumour of the return of the Staufen emperor Frederick repeatedly arose in urban opposition circles. In Alsace, on the lower Rhine, and in the Wetterau, in Swabia, and even in Lübeck around the middle of the eighties alleged 'Emperor Fredericks' were active. These, however, were soon hanged, drowned, or burnt. The most successful among them was Tile Kolup. Although he was driven out of Cologne, he was soon much sought after in Neuss and finally in Wetzlar; he was even visited by Italian supporters of the Staufen. Rudolf of Habsburg had to take military action against him, until the 'game' ended gruesomely by Tile's being burnt as a heretic and sorcerer in July 1285.

2

Continuity and Change
in Lordship

[a] FAMILY RELATIONSHIPS, HEREDITARY RIGHTS, AND FIEFS

For imperial history and the system of lordship in the empire the individual, personal behaviour and fate of kings and emperors remained of great importance, as did that of other powerful men—one only has to remember the consequences of the early death of Henry VI and the profound breach created by the death of his son Frederick II about half a century later. In both cases long conflicts ensued over the succession to the throne. In the three-quarters of a century between the death of Henry VI and the election of Rudolf of Habsburg the kingship was undisputed for only twenty-five years. Each of the opponents could point to an election by the princes. The Staufen line mainly based its claim on blood right within the narrower family. Their opponents, however, were also more or less closely related to the Staufen family. Even in an election directed against the Staufen succession to the throne, therefore, the princes felt tied to relatives of the sovereign's family. The electors and the papal Curia believed only such people capable of an effective anti-kingship.

This evaluation of power politics corresponded with the widespread dynastic attitude, which seems to have deepened in the Staufen period. When Pope Innocent III in 1202 condemned the Staufen as a family of persecutors of the Church (*genus persectorum*) and contrasted the Welfs positively to them, he alluded to this politically anchored attitude. In spite of this, the same pope could not help turning to the Staufen again.

Frederick II on his part raised the position of his family almost to sacral dimensions by having it incorporated into the expectations of the end of the world which were widely held at the time. After his return from the crusade, the Staufen family was represented in a sermon in the cathedral of Bitonto as the last imperial family in the history of mankind; it would rule until the end of world. This lent added weight to the papal opposition to the emperor, and even to his distant descendants. This religious–political attitude clearly favoured the effectiveness of the pseudo-Staufen pretenders under Rudolf of Habsburg, among the urban population.

The marriage policies which created relationships and which were intended to underpin political relations and create hereditary claims, under the Staufen were not only used to bind individual noble families within the empire closer to the royal family; they now also became a crucial instrument of far-reaching Staufen policies. For the twelve children that Barbarossa's second wife Beatrice of Burgundy bore him, he began marriage negotiations with the following: the later king of Sicily, the daughter of the king of England, the aunt of the Sicilian king and later heiress of the kingdom, the daughter of the king of Hungary, the daughter of the extremely wealthy count of Blois-Champagne, the later king of Hungary, an English prince, the heiress of the kingdom of Castile, the influential margrave of Montferrat, and also the daughter of the Byzantine emperor. Of these for various reasons only the following took place: with the heiress of the kingdom of Sicily (Constance and Henry VI); with the daughter of the count of Blois-Champagne (Margaret and Otto of Burgundy); with the margrave of Montferrat (Sophia and Margrave William II); and with the daughter of the Byzantine emperor (Irene and Philip of Swabia).

Barbarossa's grandson Frederick II first married the daughter of the king of Aragon, and by his second marriage the heiress of the kingdom of Jerusalem, and finally, after a relationship with the daughter of a margrave only legalized subsequently, the sister of the English King Henry III. By these four marriages there were altogether ten children. The emperor had at least nine other children from relationships with eight

other women. These illegitimate relationships had no re-
cognizable political background, but they certainly enabled
Pope Innocent IV to imply that the emperor had a harem of
Saracen women at his court. At the Council of Lyons the
imperial envoy countered these accusations by saying: 'The
emperor does not keep . . . the Saracen girls . . . for intercourse—
who could prove that?—but because of their dexterity and their
other artistic skills' [14: xxviii. 259]. Frederick II arranged
politically important marriages for his legitimate children as
well as for his 'bastards'—in which, however, he was not as
successful as Barbarossa. His sons Henry (VII) and Conrad IV,
installed as kings in Germany, significantly married daughters
from German noble families, so that the Norman Staufen
gained additional support in Germany.

The German high nobility also engaged in extensive marriage politics. Henry the Lion will serve as an example of this.
Henry's family-based consciousness is graphically depicted in
a miniature most probably executed in 1173 on the duke's
order. It was bound into the Gospels given by the ducal couple
to the church of St Blaise in Brunswick which Henry founded.
It represents the duke's coronation with his second wife
Matilda, the daughter of the king of England. The double duke
and his wife are receiving the crown directly from Christ: an
eloquent expression of divine right which seems to ignore the
feudal suzerainty of his imperial cousin. Looking on are the
Emperor Lothar III and his wife Richenza, and King Henry
II of England and his wife Eleanor of Aquitaine as well as his
mother Matilda, the widow of the last Salian emperor. Presented as additional witnesses are the parents of Henry the
Lion, i.e. Henry the Proud and his wife Gertrude, the daughter
of the Emperor Lothar III. In this way the royal and imperial
predecessors and relatives of the double duke are very clearly
emphasized. The claims of the Welf move on this level, as the
crowns which are placed on to his and his wife's heads by the
hand of God are similar in design to those of the royal and
imperial witnesses [626a: 124, 126 (pl.)].

Almost at the same time, around 1170, in the family monastery
of the southern German Welfs, in Weingarten (near Ravens-
burg), a comprehensive history of the Welfs was written: the
Historia Welforum, which was especially close to Welf VI. The

author traced the origins of the family back to pre-Christian times. The Welfs, he says, came from the Franks, who in turn stemmed from the Trojans. One of the earliest ancestors married the daughter of a Roman senator, called Catilina, and named his son after his Roman father-in-law Catulus (meaning 'whelp', *Welf*). The further rise of the family had mainly occurred because the Welfs had acquired for themselves huge estates and had fortified their residences. On this allodial basis, created by themselves, the Welfs had been in a position to surpass even kings in wealth and honour. Because of this, it continues, they were able to refuse homage to the Roman emperor. Around 1230 the Premonstratensian Burchard of Ursberg in Swabia brought the historical self-image of the Welfs up to date: 'This family was illustrious and of the highest nobility, so that it was always devoted to God, always served the Roman Church and often opposed the emperors' [16: xvi. 8].

The 'oppositional spirit' of the high nobility, based on ancestry and family, also expressed itself politically, for instance in a letter of 1161 sent to the French king by the Zähringer Duke Berthold IV, then still the brother-in-law of Henry the Lion. Shortly before, Barbarossa had refused to invest Berthold's brother as archbishop of Mainz after his election; so the Zähringer promised the French king, who in the papal schism favoured the anti-imperial Pope Alexander III, his full support in the dispute with the emperor, and in doing so trusted in his relatives. Many of the more powerful German princes were bound to him, he said—the Zähringer being in rank equal to a king—by affection or relationship, many also by hatred towards the emperor.

Besides the ancient means of family relationship, in the Staufen period feudal ties continued to play a large political role, probably to an increased degree. Like the popes, the Staufen used feudalism to express their superiority over otherwise independent powers. They used this instrument in the border zones of the empire and in more distant areas of interest. As under the Salians, so under the Staufen, some of the Polish dukes entered into feudal ties with the kings and emperors. One of them was Boleslav IV (1146–73). After a campaign in 1157, which he had undertaken in the interests of the Bohemian Duke Vladislav II (1140–73), a relative by marriage of Conrad III,

Frederick I forced Boleslav to swear an oath of allegiance, to pay reparations, and to hand over Silesia to Vladislav's heirs. Something similar happened to the kings of Denmark; Valdemar I (1157–82) was enfeoffed with the kingdom of Denmark in 1162. Even King Richard the Lionheart of England had to swear an oath of fealty as a condition of his release from imprisonment by the Emperor Henry VI, so that he counted as one of the imperial princes during the struggle for the throne. In 1195 the king of Cyprus, whose island kingdom had been torn out of the Byzantine empire in 1191 by Richard the Lionheart, also entered into feudal dependency on the empire. During his crusade Frederick II once more renewed this feudal dependency. On the other hand, Frederick II and also Otto IV under the pressure of circumstances temporarily acknowledged the feudal ties of the Sicilian kingdom with the papacy, even if the Staufen before and afterwards insisted that the kingdom belonged to the empire. But in this case too they did not base their legal title on a general idea of world rulership, but on hereditary right, which Henry VI had to impose against his competitor by force.

The empire did not have fixed borders in the modern exclusive sense. From this point of view as well, the intensively discussed alternatives 'national state' or 'universal state' are misleading. Thus several German high nobles and even ecclesiastical princes independently made political contacts, which could go as far as treaties with powers outside the narrower empire, especially when in conflict with the king. The higher nobility in the *regnum Arelatense* maintained close political relations with the French and also the Spanish kings. These were often deepened by feudal ties. German nobles entered into feudal relationships with the English and French kings, even if only in the form of money fiefs. It has recently been justifiably emphasized that particularly between France and Germany only a wide, indefinite border existed. 'The feudalism of the high Middle Ages was of its nature supranational and knew no borders' [330: 542].

This openness was not only restricted to border areas, in which political influence wavered according to the power-political situation: it was true for the whole of the empire. The deeper reason for this lay in the structure of imperial rule. In

Germany, and even more in Burgundy, it was typologically an 'aristocracy with a monarchic head'. For imperial Italy, especially from the Staufen period onwards, it can be better characterized as a monarchy based on independent communal, noble, and ecclesiastical holders of formally delegated lordship rights. This constitutional difference, which reflects different traditions of lordship on either side of the Alps, made very little difference to the large radius of action which the more powerful city communes of imperial Italy, themselves led by an aristocracy, were able to maintain in spite of opposing tendencies in the Staufen imperial government. The openness of imperial rule in Germany was no doubt increased by the tendency towards universalism in the Staufen period, which was not at all restricted to the Staufen. It is just as much an established fact that thereby in a complex interplay the 'aristocracy' in its various forms gained greater possibilities for development.

It was decisive for the closeness of the 'aristocracy' to the 'monarchic head' that the Staufen rulers were not able to eliminate the election rights of the German princes in the succession to the throne in favour of hereditary right despite many attempts to do so, culminating in Henry VI's plan for a hereditary empire. This disadvantage was all the more serious in that the German high nobility was able at the same time to establish its hereditary rights in imperial fiefs. In most cases the emperor was forced to redistribute escheated imperial fees to the princes after a short while, in clear contrast to the English and French kings. It was this constraint that forced Frederick I to redistribute the imperial fees of which Henry the Lion had been legally deprived. When the landgraviate of Thuringia reverted (1190), Henry VI had to give it to the brother of the late landgrave. However, from 1195 on, the emperor was able for the time being to keep the margraviate of Meissen. But in 1227 Frederick II promised Landgrave Hermann II of Thuringia, who was a minor, enfeoffment with the margraviate of Meissen, even if the father should die before the son's coming of age. The confiscation of the duchies of Austria and Styria by the same emperor after the Babenbergers died out in 1246 had to be reversed after the death of Frederick II.

Earlier research generally fixed the closing of the group of imperial princes with the trial of Henry the Lion (1180). This

meant that from this time onwards only nobles and ecclesiastical lords who were in direct feudal relations with the
king, and who were committed to service and an oath of fealty
to him only, counted as *principes*, entitled to rights in the empire.
But in reality the exclusion of the other rulers from this narrower circle of imperial princes, who were recruited mainly
from the dukes and equivalent nobles and ecclesiastical lords,
only represented a long-term trend, which was probably
hastened by the events of 1180, but which was not yet a reality
at that point. From then on the *principes regni* or *imperii* came
forward even more as a group with common interests even
against the king and which, especially from the period of disputed succession to the throne, insisted on enforcing their pre-
eminence. This was generally acknowledged for the ecclesiastical princes by Frederick II in the *Confoederatio* (1220), and for the
ecclesiastical and secular princes in the *Statutum* (1231/2) of
Henry (VII) and Frederick. The growing exclusiveness of the
princes of the empire derived from their endeavours to make
the other lords feudally dependent on themselves, and to incorporate them into their own territorial lordships, and thus to
pull them out of a direct legal relationship with the monarchy.

Closely connected with this long-term process, the theory of
the *Heerschildordnung* (the 'order of military ranks'), was formulated for the first time coherently around 1220 in the *Sachsenspiegel* of Eike of Repgow. Originally, *Heerschild* (*clipeus
militaris*) meant the right to raise vassals for military service;
but from the late twelfth century on the term increasingly
referred to the position of each vassal within the hierarchy of
the feudal system. At its head was the king. On the second and
third steps he was followed by the ecclesiastical and secular
princes, who were otherwise equal. The fourth, according to
J. von Ficker the *Normalschild*, was in danger of being mediat-
ized by the ecclesiastical and secular lords. This was followed by
further ranks: the vassals of the fourth *Heerschild* down to the
ministerials or the servicemen, the so-called *Einschildritter*. The
latter could only receive fiefs but not grant them. It has to be
kept in mind that the *Heerschildordnung*, which was taken over
by the *Schwabenspiegel* around 1270, did not mean a 'system of
compulsory norms', particularly at the lower levels, but only a
'prescribed order'. It certainly cannot be equated with social

strata, as is generally done when legal systematization is carried over uncritically into history.

The ecclesiastical princes were given the second rank in the *Heerschildordnung*, even before the secular princes—not least to take account of the fact that many secular princes held large ecclesiastical fiefs and often did only small service in return for them. The kings also made use of Church property in this way—mainly in the second half of the twelfth century. The ecclesiastical princes belonged to the *Heerschild* in consequence of their incorporation into the imperial feudal system. This took firmer shape after the Concordat of Worms, and from it Frederick I still drew advantages for imperial rule. Thus he refused to grant the *regalia* to his Babenberg relative Bishop Conrad of Passau, who had been elected archbishop of Salzburg by the chapter and the ministerials in 1164, because he did not recognize the imperial pope. In a suit under feudal law, similar to that against Henry the Lion in 1180, the emperor had the elected archbishop summoned three times and finally sentenced, as the Babenberger had occupied the archbishopric by usurpation and had neither been granted the *regalia* by the emperor nor the spiritualities by the imperial pope.

But from the struggle for the throne at the latest, the assimilation of the ecclesiastical and secular princes proved disadvantageous for the transformed royal lordship over the Church. From this time onwards, more than before, fuedalism became an instrument of the princes. Its centripetal powers, which Henry II of England and Philip II Augustus of France in their different power systems were able to strengthen, at the latest by the turn of the thirteenth century slipped out of the hands of the Roman kings in favour of the princes. The comparison demonstrates the ambivalence of feudalism. Its shape reflected the relevant power structure: its laws influenced the realities of power politics only to a limited extent.

Under Barbarossa, particularly in the fifties and sixties, the ecclesiastical princes continued to make a considerable military and financial contribution to imperial policies, then concentrated on Italy. But the limits of feudal service were already clearly outlined. On his fourth Italian campaign of 1166/7, the emperor used mercenaries to supplement the imperial army; the German contingents were also rewarded financially. The emperor primarily obtained the money necessary for this from the cities of imperial Italy. For this reason too, access to finance became increasingly important. In his wars in imperial Italy Frederick II relied only to a small extent on his German imperial vassals. For his actions against the Lombard League from the 1230s onwards, he fell back on the Saracens billeted in Lucera and the contingents of his Italian allies. While the imperial ministerials in the time of Frederick I and Henry VI still served as important supports of imperial interests south of the Alps, they only played a subordinate role in this field under Frederick II. In the same decades, again accelerated by the struggle over the throne, the ministerials, especially the imperial ones, supplanted their service bonds with fief-like or even feudal relationships.

[b] THE POSITION OF CHURCHES AND MONASTERIES

The assimilation of the imperial bishops to the nobility was also expressed in the grant of duchies to individual bishops. One example is the grant of the duchy of Westphalia to the archbishop of Cologne in the Gelnhausen charter of 1180. Archbishop Philip probably raised large sums for the imperial treasury in return. According to the inscription on his tomb, he procured the huge sum of 50,000 marks in silver for the acquisition of his duchy. After the defeat of Henry the Lion Archbishop Philip soon landed in severe territorial political disputes with the emperor, the connections of which with the rest of imperial politics have already been mentioned. A similar process in the long run resulted from the granting of the duchy of Franconia to the bishop of Würzburg in 1168. The bishops were unable to make their legal title a reality, not least because of the strong position of the Staufen ministerials. Under Henry (VII) the conflict between the bishops and the imperial ministerials again came to a head; the latter fought for their own advantage as well as for royal interests. The imperial laws of 1220 and 1231/2 were also directed against such measures by the king and the imperial ministerials.

Alongside this trend towards independence, which really only set in from the late twelfth century and especially from the period of conflict for the throne, it must not be ignored that quite a few high clerics in the reign of Frederick I still proved extremely useful in the imperial service. Among them at the beginning of Barbarossa's reign was Abbot Wibald of Stablo-Malmédy, the last imperial abbot to occupy an eminent position at the royal court in the Middle Ages. He was first succeeded by Bishop Eberhard of Bamberg. He was followed as the emperor's most important adviser for more than ten years by Rainald of Dassel, the most eminent politician of his time, who in 1156 rose to be chancellor and three years later to be archbishop of Cologne. A similar position to that of Rainald of Dassel from the middle of the sixties on, and particularly after the death of the archbishop of Cologne, was held by Christian of Buch, who also originated from a lesser noble family. In 1165 the emperor made this skilled politician, who could speak five languages, archbishop of Mainz, after having deposed his predecessor Conrad of Wittelsbach, a supporter of Alexander III. During his period of office, nearly two decades (1165–83), Christian was almost entirely occupied with the imperial service. From 1171 on he was continually in imperial Italy. When after Christian's death Conrad of Wittelsbach was finally able to return to the archbishopric of Mainz (1183–1200), he described emphatically the ruinous condition of the see, which Christian had burdened with high debts. Many estates of the archbishopric had been mortgaged, and a great number had come under the power of imperial ministerials. Finally the annual revenues of the archbishop had all been used up, except for a small remainder, by the long stay in Mainz of the imperial court and the costly festival which Barbarossa held there to celebrate the knighting of his eldest son in 1184.

As this complaint makes clear, Barbarossa had succeeded in maintaining the traditional services of the imperial churches. Besides army and court duties, which also weighed to some extent on the lay vassals, the early Staufen considerably burdened the imperial churches and abbeys with hospitality dues for the wandering royal court and its often large following. Furthermore they demanded the rights of *regalia* and *spolia*, which the kings had had to renounce after the struggle for the throne. These two terms, which were not clearly distinguished from one another, meant the right of the king to confiscate at least part of the personal property of imperial bishops and abbots on their death, and during episcopal vacancies to use the property, lordship rights, and estates of cathedrals and imperial monasteries. From the middle of the eighties onwards the papal Curia's criticism of these relics of private church rights increased, in order to recruit supporters of the papal policies. However, the papacy had limited success in this until the outbreak of the struggle for the throne.

In a letter to the Roman cardinals, the ecclesiastical princes of the empire listed the most important reasons for their pro-imperial attitude in the conflict between emperor and pope which broke out again in 1186: they would especially suffer in the dispute between the two powers; a continuation of the struggle would diminish the ecclesiastical estates and lead to the ruin of the churches. 'Since many princes, noblemen, and vassals already own much of our Church property, they daily hunger for more and are only waiting for the opportunity to pounce upon our estates to make use of them for themselves' [17: i. 447, no. 316].

Despite being the product of a specific situation, this letter demonstrates the basic community of interest between the emperor and the imperial churches. As the emperor needed the imperial Church to limit the predominance of the nobility, so the ecclesiatical princes looked to the emperor for support against the high nobility, from which, however, they themselves usually originated. Their fight against the emperor, which the papacy—the head of the official Church—demanded, posed a threat to the basis of the imperial Church's existence. This connection restricted the effectiveness of papal intervention among the imperial episcopate during the struggle for the throne, and even in the final phase of Frederick II's conflict with the papacy. The emperor on the other hand, because of the opposition of many prelates during this period, was prepared for drastic consequences, which went as far as depriving the Church of its power and forcibly 'converting' it to poverty.

Frederick I and also Henry VI were generally still in a position to invest clerics whom they trusted with the imperial churches and monasteries, especially within the narrower imperial lands and their periphery. In this they exploited the Concordat of Worms of 1122 to the limit, in so far as they felt

committed to it at all. The course of the dispute over the archbishopric of Trier between 1183 and 1189 sufficiently demonstrates that the imperial court did not hesitate to use violence
to enforce its candidate. Henry VI took prisoner the followers
in Trier and Koblenz of Archbishop Folmar, whom the pope
supported and had consecrated, he had their estates pillaged
and Folmar's house pulled down. During the struggle for the
throne the competitors for the kingship had to proceed differently in this respect as well. Thus during his stay in Trier in
October 1202 King Philip, in agreement with Archbishop John
of Trier, made a formal sworn treaty with the prelates, clerics,
abbots, minsterials, and citizens of Trier to make them favourable to a candidate for the archbishopric who would be
loyal to the king at the next vacancy of the see. For this Philip
promised his allies at Trier amongst other things a reduction
in payments to the royal toll stations at Cochem and Ham-
merstein [17: ii. 7 f., no. 7]. This treaty was all the more important for the Staufen, as already in 1198 the Welf party, through
the archbishop of Cologne, had persuaded Archbishop John
(1189–1212) to decide for Otto IV in return for financial support. Thus Innocent III in a letter of November 1202 could
rightly reproach the archbishop of Trier with conspiring with
the citizens of Trier, and some clerics and ministerials, to the
disadvantage of the pope.

After the momentous weakening of royal power in the decades of the struggle for the throne, the high noble families,
whose members generally dominated the chapters—but who
often competed with one another too—gained more influence
on episcopal elections. The importance of cathedral chapters
as election committees grew from this time onwards. Now the
papacy also interfered directly in the appointment of bishops,
though to begin with only in individual instances. But in general, development went in favour of the powerful noble families
and of associations led by them. As an example of this we may
cite the counts of Berg, whose narrower territorial political
influence reached up to the gates of Cologne. Under Archbishop Bruno III, who occupied the see of Cologne in 1191,
the first member of this comital family to do so, his nephew
Adolf rose to be provost of the cathedral of Cologne. After

Bruno's death in 1193 this nephew became his successor. Although Adolf was deposed by Innocent III in 1205 during the course of the struggle for the throne, which he decisively influenced, he was finally able to win through against Bruno of Sayn, who at first was promoted by the pope. Adolf resigned in 1216, and was followed by his cousin Engelbert. During the conflict in 1225 over the county of Berg, which he claimed to inherit, Engelbert was murdered by his cousin's son Frederick of Isenburg, who himself had influential comrades-in-arms in his brothers, the bishops of Osnabrück and Münster.

The self-confidence of the usually high noble imperial princes of the Church at the end of Frederick II's reign is perhaps most significantly expressed in the tomb, created *c.*1250, of Archbishop Siegfried of Eppstein (1230–49) in the cathedral at Mainz. Next to the archbishop stand two considerably smaller figures. These depict the anti-kings Henry Raspe and William of Holland, raised by the Rhenish archbishops. The archbishop touches the crowns of both kings, or even places them on their heads. The 'interregnum' in fact offered the powerful ecclesiastical princes a favourable opportunity to establish and expand their position in imperial and territorial politics. The difference between this and episcopal power in other European countries, a contrast created much earlier but now even greater, aroused the astonishment of King Richard of Cornwall, as an English source for the year 1257 reports: 'Look what brave and warlike archbishops we have in Germany . . .' [14: xxvii. 480].

But it would be unwise to generalize about all German bishops from the eminent position of the Rhenish archbishops. Not a few bishops, especially those in the east, in new settlement areas, during the course of the twelfth and thirteenth centuries were forced to submit to local secular lords, even if their sees had not been subject to them since their foundation. This was already true for the bishoprics founded by Henry the Lion east of the Elbe. Even some of the older Benedictine monasteries with large estates came under the rule of the princes in the Staufen period. Only very few of the large circle of Cistercian and Premonstratensian monasteries kept their independence from the princes, remaining subject to the emperor alone. The only exceptions were a few Cistercian monasteries, for example

Salem on Lake Constance, which were favoured by the more effective imperial rule in the Staufen family lands.

The office of lay advocate was of crucial importance for the integration of churches and monasteries into lordship. The lay advocates held the most effective means of superiority. In single cases already in the twelfth century, and increasingly in the thirteenth, first bishops and then a few abbots succeeded in dissolving the advocates' rights or in ousting them by force, and in bringing them under their own control, generally by means of ministerials. Only those churches and monasteries which could restrict the power of their noble lay advocates achieved a secure princely position. This decided the question of whether they could build up their own lordship. Thus for the archbishop of Trier it was a decisive success when in 1197 he bought out the rights of the count palatine of the Rhine as lay advocate of the cathedral, and in this way no longer had to share power with him.

[c] IMPERIAL RULE, TERRITORIAL POLITICS, AND
MINISTERIALS

Over against the broad effectiveness of imperial rule and the wide political field of action of many imperial princes during the Staufen period in Germany, there stood a growing attempt to intensify lordship over smaller areas. There was no difference in principle between the two approaches. Frederick I and Henry VI carried on territorial politics to a far greater extent than their predecessors in the German empire. The struggle for the throne made the continuation of this policy considerably more difficult and also narrowed its geographical basis. As a result of the strengthened position meanwhile attained by the princes, under Frederick II and Henry (VII) a conflict of interest emerged between imperial 'universal politics', whose aims could ony be achieved with the support or at least the toleration of the princes, and the resumption of royal territorial policy. The ensuing conflict between empire and papacy left only a small range of action for Staufen territorial politics, which Frederick II nevertheless exploited when the duchies of Austria and Styria reverted.

In the territorial politics of king, princes, and other powers, the churches and monasteries from the mid twelfth century attained a high position, both as objectives and as bases. At the same time the rule of castles, markets, towns, and trade routes gained increasing importance. With their fortifications often attached to castles, the urban settlements not only fulfilled military functions; they were also economic 'islands of intensity' with a relatively high economic potential, providing their masters with the financial income which became more and more important. Other forms of development, like clearing activities and the foundation of villages, were connected with this urbanization process in the old settlement areas and in the eastern colonization districts.

The territorial policy of the Staufen was concentrated on the Salian–Staufen imperial lands. Its most effective instruments were the imperial ministerials, who acted as administrators from the palaces, castles, and towns. With the exception of the Harz region around the palace of Goslar and the area around Nijmegen, the north of Germany (beyond a line from Nordhausen to Dortmund) was barred to Staufen territorial politics even after the fall of Henry the Lion. This is also true for the areas left of the Rhine and west of the lower Moselle together with Lorraine, for Bavaria south of the Danube and east of the Lech, and for Bohemia. The larger area of the Welf property between the Lech, Lake Constance, and the Danube only came under the full control of the Staufen after Barbarossa's death. Frederick I had already won important positions between Ulm, St Gallen, and Basle from the inheritance of the count of Pfullendorf, whose only son and heir was a victim of the Roman epidemic of 1167. In the Black Forest the Staufen territorial policy only spread after the Zähringen family had died out in 1218.

Within the broader sphere of action of the Staufen imperial ministerials the thinly settled wood and forest areas were the favoured fields, as they allowed a continuous lordship to be built up. The forests (*forestes*) were restricted areas, excluding other users and lords. Such royal forests for example existed in the Heiliger Wald (*sylva sacra*) around Hagenau in northern Alsace, with such characteristic names as Forstfelden, Königsbruck, and Reichshofen. In the north of this area was the forest of *Lutra* around the Lauter with the residence of the imperial ministerial family of (Kaisers-)Lautern, who distinguished themselves in Italian politics in early Staufen times. West of Speyer as far as Neudahn stretched another thinly settled area with numerous imperial ministerials, whose castles built in or on rocks still today distinguish the Staufen country. Among them is the castle triad of Trifels, Anebos, and Scharfenberg. There was also the Dreieich forest south of Frankfurt, which joined up with the Büdinger imperial forest to the north-east, and the imperial forest around Frankfurt. In the surroundings of Nuremberg the Sebalder Wald to the north-east and the Lorenzer Wald to the south-east offered the imperial ministerials favourable opportunities for development. Another forest explains the cluster of imperial ministerials in the Cham area on the Regen in the Upper Palatinate. The same is true of the Egerland, and also of the Pleissenland around Altenburg in Thuringia, with the Kammer and Leina forests. The combination of forests and mines was characteristic of the north-eastern Harz area around the imperial administrative centre of Goslar, which was installed in Salian times. This concentration on areas offering greater opportunities for development and expansion minimized possibility of conflict with the king's princely competitors in territorial politics. On the other hand it also gave royal representatives a good chance to develop their own lordships.

Staufen territorial policies, just like those of the princes and other lords, were put together from numerous small and locally effective measures. The hard struggles over details are well demonstrated by a charter of Frederick I which the emperor made out in February 1158 during his stay in Hagenau; it was for the Cistercian monastery of Neuburg, a foundation of his father and the count of Lützelburg. In it, a few months before setting off on his second Italian campaign, the emperor established among other things that the animals of the monastery were allowed to graze in the Heiliger Forest, with the exception of sheep; the monastery might procure its firewood from the forest, but building wood only with the permission and supervision of imperial representatives. Ministerials and serfs of the emperor and their property were only to be placed under the control of the monastery with the agreement of the emperor

[19: x. 1. 345 f., no. 206]. Even more detailed rules were made by the imperial court in the city charter of liberties, made out in northern Italy in 1164 [19: x. 2. 346–9, no. 447] for Hagenau, where from 1160 onwards Barbarossa extended the palace which he later often used. Hagenau was also the base for ministerials with more than local responsibilities. The emperor obliged the Cistercian monastery of Neuburg, near which Barbarossa's father Duke Frederick II of Swabia had founded the Cistercian house of Königsbruck, to renounce its property rights in the Heiliger Forst, for which he compensated it with only a small estate at Seelhofen.

In these small-scale territorial politics, purchase also played an important role: thus in 1166 Frederick I bought the village of Eschbach from the abbey of Maursmünster for 100 marks of silver. In order to round out property complexes, exchanges were often made. Thus at the beginning of 1158 Barbarossa received the castle of Badenweiler with 100 ministerials and 500 manors from Henry the Lion, out of the inheritance of his wife Clementia of Zähringen. For this he gave the Welf the castles of Herzberg and Scharzfeld, situated in the imperial forest of the Harz, the estate of Pöhlde, and furthermore an imperial ministerial with his children, allod, and fief. Since these were imperial property—i.e. not Staufen property—the Staufen compensated the *regnum* with castles, estates, markets, and his ministerial Temo of Colditz with his children and all his goods and fiefs, which altogether made up twenty villae; these were Saxon properties which had come to him by inheritance or which he had bought from Count Rabodo of Abenberg for a large sum of money [19: x. 1. 332 f., no. 199].

Just as the ministerials played an eminent role in the territorial politics of the princes, the imperial ministerials were the most effective agents of Staufen imperial territorial politics. From the middle of the twelfth century onwards, their importance in general imperial politics increased even more. Especially in Italian politics under Barbarossa and Henry VI they found new fields of action and opportunities of rising, of which Markward of Annweiler provides an outstanding example. From the eighties onwards, and even more under Philip of Swabia and Henry (VII), they gained growing influence at the royal court, among them especially the holders of imperial

court offices. Until the murder of Philip of Swabia they were
the most important agents of continuity in Staufen imperial
politics in the struggle over the throne. Philip, in a letter to
Pope Innocent III, boasted: 'We have so many ministerials
that we can hardly count them' [352: 618]. They quickly joined
the young Frederick II. In the conflict between the emperor
and his son, many imperial ministerials took the side of Henry
(VII).

In contrast to Barbarossa, Henry VI, and Otto IV, Frederick
II in the reorganization of imperial administration in Italy
from 1238 onwards favoured officials from the Sicilian kingdom, without falling back on German imperial ministerials.
This process, and the unimportance of German ministerials at
the Norman–Staufen court, were a consequence of the shift of
gravity in imperial rule from the area north of the Alps to the
centre of the Mediterranean. In the 'interregnum' the imperial
ministerials also for a long time lost their established contact
with the monarchy, which from the death of Conrad IV to the
reign of Rudolf of Habsburg possessed little power, and then
only outside the Staufen imperial lands. Either they increasingly came into dependence on territorial lords or, especially in the main area of the Staufen lands, they maintained
an independent position. With the end of the Staufen, the
special position of the imperial ministerials, grown out of unfreedom, also ended. Besides the imperial ministerials, many
counts and free lords had distinguished themselves in the service
of the Staufen emperors. Rudolf of Habsburg in his reorganization of German imperial rule relied primarily on the
lower nobility. By now many imperial ministerials had been
integrated in this. Feudal law had offered a convenient legal
framework for this change of status. In this respect too, the
imperial ministerials seem to have paved the way for the great
mass of their class who were subjected to other lords.

It must be remembered that huge social differences existed
even between the imperial ministerials, and remained until the
end of the Staufen period. The difference between imperial
ministerials like Werner II of Bolanden, Eberhard of Lautern,
and Markward of Annweiler, on the one hand, and some imperial ministerial in an unimportant castle, was immense. We
will take a closer look at the example of the Bolanden family.

Their history may at the same time elucidate some of the problems of the imperial ministerials as instruments of territorial politics in the later Staufen period.

Werner II of Bolanden (d. *c.*1198), who appears in Barbarossa's following from 1170 onwards, together with the Staufen count palatine of the Rhine was the most important instrument of Staufen territorial politics on the middle Rhine. Towards the end of the twelfth century he controlled large, concentrated estates and rights—among them the lay advocacies of several monasteries and churches—in Rheinhessen and the Palatinate, and also in other important places on the middle Rhine. According to the Bolanden register of fees, written around the middle of the thirteenth century but based on older material, Werner II held fiefs from 45 secular and ecclesiastical lords, among them the emperor and Duke Welf VI. Supported by this position, which had long been similar to the nobility and was further strengthened by the weakness of the crown after the struggle for the throne, his sons married members of noble families. In this they first trod a path which soon became open to other distinguished imperial ministerials. With these social relations the Bolanden family at the same time loosened their ties with their Staufen lords. In the struggle for the throne Werner II openly stood on the Welf side. In the dispute over the see of Mainz which broke out in 1200, he was one of the most important allies of the anti-Staufen candidate Siegfried II, who, like his successors Siegfried III (1230–49), already mentioned, and Archbishop Werner (1259–84), came from the noble family of Eppstein, to which Werner of Bolanden was related. During the minority of Henry (VII) he was among the closest advisers of the emperor's son. In the final stages of the Staufen fight against the papal party a member of the main line of the Bolanden family, Werner IV, supported the archbishop of Mainz from as early as 1243; he was joined by his brother in 1249, while other members of the family later supported the Staufen emperor and his son Conrad IV.

The rise of the leading imperial ministerials and their continuous assimilation into the nobility from the end of the twelfth century decreased their interest in imperial service, from which they could no longer expect much because of the weakening of the kingship after the struggle for the throne. The ousting of the servile law, which had never been a 'civil service' law anyway, by feudal law was an expression of their increased political range of action. With such independent functionaries no 'state' could be created. They thus followed the route which had already determined the development of the imperial churches. Just as the latter, at the latest from the investiture struggle onwards, moved more and more into a noble and princely position and thus lost their original function in imperial government, the more powerful imperial ministerials from the turn of the thirteenth century themselves attained a noble-like position and soon afterwards dropped out as reliable instruments of royal power for use against the secular and ecclesiastical princes, in spite of their owing their rise to the monarchy—as the imperial churches had before.

But also the ministerials of the other lords were far from subordinating themselves unselfishly to the will of their masters. Thus for example the Babenberg Duke Frederick II (1230–46) had to use force against his more powerful ministerials—like the Kuenringer and Maissauer—who had moved into the positions, and partly also into the properties, of the counts and other nobles against whom Frederick's father Leopold VI (1194–1230) had fought successfully. In other territories too, the ministerials joined the circle of local lords. Thus on this level as well they gained the right to participate in aristocratic politics. A decision made in 1231 under King Henry (VII) at a court in Worms, with the consent of the princes, already formulates such a demand for the agreement of the local magnates (*meliores et maiores terrae*) when decreeing new laws and titles [3: xxxii. 422f., no. 108]. The development of group representation could also join on to these traditions; but this only began in outline from the end of the thirteenth century.

[d] THE RISE OF THE COMMUNES

Along with the influence of other factors, particularly economic ones, the political events and social processes just outlined in the Staufen period favoured the establishment and proliferation of rural, and especially of urban, communes. In the course of rural development and the territorial politics connected with it, the number of communes multiplied as never before. At least in the old settlement areas this growth rate was not reached again until the late nineteenth century. In approximately twelve decades from the middle of the twelfth century to the end of our period, the number of towns alone rose from about 200 to more than 2,000. But we shall not yet enter into details on these quantitative aspects.

For the development of communes in the following centuries it was very important that urban communes were able to strengthen their political position considerably in the Staufen period, especially the larger ones. This increase in importance at the same time furthered the development of communal forms of organization which also were to become crucial.

The symbiosis of towns and lordships, which became closer from Frederick Barbarossa's time onwards, showed itself in the growing importance of the towns as stopping-places for the itinerant rulers. In this the episcopal towns continued to be important, but now, even more than under Conrad III, places which were turning into urban centres and newly founded towns emerge. At the same time Barbarossa had palaces built in numerous places to which he granted city rights and which he promoted by economic measures. This is true for Hagenau in Alsace, for Kaiserslautern, Frankfurt, Gelnhausen, Wimpfen, Eger, Nijmegen, and Kaiserswerth. Although the Staufen of the thirteenth century still made use of the urban palaces or palatine towns as residences and centres of power, they did not found new palaces. Their foundations generally were only small castle towns.

In a considerable number of royal towns the Staufen exploited the ecclesiastical lay advocacy, with which they also secured their rights over some bishops' towns, like Basle and Augsburg. Amongst those towns which came into existence on Church land were Schaffhausen, Zürich, the Alsatian towns of Münster in the Gregorienthal, Türkheim, Colmar, Schlettstadt, Rosheim, Oberehnheim, Weissenburg, and Selz, and also Sinsheim, Weil, Feuchtwangen, and Wetzlar. Against this method of controlling cities, which secular princes also practised, the ecclesiastical lords protested, so that Frederick II forbade such a use of the lay advocacy in the *Confoederatio* of 1220. Less controversial were purchases and exchanges, and also the reversion of imperial fiefs, with which the Staufen increased the number of royal towns especially in the imperial areas. Frederick I also entered into the inheritance of the urban politics of the high nobility in the case of Lübeck. In 1188 Barbarossa expressly confirmed the freedoms previously granted to the port by Henry the Lion, who had founded it three decades before, since when it had risen to be an important trading centre.

While under Frederick I a very large proportion of town foundations in the German empire were brought about by the emperor, from 1242 onwards the Staufen had to renounce such activities completely. In the next three decades, when the number of towns in central Europe rose from about 900 to more than 2,000, the German kings remained completely excluded from this increase in power. The preponderance of princely, other noble, and clerical founders of towns became evident from Henry VI's death. Before the outbreak of the struggle for the throne the crown in Germany possessed important rights in about a quarter of the then existing towns, while around the middle of the thirteenth century this had sunk to about one-tenth.

The numerous town foundations of the Staufen, the princes, and other lords document sufficiently the huge interest the traditional powers had in fortified urban centres, which in the smallest space were highly effective both for military uses and as sources of money. For the same reasons they were in principle intent on far-reaching control of the towns. In this, however, they had to consider the advantages of the urban dwellers too. This was all the more necessary when their rule was unstable or threatened by competitors, and they had to secure the loyalty and support of the citizens. In the basic situation thus outlined, new opportunities arose for the political ruling classes to maintain their advantages and those of the urban community and to enforce new legal rights. The citizens, for their part, were extremely vulnerable outside their own city walls. The smaller, often new towns with primitive walls, but also older, generally bigger and better fortified towns, were dependent on securing themselves within the regional power structure.

In this complex situation, relations between the traditional powers and the widely differing towns varied greatly. Among them the episcopal cities in the old settlement areas—especially those on the Rhine, Main, Moselle, and Danube—were the most important politically, mainly because of their economic importance, and because they were situated in regions which were decisive for the balance of power in the German empire.

Against the background thus outlined, the clichés about relations between the 'feudal' powers and the towns, which are still to be found even in the latest literature, prove to be quite inadequate. The generalization that the towns were 'anti-feudal' or that the traditional powers were 'anti-town' ('anti-bourgeois') does not need extensive refutation, although this pattern of interpretation, originating in the eighteenth and nineteenth centuries, even today has an after-effect on research in a modified form. It is also disputable whether individual rulers at times exercised 'pro-town' or 'anti-town' policies.

Thus before 1180 the Emperor Frederick I, because of his experiences with the Italian communes, is said to have been 'a decided opponent of confederation as a movement of bourgeois independence' [567: 42]. Against this it can be argued first that the same emperor, even at the time of the Diet of Roncaglia, and even in imperial Italy, did not question the existence of the city commune as such. Rather in the fifties and sixties he put a large number of city communes on to the same level as the traditional noble and clerical powers in imperial Italy by integrating them into feudal law. And the proofs often adduced from the German empire—the events in the metropolitan cities of Mainz and Trier—are not convincing.

Some references to Trier will have to suffice for this. As already in 1157, Frederick I in autumn 1161—during his long fight against the Lombard metropolis of Milan—forbade the 'confederation of the citizens of Trier, which is also called a *Schwureinung* (alliance by oath)'. With both of these prohibitions Barbarossa was reacting to one of several points of conflict between Archbishop Hillin of Trier and the emperor's half-brother Conrad. As count palatine of the Rhine (from 1156) the Staufen Conrad continued the territorial-political quarrels with the archbishop of Trier. In this he had recourse to his position as lay advocate of Trier cathedral, which gave him important rights in the city of Trier. The ruling stratum in Trier, whose independent political actions we have met before, exploited the competition and, appealing to the count palatine, began their confederation, with which they tried to enforce new rights against the interests of their archiepiscopal lord. Faced with his own precarious situation and burdened with the papal schism, the emperor had a strong interest in ending the dispute between the two princes. He finally brought about a compromise between them. In return for the promise of other advantages, the Count Palatine Conrad had expressly to withdraw his consent to the confederation of Trier. In an attempt to prevent further conflicts, the emperor ordered that the confederation was not to be renewed, neither at the instance of the archbishop nor of the count palatine. This means that Barbarossa thought it possible that even the archiepiscopal lord of the city could draw, or at least expect, advantages from the support of the *communio* or *coniuratio* in the town. Therefore the emperor did not turn against all confederations on principle, but only against the *coniuratio* of Trier, which might have considerably altered the power balance between the competing princes. Thus it is not surprising that some years later the same emperor, in a charter for the inhabitants of his 'palatine town' of Hagenau, automatically assumes the existence of a citizens' commune with its own town rights (*civile ius*) [19: x. 2. 173–5, no. 337; see 3: xxxii. 264–7, no. 69].

Nor is the emperor's prohibition of the confederation at Trier in contradiction to the fact that in the eighties and nineties Barbarossa and Henry VI, though under different political circumstances, granted favourable privileges to such episcopal cities as Worms, Speyer, Cambrai, Cologne, Metz, Verdun, and Bremen. In 1182, the same year in which Frederick I confirmed and extended Henry V's privilege in favour of the citizens of Speyer, he forbade the city of Trent (which belonged to the German empire) for all time the consular constitution which had long been in existence for the neighbouring cities of imperial Italy, when they had long been recognized by the emperor.

A few months after Henry VI's death, in a fundamentally changed situation, Philip of Swabia at the beginning of 1198— i.e. at the start of the struggle for the throne—made a treaty with the citizens of Speyer in obvious agreement with the local

bishop. In this the citizens committed themselves to support the
Staufen militarily and economically. In return Philip, besides
earlier privileges, also confirmed a freedom (*libertas*), said to
have been granted by his imperial brother. It contained the
right of the people of Speyer to elect a committee of twelve, to
look after the city community (*universitas*) as best it could, and
to rule the town with its advice (*consilium*). Philip of Swabia, if
not Henry VI, in this way legalized the town council, and thus
in effect also a constitution, which was created on the model of
the consulate in the Italian and southern French towns. A little
more than two decades later, Frederick II granted the laws of
the city of Speyer to the former village of Annweiler, which
was closely connected with the castle system around the high
Trifels, where Richard the Lionheart had been kept prisoner.

As in the case of the ministerials, the struggle for the throne
furthered and made necessary the political independence of
the towns. During this period, we may remember, Cologne,
economically the most important town, by its decision for the
Welf Otto IV exercised a considerable influence on the fate of
the empire. What was happening here on the highest level was
only a symptom of the increase in importance of the economically and also militarily effective urban communities in
times of political crisis, when competing groups had to rely on
intensive use of their potential. This explains how the relations
between the candidates for the throne and individual city communes—as for example Trier—were laid down in treaties and
could almost look like contracts.

The increased military dangers during the struggle for the
throne caused the towns to push forward with the building of
walls, which can be proved for Cologne, Strasbourg, Mainz,
Liège, Verdun, Metz, Bremen, and Passau. To finance these
expensive communal works, which might also be undertaken
with the consent of the lord, the urban communes generally
introduced taxes on consumption in the form of excise duties.
Such an expansion of their competence contained the germ of
new conflicts with the ecclesiastical urban lords, who claimed
immunity from taxation and jurisdiction for clerical institutions
and persons.

The growing functions and responsibilities favoured a
strengthening of communal administration. Very varied solutions were found for this, like the creation of sworn collegiates

(*iurati*) and the introduction of councils. The council, with regularly changing officials, was adopted around the turn of the thirteenth century by Speyer, Lübeck, Utrecht, and Strasbourg. Besides the consuls, as in Strasbourg, however, the sworn colleges (*Schöffenkollegien*) continued in existence. Generally those families were active in the consulate which also held the posts of jurors (*Schöffen*). The consular constitution in the following years spread especially fast in the north German towns. In the newer towns it often resulted from taking over town laws, so that for example Rostock already in 1218 had a council on the model of Lübeck. The Teutonic Order in 1233 granted the right to a free election of judges to the citizens of Thorn and Kulm. This oldest Prussian town charter was to become a model. On this basis jurors' colleges and also urban councils could come into existence. In southern Germany town councils became more widespread only around the middle of the thirteenth century. The interregnum brought about changes, especially in the imperial towns, where the king was lord and where he safeguarded his rights by means of officials. But in bishops' towns, like Cologne, Strasbourg, Augsburg, Regensburg, Passau, Salzburg, Constance, Worms, Speyer, Liège, Osnabrück, Bremen, and Minden, the town communes were able to obtain in disputes with their lords more favourable conditions and extensive powers for themselves.

The imperial laws of 1231/2, with their radical decrees against urban communes in favour of the mainly ecclesiastical town lords, had long proved to be generally ineffective before the death of the Emperor Conrad IV. By 1242, when the anti-Staufen party among the German princes openly declared itself, they had lost their political importance for the emperor. Frederick II, who had among his supporters large urban communes in upper Italy, contrary to the wording of these laws in 1245 expressly allowed the city of Regensburg, after its bishop had changed over to the papal side, to elect councillors and to install mayors for the honour of the empire and the benefit of the town.

From then onwards, the basic situation which obtained in the period of the struggle for the throne kept being repeated. However, the larger cities now had more political weight. This was based not least on financial contributions such as can be seen in the imperial tax list of 1241/2. According to this the cities of Frankfurt, Gelnhausen, Wetzlar, and Friedberg paid a total of 740 silver marks, the Jews who lived there paying the king further sums on top of that. Now King Conrad IV and Frederick II as well as some city lords made pact-like treaties with single towns. The relationship of the Staufen to the episcopal city of Worms is an example; together with its bishop, Landolf, of ministerial origin, it remained on the Staufen side. In 1244, only about a year after the arrangement of a pact between the emperor and the city of Worms, Archbishop Siegfried III, who wanted to detach his cathedral town of Mainz from its alliance with Conrad IV and to bind it into his anti-Staufen policy, granted it great privileges, among them a city council (*consilium civitatis*). On this basis the city was able to pursue its own political life until the fifteenth century, independent of the archbishop.

The legal uncertainties and political dangers which increasingly appeared after Conrad IV's death were probably the most important reasons for the initiative of the middle Rhineland towns, with Mainz at their head, in founding the Rhenish Federation (*Rheinischer Bund*). This, the first large German town federation, differed in its general aims from the middle Rhenish Federation as well as from that of the Liège towns in the later twenties. On the middle Rhine around 1225 neighbouring royal and episcopal towns had entered into a treaty. The alliance of Liége (1229/30), differently again, tried to provide security for the rights of its members against their common lord. Thus it contained elements of the development of an urban order on a territorial basis. These beginnings, however, only attained more established forms in the German empire in the later medieval centuries, which also holds true for the mutual co-operation of the towns within the imperial constitution.

The village and rural communities took part in the rise of communal co-operative life, which was mainly the work of the larger towns. The borders between village and town, between citizen and peasant, were in many cases fluid—especially in the older villages and the newly founded towns, or those settlements recently endowed with urban rights. Many villages almost overnight became towns in the legal sense by royal or princely decree without there having been any considerable change in the economic and social situation of their inhabitants, at least to begin with. In the eastward colonization movement, towns and villages in many areas were founded simultaneously. In Silesia, particularly after the retreat of the Mongols, these towns had 10–20 villages assigned to their municipal areas, for which, as for the town, a German urban law (normally the Magdeburg law) was in force.

According to W. Schlesinger's definition, the rural community was 'a lasting, locally bound association which was in a position to maintain authority, and especially legal rights, over its members'. 'It is a co-operative legal peasant community, with the capacity to act in common and certain rights of self-administration, and which exercises coercive power.' This description can be applied to the urban community without significant changes. In fact both forms of community had deeply rooted similarities from their beginnings in the high Middle Ages until the nineteenth century. In the village and rural communes, old forms of neighbourhood and co-operative exploitation rights—especially of the common—and also communal economic or military functions served as a point of departure. Parish organization was of special importance. This connection becomes especially evident in those cases where the village could elect its priest. An essential impulse for the development of rural communes came from the changes in the organization of courts and the rights of stewards from the late eleventh century onwards and also from the levelling in personal legal status within the manorial *familiae*. Such anticipations acquired new opportunities to develop in the internal and eastward colonization from the middle of the twelfth century onwards. Rural development in regions previously little used, and sparsely settled, favoured and demanded co-operative action and the definition of areas whose settlers and inhabitants had as far as possible a single legal status.

The numerous *villae novae* in the Latin parts of the empire and in eastern France are to be seen in this context. The charter of liberties given to the *maior*, the jurors (*Schöffen*), and the inhabitants of Beaumont in the Ardennes by the archbishop of Reims in 1182 offers one model among others. The inhabitants of this place, already fortified in the middle of the twelfth century, who also undertook forest clearance, received in this *Loi de Beaumont* a uniform legal status with freedom of movement and unrestricted marriage rights. Their payments and services were fixed: rent, entry fines, and a fee on change of property, one-sixth of the cereal harvest of the old land and one-seventh of the newly cleared arable, and fees for the use of mills and ovens (seigneurial rights) each being about 5 per cent of the flour or the bread, amongst others, show the transformation from the old manorial conditions to the new forms of rural peasant existence. In return the archbishop secured for them inheritance rights and a local court as well as protection for the market. The inhabitants were allowed to elect the *maior*, responsible for legal judgements and for collecting dues, and the jurors (*iurati*). These were supposed to remain in office for one year, unless decided otherwise by the electors [compare 3: xxxi. 250-7, no. 95].

This complex of community rights was subsequently granted to about 500 places, primarily in the French–German border area and in the county of Luxemburg. From about the middle of the thirteenth century the charter of freedom also had an influence on town charters granted by the count of Luxemburg. Such models are not as clearly visible in the old settlement areas of Germany. Nevertheless a similar legal status can be seen, especially in the *Freiheiten*, and valley communities. In the drained areas on the North Sea coast with their huge communal works, the title *consules* is found for the annual officials of the parish in the first half of the thirteenth century; the holders originated from families of better-off farmers. In the new settlement areas in the east a widespread though unstandardized settlement law (*ius Teutonicum*) came into being, which, as a special village law for the alien settlers, also contained the basis for the village community. It was apparently able to draw on earlier communal developments in the new settlement areas, while taking over models mainly but not exclusively from Franconia and the Main region in the old settlement areas.

The variations in the forms and circumstances of village and rural communes corresponded to the diversity of communal responsibilities. They might be limited to the regulation of neighbourhood access to the common and to judicial functions in petty cases, but they might also cover more serious matters.

Procedural rules might be highly developed. Thus Eike Repgow in the *Sachsenspiegel* mentions as normal that all instructions by the headman, made by him with majority consent for the benefit of the village, were binding on the minority. As apparently in most cases, powers of decision lay with the holders of peasant tenements. As among the urban inhabitants, among these also the *maiores* and *meliores* stood out, and probably held all the community offices.

The position of city, village, or rural community within the power structure was dependent on the social quality of their leading groups. But in spite of various parallels the differences remained noteworthy, as the village and rural communities were generally more strongly exposed to the grip of the lords of the land, village, or region than the towns were. In zones of fragmented lordship in the old settlement areas—especially in the Staufen imperial region—in the following period smaller and younger towns were also able to stand their ground for relatively long periods against the territorial lords. Outside these areas, however, even larger urban centres remained under strong control by their lords. Territorialization in the Staufen period did not on the whole hinder the development of co-operative, communal institutions in the country and in the towns; rather it created the pre-conditions and mediated the impulses for it. The economic factors which also influenced this will be dealt with in the next chapter.

3

The Expansion of the Economy

[*a*] POPULATION GROWTH, RURAL DEVELOPMENT,
AND URBANIZATION

The numerous new foundations of villages, markets, and towns, as well as their expansion, offer the most convincing evidence for the strong increase in population after the middle of the twelfth century. They cannot, however, simply be transposed into a population graph, as they are considerably influenced by other factors, especially military ones and those concerning territorial politics—as the extensions of town walls and the new urban foundations make clear. Nevertheless we can conclude from the enormous expansion of settlement in eastern Germany and eastern central Europe that the population in the German empire increased from the middle of the twelfth century even more than in the previous century.

The extension of the arable area in internal and eastern colonization, and improvement of agricultural methods, created sufficient food for more people. In spite of this, even in the second half of the twelfth century and the first third of the thirteenth century rising prices, famines, and periods of hunger occurred again and again in the old settlement areas in the west. After the widespread famines of 1162 and 1175/6, in many areas of western Germany as far down as Austria a long period of hunger raged between 1195 and 1198, with particularly severe effects. In the first half of the thirteenth century the supraregional famine of the years 1225/6 was apparently an exception, while huge price increases and famines went on occurring in single areas. On the whole it seems that the supply situation in basic foodstuffs was improving. From the middle of the century, grain imports into northern

Germany from the new settlement areas in the east contributed to this.

Internal colonization in the old settlement areas did not succeed in finally banishing the danger of weather-related famines. The newly worked fields were often dependent on especially favourable weather. Furthermore the inhabitants of the towns were increasingly dependent on the surplus production of the peasant population. The clearings, mostly carried out under seigneurial supervision and control, often led to a decrease in usable areas outside the arable. With the reduction in forest and wasteland the pasture grounds decreased, as did the food reserves for times of need—like small game, roots, and berries—and the supply of timber and fuel. Against this background, it often came to disputes between manorial and village lords on the one hand and village communities on the other about common rights, which noble and ecclesiastical powers tried to restrict with the help of their power of the ban. The limits of expansion were thus clearly outlined in the course of the thirteenth century.

Around the middle of the same century similar symptoms also appeared in urbanization in the western old settlement areas. Because colonization in some areas—such as in the Maas-Schelde region and on the Rhine and the Danube—had reached a relatively high level already by 1150, the growth rate in the western imperial area stayed below the central European average. Around 1150 in the area left of the Rhine between Mainz and Basle there were seven towns in an area of *c.*280 kilometres in length by 40 kilometres in width. In the following hundred years, in the last decades of which the growth rate was particularly high, a total of 34 towns were added, equalling about a sixfold increase. On the other hand the number in the north German area between the IJssel and the Elbe north of a line Deventer-Osnabrück-Minden during the same period only showed an increase of 12, which did not more than double the number. Such differences can still be observed in urbanization after the middle of the thirteenth century. From about then onwards, however, most of the new foundations in the more urbanized old settlement areas remained small towns with a lesser urban provision. Many of them had a village settlement as their basis. Sometimes several villages were even broken up in favour of a new urban foundation. This means that at the end of our period in these areas a certain saturation point had been reached in urbanization.

This cannot be said for the regions east of the Elbe and Saale, although here as well huge regional differences are observable. With very few exceptions—like for example Lübeck, Altenburg, and Meissen, which were not too far from the borderline—by the middle of the twelfth century in this area there were no towns which according to current archaeological findings could be compared with those in the west, and this in spite of the existence of large trading and industrial settlements. Up to the middle of the thirteenth century about 250 new towns were founded east of the Elbe and Saale and north of the line Eger–Prague–Troppau, on the initiative of such lords as the Obodrites in Mecklenburg or the Polish Piasts in Silesia. East Pomerania, East Prussia, Courland, and inner Poland up to this date were still empty of towns. The eastward colonization, and urbanization with it, reached this area later. It has recently been well characterized as a civilizing westernization of eastern central Europe. We may remember that the smaller German imperial area was at the same time strongly influenced by areas of higher civilization in the west, and possibly even more in the south.

This 'westernization' was not only carried out by the towns. Rather its strongest base was the agricultural development which ran parallel to it, and which was carried out mainly by German settlers. With the simultaneous foundation of towns and villages, the preconditions for an intensive relationship between town and country was created, such as had already developed in the old settlement areas. In this way agriculture in the eastern areas of new settlement was right from the beginning orientated towards the market at a relatively highly monetary level.

The immigrants with their 'German laws' (*ius Teutonicum*) received more favourable conditions than the Slav peasants. Soon this legal status was occasionally also granted to the indigenous population. But besides this, for example in Silesia, older forms of serfdom with compulsory labour services continued and in the late Middle Ages served as the basis of new forms of unfreedom. With the free hereditary tenement, which included the right to sell the land and leave their tenements, and with freedom from the otherwise normal compulsory labour, which could become particularly onerous in wartime, the new settlers had in practice free legal status. For their mostly large holdings they were also exempted from rent in the first years after settlement, the terms of which varied between four, five, ten, or even sixteen years, depending on the circumstances.

The organization of rural or urban settlement was often in the hands of agents (*locatores*) of noble, urban, or even peasant origin, who acted on behalf of princes, nobles, or bishops. In return for their activities, which went as far as recruiting settlers in the old settlement areas, they received free tenements or other privileges, and not least hereditary office with generally lesser judicial powers (as *Schultheiß* = village mayor), so that they were also responsible for collecting payments.

Among the clerical institutions the Premonstratensians and especially the Cistercians played a role, by no means small, though overestimated in the past, in the settlement activities in the east. From the middle of the twelfth century, the Cistercians for the first time founded large numbers of settlements in the area beyond the Elbe and the Saale. Many of the first Cistercian monasteries were also the domestic and burial monasteries of lords: such as Altzelle (1162, for the margrave of Wettin); Doberan near Rostock (1171, the lords of Mecklenburg); Oliva near Danzig (in the seventies, dukes of Pomerelia); Leubus (not later than 1175, the Polish duke of Silesia); Lehnin near Brandenburg (1180, the Ascanian Margrave Otto of Brandenburg). In most new foundations demesne farming played a smaller role than the rent incomes from landed property and lordship rights.

According to recent estimates, during the twelfth and thirteenth centuries only about 200,000 immigrants from the western old settlement areas participated in the colonization of the east. According to this, only about 2,000 settlers per year moved to the east, which, given an overall population of ten million, corresponded to only 0.02 per cent. Even if this rate was multipied by five, emigration would still be within the normal growth rate of the population. Based on these statistics it seemed to be possible to conclude that emigration was not caused by overpopulation or peasant oppression in the countries of origin.

Against this, though, it must be said that the condition of the population in the old settlement areas was not at all uniform, and furthermore—as is shown by price increases and famines—it varied greatly in time. Misfortunes restricted in space or time could well give the decisive impulse for the exodus. Anyway it was not only objective conditions in the emigration areas and verifiable chances in the east that were crucial in motives for emigration. One also has to consider how the emigrants experienced their situation in their homeland, and what expectations they harboured on the basis of the available information about their chances in the settlement of the east. A satisfying answer is still awaited; this is made difficult by the source material. At any rate, emigration to the east is not sufficient proof of generally unfavourable conditions among the population in the old settlement areas.

[b] THE ADVANCE OF THE MONEY ECONOMY

In the middle of the twelfth century many mints existed in the German imperial area, with concentrations in the Maas, Rhine, and Danube areas and also in Saxony. Around the year 1140, however, there were still only 25 active mints. This situation changed radically in the Staufen period. Mints which had closed down were revived, but mainly, numerous new mints were founded. Two hundred and fifteen mints on German soil have recently been proved for the period between 1140 and 1197. One hundred and six of them were in clerical hands (61 episcopal and 45 monastic), 81 were under the control of secular lords, and 28 under royal control. Between 1197 and 1270 the number doubled again, to a total of 456. These were divided into 152 mints of clerical lords (106 in episcopal hands, 46 monastic), 277 in the hands of secular dynasts, and 37 royal mints. The main beneficiaries of the time after the struggle for the throne therefore were the bishops and the secular princes, while the monasteries stagnated and the kingship gained only few new mints. The great increase in the number of minting places occurred in close connection with the equally vigorous wave of urban foundations, in which too the kingship from the turn of the thirteenth century had only a small part.

With the exception of the royal mint of Schwäbisch Hall, the new mints had nothing like the same importance as the coinage of the large episcopal cities, among which Cologne and Regensburg stood out. The predominance of the mints in the episcopal towns mainly expressed itself in the new coins—again with the exception of Schwäbisch Hall—being struck on the model of those of the 'mother towns'. In most cases the royal mint followed this pattern too. Thus the Staufen mints in the diocese of Strasbourg at Schlettstadt, Hagenau, and Offenburg struck on the model of Strasbourg. In this way the predominance of the episcopal coins was often reduced or undermined in the Staufen period, a process in which the royal mints took part. Thus the Nuremberg penny gained considerable distribution at the expense of the *denarii* of Bamberg and Regensburg; the penny of Cologne had stiff competition from the royal mints of the surrounding area—like those of Aachen, Duisburg, and Nijmegen.

The greatest long-term success of Staufen minting was attained with the mint at Schwäbisch Hall, which Barbarossa founded in 1180 at the power centre of the Staufen family territory. The mass production of this mint in the course of a century radically changed the mint system in Germany. Right from the beginning this penny, which was independent in form, image, weight, and alloy, circulated far beyond the diocese of Würzburg. Its success depended not least on its low value, with which it ousted the good coins ('Gresham's Law'). Thus the policy of light money won through. At the end of the Staufen period the 'Haller' ('Heller') almost gained the rank of an imperial coin, the circulation of which was no longer locally limited. Staufen minting policies were probably in general carried out by the imperial ministerials who were resident in the palace towns and the royal cities. The princes often protested against the royal mint policy, which just like that of the ecclesiastical and secular lords was clearly motivated by territorial politics. Their interest can be read in Frederick II's concessions of 1220 and 1231/2. This also expressed the growing influence of the money economy on politics.

The decline of high-value coins, as a phenomenon parallel to the 'mint boom' and to urbanization, corresponded to the demand of much of the population for small coins with which they could participate in market trading for their daily needs. The advancing money economy in central Europe during the Staufen period therefore reflects a modernization process, which also showed itself in division of labour, social mobility, and in attitudes and values. But the gap in monetary development between central Europe and the Mediterranean world still remained noticeable even at the end of the Staufen period. The gap was probably least in islands of monetary and economic intensity, for which Cologne is the best example with its outstanding coins, which spread as far as England.

[c] CHANGES IN AGRICULTURE

A number of changes affected agriculture in the empire north of the Alps in the Staufen period; they began earlier, but now gained greater weight. Here we shall mention: the ousting of the villication system in favour of rent-receiving and various forms of lease; greater orientation of agriculture towards markets, with the beginnings of specialization; the application of new techniques and growing methods, which made the expansion of the settled areas easier and increased productivity; and alterations in the burdens of the peasant economy.

The decline of the independent manorial economy and the granting of tenements generally for fixed dues or money rents, and also the commutation of compulsory labour in return for money, favoured the transformation to rentier landlordship. With this a system is meant which, like the villication system, must only be taken as an ideal. In reality, especially in the Staufen period, many mixed forms existed in between the two ideal types, which themselves showed numerous variations. Manorial autarky in many cases remained in existence. This was to be found especially often close to centres of lordship, i.e. monasteries, towns, and castles. Many traditional estates kept their basic form, but adapted to the market.

This direction of development was also followed by the independent economy of the Cistercians. Thus the monastery of Himmerod already in the twelfth century owned houses in Trier, Andernach, Bonn, and Speyer, which served as bases for the exchange of goods on urban markets. A little later in Speyer alone there were 19 houses belonging to monasteries. Twelve of them belonged to nine Cistercian abbeys. More and more often the Cistercians extended their system of granges at the expense of hitherto independent peasants, who were probably driven out of their farms and given compensation. If the twelfth-century influx of lay brothers (*conversi*), who ran a considerable part of the independent economy, was greater than the need for labour, which early on was often carried out by paid labourers, in the later thirteenth century a shortage of *conversi* appeared among the Cistercians. This compelled these reformed monasteries, which from the same time onwards increasingly neglected their original ideals, to lease their granges, especially the more distant ones. Otherwise the white monks, who managed their economy in an effective and often exemplary way, used the opportunities of the urban market so cleverly that many abbeys were considered rich by the second half of the twelfth century. Active participation in supra-local trade—primarily in wool, partly also in horses—contributed to this.

The lesser nobility also pursued an independent economy. They went on attaching great importance to renders of products in kind, which they themselves marketed. This advantageous way of trading apparently had a lasting effect on the attitudes of smaller landowners. According to the *Kleiner Lucidiarius* of 'Seifried Helblinc', a collection of didactic poems with numerous criticisms of the time by an otherwise unknown knight from Lower Austria of the end of the thirteenth century, ministerials and knights at the court of the lord—as the author laments—preferred to talk about the price of eggs, cheese, piglets, and wheat. They were especially interested in how to get a cow to give more milk; their attitude was directed towards earnings and profits.

Among the reasons for the decline of the large estates, the difficulties of the landowners with large-scale, extensive, costly administration are not to be underestimated. The earlier problems increased, because the leading groups within the familia— primarily the ministerials—used the administrative positions given to them to lead a quasi-noble life. After the middle of the twelfth century the abbot of the large imperial monastery of Fulda complained about this. When he entered upon office, allegedly the store-rooms of the monastery were so empty that the monks had nothing to live on. 'No wonder,' the abbot continues, 'as lay people had all the dairy farms of the monastery and gave and kept for themselves what they liked.' The high nobles had appropriated the monastery estates under the pretence of enfeoffment. But the less powerful (*pauperiores*) had made clearings and settlements in the woods and forests of the monastery. Despite great efforts the abbot had not succeeded in getting back all the stolen property, 'as all the ministerials of the monastery support one another, all only looking after their own and not that which is Christ's. Yet I did get back something from single farms, sometimes more, sometimes less' [3: xxxi. 212–19, no. 80].

The various forms of free tenancy offered a way out of these difficulties for the tenants too. By taking up elements of Roman law, as had already happened much earlier in the Latin lands, this route was first followed by ecclesiastical landowners on the periphery of the larger towns, from the turn of the thirteenth century onwards. Vineyards were sometimes leased already in the late twelfth century. The leaseholder generally had to deliver half or one-third of the harvest to the owner. Not long afterwards in the Rhineland holdings were given to peasant and also urban leaseholders on terms of three, six, or nine years. In these 'modern' leasehold contracts, normally the inventory of the farms, with animals and tools, was put at the disposal of the leaseholder. Soon the leaseholder was confronted with detailed orders concerning the running of the estate in order to maintain the stock and at the same time fulfil all the payments. The leaseholder under these circumstances had to be specially bent on increasing productivity.

To improve agrarian yields in the twelfth and thirteenth centuries, various methods, some of them known earlier, were used to a greater extent. Among them were more effective fertilization, keeping animals in stalls, and growing fodder plants and pulses. Pictures from the thirteenth century also suggest the increasing use of heavy ploughs with a coulter and soil-turning mould-board, which on heavier soils made larger yields possible. Besides this, the four-wheeled wagon, often drawn by oxen, was increasingly used as a means of transport in agriculture.

The burdens from the side of the landowners decreased in the old settlement areas as well. But in place of these, other demands on the peasant population appeared, mainly made by officials and local lords, and these could be economically decisive. The raising of tax-like tributes by the officials or the owners of the court, the village, or the local area, who often enough staged their competition on the backs of the peasants, led to aggravated burdens. Added to this were market dues, devaluations of coinage, and tolls, which ecclesiastical and secular lords tried to increase to make them into lucrative financial incomes. The more the peasant economy orientated itself towards the need of markets and cities and became dependent on them, the more these dues affected it.

It was not only agriculture that was vital for the economic situation of the rural population. To a growing extent important industries and crafts were carried on in the country and in rural settlements. Among them were the production and processing of iron and precious and non-ferrous metals; wool-spinning, pottery, ceramics, and glass-making; producing indispensable salt by means of salt-pans, and production of charcoal, amongst other things. Therefore in industry too there was a transition from a rural to an urban economy, which at the same time served as a 'midwife' to the towns, and which animated trade.

[*d*] THE EXPANSION OF TRADE AND INDUSTRY

Rural development and progressive urbanization, the strong move towards the development of a money economy, and the growing orientation of agriculture towards the market are all certain proofs of the increase in industrial activities and local trade. The latter also strengthened the foundations of long-distance trade. From the second half of the twelfth century onwards there are increasing signs of closer contact between the German economic region, which was gradually spreading eastwards and becoming denser, and the Mediterranean area and the west of Europe. As well as benefiting from the many-sided trade connections with the south and the west, where the fairs of

Champagne arose as the most important exchange centre between the Mediterranean, rich in traditions, and the promising
economic areas of north-western Europe, German trade, the
merchants active in it, and also the fast-growing towns especially of the Baltic area, gained great advantages from the
rapidly progressing 'westernization' of eastern central Europe,
which in turn received essential impulses from this trade.

From the late twelfth century German merchants became
more active in trade between Germany and Italy. Via Genoa
and Venice they gained access to the most important centres
of Mediterranean trade, which itself, however, remained in the
hands of the Italian sea-trading cities. At the latest around
1230 trade between northern Germany and north-west Italy
down to Genoa became easier when settlers succeeded after
extensive building works in erecting a bridge made of iron
chains passable by carriers and pack animals over the St Gott-
hard pass in the area of the Schöllen Gorge. German merchants
were active in Venice long before the existence of their market
and warehouse, which was founded between 1222 and 1225 on
the Grand Canal near the Rialto bridge, and was known as
the Fondaco (from the Arabic *fundūq*) dei Tedeschi. Bernard
'the German', who around the turn of the thirteenth century
rose to be the richest inhabitant of the city, was a great exception among them. This merchant, who had appeared as
a money-lender to southern German high nobility, probably
obtained his huge capital, the equivalent of about 650 kilo-
grams of pure silver, mainly from importing silver from the
mines of the eastern Alps into the Adriatic.

The Danube trade also experienced a large upturn. Among
the south German merchants, those from Regensburg took the
lead. This is demonstrated by the market laws for Enns, decreed
in 1191 by Duke Ottokar of Styria, in which the organization
of the market traffic was granted to the *Hansegraf* of Regensburg. The merchants of Maastricht, Aachen, and Ulm as well
as other strangers were also given prominence in this. Merchants from Metz, Amberg, and Nuremberg also took part in
the trade via the Danube, reaching as far as Russia; just like the
other long-distance traders, they had to rely on the crossroads
of Regensburg. The most important destination of the Regensburg merchants in the east was Kiev. There in 1179 a

Regensburg merchant who belonged to the *familia* of the monastery of St Emmeram had long been resident; and from there he kept up contacts with his home town. In Kiev the long-distance merchants gained access to the stream of goods from the eastern Mediterranean area, which came via Constantinople and the Black Sea; from Russia they mainly bought fur and wax. On the Danube the Regensburgers sold cloth from the countries of north-west Europe.

These textiles, of extremely varied quality, were sold as far as Regensburg and even beyond by Rhineland merchants, among whom those from Cologne were outstanding. But the Regensburgers were also included in the Rhine trade. With the rise of the fairs of Champagne, merchants from the western parts of the empire, where at the same time the trading activities of the Jews were curtailed, gained direct access to the most important centres of exchange in goods and money in western Europe. There the Germans received practical demonstrations of the highly developed payment and credit system, and the organization of trading enterprises. The Italians remained in a leading position in this, and soon also began to compete with the Jews in Germany as money-lenders.

In the north European exchange of goods between west and east the German merchants were not only favoured by their central position, but also by their head start in civilization. Lübeck, which was only founded in 1160 by Henry the Lion, grew into the most important centre; its interests were promoted by Henry also for power-political reasons. This new foundation on the Trave became a bridgehead of the long-distance trade between the great manufacturing areas of north-western Europe and the Baltic. The east primarily produced raw materials (fur, wax, hemp, flax, and also ore) and staple food (grain, fish, and honey). Around 1300 there were about 40 grain warehouses in Lübeck, which probably housed grain destined for export. The large cogs which came into use in the Baltic and North Sea traffic from the end of the twelfth century onwards, with their length of 20 metres and width of 6 metres, could take up to a hundred tonnes of freight, and now made bulk transport across the high seas possible. This technical progress not only favoured the development of the north German maritime towns, but also changes in the organization of trade.

The island of Gotland with Visby was a main base for the seafaring trade of the Baltic. In the sixties Henry the Lion intervened on behalf of the Gotland merchants. The society of merchants from the Roman Empire who frequented Gotland (*universi mercatores imperii Romani Gotlandiam frequentantes*), in which merchants from Lübeck, but also Westphalians and Saxons worked together under elected *Oldermänner*, became one of the organizational cores of the 'German Hanse'. As early as 1189 the merchants from Gotland and Germany received a guarantee of protection for their persons and goods from the Russian prince Yaroslav, primarily for the trade with Novgorod. In this fast-developing city on the Volkhov close to Lake Ilmen the Germans soon afterwards founded a settlement of their own by the market, in the 'St Petershof'. This served both as living quarters and as an office for the summer and winter travellers. The Gotlandic society also participated in the crusade against the Livonians (1199) by equipping several hundred crusaders, and by the transport of troops.

From the beginning of the thirteenth century merchants from the Baltic also traded in the North Sea, for which to begin with they used the road from Lübeck to Hamburg. Up to then the merchants of Cologne had ruled the trade with England almost on their own. In this they were supported by privileges of King Henry II of 1157 and 1175 and of Richard the Lionheart. For some decades they had had a guild-hall available in London, above the Thames bridge, which later developed into the Hanse office.

The attempts of the Cologne merchants forcibly to exclude from the England trade unwanted competitors from the Baltic, especially those from Lübeck, were unsuccessful in the long run. In 1237 King Henry III, Frederick II's brother-in-law, granted the Gotlanders protection and freedom from toll for all goods bought and sold by their members in his realm. Three decades later he first granted the Hamburg traders (1266) and then also those of Lübeck (1267) the right to found a Hanse, on the model of the Cologne merchants. The competition of the north German merchants in the England trade was only alleviated in 1282 by the foundation of a single 'German Hanse' in London.

From the beginning of the thirteenth century the trading activities of German merchants in Flanders, then the largest cloth-producing area in Europe, also increased considerably— especially merchants from Cologne, Bremen, Hamburg, and Lübeck. Unlike in England, sharp disputes between the German merchants did not occur in the Flemish harbours. Bruges became their trading centre, and also Damme. In 1252 and 1253 they received comprehensive privileges—legal securities, reduction of tolls at Bruges and Damme, scales of their own in Damme. In the following period the German trade grew with the boom which put the city of Bruges on its way to becoming the 'world market-place of the West'.

The gradual transformation of the German Hanse from a more or less loosely organized association of individual merchants from different towns, into an association of cities, came to pass only in post-Staufen times. The first signs, however, showed themselves in the decline of the Gotland society on the one hand and in the rise of urban leagues, primarily in the northern German area, on the other. The Westphalian city league (Münster, Osnabrück, Minden, etc.), created in 1246, was a precursor. Similar leagues were concluded among Saxon towns too in the second half of the thirteenth century. Even more important became the league of the 'Wendish towns'. It had its origin in the pact between Hamburg and Lübeck, first made in 1230 and subsequently renewed several times; it covered the protection of the trade routes between the two cities (1241) and a coin-minting agreement (1259). The sometimes sharp rivalries of Lübeck with the other Baltic towns of Rostock and Stralsund—the latter was even destroyed by Lübeck in 1249—was replaced towards the end of the fifties by reconciliations and treaties. In 1265 these culminated in a permanent treaty in which an annual meeting was agreed. As well as Lübeck, Rostock, and Stralsund, also Wismar, Kiel, Hamburg, and Lüneburg, and then Greifswald, Stettin, and Anklam took part in it.

In the surviving source material of the twelfth and thirteenth centuries, the influence of political factors, conjunctions, and powers on the development of trade emerges more clearly than ever before. This is not just a consequence of developing literacy, but also of fundamentally changed political conditions.

Now in the German part of the empire too, though not to the same extent as at the same time in imperial Italy, treaties were made between towns, which influenced trade. The people of Cologne made such treaties early on with Trier (1149), Dinant (1171), and Verdun (1178). On the whole even more effective, however, were the measures taken by kings and princes to promote trade in the towns subordinate to them, and to gain financial profit from them. In this respect the kings still had a legal advantage over the territorial lords.

Among the Staufen rulers, it was Barbarossa who succeeded in doing most in this respect. He was probably able to base his measures on the counsel of merchants. Thus, in 1173, the emperor made a settlement with Count Philip of Flanders by which he intended to further the development of the royal towns of Aachen and Duisburg. According to this, merchants of Flanders, to whom the emperor granted more legal security, like exemption from judicial duel, should give preference to the four fairs which had been founded in the cities; this was probably directed against the interests of the archiepiscopal metropolis of Cologne. Alongside such measures, and similar ones taken by Henry the Lion particularly in favour of his new foundation of Lübeck, Barbarossa had earlier intervened in favour of trade in a general sense, while also looking after his own interests. Already in 1155 the emperor reacted to the complaint of merchants that new, unjust, and 'senseless' tolls were demanded on the Main from Bamberg to Mainz. Basing himself on a judgement by the princes, the emperor thereupon ordered that all holders of toll had to prove their legal right to do so. As nobody could prove their legality in this way, Barbarossa declared all toll on the Main invalid, but with the exception of two temporary ones and the imperial toll at Frankfurt [3: xxxii. 236–41, no. 62].

The imperial chancery produced an even more general argument when in 1165 Barbarossa declared the removal of obstructive dams and fortifications on the lower Rhine. In future the river—as it had always been—should be a free and royal route. The emperor justified this intervention by citing his duty to care for the good of the whole of the fatherland and the needs of the poor and weak (*salus totius patriae ... et necessitates pauperum*) [19: x. 2. 422f., no. 496]. Arguments like this are similar to the motivation formulated by Frederick II in his privilege of 1245 for the city of Speyer, which was to be spread among numerous towns. In this the Staufen justifies the creation of a 14-day autumn fair in Speyer by the general benefit which occurs from promoting the exchange of goods. The beginnings of 'political economy' are thus already noticeable in Staufen policy [567: 49]. In practice, though, with the Staufen and other sovereigns in Germany motives of territorial and fiscal policy prevailed, which was mainly a consequence of the particular power structure in the German empire. In order to win through in the constant competition among themselves, it became more and more important for the lords to gain an income from the expanding trade by means of rights of conduct, tolls, and mint and market dues.

Now the lords who won great advantages were those who controlled rich deposits of iron ore, silver, non-ferrous metals, or salt. In the Siegerland, in the western Harz, in the upper Palatinate, in Styria, and in Carinthia the mining of iron ore was increased. Iron was increasingly produced by underground mining. At the same time smelting was considerably improved by bellows driven by water power. Such technical innovations also benefited the production of silver and non-ferrous metals. Besides the Rammelsberg at Goslar, deposits were now also exploited on a large scale at Freiberg in Saxony (from 1168 on), and from the thirteenth century onwards in Bohemia. Similar progress was made in salt mining. The Welf salt mines at Lüneburg, the Staufen ones at Schwäbisch Hall—the origin of a very successful coinage (the *Heller*)—Reichenhall in Bavaria, and later Hallein near Salzburg were the most important centres.

The demand for salt, which indirectly gave the *Heller* its name, grew with the rising population, which was dependent on large quantities of it for conserving meat and fish. The improved raw materials opened up new possibilities of development in the metal-processing industries, which were not least used for export. Besides the older centres in the Maas towns and in Cologne, new, specialized towns—like Solingen and Nuremberg—arose. The highly developed craft skills are shown for example in the monumental statue, weighing 16 hundredweight, of the lion of Brunswick, probably cast in a

Brunswick workshop; it was the first 'standing sculpture in the round' (on a pedestal in the open air) of the Middle Ages. Other admirable examples are the works of the goldsmith and enamel painter Nicholas of Verdun, who in 1181 finished his work on the altar of Klosterneuburg. Perhaps Nicholas also worked on the greatest reliquary preserved from the Middle Ages, the shrine of the Three Kings at Cologne, for which around 1200 King Otto IV apparently donated three crowns of gold and precious stones. Both works of art and also the separate shrine at Siegburg which was made for Archbishop Anno of Cologne who was canonized in 1183 are outstanding evidence of classicizing goldsmith work from the turn of the thirteenth century. At the time this tendency was apparent in other forms of art too, like early Gothic architecture, sculpture, and painting, and it went with a new turning towards nature, sensuality, and physical beauty, as they also found literary expression.

Romanesque architecture, and Gothic, which from the second third of the thirteenth century onwards spread into Germany from France, are excellent proofs of the high standard of building crafts. They found much demanding work in the numerous castles and palaces, in the construction of monasteries and country churches, and especially in the fast-spreading markets and towns. In this the buildings of the townspeople, town halls (like those at Cologne and Worms) as well as walls, played an increasing role.

Urbanization created numerous new production centres and markets for the textile industry too. As in the metal industry, export-oriented crafts in this field also expanded. Mass production promoted the division of labour, so that now the sources mention more 'specialists', like fullers, weavers, dyers, shearers, and the merchant tailors who were primarily engaged in trade. In the Cologne textile industry, besides the prevailing woollen cloth, *Tirtei*—a mixture woven from wool and linen for coarser work and peasant clothing—was produced as well. In the twelfth and thirteenth centuries another exporting area developed by Lake Constance, specializing in linen processing. It developed out of domestic weaving in the villages, markets, and monasteries in close correlation with urban politics, especially that of the Staufen. The linen industry of that area in the later thirteenth century obtained a large share of the contemporary 'world market'.

[e] EXTENT AND LIMITS OF EXPANSION

Economic growth in Germany unmistakably accelerated considerably from the middle of the twelfth century. In the areas east of the Elbe and the Saale a development almost by leaps and bounds began, which was probably so far unique in the history of the Middle Ages. The civilizing 'westernization' was introduced there by immigration, and by direct take-over of 'western' models and experiences which were at a high level right from the beginning. With this, however, were connected severe and bloody battles, political domination, and religious repression.

The expansion of economic life in the old settlement areas was steadier. Here from the middle of the thirteenth century the limits of expansion were outlined in colonization and in the urbanization connected with it. In trade and industry there were still good opportunities. The greatly increased exchange of goods with neighbouring countries created an extremely effective impetus towards the economic assimilation of Germany to the Mediterranean and Western cultural areas. In some industries—such as in areas of metal processing and in cloth production—some towns attained an internationally competitive level. This established Germany's mediating role between the Mediterranean and the North and Baltic Seas, between the fairs of Champagne and the eastern countries beyond the Elbe and Saale.

From the modern point of view the fundamental economic transformation achieved great progress. It should not be forgotten that this often resulted from extreme need, especially periods of famine, which drove people to new and often risky ways of securing their existence. Not seldom these advances also necessitated sacrifices. The dark side can most clearly be seen in the settlement of the east, which in the long run, however, procured advantages for the Slavic population of those regions as well. Even many immigrants into the towns had to face high risks, if they could not secure themselves sufficiently against the ups and downs of the labour market and against breakdowns in the supply of staple foods. The successful advance of the economy produced new constraints and forms of dependence for many people in town and country. The influence of this economic transformation on ecclesiastical and religious life was not always favourable either, as the constant complaints about the greed of clerics and laymen make clear.

4

Church Life, Piety, and Education

[a] CRISIS AMONG THE TRADITIONAL MONKS AND
CLERGY

'At this time, the glory of the clergy, but especially that of the
old monasticism, began ... to grow pale.' This entry in the
annals of the Bavarian Premonstratensian monastery of Schäft-
larn in 1229 [14: xvii. 339] expresses an opinion which around
the middle of the thirteenth century was widespread in Germany. The rapid expansion and increasing effectiveness of the
mendicant orders in the German towns from the beginning of
the twenties of the same century spoke for this. Now in Germany too it was found that the traditional clergy and traditional forms of monasticism could not sufficiently fulfil the
altered and increased tasks of the Church in spiritual care. This
finding was strengthened by the appearance of heretical groups
in the bigger German towns from the second half of the twelfth
century. They no longer contented themselves with criticism,
which had already grown loud, but rejected the Catholic
Church entirely as a means of salvation, and set against it their
own organization.

The reasons for this crisis among the 'old' clergy and monasticism are to be found mainly in the fact that the internal
ecclesiastical reforms, which had mostly begun around the turn
of the twelfth century, in Germany too had ebbed away from
the middle of the same century. Although the Cistercians, Premonstratensians, and Augustinians here as in other parts of
Europe continued to found new settlements, it was significant
that the Augustinian canons, who were especially active in
urban environments, remained largely ineffective in the new

settlement areas in the east where the Cistercians were particularly successful. Even the reform centre of Springiersbach
after the death of its first provost Richard (d. 1158) experienced
a steep decline from which it never recovered. About the
same time the abbey of Hirsau, which in the first half of the
twelfth century had reformed numerous Benedictine monasteries and influenced many new foundations with its rule,
sank into a place of only provincial significance. From the
first decades of the thirteenth century, in many Benedictine
monasteries the symptoms of monastic and at the same time
economic decline began to accumulate.

With the Cistercians and Premonstratensians major economic difficulties seem to have appeared more often from the
middle of the thirteenth century. Deviations from the original
statutes can often be observed even before they were revised
and altered. Although the Cistercian monasteries in the western
old settlement areas were mostly situated away from the larger
towns, many of them had intensive contacts with urban markets
and also with the townspeople, from whose number came the
most important donations to the white monks in the thirteenth
century. In the east from an early date they stood in close
connection with the families rising to local lordship. This was
also expressed in the function of the Cistercian houses as burial
places and family monasteries for these dynasts; the Cistercians
generally were very close to the courts of the rulers. The new
foundations here, in contradiction of the statutes, were not in
remote places, but mostly on the big trading routes or close to
towns. Just as irregular was the abandonment of economic
self-sufficiency in favour of rent income, in which the Cistercians assimilated to the Benedictine monasteries earlier in
the east than in the old settlement areas.

In spite of this open tendency to become more worldly, at
the turn of the thirteenth century the Cistercians, contrary to
their original intent, in Germany too opened themselves towards new religious aims by taking convents of nuns into their
order. Even after the decision of the General Chapter in 1228
not to include any nunneries in their order, until 1251 they
allowed exceptions following papal interventions. Even without
such a formal tie, which included the duty of spiritual care by
the monks, other women's communities took up the Cistercian

rules, which had almost become a fashion. Only after the middle of the thirteenth century did the white monks leave the spiritual care of the religious women's movement completely to the Dominicans and Franciscans. Up to then more women's than men's monasteries had come into existence in Germany. Thus around 1250 there were altogether almost 100 Cistercian nunneries in the dioceses of Cologne, Mainz, Trier, Constance, and Würzburg, not a few of them situated in towns or at least close to settlements. The nuns mainly came from noble and ministerial families. In the second half of the thirteenth century discipline in the women's convents was gradually undermined by the fact that nuns—and also the lay brothers and sisters— were allowed to have private property which after their death would fall to the monastery.

The ebbing away of the old and the lack of new impulses towards reform, from the middle of the twelfth century up to the time when the mendicant orders arose in the second quarter of the thirteenth, overlapped with the phase in which the higher ecclesiastics of the older parts of the German empire were on the whole more concentrated on expanding and securing their power positions than were those of neighbouring countries. The often sharp criticism of the papacy and the Roman Curia was incited again and again by political disputes between the empire and the papacy. The reproach that Rome was not ruled by Peter but by Mammon was widespread in Germany in the 1150s, as the *Trierer Stilübungen* suggest. Some decades later Walther von der Vogelweide (d. *c.*1230) also joined in this criticism of Rome.

But the reproaches of clerics and lay people were mainly directed against the secularized clergy, who neglected spiritual care and also otherwise misused their office. This was made with different emphases by for example the Benedictine nuns Hildegard of Bingen and Elizabeth of Schönau (d. 1164), the poets Heinrich von Melk (*c.*1160) and Walther von der Vogelweide, the Cistercian Caesarius of Heisterbach (d. after 1240), the anonymous writer of Passau—possibly a Dominican (*c.*1260/ 1266)—and the great Franciscan popular preacher Berthold of Regensburg (d. 1272). The critical voices came almost without exception from the old settlement areas, where economic and social transformation had occurred on a level most easily comparable with that in the neighbouring countries in the south and west.

[b] RELIGIOUS MOVEMENTS BETWEEN ORTHODOXY AND HERESY

As in the previous century, the German empire in the Staufen period received its most important religious impulses from imperial Italy and the West. The Cathars (the German word *Ketzer* (heretic) is derived from this term), who appeared in Germany as heretics right from the beginning, apparently survived the first persecutions of 1143 at Cologne, at least in part. In 1163, however, they were discovered again. Some of them were tried in the cathedral and later burnt near the Jewish cemetery. Before that they had even succeeded in founding schools and in winning over respected citizens. Hildegard of Bingen preached against the heretics of Cologne, and about the same time or a little later, the Cathars were noticed in Mainz and Koblenz, and also in Passau and Vienna. In the first half of the thirteenth century they were found on the Rhine as far as Strasbourg, in Trier, in villages around Passau, and also in Goslar and Erfurt. But in Germany these obvious heretics, who were accused of severe offences by the Church, caused no great danger for the official Church.

The activities of the Waldensians, who grew out of the poverty and penitence movement, were probably more threatening. As early as 1192 a synod in Toul condemned the 'Waldoys'. The bishop of the neighbouring diocese of Metz became aware of them in 1199, but at first without being able to place them firmly. Men and women of lay status were holding assemblies there, as can be concluded from a correspondence between the bishop and Pope Innocent III. They read to one another from French translations of the Bible. They preached in spite of the prohibition of the priests, to whom they denied obedience, referring to the Bible. They despised all who did not belong to their circle, being convinced that they could impart the words of salvation better than the foolish priests. So far the local Church was satisfied with burning the Bible translations.

The spread of the Waldensians in Germany during the thirteenth century probably overlapped with that of the Cathars. Among the heretics who around 1231 had three different meeting places (*scolae*) in Trier, there were no doubt Waldensians. The Franciscan David of Augsburg (d. 1272), the teacher of the popular preacher Berthold of Regensburg, testifies to the activities of the male and female Waldensians in such schools: 'Day and night they do not stop teaching and learning.' Berthold himself apparently thought there were many uneducated people among the 'heresiarchs', when he called on them : 'Go back to ploughing and weaving.'

Besides these two main groups, who were not always sharply differentiated by members of the official Church, from the beginning of the thirteenth century other, smaller sectarian communities appeared in Germany, again primarily in towns. The followers of Ortlieb of Strasbourg, who had been condemned by Pope Innocent III (i.e. before 1216), attracted a lot of attention. Another heretical group was strongly influenced by the religious and political disputes between empire and papacy in the 1240s; they had their centre in Schwäbisch Hall, the Staufen salt-making town and important minting place. They turned upside-down the papacy's accusation that Frederick II and his son Conrad IV were heretics; for its anti-Staufen propaganda the papacy relied on the mendicant orders. For them the pope was a heretic, the bishops and prelates simoniacs. True salvation, they said, rather derived from the Staufen rulers. The heretics who appeared in the Swabian village of Ries, near Nördlingen, a few decades later (around 1270), whose teachings were marked by excessive mysticism and pantheistic spiritualism, were in close connection with religious movements. Noticeably many women took part in the secret meetings, which points to the expansion of mysticism in the Béguine and other women's convents which was soon to occur.

In contrast to the south of France, the persecution of heretics in Germany, where they were discovered only singly and in small groups, was not carried out systematically. Only a short time after the end of the crusades against the Albigensians (1229), however, Germany witnessed proceedings similar in form. Prompted by the archbishop of Bremen, Pope Gregory IX in October 1232 called a crusade against the allegedly heretical Stedinger (between the Weser and the Hunte area). After the first military advance had been unsuccessful and the count of Oldenburg had met his death, the pope in June 1233 renewed his call, for which now sermons were preached even in Holland, Brabant, and Flanders. The army thus recruited, with expectations of complete indulgence and probably also rich booty, completely defeated the Stedinger peasants in May 1234 near Altenesch. These 'crusades against heretics' were clearly motivated by territorial politics. They were directed against those peasants, some wealthy, who in rejecting new demands since the beginning of the thirteenth century had again and again rebelled against their lords. The accusation of heresy, which had already been raised at the Lenten synod of 1230 or 1231, was based on the persistence of the Stedinger people in excommunication, on their attacks on churches and clerics, and on their belief in demons, sorcery, and prophecy— i.e. on obvious superstitions which were and remained widespread elsewhere among the peasant population.

The simultaneous actions of the cleric Conrad of Marburg, which created a huge sensation, were not so superficially motivated. Based on the authority of Gregory IX, Conrad, who at the same time urged the canonization of his spiritual disciple Elizabeth of Thuringia, in 1231 introduced the Inquisition into Germany; this was the first instance in Europe of the practice of papal extraordinary jurisdiction. Conrad and his helpers practised this rigorous judicial procedure, which hardly allowed the anonymously accused any chance of defending themselves, primarily in the Rhine country and in the diocese of Trier. When he also accused high nobles—like the count of Sayn—those threatened had him murdered, on 30 July 1233. The huge resentment caused by Conrad's inquisitorial practices probably played quite a part in sheltering Germany until far into the fourteenth century from similar persecution. As a relieved contemporary in Trier put it: 'After that (Conrad's death) the stormy persecution ceased, and these extremely dangerous times . . . began to leave room for a milder attitude' [14: xxiv. 402].

The Béguines and Beghards too were spared persecution until towards the end of the thirteenth century. These religious communities, which came into being around the turn of the century in the Maas–Schelde area as part of the widely spread religious poverty movement, can be shown in other German cities by charter evidence from the twenties. It is probably not by chance that the earliest proof comes from Cologne (1223), but it is soon followed by other pieces of evidence from Osnabrück (1233), Münster (1245), Trier (1252), Hamburg (1255), Lübeck (1270), and Goslar (1274). Around the middle of the century about two thousand Béguines and Beghards are said to have lived in Cologne and its surroundings. In Germany too by far the larger part was made up of women.

Besides the Béguines and the numerous other women's communities which from around the turn of the century in various towns linked up with the Cistercians and later the mendicant orders, there were further innovations in religious life in Germany. Thus the order of St Mary Magdalen came into existence on the initiative of the Hildesheim canon Rudolf, who in the mid twenties was active preaching the crusade in the archdiocese of Mainz. This offered 'repenting women'—former concubines and other 'fallen women'—the chance of a communal pious life—to begin with according to Cistercian, and then Augustinian rules. After a short time the order had many convents in German towns. Besides these actual 'repenting women', soon afterwards those from better social milieux entered the convents as well.

From the beginning of the thirteenth century the new religious ways of life were at home in the towns in Germany too. They were, however, not limited to the towns and it is not only the urban environment which accounts for them. The poverty ideal struck a chord and found much support among the rural nobility too, which certainly benefited the urban communities. There were, however, only a few members of the high nobility who themselves took up a life of voluntary poverty and penitence. All the greater then was the sensation caused by the actions of Elizabeth, the Hungarian king's daughter and wife of the Landgrave Ludwig IV of Thuringia (d. 1227). In the great famine year of 1226 she had so much grain distributed from the landgrave's barns to the poor that their need was relieved. After she was widowed—she was the mother of three small children—she dedicated her life in voluntary poverty and daily work to the care of the poor and sick in the small hospital, which had been founded outside Marburg (1228) with her own modest means; in 1231 she died of exhaustion, only 24 years old. From the beginning she had put her hospital under the patronage of Francis of Assisi, who shortly before had been canonized by Pope Gregory IX. Only a few years after her death the same pope conducted the canonization of Elizabeth on 27 March 1235 in Perugia. The translation of her remains followed on 1 May 1236 in the presence of the Emperor Frederick II, Hermann of Salza the Grand Master of the Teutonic Order, the archbishops of Cologne, Mainz, Trier, and Bremen, and numerous other ecclesiastical and secular lords. Her grave had already become the centre of a pilgrimage. Directly after her canonization, the foundation stone was laid for the future church of St Elizabeth, one of the earliest Gothic buildings in Germany, planned after northern French models.

The hospital of St Francis at Marburg had already gone over to the Teutonic Order. The same knightly order had begun to erect hospitals in many German towns, as testified by early mentions in Koblenz (1216), Wiesbaden (1218), Cologne (1218), Speyer (1220), and Goslar (1227). The other large knightly orders up to the middle of the twelfth century also had hospitals in many bigger German towns. Apparently older monasteries which were situated close to the larger towns or on important routes now also once again became interested in hospitals. Thus in 1240 the abbey of St Maximin in the outskirts of Trier erected a hospital to the honour of St Elizabeth. From the late twelfth century members of the urban ruling classes also involved themselves in the building and running of urban hospitals, usually in the form of brotherhoods. The 'bourgeois' hospital order of the Holy Spirit, which came into being around the turn of the century in Montpellier, also contributed. In this way urban hospitals, generally based on brotherhoods, came into being for example in Nördlingen (1233), in Mainz (1236), at about the same time in Frankfurt and Ulm (1240), and soon afterwards in Goslar too (1254).

This brief survey shows how strongly the new religious ways of life in Germany still in the course of the thirteenth century were dependent on stimuli, models, and organizational forms from southern and western neighbouring countries, which on the whole had a more developed civilization. The first appearance of flagellant processions in southern Germany during 1260/1 gives the same impression. This penitence and peace movement was a reminiscence of the religious emotions which took hold of much of the population, starting from Perugia in 1260 and then spreading quickly to the other central and northern Italian towns. It was influenced by eschatological ideas. For several reasons it found little resonance in Germany.

[c] THE MENDICANT ORDERS

Among the four large mendicant orders, the Carmelites and Augustinian Hermits, which only came into being around the middle of the thirteenth century, lagged far behind the Franciscans and the Dominicans until the beginning of the seventies. Like other such orders, they can therefore be left out of the following discussion.

The first settlements of the Franciscans and Dominicans in Germany occurred almost at the same time, in the years 1220-1. An earlier attempt by the Franciscans in 1217 had failed because of their lack of knowledge of the language, and also because of the mistrust with which they were met by the German clerics by reason of their unusual life-style. In their second, successful attempt in 1221, the Minorites, mainly Italians, were led by Caesarius of Speyer (d. *c.*1239). He had studied in Paris. During a stay in Syria he had been accepted into the order by Brother Elias, later the general of the Franciscans (1232–9). By the time Caesarius returned to Italy (1223), the Franciscans had founded their first settlements in Augsburg, Regensburg, Würzburg, Mainz, Worms, Speyer, Strasbourg, and Cologne. With the support of the bishop of Hildesheim there then followed the expansion of the order into Saxony and Thuringia. From the forties onwards the Minorites also had convents between the Elbe and Saale and the Oder. Already in 1230 rapid growth brought about the division of the province of Germany into those of Saxony and the Rhineland; the latter was again split up in 1247 into the provinces of Cologne and Strasbourg.

Around the middle of the century about one hundred Franciscan convents existed in German towns with approximately two and a half thousand friars. In the next fifty years the number of monasteries doubled again. A comparison with other Western European countries, where the mendicant orders only slowly increased in number from 1275, shows that the continuing expansion of the Franciscans and the other mendicant orders in Germany was largely a consequence of the ongoing urbanization, particularly in the south and east. The number of Dominican monasteries (priories) remained considerably smaller than that of the Franciscans. By the middle of the century they possessed only forty priories in Germany, i.e. less than half of the Franciscan number. The Dominicans, however, deliberately concentrated right from the start on the larger and more important towns. They had more influence than the Franciscans in Prussia and the Baltic countries.

In Germany the mendicant orders, with their new forms of spiritual care, grown up and tested out in highly urbanized regions, made essential contributions to the improvement of pastoral work. Here they met a situation in which the shortcomings of traditional religious teaching and care, especially of the urban population, had become obvious through the fast-growing urbanization. At the same time they were able to influence this process here at a relatively early stage, without the defects having been established in the younger and generally still small towns. It is therefore no accident that the objections of the local clergy to the mendicant orders on the grounds of confessions, preaching, and funerals were expressed most sharply in the older towns like Cologne (1225) and Strasbourg (up to 1254). The poverty ideal, firmly observed at first, freed the mendicant orders from conflicts with the urban communes over the judicial and tax privileges of the churches and monasteries.

The many links of the mendicant orders with the cities, whence they influenced the population of the surrounding areas too, and their unavoidable relations with the hierarchy of the Church, could obviously give the mendicant orders a mediating role between city communes and the ecclesiastical lords of the towns. Thus the Dominican Albertus Magnus in the fifties and again in 1271 acted as an arbitrator between the city of

Cologne and its archiepiscopal lord. But the Franciscans and Dominicans, in spite of temporary reservations, were not in a position to remain neutral in the conflict between the Staufen and the papacy. At the latest from the deposition of Frederick II at the Council of Lyons they were committed to the service of the papacy and to the fight against the Staufen, against whom they also acted as crusade preachers. This political partisanship affected their reputation, especially in the Staufen parts of the empire.

The Franciscan John of Diest distinguished himself as chaplain of the anti-king William of Holland, for which in the end he was rewarded with the bishopric of Lübeck (1254-9). Otherwise only a few Franciscans and Dominicans were made bishops, and then mostly in politically unimportant sees. The Franciscan Heinrich Knoderer, who as an adviser of Rudolf of Habsburg was raised to the see of Basle, and later even to the archbishopric of Mainz (1286-8), was a rare exception.

He took part in the battle of Dürnkrut (1278) with a military contingent of his own; the contradiction between the model of Francis of Assisi and the traditional activities of a German imperial bishop was insoluble. This conflict was certainly one of the reasons why Albertus Magnus after only one year asked the pope to release him from his office as bishop of Regensburg (1260-2).

Heinrich Knoderer, the son of a baker or miller from Isny (Allgäu), who had studied in Paris, and Albertus Magnus were among the few members of the mendicant orders whose social origin can be roughly determined. The only certainty is that members of all social classes up to the high nobility were accepted into the mendicant orders. A large part of the leading members in the convents probably originated from ministerial and knightly families and from the rest of the urban patrician class. These social groups were probably more strongly represented in the Dominican order than among the Franciscans, who it seems accepted men of lower origin in larger numbers. Among the Dominicans, Germans early took up leading positions, which might be traced to the influence of Jordan of Saxony. In the German provinces of the Franciscans, in contrast, friars from Italy remained dominant for a longer period.

The two mendicant orders' differing attitudes towards the priesthood and education were also affected by these differences.

[d] SCHOOLS, LEARNING, AND EDUCATION

As in other countries, the percentage of priests among the Franciscans in Germany, especially at first, was considerably lower than that among the Dominicans. Jordan of Saxony, in his 15-year career as Minister General of the preaching order, endeavoured to recruit students at the new universities in France, Italy, and England. Among them apparently were relatively many Germans, who because of the high cost of study usually came from well-to-do families. As the only school of the Dominican order then in existence, St James at Paris, was soon overburdened, in 1248 a school for the German province was founded in Cologne. Its first rector was Albertus Magnus. Before he entered the order, he had studied in Italy, and from 1233 he taught in different German schools of the order before gaining his doctorate in Paris in the forties. Thomas Aquinas was at first one of Albertus's pupils in Cologne.

At first the work of the Franciscans in Germany suffered particularly from the lack of priests. In the carefully chosen group with which Caesarius of Speyer began his mission in Germany in 1221, there were 15 laymen and only 12 priests. The Franciscans in Germany had no teacher of theology until 1228. In this year the Minister General entrusted the Englishman Simon with this task, which he took up at the convent in Magdeburg. A few years later Simon's fellow countryman Bartholomaeus Anglicus (b. before 1200, d. after 1250) began his work; he had been teaching shortly before in Paris. He distinguished himself especially as the author of a widely distributed, scientifically orientated encyclopedia. Berthold of Regensburg was probably educated in Magdeburg. From 1240 Berthold was active as a popular preacher in Augsburg and many other southern German towns and districts, at times together with David of Augsburg (d. 1272), who at first was novice master in the house at Regensburg. Berthold's sermons, in which he mainly addressed the urban middle and lower classes, were so sought-after that they often had to be held in the open air. He had a lasting influence on popular religious teaching by sermon collections of his own, and copies made and collected by clerics and colleagues.

Although study in the mendicant orders was primarily directed towards the practical needs of preaching, spiritual care, and fighting heretics, it nevertheless had a great effect on the religious instruction and care of the urban and suburban population. Not only that, but because of their close connections with the spiritual centres of western Europe and the active exchange of thought within the mendicant orders, increased by the high mobility between convents, the mendicant orders also made an important contribution to the lasting integration of the German lands into Western European civilization.

The achievements of the mendicant orders become even clearer when compared to the older orders, the canons, and the parish clergy. The German cathedral schools on the whole stuck to their traditional approach. By the middle of the thirteenth century the cathedral school of Bamberg was of only regional importance. Once the school of the 'imperial Church system', it obviously had not only neglected the new theology but also not developed the study of Roman law, which began in Bologna in the second half of the twelfth century; this was probably partly because there had been no concern for it in imperial politics since the struggle for the throne. Church law became more important, for which handbook-like texts were supplied, mainly via France. At the same time it became habitual in Germany for many clerics—and also laymen—to spend a few years of study at the schools and universities of France and Italy.

The new approaches met with success, not only among the mendicant orders in the growing urban centres. Already before 1220/1 in towns like Ghent and Erfurt the interest of the population was expressed in the urban schools. In 1191 the citizens of Ghent had their previously denied right to found schools granted by charter. In 1262 the council of Lübeck gained *de facto* control over the school of St James's church. Not only simple reading and writing skills, which became more and more necessary for merchants and other crafts- and tradespeople, were taught there, but also Latin.

In the course of the thirteenth century, in Germany considerably later than in the urbanized areas of the Latin countries, the clergy's monopoly of literacy was first breached on a broad front. The urban ruling classes played the biggest part in this. The need derived not only from daily business, but from the increasing work of the city communes. Thus the city of Lübeck around the middle of the thirteenth century tried, albeit without success, to recruit a jurist well versed in civil and Church law, trained in the north Italian universities. The bigger city communes especially needed versatile and competent town clerks, who could act as legal advisers and 'diplomats'. From the second quarter of the thirteenth century such town clerks are found more and more often in Germany. One of them was Henry of Boitzenburg, who worked in Erfurt between 1265 and 1282. He was a noble who had become a master and doctor of canon law in Paris and Italy.

From the middle of the thirteenth century we find the first evidence in Germany of written town chronicles. It is not by accident that, besides Worms, it comes from Cologne, the biggest city in Germany. The new literary genre is probably most developed in the *Boech van der stede van Coelne*, probably written between 1277 and 1287 by the town clerk of Cologne and later priest, Godefrit Hagen (d. before 1301). In this matter too there was a difference of about 100 years between Germany and imperial Italy.

Written history in Germany stayed far behind the great achievements of Staufen court historiography after the time of Otto of Freising and his successor Rahewin. Although they found successors in the Benedictine abbot Otto of St Blasien (d. 1223) and the provost Burchard (d. 1230) of the Premonstratensian monastery of Ursberg, these works attracted little notice in the thirteenth century, which was essentially a consequence of the course of imperial history. On the other hand the Welf family history, the *Historia Welforum*, probably written between 1167 and 1174 in the monastery of Altdorf-Weingarten, by the Welf family seat, attracted much greater interest. Those and similar works, like that of Gislebert of Mons (d. 1223/5) on the counts of Hainaut, or the almost contemporary chronicle of Livonia, already point to the fashion for regional history, which set in strongly from the beginning of the fourteenth century.

Historical narrative in the German language addressed a wider lay public. After the *Annolied* ('Song of Anno'), written around 1080, which research on the manuscripts so far suggests was not very widely distributed, the 'translations' of clerical history for the lay world, in which their main addressees were ministerials and knights, probably only began on a broader basis around the middle of the twelfth century. According to the latest dating, the first German rhymed chronicles were the imperial chronicle of a priest from Regensburg, the Song of Alexander by the cleric Lamprecht, and the Song of Roland by the cleric Conrad.

The boundary between this historical poetry and 'courtly' epics was fluid. Just as with the Song of Alexander and the Song of Roland, the patterns and models probably came mostly from areas of French speech. At least in the twelfth century, the reception of these patterns took place primarily via the Rhine country but also to the south (Bavaria) and to the east (Thuringia). Up to the end of this century the epic poets were predominantly clerics. Hartmann von Aue (d. after 1210), who called himself 'knight' and *dienestman* ministerial, was probably the earliest exception. Later, when the education of laypeople in Germany had made greater progress, Rudolf von Ems (d. 1250/4) was both 'ministerial' and 'a man with knowledge of the Latin language'. The greatest German epic writer, Wolfram von Eschenbach (d. *c.*1225), was an 'uneducated', very well informed layman.

In general the authors of epics were constantly dependent on patrons, and were therefore always bound to the courts of princes for long periods. Thus the 'cleric' Heinrich von Veldeke (d. before 1210) finished his romance of Aeneas, the *Eneit*, between 1184 and 1190 at the court of the landgrave of Thuringia. About ten years previously Heinrich had completed two-thirds of his work at a princely court on the lower Rhine, before it had been taken away from him by a count interested in literature and had then come into the possession of the landgrave. The *Minnesänger* and epigrammatists on the other hand were less dependent on continuous patronage. Not a few of them belonged to the high, and even the highest, nobility.

The later Emperor Henry VI wrote *Minnelieder* in his youth; his son Frederick II made such poems in the Sicilian language.

Until about the end of the twelfth century the courtly lyric, which began in Germany at about the same time as the secular epics, had its centre in the Staufen south-west. Friedrich von Hausen apparently held a key position in this. He often stayed at the imperial court, even when it was in Italy. In 1190 he had a fatal accident when accompanying the emperor on crusade in Asia Minor. Other members of this Staufen court circle were Ulrich von Gutenburg, Bligger von Steinach, Bernger von Horheim, Heinrich von Rugge, and Hartwic von Rûte.

The emperor's court helped the Provençal-style *Minnesang* to break through in the last decades of the twelfth century. It is possible that the continual contact of the Staufen court with Italy played an important role in taking over this model. There, especially at the court of the margrave of Montferrat, a contemporary centre of Provençal poetry was to be found. The poetry thus influenced attained its highest development in Albrecht von Johansdorf, Hartmann von Aue, Heinrich von Morungen, Reinmar von Hagenau, and finally in Walther von der Vogelweide, the most important German poet of the Middle Ages and the real founder of German epigrammatic poetry. After leaving the Babenberg court in Vienna (1198) Walther also experienced the darker side of the life of an 'itinerant' professional poet. It was probably brightened, but only for a short time, by the fief granted to him by Frederick II.

During the thirteenth century in Germany too, 'courtly' poetry developed closer connections with the towns, and especially with the urban ruling classes. This connection came about through the development of the courts of various princes into towns, and the beginnings of the 'residence' towns of the secular princes now began to appear in outline. In the episcopal towns the closeness of court and town had long existed. Behind it stood numerous links between leading urban families and life at the courts. Thus it does not seem unusual when Rudolf von Ems in his *Willehalm* mentions 'maister Hesse von Strasburg', who is known to have been town clerk there, 1230–40, as an authority on literature and criticism. Strasbourg was also the centre of the early transmission of *Tristan*, by Gottfried von

Strassburg, who seems to originate from the Strasbourg bourgeoisie. In his rhymed novel *Der Guote Gêrhard*, Rudolf von
Ems, who according to his own words was incited to write
this didactic poem by the ministerial Rudolf of Steinach from
Constance, puts a Cologne merchant at the centre. The son of
this merchant, distinguished by *güete* (goodness) and *diemüete*
(humility), was dubbed and thus became a knight, so that he
could marry a noble lady. Around the middle of the same
century Ulrich von Türheim (d. 1286) testifies that 'Otte der
Bogenaere' supplied him with the French model for his *Re-
nnewart*. This citizen of Augsburg, who also had contacts with
the pro-Staufen court of Hohenlohe, was therefore close to a
poet who had been supported by King Henry (VII) and the
influential imperial ministerial Conrad of Winterstetten.

In another respect too, the courtly poetry reflects a change
of orientation. From the middle of the thirteenth century onwards the courts of the big territorial princes in eastern Germany and eastern central Europe—Brandenburg, Thuringia,
Meissen, and Silesia, Bohemia, and Poland—became important literary centres.

5

New Beginnings in the Social System

One of the consequences of the great changes among literate groups was the fact that we have from the Staufen period social doctrines whose writers distinctly differ from older authors in their social and religious horizons.

This holds particularly true for Eike of Repgow, a layman educated in Latin and law; he was possibly a pupil at the cathedral school of Halberstadt of the legal scholar John Zemecke (Teutonicus), who was temporarily (1215/16-1220) active in Bologna. Like the ministerial's daughter Tenxwind of Andernach, Eike did perhaps not belong to the free nobility. In the most important lawbook of medieval Germany, the *Sachsenspiegel*, which Eike wrote and also translated from Latin into Low German, he refuted the traditional justification of serfdom (*Egenscap*) in scholastic fashion with biblical, historical, and legal arguments as well as with common sense. For Eike the decisive arguments were the exact likeness of man to God, and Christ's act of redemption. Unfreedom, he said, could not be justified on any authority—not even the Old Testament. For him the very great differences in the legal position of the unfree, which he himself had observed, were evidence of the unjustness of serdom as a whole. The unfreedom of men had only come into being by force, imprisonment, and other unjust acts of violence. On this an established right had been based, which was now unjustifiably maintained.

This opinion was highly successful in the numerous manuscripts in which the *Sachsenspiegel* was distributed. Around 1275 it was taken over and extended in essentials in the *Kaiserliche Land- und lehnrechtsbuch*—the *Schwabenspiegel*, written by an Augsburg Franciscan and based on the *Sachsenspiegel*. The author added that service to a master is solely legitimate in return for the granting of protection. If the lords 'die Lant nit schirment' (did not protect the country), they had no right to service. Not personal dependence but only effective protection could be regarded as a legal basis for personal services. The Franciscan thus pursued the functional scheme of interpretation, which had been handed down from the eleventh century, to its extreme conclusion.

Berthold of Regensburg's social doctrine was also based on this. His sermons were edited in the seventies by Franciscans from Augsburg. In these, unfreedom is meaningless as a basis for social distinctions. Berthold, however, admonished the peasants to remain loyal towards their masters. He criticized them for often avoiding their duties by putting themselves under another master. But this, he said, was often the fault of the lords for making excessive demands. The popular preacher holds on to a hierarchical order, in analogy with the heavenly choirs. This order remains essentially distinguished by the traditional dualistic pattern: the *hoehsten* (highest) and the *hersten* (most pure) are those entrusted by God with the clerical and secular tasks of ruling the world—priests, monks, and secular lords. Among the latter are emperors and kings as well as princes, knights, and lords and all other holders of power and jurisdiction, among them the town communes, which are not specifically mentioned. The element of birth therefore steps into the background with these groups in favour of the idea of office. For undertaking their tasks the holders of offices and power have the right to demand services from the rest of the population—the 'poor' people.

When saying 'poor' the Franciscan certainly does not mean the economically weak. The popular preacher, experienced in the ways of towns, places the clothes-makers, like weavers, furriers, shoemakers, and others, at the head of these six groups. They are follwed by smiths, carpenters, goldsmiths, moneyers, stonemasons, and turners. After them follow the merchants, especially the long-distance merchants; then the food trades—bakers, brewers, butchers, including the small shopkeepers.

Subordinated to them are the peasants. In the last place among the nine earthly 'choirs' are pharmacists and physicians. In the tenth choir, the fallen angels, the Franciscan, according to his hierarchical principle of usefulness, firmly places minstrels and jugglers, but also all those—therefore also those priests, monks, and lords—who do not carry out their office in a Christian sense.

The idea of office in this way supports the egalitarian tendencies on the model of the original Church, which before the Franciscans had found expression in the poverty movement. This idea also formed the starting-point for a more differentiated and meaningful integration of other social groups which had gained in importance, particularly in the towns. This process was favoured by the pastoral activities of the urban mendicant orders.

It must, however, be borne in mind that such religiously motivated interpretations and attitudes, coloured by new experiences, were by no means accepted by all contemporaries. It is significant that Eike of Repgow could not support his point of view from contemporary authorities. Rather he turned against a century-old tradition, which relied on the authority of the Bible and customary law. At about the same time (1224) the bishop of Münster sharply condemned and punished with excommunication, on God's and his own authority, those serfs who 'pull their neck out of the yoke of serfdom' by fleeing into the towns [3: xxxi. 296-9, no. 111]. The birthright principle also gained great importance in the definition of the 'lordly class' (*Herrenstand*) and of knighthood in the thirteenth century.

[*b*] MINISTERIALS, 'KNIGHTHOOD', AND NOBILITY

From the middle of the twelfth century onwards in Germany too there were repeated attempts from various sides to restrict the great mobility within the ruling classes and to impose a stricter order. One need only remember the development of the *Reichsfürstenstand* (the group of imperial princes), in which powerful nobles striving for sovereignty linked up together, so that finally further nobles could only be accepted into this exclusive association by appointment through the king with the consent of the existing imperial princes. This delimitation of the group of imperial princes ran almost parallel in time with the efforts of the unfree knights to be legally distinguished from the peasants. At the same time a large number of ministerials in the country and also in some towns succeeded in joining noble free families. The rise of the ministerials led to a great expansion of the nobility. It also strengthened the tendencies towards differentiation within noble society. This process, however, only gained clear outlines in the later Middle Ages.

The most important motive forces for these fundamental changes within the noble élite were territorialization, the feudalism which it shaped, and also rural development and economic factors. Also influential was the advance of a courtly-noble common consciousness, which from the middle of the twelfth century increasingly gained shape in literature based on patterns and influences from the Latin countries. As the effectiveness of these factors varied considerably by region, the social tendencies just outlined expressed themselves in different forms, and partly with wide chronological variations.

The ministerials were probably the most dynamic force. In the old settlement areas, where the more powerful noble or ecclesiastical princes controlled more than 100 ministerial families, they were generally more numerous than in the eastern new settlement areas, for example in the Mark of Brandenburg. As personal unfreedom was to a large extent meaningless there, even among the peasant population—at least as far as they lived according to German law—organization according to professional groups could be enforced unhindered. For the same reasons in the territories beyond the Elbe and Saale a relatively homogeneous knighthood developed, which in itself, however, was graded according to rights in property and jurisdiction.

Within the old settlement areas the ministerials assimilated more to the noble free vassals if their masters pursued intensive, large-scale territorial politics and controlled sufficient fees. The forms and conditions of imperial rule, as has been pointed out, favoured the tendency towards independence and the rise of the numerous imperial ministerials in the Staufen areas. But now many ministerials who had not received sufficient fees from their lords became the vassals of other lords, which meant that their personal servitude became in practice meaningless. In this the ministerials of the archbishop of Cologne were supported by the wording of a law of service given in 1165. This assimilation to noble vassals also offered a basis for marriages between ministerials and nobles. As the ministerial partners were still bound to their lords for part of their property, even members of powerful imperial ministerial families needed the consent of their royal lord, or a formal liberation, even after the middle of the thirteenth century. But the 'growing together' of ministerials and noble vassals was not impeded by such relics. Looking at the development of definitions, in the thirteenth century this process was expressed by the ousting of class titles such as *ministerialis* on the one hand and *liberi* or *nobiles* on the other, in favour of the title *milites* referring to both groups.

The merging of the unfree nobility, the ministerials, into the free nobility brought about an increasing similarity of the noble élite of the German empire to that of France and Italy, in so far as the ministerials never played an important role there, except in border areas. One could interpret the 'disappearance' of the ministerials, which happened simultaneously in the towns too, as an expression of the 'westernization' of Germany. No doubt the essential factors which influenced this process were based on special conditions and developments in Germany in the twelfth and thirteenth centuries, but causes which originated in the neighbouring Latin lands of France and Italy, and affected them earlier, clearly had an effect as well—especially the crusade and poverty movements with their manifold religious and social consequences.

In this context the activities of the ministerials in founding churches and monasteries, which increased greatly from the twelfth century, and also their entry into the monasteries, was of a value which can hardly be overestimated for their rise. Premonstratensian and Cistercian monasteries, and not least the knightly and mendicant orders, offered the ministerials a rich and also 'profitable' field of action. It seems that this social and religious basis also furthered the rise of individual sons of ministerials to higher positions in the Church hierarchy, although even in the thirteenth century they reached episcopal rank, or succeeded in standing their ground in it, only in a few cases.

The process by which the ministerials grew into the feudal nobility, favoured by many factors, was closely connected with the reception in Germany of courtly poetry from the Latin lands. From the turn of the thirteenth century the ministerials obtained great influence on the adoption, shaping, and distribution of this poetry, in which general knightly and noble self-images, values, and behaviour were given literary form. Soon eminent ministerials like Rudolf of Steinach, a ministerial of the bishop of Constance, and the imperial ministerial Conrad of Winterstetten, appeared as patrons of this courtly, knightly poetry. Conrad was probably the first among his fellows to become an influential figure in courtly poetry; he formed the centre of a 'society' marked by similar literary interests.

[c] PEASANTS AND THE RURAL POPULATION

It was virtually a necessary accompaniment of the rise of the ministerials into the feudal nobility and their knightly life-style, that the knights were distinguished, or tried to differentiate themselves, from the rest of the rural population. As the great majority of knights, at least in the old settlement areas, were themselves of unfree origin, and as there were free as well as unfree people among the peasants (*rustici*), the only distinguishing characteristics left were professional activities and endowment with property and lordship rights (fiefs). However, in a time of great economic transformation, and expansion and intensification of lordship, these distinctive marks were of little use in sealing off the status of knighthood from below.

Barbarossa's Constitution against Arsonists of 1186 suggests that many sons of clerics and peasants received the belt of knighthood and in this way found acceptance into the knightly class. There is little evidence that this changed considerably in the following period, despite the emperor's prohibition. Naturally, the sons of knights had more chance in the long run of leading a knightly life, which strengthened the element of birthright. In Hainaut at the turn of the thirteenth century, however, the possibility was allowed for that the sons of knights might not become knights; in this case they were put in the same legal category as the peasants.

On the other hand, in the duchy of Bavaria at least, many peasants around the middle of the thirteenth century (1244) treated themselves to such an expensive life-style that, probably for the first time in a public peace, decrees were made against their long hair, their precious clothes, and their display of knightly weapons. Heads of households were, however, allowed to wear a sword when going to church. They were permitted to keep all kinds of weapons at home—including chain armour and an iron helmet—in order to be armed in case of a general emergency, for defence against external enemies, and for enforcing court sentences.

The legal demarcation between knights and peasants was thus often in contradiction to the economic and social similarity between well-to-do peasants, who often held an office as well, and the economically not so well-off knights who had only small fiefs. This tense situation found expression in the pejorative attitude to peasant behaviour in courtly literature. But more important in the long run was social assimilation, by marriage, and not least by princes dubbing peasants to knighthood. Many peasants became knights in this way, while some knights became 'countrified'.

The situation of peasants with large farms was on the whole particularly favourable in the Staufen period, despite the sometimes new burdens which were loaded on to them by various lords. It is more difficult to judge the situation of the rest of the rural population, with their extremely varied conditions of life. As the sources testify, those country-dwellers who had small farms, or none at all, escaped from their burdens by fleeing when circumstances allowed.

Already before 1158 the male and female serfs of the Cologne monastery of St Maria im Kapitol, who belonged to two farms near Cologne and who had to pay the relatively high rent of ten *Pfennige* (pence) per head, did exactly that. When the abbess afterwards put an additional burden on the remaining peasants with holdings, in order to even out the loss created by the flight and also by mismanagement, these independent peasants fled as well. Faced with this threatening situation the monastery decided to invest heavily in improving the livestock and the other equipment of the farms. They reduced the rent to two *Pfennige* per head, but demanded the less burdensome once-for-all dues of the best beast or best dress, and a marriage due of six *Pfennige*. Under these more favourable conditions the serfs declared on oath that they were prepared to work with all their might to deliver the fixed payments in money or in kind to the monastery, leaving the surplus to themselves [3: xxxi., no. 85].

As this example shows, migration from the country—like participation in the settling of the east or in inland colonization—was not necessarily caused by oppression by the lords. The flight was often rather a consequence of expectations the rural inhabitants had about town life, and in which they were encouraged by the lords of the towns and by the communes. To those country-dwellers concerned with trade and industry, the bigger towns especially seemed promising. This is expressly stated by a young man in 1181: he preferred the merchant's profession to that of a peasant, as while doing business in town he had developed a strong dislike of rural life. He therefore sold his property rights in a tenement with 27 acres (*Tagwerk*) of arable land, thereby increasing his capital for life in the town [26: 104]. But the towns held a fascination for rural dwellers not only for economic reasons. Behind their walls they offered the immigrants stronger, in many cases even certain, protection against feuds and the dangers of war.

The growing competition between the numerous lords of markets and towns, who in some old settlement areas by the first decades of the thirteenth century only disposed of very small catchment areas for urbanization, caused them to promote the immigration of rural dwellers by more and more profitable offers. Among these attractions was the possibility, which local and urban laws contained from the late twelfth century, of shaking off the remaining manorial duties and dependences in urban 'freedom' after a year and a day—but sometimes after a considerably longer term. Even if the manorial lord managed to find his serf within this period, he often still had to produce proof for his claim before local or urban courts. Even if the court then decided in favour of the manorial lord, such serfs could in many cases remain in the town while acknowledging their duties. In this way they had the chance to free themselves in the long run from legal restrictions, which were especially disadvantageous concerning their rights of inheritance. The immigrant serfs could safeguard their situation in a town by putting themselves under the protection of a monastery or church, by becoming rent-paying tenants. Others might enter into a protective relationship with one of the more powerful citizens, who recruited their *Muntmannen* (those dependent on protection) from other strata of the urban and rural population as well.

This was the meaning of the phrase *Stadtluft macht frei* ('town air makes free'), which was only formulated in the nineteenth century. The result was an improvement in the legal situation of the people living in rural settlements as well. Significant for this were the development of village and rural communes, and the grant and confirmation of rights to villages. From the beginning of the thirteenth century larger towns granted participation in urban privileges to individual inhabitants and communes in the surrounding areas, for which these 'outside citizens', or *Pfahlbürger*, mostly entered into financial obligations. The princes successfully resisted this process in Frederick II's and Henry (VII)'s imperial laws, without completely preventing its continuation, so threatening for the lords' interests.

The clearing activities of peasants in the old settlement area also had a long-term positive effect. This 'freedom by assarting', however, was more dependent than the 'urban freedom' on favourable relations with protecting lords, as otherwise the demands of the local lords might become excessively heavy burdens. Thus the archbishops of Bremen tried to transform the hereditary fees, which had been granted to the peasants of Stedingen by the charters of settlement, into dependent leases and thereby to bring the free peasants into manorial dependence. The resistance that the Stedinger peasants put up against this, as already mentioned, was broken by force in the crusades of 1232/4.

[d] TOWN-DWELLERS AND CITIZENS

The wide catchment area for immigration into the city of Cologne gives an impressive picture of the attraction exerted by the larger towns as early as the twelfth century, even if Cologne, as the biggest German town, was an extreme case.

The evidence for the places of origin of citizens of Cologne shows that the Rhenish metropolis attracted immigrants from the upper Rhine area as far as Basle and Zürich, from the south-east as far as Würzburg, Nuremberg, and Regensburg, from the east as far as Erfurt and Goslar, and from the north and north-east as far as Bardowick and Groningen, and even from Denmark and Norway. In the south-west the immigration area reached as far as Metz, Bar, and Verdun, in the west and north-west as far as St Quentin, Valenciennes, and Ypres. Apparently individual Englishmen also settled in Cologne. The most important immigration areas besides the middle and lower Rhine were the numerous urban centres, highly developed at an early stage, on the Maas and in the area between the Maas and the Schelde.

Many of the immigrants from distant places were merchants, who as citizens of Cologne went on trading with their original towns. The parents of Marcmann Lämmchen, who is witnessed as a juror and senator (*Schöffensenator*) of Cologne between 1140 and 1178, and who therefore belonged to the inner group of political leaders, originated from the Maas town of Huy. The Minnevuz family, who had immigrated from Basle at the beginning of the twelfth century, experienced a similarly steep rise. The foundation in this case too was laid by marriage in the first generation into a high-ranking Cologne family. One of the immigrant's sons in the second half of the twelfth century was a Cologne *Untergraf*. His grandson was a ministerial and knight and married his daughter to one of the members of a noble family living as townsmen in Cologne.

As in many other towns of the old settlement areas, the ministerials made up a high percentage of the smaller urban ruling groups in Cologne too. There they were organized in the *Richerzeche* (union of the rich and powerful), known in documents from 1180 onwards, which supplied the two mayors, most of the jurors, and later also many members of the town council. Several members of the *Richerzeche* were evidently ministerials of the archbishop of Cologne or of other churches or monasteries of the town, in some cases even imperial ministerials. They had rights over market stalls, had large landed property at their disposal, and were also active as moneylenders. The Cologne citizen Konrad Unmaze ('immodest'), who was one of the mayors several times, was a ministerial. In 1174 he was able to lend Archbishop Philip the huge sum of 650 marks of silver, for which as well as houses he received the Rhine toll as security.

In other large towns ministerials were also represented in large numbers in the moneyers' guilds, which usually had a monopoly of money-changing and the silver trade, and who participated in financing the mint. Such co-operatives are found for example in Worms, Speyer, Trier, Regensburg, Passau, Augsburg, and Vienna. For many urban ministerials active participation in market and money trading, participation in the political leadership of the town, and personal ties to the lord of the town or other lords, from whom they held servile fees and soon other fees too both inside and outside the town, were thus closely connected. It must be remembered, though, that participation in trade and finance was only important in the bigger towns. There close social connections existed between ministerials and rich merchants. In the numerous smaller towns, especially those attached to castles, the activities of the ministerials resembled much more those of their country-dwelling fellows, the distance between them and other urban ruling groups remaining large.

The ministerials probably formed the most important link for integrating the towns into the existing power structure, and also enabled them to win greater independence outside the towns. The special conditions in the towns on their part promoted the loosening of the ministerials' servile bonds. But at the same time they contributed to the reduction of ministerial privileges, one of them being a special legal status. Thus the town laws of Strasbourg of 1270—eight years after the defeat of the bishop by his town at the battle of Hausbergen—made the city court binding on all inhabitants, expressly also on the *gotshuzdienstman* ('ecclesiatical ministerial'). Upon this, a number of ministerials left the town, but the others remained in Strasbourg as knights.

Already before then feudal law had pushed legal serfdom into the background, among the urban ministerials too. Citizens who did not originate from ministerial families could also enter into feudal ties, as a privilege of Henry (VII) of 1228 for the citizens of Basle specially emphasized. These processes were connected in the larger towns with a reduction in the powers of the lords of the towns, the old ministerial relationships and privileges thereby losing their basis. Only in those towns where the feudally anchored ruling groups succeeded in securing sufficient room for manœuvre against the lord of the town and also against the town commune, did an urban nobility begin to develop, from about the middle of the thirteenth century onwards. This urban aristocracy was closely connected with the lower nobility in the countryside. By exercising allodial and feudal property and lordship rights, this ruling group reached far beyond the town walls. With this they simultaneously opened up possibilities of influence in the town to lords from outside it. Such deepened social relationships between town and country formed a sound bridge for the passage of knightly poetry into the urban milieu.

In this way in many German towns in the old settlement areas—for example in Strasbourg, Augsburg, and Regensburg—a development began which had taken place much earlier in the Latin lands. There to begin with the urban nobility had strengthened the political power of the communes, but soon considerably weakened their inner cohesion. Conflicts between leading families, perhaps most visible in Cologne, were already clear in outline in the first half of the thirteenth century.

The predominance of a few families which tried to mark themselves off from those below by birth did not exclude the rise of new groups, who had usually become rich in trade, into this association, particularly as members of such families might get into economic difficulties and suffer social decline. In most larger towns, as well as such co-operatives as the *Richerzeche* in Cologne in which the families were organized, there were also other guilds or variously named brotherhoods for the other merchants. Traders' and drapers' guilds were widespread in central German towns like Halberstadt and Magdeburg. These endeavoured to monopolize not only the wholesale trade, but also the retail business. They therefore also strove to secure their predominance over new groups, which mainly came from the craft population. Around the middle of the twelfth century about 200-300 merchants were members of the guild in Cologne, among them probably only a few craftsmen who were also active in trade.

At the same time craftsmen in large numbers began to organize themselves in brotherhood-type corporations in the bigger towns. In Cologne, besides the linen-weavers (1149), foundation charters down to the middle of the thirteenth century exist for the turners (1179/82), felt-shoemakers (1225), wool-weavers (1230), and tailors (1247). Further evidence allows us to suppose that in Cologne at that time more than a dozen corporations were in existence. It depended on the power structure of the individual town whether, as in Cologne from at least 1149, they were controlled by the leaders of the town commune or by the ecclesiastical or secular lords. In by far the majority of cases they were also legitimized in the thirteenth century by the lords of the town, as demanded by the imperial laws of 1231/2.

The corporations of craftsmen in one form or another, and they are given extremely varied names in the sources (*Amt, Zunft, Gilde, Innung, Bruderschaft, Handwerk*, etc.), were shaped by a varying admixture of collective or lordly influences. In the older episcopal towns these corporations could build on to earlier forms organized by the lords for market business and the supply of the court. In towns like Strasbourg, Trier, and Worms, the 'chamber craftsmen' (*Kammerhandwerker*) were examples; with their service links with the episcopal court, they enjoyed economically important privileges. Such older organizations were still effective to a certain degree in Staufen times, but on the whole they were overlain and transformed by the self-generated bonds of the craftsman brotherhoods with their specific economic, social, and religious aims.

The corporations in Germany developed into an effective 'cement' for a wide urban middle class, which only in Staufen times acquired firm outlines. The craftsmen in the bigger German towns, however, did not attain great political weight, which was caused among other things by the differences and limitations of their various interests. Only in Cologne from the middle of the thirteenth century did they temporarily gain greater political importance, in disputes between the archiepiscopal lords of the city and the leading families, as well as among the families themselves. This, however, was partly the result of members of the families having had themselves made heads of guilds, and then using them in this way for their own interests. But this also expressed a transformation in the importance of new classes and groups, who had only recently acquired the opportunity to develop on the urban periphery.

The various corporations and brotherhoods of merchants and craftsmen created behind the town walls a dense network of self-help, in which more and more groups previously much in need of protection, and economically heavily dependent, gained overall security. In spite of their strong self-interest they laid a foundation on which the general needs of the urban population could be expressed against the egoism of the great families. In this way they made an indispensable contribution to the 'openness' of urban society, which in the following centuries had to withstand great pressure from the territorial lords and also from the internal urban tendency to develop domination and authority. In this respect the German towns on the whole proved more resistant than the cities of imperial Italy. In Staufen times the latter had the more developed economy and the higher civilization, but they suffered from the fact that their internal social differences were checked to a much lesser degree by the lords of the towns and other powers.

[e] THE JEWS AS AN ALIEN MINORITY

The endeavours of guilds and corporations to enforce monopolies and other professional privileges had a restricting influence on the economic activities of the Jews, contributing to the fact that the Jews were more and more pushed into usury, which was forbidden to Christians by the church. The more the Christian communes organized themselves internally, the more the outsider role of the Jewish communities developed. The crusade, the campaigns against heretics, the definition of dogma, as well as the institutional hardening of the Roman official church, all increased the isolation of the Jewish minority. One sign of this is the decree made in 1215 at the fourth Lateran Council, that Jews and Saracens ought to be distinguished from Christians by their clothes. The demand, first made in France, that Jews ought to wear a yellow ring is most probably based on this. Another consequence was the confiscation of the Talmud everywhere in France in 1240, and the subsequent condemnation and burning of all available copies of this sacred masterpiece of the post-biblical Jewish tradition.

Immediate dangers for the Jews arose from such an unfavourable background when anti-Jewish lords controlled an efficient administration and other political instruments that might enable them to take measures to enforce their own interests against the Jews. Right at the beginning of his reign (1180) King Philip Augustus did just this. He had all the Jews in the area he controlled arrested, extorted a high ransom from them, reduced debts to them to the one-fifth which he himself claimed, and finally in 1182 ordered their expulsion. Later attempts at recall alternated with severe restrictions and burdens on the Jews, over whom the monarchy tried to enforce its direct supremacy even outside the crown lands. In England there were pogroms in 1189/90, and at the beginning of the thirteenth century King John began a policy of subjecting the Jews to harsh control by the central administration and exploiting them financially. On the other hand, in the parts of the Iberian peninsula which were newly settled in the course of the *reconquista* they obtained generally favourable opportunities for development, so that numerous Jews immigrated into the Christian kingdoms from the southern Islamic areas.

The position of the Jews in the German empire during the Staufen period is best compared with that in the Christian areas of Spain. In the long and changeable history of the Jews in Germany this period marked an apogee, which by the last quarter of the thirteenth century was already past. The Jews in Germany were important pace-makers in urbanization. After the middle of the twelfth century their communities grew in the towns which already existed, while simultaneously they settled in those newly coming into existence or being founded. The western German old settlement areas on the Rhine, and the south-west, contained the main concentration of Jewish settlements. In north-west Germany and in the central areas of the Hanse, Jewish communities came into being only after the middle of the thirteenth century and even then their numbers remained small. The same seems to have been true of the eastern new settlement areas, where the Jews were granted favourable conditions in Bohemia and especially in Prague.

The well-to-do Jews had inheritance rights in land, houses, gardens, vineyards, and other real estate. In many towns, such as Cologne, Regensburg, and Worms, the Jews participated with their own weapons in the defence of the town against external enemies. Although in Germany too they were being pushed out of trade, they remained active for some time yet, as for example is shown by the payments of pepper and silk by the Jews of Trier to the archbishop. Sometimes they were concerned with minting, even if only as suppliers of silver. Around 1180 the imperial ministerial Kuno of Münzenberg employed a Jew as mint-master, or as a lessee. The dukes of Austria, and obviously other princes as well, made use in their administration of the financially experienced Jews, who were well acquainted with accountancy, and this despite papal protests (1233). Such activities were presumably the necessary accompaniment of the Jews' money-lending deals with princes. From the middle of the thirteenth century the authorities in Germany also began to react to money-lending (generally against security) by restricting interest rates. In 1255 the Rhenish League brought its influence to bear when it fixed the limit of annual interest for weekly loans at 43.4 per cent and for yearly loans at 33.3 per cent.

The Jews were spared serious persecution during the later crusades, in contrast to the first two. At the beginning of 1188, during the preparations for the Third Crusade, the majority of the Jews of Mainz felt cause to flee to Münzenberg, the castle and town of the imperial ministerial Kuno. But those Jews who remained in Mainz were also protected against their enemies by Frederick I and Henry VI.

The accusation that the Jews murdered children for healing or ritual purposes had been spreading from the 1140s in England and France. In 1235 it was the pretext for serious pogroms in Lauda, in neighbouring Tauberbischofsheim, and in Fulda. The events in Fulda caused the Emperor Frederick II to order a thorough investigation. He had the accusation of ritual murder examined for its truth, first by princes, nobles, and clerics. After these reached no clear results, the emperor entrusted the investigation to respected Jews who had been converted to Christianity, and who had been called together from many western countries. These experts, who were opposed to Judaism but were well acquainted with its laws, customs, and scriptures, confirmed to the emperor that the accusation was completely unreasonable. Thereupon the emperor in July 1236 with the consent of the princes acquitted all the Jews of Germany of this nonsensical accusation, which was widespread outside Germany too [3: xxxii. 496–503, no. 123].

In spite of this, alleged ritual murders were later again the cause of severe local persecutions, certainly in Pforzheim and Weissenburg in Alsace (1267 and 1270). On the whole, the persecutions of Jews up to the end of our period were restricted to relatively few and—with the exception of Frankfurt (1241)—to smaller places, like Kitzingen, Ortenberg in Hessen (1243), and Arnstadt in Thuringia (1264), as well as Koblenz and Sinzig (1265).

No doubt the intercession of the Staufen for the Jews contributed to their relatively favourable position in Germany. The emperors were also following their own interests in this, as, like the contemporary Plantagenets and Capetians, they tried to enforce their direct control over the Jews and to use that as the basis for their financial demands. The claim that the Jews were directly subject to the emperor alone, already raised by Frederick I, was strengthened by Frederick II during his intervention in the accusation of ritual murder just mentioned. In doing so he claimed that all the Jews of Germany were servants (*servi*) of the imperial chamber, thus falling back on a widespread ecclesiastical view according to which the Jews were condemned to eternal servitude.

In declaring them servants of the chamber the imperial court primarily intended to express the emperor's right to their services. In reality, though, many German Jewish communities had for a long time already been subject to ecclesiastical lords, like those in Cologne, Mainz, and Trier; others, though mostly smaller ones, were subject to lay princes. Thus there were hardly more than two dozen Jewish communities listed with tax dues in the imperial tax list of 1241/2. The returns of the Jews came to 'only' 12 per cent of the entire imperial income. The towns listed in it paid five times as much as the Jews.

The acquittal from the accusation of ritual murder, and the fixing of the Jews' constitutional position by Frederick II in

1236 created the basic guidelines for the Jewry-law of the duke of Austria (1244), which was in turn adopted by the kings of Hungary (1251) and Bohemia (1254), and by the Polish prince of Kalisch (1264). The imperial law thus became the basis of the legal position of the Jews in eastern Europe. Only later was the idea that they were 'servants of the chamber' interpreted and used in the sense of allowing the monarchy unrestricted rights over the Jews.

Under the relatively favourable conditions of life in Germany the Jews were able to achieve a high point in their religious culture. Around the middle of the twelfth century at a rabbinical council at Troyes, the Jewish communities of Speyer, Worms, and Mainz were granted the leadership of the Jews in Germany, which they exercised until about the middle of the thirteenth century. In these towns, as well as in Regensburg, Würzburg, and later in Vienna, there existed much-frequented Talmudic schools. Up to about the middle of the thirteenth century the Jews of Germany often perfected their religious education in the schools of French communities. Meir ben Baruch did this, before the Talmud burnings of 1242 in France, which he experienced as an eyewitness. Meir (c.1220–93), who was named after Rothenburg where he long lived, was for nearly half a century the generally accepted leader of the German rabbis. It is significant for the deteriorating situation of the Jews in Germany that around the middle of the eighties Meir felt obliged to emigrate. He was caught and kept in prison until the end of his life. The times were past in which a Jew, Süsskind von Trimberg (c.1200–50), could appear as a *Minnesänger* in the German language at German courts.

IV
GERMANY IN THE CONTEXT
OF EUROPE

In the more than two centuries described in this book, the life of the people in the German empire underwent a great transformation in all important respects. The change in ways of life was more far-reaching than ever before in medieval history. It seems that only in the nineteenth and twentieth centuries did changes attain a similar dimension. Reservations about this thesis derive from the difficulty of proving it. This can only be done in a general survey of German history. The thesis also implies that the transformation which took place in these central medieval centuries had a fundamental and formative effect on later German history. The complex German cultural area during this period grew from its peripheral position into the centre of Christian Europe, where it gained a mediating role. Again and again it received stimuli from the West and from the rich cultural landscapes of the Mediterranean area, where simultaneously the old traditions of Jews, Muslims, and Christians were revived and passed on to the Christian West. These impulses were relayed to the north and east via Germany. But here they were also shaped and handed on in an assimilated form. Classical civilization, originating in the Mediterranean area and several times passed from hand to hand in this way, was renewed and strengthened and made fertile for the expanding West. European connections supported this transformation in the German empire from relatively primitive conditions, and led it into new paths of European history.

When Frederick II died in his distant hereditary kingdom it was already decided that the *regnum teutonicum* was an 'aristocracy with a monarchic head'. The electoral right of the princes was established in customary law; the outlines of the system of electoral princes could already be discerned. The plan for a hereditary empire, such as Henry VI had unsuccessfully tried to impose half a century before, was now an illusion. The hereditary rights of the secular princes, and the legal claims of the ecclesiastical ones to imperial fiefs and offices, had become unassailable. The laws governing appointment to imperial offices, anchored as they were in feudalism, had been ousted by the allodial hereditary rights of the secular princes. Thus the Wittelsbach brothers Ludwig II (1253–94) and Henry XIII (1253–90), in breach of the relevant imperial law, split their duchy without opposition into Upper and Lower Bavaria: besides Upper Bavaria, Ludwig II secured for himself the palatinate of the Rhine. Such partitions later occurred again and again in other secular territories.

The ecclesiastical principalities meanwhile remained impartible. The great majority of them were situated in the old settlement areas, where they clustered in the Salian–Staufen imperial territory. Their singular position in European history stemmed from their roots in Ottonian and Salian imperial lordship over the Church, the effects of which have strongly influenced German history until today. After the investiture struggle the ecclesiastical princes in the old settlement areas did not only help to undermine imperial rule; they also hindered the construction of large territories in the hands of secular princes, and even prevented them entirely except in a very few cases. As the kingship was to a large extent ineffective in the new settlement areas east of the Elbe and Saale, the ecclesiastical powers lacked support in their competition with the princes. Rather they became the instruments and constituent parts of comparatively homogeneous secular territories; this was to have significant consequences in the history of the Reformation.

Around the middle of the thirteenth century, after the decline of Staufen imperial rule, the migration of the political centre of gravity in the German empire, from the old settlement areas in the west to the former border regions with their relatively large territories, was already visible in outline. The solicitude, based on ties of blood, of the Wittelsbacher Ludwig II for Conradin, the last descendant of the Staufen family, was a symptom of this. Even more significant was the extraordinary role played by King Ottokar II of Bohemia in the decades of the interregnum, before the reign of King Rudolf of Habsburg. Although the Habsburg was victorious over the Bohemian king in the battle on the Marchfeld near Dürnkrut on 26 August 1278, the direction of late medieval imperial politics, with its centres at Vienna and Prague, was already outlined if not yet completely established.

Around the middle of the thirteenth century it was already clear that imperial rule in the kingdom of Burgundy—in the south-western lands of the Rhône and the western Alpine area, with their close connections with the Mediterranean and northern Italy—was doomed to failure despite Barbarossa's successes and, temporarily, also those of his grandson Frederick II. The Capetian Charles of Anjou, together with the papacy, was the grave-digger of the Staufen empire in Italy. From Frederick II's time on, this was anyway based on the Norman–Staufen hereditary kingdom. The close but tense relations between the universalism of empire and papacy, which both had their centre in the Mediterranean area and especially in Italy, had been torn apart in the 'final struggle' between the Staufen and the papacy. Henry VII and Ludwig of Bavaria took it up again, but under completely different circumstances.

The universalizing tendencies which under the emperors and kings of the Salian and Staufen period were increasingly directed towards the central Mediterranean area, and there met the crusading movement from Western Europe, were subsequently narrowed down. Their connections and effects, however, influenced the further course of German and European history. The universalism of imperial policy favoured the rise of ecclesiastical and secular lordships and the development of local powers. These were able to secure for themselves a growing share of rural development, urbanization, and economic expansion generally, so that, particularly after the Welf–Staufen struggle for the throne, the monarchy fell irretrievably behind. In the new settlement areas the development of political power bypassed the monarchy. It had been decisively weakened even before the beginning of continuous expansion into the country east of the Elbe and Saale, by the disputes of the 'investiture struggle', so that the settlement of the east only shifted the power relations between monarchy and independent princes even more to the disadvantage of the imperial power, which was only firmly established in the old settlement areas.

In the nineteenth and twentieth centuries the Roman emperors and kings of the central Middle Ages have often been blamed for not creating the basis of a strong monarchy, and thus for preventing the development of a German national state. This anachronistic approach, which especially condemned Barbarossa's imperial policies, does not need to be discussed here.

From this fixed point of view it was also overlooked that the kingdom of the Franks and the Roman empire had essentially determined the growing self-consciousness of the Germans. From here, the neighbouring nations and races of Franconia, Saxony, Bavaria, and Swabia developed a constructive common consciousness of being 'Teutonici' or 'Theodisci'. Even the name 'Teutonici' (etc.) emerged in close connection with the imperial policy of the Ottonians and Salians in Italy. Here, it was first fixed as denoting members of a linguistic community. The decisive impulse towards the formation and expansion of the political concept of the *regnum teutonicum* (etc.) came from the Gregorian papacy. The purpose behind it, to confine the authority of the kings to northern alpine, predominantly German-speaking territory, could, however, not prevail. Whereas from the twelfth century the concept of the *regnum teutonicum* became ever more widespread and was also used by the imperial chancellery, it still retained the significance of *regnum Francorum* and therefore the imperial claim too. From the same time the association of *regnum* and *imperium* was taken up and spread by the royal chancellery, expressed in the title of *rex Romanorum*. Imperial political connections were therefore fundamentally responsible for the fact that in Germany—as in many other west and middle European countries—from the turn of the twelfth century a common historical consciousness developed. It was based not on an independent national history but on the construction of a Roman tradition. Caesar was close to the heart of this tradition. This prototype of all emperors was supposed to have laid a foundation for the nations of Franconia, Saxony, Swabia, and Bavaria in his imperial Roman policy for the community of *diutischi lieuti*. Many German cities traced the history of their foundation back to Caesar and the

Romans, and based their self-esteem on it. And with the alleged decrees of Caesar even the self-consciousness of the German knight was bolstered, as the Ebersheim Chronicle confirms [345 and 14: xxiii. 427–53]. And in this way too imperial policy fostered the incorporation of the Germans into the essential strands of the tradition of European history.

Imperial policy, over and above this, was also a vital factor in the foundation and development of co-operative and communal ways of life in Germany. The lengthy conflicts between empire and papacy formed only the highest level of the far-reaching disputes between the secular and ecclesiastical powers. Alongside religious and spiritual movements and economic processes, they provided an effective stimulus for the development of freedoms in Church, government, society, and culture. As the conflict between empire and papacy was concentrated on the central area of the German empire it not only widened the field of action of the regional and local powers, here more than in other West European countries, but at the same time also particularly strongly favoured the development of guilds, brotherhoods, and communities, which form an extremely valuable tradition of democratic life in Germany, often undervalued in the recent past. The basic forms of the guilds, brotherhoods, and communities had independent roots in the given power and social structures of the German empire, as in other countries of the old Carolingian empire; nevertheless their establishment and development were favoured by multiple influences and models from the West and the Mediterranean. One only need remember the new stimuli towards Christianization provided by Church reform, by the inspiration of the early Church, by the religious poverty movement, and by the mendicant orders. The expansion and intensification of trade relations should also be mentioned, in which the Italian maritime trading cities—primarily Venice and Genoa—and the fairs of Champagne formed important focal points. The Jews, who immigrated, first mainly from the south and then also from the west, and later the activities of the 'Lombards' and the 'Cahorsins' had a lasting impact on trade and the monetary economy of Germany. Finally the Peace of God should be mentioned, and the urban consulates which derived from the Roman legal tradition, and the whole influence of Latin urban culture, mainly radiating from northern Italy into the empire north of the Alps.

The political importance of the guilds, brotherhoods, and communes was considerably increased and made firm in the long term by the rapid growth of existing rural and urban settlements and the large number of new ones. Rural development and urbanization, in close correlation with population growth, reached degrees which fundamentally changed the landscape and the economic structure of the old settlement areas, and even more of the new areas in the east. Along with the increasing size and density of settlements went an enormous increase of agricultural and industrial production and productivity, and also an intensification of the money economy, trade, and the division of labour. These processes occurred with unusual dynamism in almost all European countries during the central Middle Ages, but it was in Germany that they led to the greatest transformation.

This exceptional position was based mainly on the primitive stage of rural development and urban culture in Germany in comparison to its western and even more to its southern neighbours before the changes of the central Middle Ages; in contrast to those of the ninth and tenth centuries, these changes were not endangered by invasions of alien peoples—such as previously by the Vikings and Hungarians. Rather the German settlement area was extended far into the Slavic lands in connection with the expansion of princes such as the dukes of Saxony, the margraves of Brandenburg, the counts of Schwerin and Holstein, and the lords of Mecklenburg, who also succeeded in maintaining themselves against the competition of the king of Denmark. To the east and south-east the settlement of German peasants, merchants, knights, priests, and monks occurred in a different political context. The 'westernization' of eastern central Europe which this furthered, as has been mentioned, led Germany from its peripheral position in the east of Latin Christendom into a central position between west and east, which was exploited and developed not least by the Hanse merchants and cities.

When in the third quarter of the thirteenth century the expansion into the eastern areas of new settlement was making great progress—later even surpassed—rural development and urbanization in the old settlement areas were already nearing the limits of growth set by the size of the population, the nature of the country, and climatic conditions. Therefore economic development in these regions in subsequent centuries often went along more 'conservative' paths, orientated towards the transformations achieved in the high Middle Ages. The old settlement areas, the seedbed of eastern colonization, were prepared and supported in their roles by their wide contacts with western and southern neighbouring areas. We should remember the pioneering activities of the settlers from Flanders and from the Rhine mouth, but especially of the Cistercians and Premonstratensians who originated from the Latin lands, and the crusading movement. The latter 'branched off' from France and the Mediterranean in the wars against the pagans in the east—with the essential participation of the Cistercians— even before the knightly orders, especially the Teutonic Order, took over and developed the inheritance of the crusading movement.

Almost all the monasteries, orders, and churches—with the exception of the early hermits' communities, which, however, were not common in Germany—played a considerable part in rural development, eastern settlement, and urbanization. In this they chose different approaches and emphases, the early Cistercians in rural isolation and the mendicant orders in the towns marking the extremes. The great rise in the number of monasteries and churches, among them especially the parish churches in the cleared and newly settled areas, resulted from this participation, and occurred in Germany more than in other European countries. In Germany as well as in the rest of Latin Christendom, this quantitative growth was an expression of great change and intensification in religion. In this way the German part of the empire had by the last quarter of the thirteenth century acquired a basic religious and ecclesiastical infrastructure which was hardly extended at all in the following centuries, except for some further increase mainly in the mendicant orders.

The essential models and impulses for the extremely vigorous ecclesiastical and religious transformation, which had such far-reaching consequences in the German empire from the middle of the eleventh century onwards, came almost without exception from outside, from the west and south. Instances of this are Fruttuaria and Cluny, models for the reformed monasteries of Siegburg, St Blasien, and Hirsau, as well as the emergence of the Cistercians and Premonstratensians, the hospital and knightly orders, and not least the mendicants. The only exceptions to this were some branches of the reformed regular canons in the late eleventh and early twelfth centuries. The religious poverty movement, generally led by wandering preachers and which found a huge echo among women, came from the Latin West into the German empire. This is also the case with the Waldensians, who were made heretics, while the Cathars, who from the beginning were more dogmatically heretical, probably pushed forward into Germany from the south-east. In comparison to southern France and northern Italy, Germany remained a side-show in heretical activities; but even here the most prominent centres were the more strongly urbanized old settlement areas like the Rhine, Moselle, and Danube regions.

The waves of religious renewal at the same time prepared the path for spiritual stimuli, which reached Germany through the convents and religious communities. They made personal contacts more frequent and promoted the exchange of ideas and also the spread of manuscripts, from which spiritual life in Germany drew great advantages. The most lasting effects in this respect came through the Dominicans and Franciscans. The school of the Dominicans at Cologne became the earliest forerunner of the German universities. It is significant that the first university was only founded around the middle of the fourteenth century: i.e. one and a half centuries after the establishment of the first universities in Italy, France, England, and Spain (Salamanca, 1220). Before this the city schools of France and Italy were the favoured goals of German students, who there made direct contact with the spiritual centres of the West. Among them were some who later achieved great accomplishments themselves, influencing European spiritual life in ways still felt today. Hugh of St Victor, from Saxony, was one, and the Swabian Dominican Albertus Magnus another. There was also William of Moerbeke from Brabant (*c.*1215–*c.*1286, from 1277 archbishop of Corinth), who belonged to the same order, who for a while worked with Thomas Aquinas, and who was the most important translator of Greek scholarly and scientific works in the Middle Ages; amongst other works, he translated the writings of Aristotle and their commentaries.

The Latin West was also a model in the field of courtly literature, the centres of which in Germany were in the west. The fact that this literature of the noble knightly élite in the course of the thirteenth century struck a chord in the towns too, its content becoming adapted to this milieu, was significant for the future. In Germany too the towns rose as literary centres, more strongly influenced by lay people. This was based on the schools situated in the towns, in some cases already run by the towns, which increasingly met the needs and interests of urban society. The gap between this and the literary culture of the old urbanized areas, especially in Italy, was still great even in the middle of the thirteeenth century; but the first important steps on the long road to general parity had been taken.

The assimilation also showed itself in the adaptation of forms and motifs in art. Support for emphasizing the spread of classicizing trends comes from Nicholas of Verdun, who came from the Romance lands of the western empire and whose influence reached far into the east of the empire right up to Klosterneuburg. The Byzantine influence must also be mentioned, for it grew stronger from the turn of the thirteenth century in German regions too—not least in Saxony and Thuringia—taken up and in part adjusted to native forms or combined with them. About the same time (1209) in the archiepiscopal city of Magdeburg on the Elbe, the cathedral was built in Gothic style on a French pattern, so that it was also in the eastern regions that influences from East and West met at close quarters and were combined in the syncretic development of forms. Still, the acceptance of the Gothic style, admired as *opus francigenum* by Germans too, was generally slower in Germany than in England, Spain, and—on a smaller scale—even in Hungary, though with greater readiness than in Italy. Within the German regions, varying to a great extent in this respect, Romanesque churches were still being built far into the thirteenth century, as for example in the archbishopric of Salzburg, which was closely linked to Italy. Thus, decades after the start of Magdeburg cathedral, of the Trier Liebfrauenkirche (from 1233, strongly influenced by Reims), and of Strasbourg cathedral (from 1230), the Romanesque manner prevailed in some parts of the empire. In places in the Rhineland, as late as the first preparations for building the Gothic Cologne cathedral (after 1248), single Gothic forms were often merely integrated into the basic structure traditionally dominated by the Romanesque. Much stronger was the break with native traditions in the adoption of French models in sculpture. Often these works of art, among them presumably the famous Naumburg figures of the founders, were made by groups of itinerant workmen (workshops) who had been trained in France [no. 292].

The profound transformation and reorganization of social relations in Germany in the central Middle Ages were formed by all-embracing European influences, by the continuation of native German traditions, and by specifically German circumstances—such as the large extent of internal colonization, and especially the colonization of the east. To recount all the factors which were important for these fundamental processes would involve everything dealt with in this book; we shall mention only the following, in almost deliberate order and choice: the crusading movement and courtly literature, the growing political role of the communes, the rise of the imperial princes, social mobility through military and administrative service, population growth, the boom in trade and industry, rural development and urbanization, the increased consciousness of the equality of human beings, the extremely great increase in monasteries, orders, and other religious communities with their very varied aims and points of contact with society, and the spread of literacy among lay people.

In this complicated context the period from the middle of the eleventh century to the end of the Staufen age for the great majority of the population in Germany was a period of liberation from personal dependency, or of its weakening. The burdens and restrictions of unfreedom were considerably lessened and loosened. In most towns and many rural areas too serfdom became unimportant, or could be thrown off even without a formal legal act. In the settlement of the east it did not apply to the German immigrants in the first place, which soon had a positive effect on the native population too. The ministerials, and also other groups within the *familia*, in many cases enforced their title to rights and possessions and, by reducing their obligations, reached a privileged position which made their further rise easier. Numerous ministerials finally became nobles. With the greater enforcement of personal freedoms, social relations in Germany assimilated to those of the other areas of the former Carolingian empire, where serfdom had already lost its meaning, or had never had much importance.

In both places economic factors, poverty and wealth, became the predominant indicators of social position; especially at times of shortage, famine, and plague, poverty was the obvious fate of large numbers. The helplessness, passivity, or irresponsibility of the *pater familias* made all the more demands on Christian *caritas*. From the twelfth and thirteenth centuries onwards in Germany too the ecclesiastical, corporate, and finally the first urban hospitals and other institutions in growing numbers began to react to this, though still insufficiently. They came into being out of an intensified religious consciousness of brotherhood; in Germany the stimuli and models came from outside, like the Hospitallers and the mendicant orders. After the dissolution of the *familia*, finding protection for persons and property elsewhere became all the more important. Support and help from within the narrower family, from relations, a brotherhood, or a commune, and also from the powerful, became more important for existence. One way or another, new and different obligations arose, which, however, were based more on mutuality and agreements fixed in contracts or contract-like agreements.

Life in the walled and fortified towns generally offered more favourable conditions for gaining and securing the basis for existence, and a legal position, than the country. Although in comparison to urbanized areas in the Latin countries towns in Germany managed only a late revival, or even developed for the first time, the military, economic, and political power of the towns offered the basis for a vigorous development of the bourgeoisie. The bourgeoisie, which in Germany grew out of the 'feudal' world and long remained connected with it, has been established in German history ever since, and became one of the historical roots of modern citizenship.

The interlocking of town and country sometimes showed itself in the rise of ministerials living in the towns into the urban nobility, in which families of other origins found themselves too. With this, only late and only hesitantly, a similarity with the old cities in the Mediterranean area, where the nobility had long been at home, developed in these towns. The process was part of an enormous expansion and reorganization of the noble élite in Germany, which again was an adaptation to the Western European countries. That this was influenced particularly by the West can be read in contemporary knightly literature. Despite the attempts to separate the knights and peasants legally from one another, the boundaries in reality always remained open. Moreover, by the end of the Staufen period, despite the *Heerschildordnung*, attempts to classify the nobility along more status-orientated lines had resulted only in the rise of the class of imperial princes—a German peculiarity. Otherwise noble society remained flexible.

Something similar is also true for the clergy and monks, where the new religious stimuli again and again broke through social boundaries, or at least questioned them. The limitations of the Christian society are probably expressed most clearly in the persecution and restriction of Jewish outsiders, to whom, later, even worse things happened.

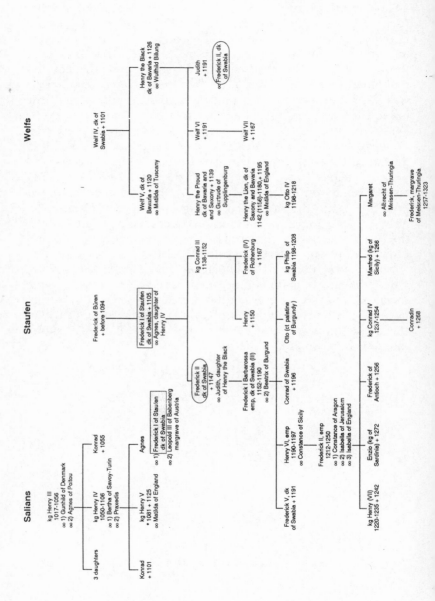

BIBLIOGRAPHY

PREFATORY NOTE

The bibliographical notes where possible include only more recent scholarly editions and specialist literature. After the first section, 'Sources and General Literature', which supplies the basic comprehensive material, there follow more specialized references assigned to single chapters and sub-sections. Titles once mentioned are not repeated. There are no cross-references, so it is advisable to combine the entries in the general part and those of the chapters or sub-sections. Only in some cases are essays from collections noticed separately. Source collections containing German translations have been preferred.

The bibliography has been kept short for lack of space, i.e. it only gives the most necessary information. Subtitles have generally been omitted, several editors or places of publication have generally been reduced to one (marked *et al.* etc.). With better-known source collections and Festschriften it seemed permissible to omit the editor's names completely. Reprints are not mentioned.

The bibliography is continuously numbered. These serial numbers serve as references for the sources and literature in the text.

SOURCES AND LITERATURE

Sources

1. *Acta imperii inedita saeculi XIII et XIV*, vols. i–ii, ed. Eduard Winkelmann (Innsbruck, 1880–5).
2. *Annali Genovesi di Caffaro e de' suoi continuatori dal 1099 al 1293*, new edn., ed. Luigi Tommaso Belgrano, vols. i–ii (Fonti per la storia d'Italia, Scrittori, sec. XII e XIII, 11–12; Genoa, 1890, 1901).
3. *Ausgewählte Quellen zur deutschen Geschichte des Mittelalters*, Freiherr vom Stein-Gedächtnisausgabe, ed. Rudolf Buchner *et al.*:
    vol. xii, *Quellen zur Geschichte Kaiser Heinrichs IV.* (Darmstadt, 1968).

vol. xiia, *Quellen zum Investiturstreit*, part 1 (Darmstadt, 1978).

vol. xiii, Lampert of Hersfeld, *Annalen* (Darmstadt, 1973).

vol. xvii, Bishop Otto of Freising and Rahewin, *Die Taten Friedrichs oder richtiger Cronica* (Darmstadt, 1974).

vol. xix, Helmold of Bosau, *Slawenchronik* (Darmstadt, 1973).

vol. xxii, *Lebensbeschreibungen einiger Bischöfe des 10–12. Jahrhunderts* (Darmstadt, 1973).

vol. xxvia–b, *Urkunden und erzählende Quellen zur deutschen Ostsiedlung im Mittelalter*, 2 vols. (Darmstadt, 1975, 1970).

vol. xxxi, *Quellen zur Geschichte des deutschen Bauernstandes im Mittelalter* (Darmstadt, 1967).

vol. xxxii, *Quellen zur deutschen Verfassungs-, Wirtschafts- und Sozialgeschichte bis 1250* (Darmstadt, 1977).

4. Brühl, Carlrichard, and Kölzer, Theo, *Das Tafelgüterverzeichnis des Römischen Königs* (Cologne etc., 1979).

5. Colorni, Vittore, *Die drei verschollenen Gesetze des Reichstages bei Roncaglia*, German translation by Gero Dolezalek (Unters. zur dt. Staats- und Rechtsgesch. NF 12; Aalen, 1969).

6. *Historia Diplomatica Friderici Secundi*, ed. Jean Louis Alphonse Huillard-Bréholles, vols i–vi (Paris, 1852–61).

7. Jasper, Detlev, *Das Papstwahldekret von 1059. Überlieferung und Textgestalt* (Beitr. z. Gesch. u. Quellenkunde des Mittelalters, 6; Sigmaringen, 1986).

8. *The Jews and the Crusaders, The Hebrew Chronicles of the First and Second Crusades*, trans. and ed. Shlomo Eidelberg (Madison, Wis., 1977).

9. *Kölner Schreinsurkunden des 12. Jahrhunderts*, ed. Robert Hoeniger, vols. i–ii (Pub. der Ges. für Rhein. Geschichtskde. 1; Bonn, 1888–94).

10. *Die Konstitutionen Friedrichs II. von Hohenstaufen für sein Königreich Sizilien*, ed. and trans. Hermann Conrad *et al.*; Suppl. vol., part 1, ed. Thea von der Lieck-Buyken (Studien und Quellen zur Welt Kaiser Friedrichs II., 2, 2. 1; Cologne etc., 1973, 1978).

11. Kretzschmar, Robert, *Alger von Lüttichs Traktat 'De misericordia et iustitia'. Ein kanonistischer Konkordanzversuch aus der Zeit des Investiturstreits. Untersuchungen und Edition* (Quellen und Forschungen zum Recht im Mittelalter, 2; Sigmaringen, 1985).

12. Migne, Jacques Paul, *Patrologiae cursus completus, Series Latina*, vols. clxxxv, clxxxix (Paris, 1855, 1854).

13. *Monumenta Germaniae Historica.*

14. *Scriptores*: vols. iv–vi (Hanover, 1841–4); vol. viii (Hanover,

1848); vols. xi–xii (Hanover, 1854–6); vol. xvii (Hanover, 1861); vols. xxii–xxiv (Hanover, 1872–9); vols. xxvii–xxviii (Hanover, 1885–8).

15. *Libelli de lite imperatorum et pontificum saec. XI et XII conscripti*, vols. i–iii (Hanover, 1891, 1892, 1897).

16. *Scriptores rerum Germanicarum in usum scholarum*, vol. xvi, Burchard of Ursberg (Hanover etc., 1916).

17. *Constitutiones et acta publica imperatorum et regum*, vols. i–ii (Hanover, 1893, 1896).

18. *Fontes iuris Germanici antiqui in usum scholarum separatim editi*: vol. XIII, *Die falschen Investiturprivilegien*, ed. Claudia Märtl (Hanover, 1986).

19. *Diplomata regum et imperatorum Germaniae*:
    vol. vi, *Die Urkunden Heinrichs IV.* (Weimar, 1941–53).
    vol. viii, *Die Urkunden Lothars III. und der Kaiserin Richenza* (Berlin, 1927).
    vol. ix, *Die Urkunden und Briefe Konrads III. und seines Sohnes Heinrich* (Vienna etc., 1969).
    vol. x, 1–4, *Die Urkunden Friedrichs I., 1152–1158, 1158–1167, 1167–1180, 1181–1190* (Hanover, 1975, 1979, 1985, 1990).
    vol. xi, *Die Urkunden Heinrichs VI, und der Kaiserin Konstanze*, vol. xi, 3, *Die Urkunden der Kaiserin Konstanze*, ed. Theo Kölzer (Hanover, 1990).
    vol. xviii, *Die Urkunden Heinrich Raspes und Wilhelms von Holland*, ed. Dieter Hägermann *et al.*; vol. xviii, 1 (Hanover, 1989).

20. *Laienfürsten- und Dynastenurkunden der Kaiserzeit*: vol. i, *Die Urkunden Heinrichs des Löwen, Herzogs von Sachsen und Bayern*, parts 1–2 (Leipzig, 1941; Weimar, 1949).

21. *Epistolae: Briefe der deutschen Kaiserzeit*, vol. iv, 1–3, *Die Briefe des Petrus Damiani*, ed. Kurt Reindel (Munich, 1983, 1988, 1989); vol. iv, 4 (in print).

22. *Quellen zur Geistesgeschichte des Mittelalters*: vol. vi, Sextus Amarcius, *Sermones* (Weimar, 1969).

23. *Regestum Innocentii III. papae super negotio Romani imperii*, ed. Friedrich Kempf (Misc. Hist. Pont. XII, Collect. 21; Rome, 1947).

24. *Das Register Innozenz III.*, vol. i (1198/99), vol. ii. 2 (1199/1200), ed. Othmar Hageneder *et al.* (Pub. der Abt. für Hist. Stud. des österr. Kulturinstituts in Rom, Abt. 2, Reihe 1; Graz etc., 1964, 1979).

25. *Rerum Italicarum Scriptores*, ed. Ludovico Antonio Muratori,

new edn. by Giosue Carducci *et al.*, vol. vi. 2 (Annales Pisani; Bologna, 1936).

26. Ruser, Konrad, *Die Urkunden und Akten der oberdeutschen Städtebünde*, vol. i (Göttingen, 1979).
27. *Scrittori d'Italia*, vols. 232–3, Salimbene de Adam, *Cronica*, new edn., ed. Giuseppe Scalia (Bari, 1966).
28. *Die Traditionen des Hochstifts Regensburg und des Klosters S. Emmeram*, ed. Josef Widemann (Quellen und Erörterungen zur bayerischen Gesch. NF 8; Aalen, 1969).
29. *Die Traditionen des Klosters Tegernsee, 1002–1242* (Quellen und Erörterungen zur bayerischen und dt. Gesch. 9, i. 1; Munich, 1952).
30. Weise, Erich, 'Urkundenwesen und Geschichtsschreibung des Klosters St. Pantaleon zu Köln im 12. Jahrhundert', *Jb. des kölnischen Geschichtsvereins*, 11 (1929), 1–105.
31. *Die Zwiefalter Chroniken Ortliebs und Bertholds*, newly ed., trans. and comment. by Erich König *et al.* (Schwäbische Chroniken der Stauferzeit, 2; Stuttgart etc., 1941).

Regesta

32. Böhmer, Johann Friedrich, *Regesta Imperii, IV. Ältere Staufer: 1125–1197*, section 2, *Friedrich I, 1152 (1122)–1190*, parts 1–2, fasc. 1, *1152 (1122)–1158*, newly revised by Ferdinand Opll *et al.* (Vienna etc., 1980); section 3, *Heinrich VI.*, newly revised by Gerhard Baaken (Cologne etc., 1972); *Namenregister, Ergänzungen und Berichtigungen, Nachträge*, revised by Karin and Gerhard Baaken (Cologne etc., 1979); *V: 1198–1272*, sections 1–5, *Philipp, Otto IV., Friedrich II., Heinrich (VII.), Conrad IV., Heinrich Raspe, Wilhelm und Richard*, newly ed. and supplem. by Julius Ficker and Eduard Winkelmann (Innsbruck, 1881–1901); section 6 (4 vols.), *Nachträge und Ergänzungen*, revised by Paul Zinsmaier (Cologne etc., 1983).
33. *Regesta pontificum Romanorum* (up to 1198), ed. Philip Jaffe (Berlin, 1851); 2nd edn., vols. 1–2, ed. Samuel Löwenfeld *et al.* (Leipzig, 1885–8; Graz, 1956).
34. *Regesta pontificum Romanorum*, ed. Paul Fridolin Kehr *et al.*, section ii, *Germania pontificia*, vols. 1–4, 6 (Berlin, 1911–81, incompl. etc.), vols. 1–3 (Berlin, 1960).
35. Stumpf-Brentano, Karl Friedrich, *Die Reichskanzler vornehmlich des X., XI. und XII. Jahrhunderts*, vols. i–iii (Innsbruck, 1865–83).

Source Bibliographies, etc.

36. Potthast, August, *Bibliotheca historica medii aevi*, vols. i–ii (Berlin², 1896).
37. *Repertorium fontium historiae medii aevi*, vol. i, *Series collectionum* (Rome, 1962); *Additamenta 1 (1962–1972)* (Rome, 1977).
38. *Typologie des sources du moyen âge occidental*, ed. Léopold Genicot, fascs. 1– (Turnhout, 1972–).
39. Wattenbach, Wilhelm, Holtzmann, Robert, and Schmale, Franz-Josef, *Deutschlands Geschichtsquellen im Mittelalter (900–1125)*, parts 1–3 (Darmstadt, 1967–71).
40. Wattenbach, Wilhelm, and Schmale, Franz-Josef, *Deutschlands Geschichtsquellen im Mittelalter (1125–1273)*, vol. i (Darmstadt, 1976).

Bibliographies, etc.

41. Dahlmann-Waitz, *Quellenkunde der deutschen Geschichte*, 10th edn., vols. i–vi (Stuttgart, 1969–87), in particular sect. 202, 203, 238.
42. Ehlers, Joachim, *Frankreich im Mittelalter (Literaturbericht) (HZ*, extra ser., 11; Munich, 1982).
43. Grundmann, Herbert, *Bibliographie zur Ketzergeschichte des Mittelalters (1900–1966)* (Sussidi eruditi, 20; Rome, 1967).
44. Haverkamp, Alfred, and Enzensberger, Horst, *Italien im Mittelalter (Literaturbericht) (HZ*, extra ser. 7; Munich, 1980).
45. Mayer, Hans Eberhard, *Bibliographie zur Geschichte der Kreuzzüge* (Hanover², 1965); Supplement, Mayer, Hans Eberhard, 'Literaturbericht über die Geschichte der Kreuzzüge', in Walther Kienast (ed.), *Literaturberichte (HZ*, extra ser. 3; Munich, 1969), 641–731.

Atlases, Handbooks, Reference Books

46. *Allgemeine deutsche Biographie*, vols. i–lvi (Leipzig, 1875–1912).
47. *Atlas zur Kirchengeschichte*, ed. Hubert Jedin *et al.* (Freiburg etc., 1970).
48. *The Cambridge Economic History of Europe*, ed. Michael Postan *et al.*, vols. i–iii (Cambridge², 1966–1987).
49. *The Cambridge Medieval History*, ed. Henry M. Gwatkin *et al.*, vol. v (Cambridge, 1968).
50. *Deutsche Verwaltungsgeschichte*, ed. Kurt G. A. Jeserich *et al.*, vol. i (Stuttgart, 1983).

51. *The Fontana Economic History of Europe*, ed. Carlo M. Cipolla, vol. i (London etc., 1973).
52. Fuhrmann, Horst, *Germany in the High Middle Ages, c.1050–1200*, transl. Timothy Reuter (Cambridge Medieval Textbooks; Cambridge, 1986).
53. Gebhardt, Bruno, *Handbuch der deutschen Geschichte*, ed. Herbert Grundmann, vol. i (Stuttgart[9], 1970).
54. *Der große Ploetz* (Freiburg etc.[30], 1986).
55. *Die großen Deutschen*, ed. Hermann Heimpel *et al.*, vols. i–v (Berlin, 1966).
56. *Großer Historischer Weltatlas*, ed. by Bayerischer Schulbuch-Verlag, part 2 (Munich, 1970); *Erläuterungen*, ed. Ernst Walter Zeeden (Munich, 1983).
57. *Handbuch der bayerischen Geschichte*, ed. Max Spindler, vol. i (Munich[2], 1981); vol. ii (Munich, 1966).
58. *Handbuch der deutschen Wirtschafts- und Sozialgeschichte*, ed. Hermann Aubin *et al.*, vol. i (Stuttgart, 1971).
59. *Handbuch der europäischen Geschichte*, ed. Theodor Schieder, vol. ii (Stuttgart, 1987).
60. *Handbuch der europäischen Wirtschafts- und Sozialgeschichte*, ed. Hermann Kellenbenz, vol. ii (Stuttgart, 1980).
61. *Handbuch der Geschichte der böhmischen Länder*, ed. Karl Bosl, vol. i (Stuttgart, 1967).
62. *Handbuch der Kirchengeschichte*, ed. Hubert Jedin, vol. iii. 1–2 (Freiburg etc.[2], 1973; spec. ed. 1985).
63. *Handbuch der Quellen und Literatur der neueren europäischen Privatrechtsgeschichte*, vol. i (Munich, 1973).
64. *Handwörterbuch zur deutschen Rechtsgeschichte*, ed. Adalbert Erler *et al.*, vols. i–iv (Berlin, 1971, 1978, 1984, 1990).
65. *Lexikon des Mittelalters*, vols. i–iv (Munich etc., 1980, 1983, 1986, 1989), vol. v up to 'Kiel'.
66. *Lothringen–Geschichte eines Grenzlandes*, ed. Michel Parisse (German edn.: Hans Walter Herrmann) (Saarbrücken, 1984).
67. *Neue deutsche Biographie*, vols. i–xv (Berlin, 1953–87).
68. *Sachwörterbuch zur deutschen Geschichte*, by Hellmuth Rössler *et al.* (Munich, 1958).
69. Schlesinger, Walter, *Ausgewählte Aufsätze*, ed. Hans Patze *et al.* (VuF 34; Sigmaringen, 1987).
70. *Storia d'Italia*, ed. Nino Valeri, vol. i (Turin[2], 1967).
71. *Storia d'Italia*, ed. R. Romano *et al.*, vols. i–ii, v (Turin, 1972–74), cf. also Annali, vols. i, iv, vi, viii, ix (Turin, 1978–86).
72. *Storia d'Italia*, ed. G. Galasso, vols. iii–v, vii, 1 and 2 (Turin, 1981–87).

General Histories

73. Abulafia, David, *Frederick II. A Medieval Emperor* (London, 1988).
74. Alexandre, Pierre, *Le climat en Europe au Moyen Age: contribution à l'histoire des variations climatiques de 1000 à 1425, d'après les sources narratives de l'Europe occidentale* (Recherches d'histoire et de sciences sociales = Studies in history and the social sciences, 24; Paris, 1987).
75. Beck, Hans-Georg, *Das byzantinische Jahrtausend* (Munich, 1978).
76. *Beiträge zum hochmittelalterlichen Städtewesen*, ed. Bernhard Diestelkamp (Städteforsch. A 11; Cologne etc., 1982).
77. *Beiträge zum spätmittelalterlichen Städtewesen*, ed. Bernhard Diestelkamp (Städteforsch. A 12; Cologne etc., 1982).
78. *Beiträge zur Bildung der französischen Nation im Früh- und Hochmittelalter*, ed. Helmut Beumann (Nationes, 4; Sigmaringen, 1983).
79. Blaschke, Karlheinz, *Geschichte Sachsens im Mittelalter* (Munich, 1990).
80. Bogyay, Thomas von, *Grundzüge der Geschichte Ungarns* (Darmstadt³, 1977).
81. Borst, Arno, *Lebensformen im Mittelalter* (Frankfurt am Main etc., 1979).
82. Bosl, Karl, *Europa im Aufbruch* (Munich, 1980).
83. Bosl, Karl, *Frühformen der Gesellschaft im mittelalterlichen Europa* (Munich etc., 1964).
84. Bosl, Karl, *Die Grundlagen der modernen Gesellschaft im Mittelalter* (Monographien zur Gesch. des MA, 4; Stuttgart, 1972).
85. Brühl, Carlrichard, *Deutschland und Frankreich. Die Geburt zweier Völker* (Cologne etc., 1990).
86. *Byzanz*, ed. Franz Georg Maier (Fischer Weltgesch. 13; Frankfurt am Main, 1973).
87. Classen, Peter, *Ausgewählte Aufsätze*, ed. Josef Fleckenstein *et al.* (VuF 28; Sigmaringen, 1983).
88. Classen, Peter, *Studium und Gesellschaft im Mittelalter*, ed. Johannes Fried (Schriften der MGH, 29; Stuttgart, 1983).
89. *La cristianità dei secoli XI e XII in occidente: coscienza e strutture di una società* (Pubbl. dell'Università cattolica del S. Cuore, Serie terza, Misc. del Centro di studi medioevali, 10; Milan, 1983).
90. *Determinanten der Bevölkerungsentwicklung im Mittelalter*, ed. Bernd Herrmann *et al.* (Acta humaniora; Weinheim, 1987).
91. *Deutsche Geschichte*, vol. i ((East) Berlin³, 1974).

92. *Die deutsche Ostsiedlung des Mittelalters als Problem der europäischen Geschichte* (VuF 18; Sigmaringen, 1975).
93. Doren, Alfred, *Italienische Wirtschaftsgeschichte* (Jena, 1934).
94. Duby, Georges, *Le Temps des cathédrales: L'art et la société, 980– 1420* (Paris, 1976).
95. Ehlers, Joachim, *Geschichte Frankreichs im Mittelalter* (Stuttgart, 1987).
96. Ennen, Edith, *Die europäische Stadt des Mittelalters* (Göttingen[3], 1979).
97. Ennen, Edith, *Gesammelte Abhandlungen zum europäischen Städtewesen und zur rheinischen Geschichte*, ed. Georg Droege *et al.* (Bonn, 1977).
98. Ennen, Edith, *Frauen im Mittelalter* (Munich[3], 1987).
99. *L'eremitismo in occidente nei secoli XI e XII* (Pubbl. dell'Università cattolica del S. Cuore, 4; Milan, 1965).
100. *Festschrift für Hermann Heimpel*, vols. i–iii (pub. of the MPIG 36. i–iii; Göttingen, 1971, 1972).
101. *Friedrich Barbarossa*, ed. Gunther Wolf (WdF 390; Darmstadt, 1975).
102. Fuhrmann, Horst, *Deutsche Geschichte im hohen Mittelalter von der Mitte des 11. bis zum Ende des 12. Jahrhunderts* (Göttingen, 1978; 2nd rev. and bibliog. suppl. edn., 1983).
103. *Geschichte des jüdischen Volkes*, ed. Haim Hillel Ben-Sasson, vol. ii (Munich, 1979).
104. *Geschichte, Wirtschaft, Gesellschaft*, Fs. for Clemens Bauer (Berlin, 1974).
105. Graus, František, *Lebendige Vergangenheit* (Cologne, 1975).
106. Grundmann, Herbert, *Ausgewählte Aufsätze*, parts 1–3 (Schriften der MGH 25, 1–3; Stuttgart, 1978).
107. Hampe, Karl, *Das Hochmittelalter* (Cologne[5], 1963).
108. Haverkamp, Alfred, Lamma, Paolo, and Manselli, Raoul, *Beiträge zur Geschichte Italiens im 12. Jahrhundert* (VuF, extra ser., 9; Sigmaringen, 1971).
109. *Histoire de la Bourgogne*, ed. Jean Richard (Univers de la France et des pays francophones, 42: Histoire des provinces; Paris, 1978).
110. *Histoire Générale de l'Europe*, ed. Georges Livet *et al.*, vol. i (Paris, 1980).
111. *Historia Mundi*, ed. Fritz Valjavec, vol. vi (Bern, 1958).
112. *Historische Forschungen für Walter Schlesinger* (Fs.) (Cologne etc., 1974).
113. *Das Hochmittelalter*, ed. Jacques Le Goff (Fischer Weltgesch. 11; Frankfurt am Main, 1965).

114. *Institutionen, Kultur und Gesellschaft im Mittelalter*, Fs. for Josef Fleckenstein (Sigmaringen, 1984).

115. *Investiturstreit und Reichsverfassung*, ed. Josef Fleckenstein (VuF 17; Sigmaringen, 1973).

116. Jakobs, Hermann, *Kirchenreform und Hochmittelalter, 1046–1215* (Oldenbourg—Grundriss der Geschichte, 7; Munich etc.[2], 1988).

117. Jones, Philip, *Economia e società nell'Italia medievale*, tr. Carla Susini Jones and Aldo Serafini (Biblioteca di cultura storica 141; Turin, 1980).

118. Keller, Hagen, *Zwischen regionaler Begrenzung und universalem Horizont: Deutschland im Imperium der Salier und Staufer 1024–1250* (Propyläen Geschichte Deutschlands 2; Berlin 1986).

119. Leuschner, Joachim, *Deutschland im späten Mittelalter* (Göttingen[2], 1983).

120. Leyser, Karl, *Medieval Germany and its Neighbours, 900–1250* (London, 1982).

121. Leyser, Karl, 'The Crisis of Medieval Germany' (Raleigh Lecture on History 1983), in *Proceedings of the British Academy, London*, 69 (Oxford, 1984), 409–43.

122. Miller, Edward, and Hatcher, John, *Medieval England* (Harlow, 1978).

123. Ostrogorsky, George, *History of the Byzantine State*, tr. Joan Hussey (Oxford[2], 1968).

124. Prinz, Friedrich, *Böhmen im mittelalterlichen Europa. Frühzeit, Hochmittelalter, Kolonisationsepoche* (Munich, 1984).

125. Prinz, Friedrich, *Grundlagen und Anfänge. Deutschland bis 1056* (Neue Deutsche Geschichte, 1; Munich, 1985).

126. *Probleme des 12. Jahrhunderts* (VuF 12; Constance etc., 1968).

127. *Probleme um Friedrich II.*, ed. Josef Fleckenstein (VuF 16; Sigmaringen, 1974).

128. *Propyläen Weltgeschichte*, ed. Golo Mann *et al.*, vol. v (Berlin, 1963).

129. *Recht und Schrift im Mittelalter*, ed. Peter Classen (VuF 23; Sigmaringen, 1977).

130. Rhode, Gotthold, *Geschichte Polens* (Darmstadt[3], 1980).

131. *Das Rittertum im Mittelalter*, ed. Arno Borst (WdF 349; Darmstadt, 1976).

132. *Schulen und Studium im sozialen Wandel des hohen und späten Mittelalters*, ed. Johannes Fried (VuF 30; Sigmaringen, 1986).

133. Seidlmayer, Michael, and Schieder, Theodor, *Geschichte Italiens* (Stuttgart[2], 1989).

134. *Die Slawen in Deutschland. Ein Handbuch*, ed. Joachim Herrmann (Berlin, 1972).

135. *Soziale Ordnungen im Selbstverständnis des Mittelalters*, ed. Albert Zimmermann, vols. i–ii (Misc. Mediaevalia, 12. i–ii; Berlin, 1979, 1980).

136. *Stadt im Wandel. Kunst und Kultur des Bürgertums in Norddeutschland, 1150–1650*, ed. Cord Meckseper, 4 vols. (Stuttgart-Bad Cannstatt, 1985).

137. *Stadt und Herrschaft*, ed. Friedrich Vittinghoff (*HZ*, Suppl. 7 NF; Munich, 1982).

138. *Stadt und Städtebürgertum in der deutschen Geschichte des 13. Jahrhunderts*, ed. Bernhard Töpfer (Forsch. zur ma. Gesch. 24; (East) Berlin, 1976).

139. Stoob, Heinz, *Forschungen zum Städtewesen in Europa*, vol. i (Cologne etc., 1970).

140. *Stupor mundi*, ed. Gunther Wolf (WdF 101; Darmstadt, 1966, rev. edn.[2] 1982).

141. Tabacco, Giovanni, *Egemonie sociali e strutture del potere nel medioevo italiano* (Turin, 1979).

142. Töpfer, Bernhard, and Engel, Evamaria, *Vom staufischen Imperium zum Hausmachtkönigtum* (Weimar, 1976).

143. *Untersuchungen zur gesellschaftlichen Struktur der mittelalterlichen Städte in Europa* (VuF 11; Sigmaringen[2], 1974).

144. *Wahlen und Wählen im Mittelalter*, ed. Reinhard Schneider et al. (VuF 37; Sigmaringen, 1990).

145. *Wort und Begriff 'Bauer'*, ed. Reinhart Wenskus et al. (Abh. der Akad. der Wiss. Göttingen, phil.-hist. Kl., 3. Folge, 89; Göttingen, 1975).

146. *Die Zähringer. Veröffentlichungen zur Zähringer-Ausstellung*, vol. 1: *Eine Tradition und ihre Erforschung*, ed. Karl Schmid; vol. 2: *Anstoß und Wirkung*, ed. Hans Schadeck et al. (Sigmaringen, 1986).

147. *Die Zeit der Staufer*, vols. i–iv (Stuttgart, 1977); vol. v (Stuttgart, 1979).

I. THE AGE IN EUROPEAN PERSPECTIVE

I. 1. The Expansion of the West in the Mediterranean area

148. Althoff, Gerd, 'Nunc fiant milites, qui dudum extiterunt raptores', *Saeculum* 32 (1981), 317–33.

149. Brundage, James A., *Medieval Canon Law and the Crusader* (Madison etc., 1969).

150. *I Comuni Italiani nel Regno Crociato di Gerusalemme*, Atti del Colloquio 'The Italian Communes in the Crusading Kingdom of

Jerusalem' (Jerusalem, May 24–May 28, 1984), ed. G. Airaldi *et al.* (Collana Storica di Fonti e Studi, 48; Genoa, 1986).

151. Erdmann, Carl, *Die Entstehung des Kreuzzugsgedankens* (Forsch. zur Kirchen- und Geistesgesch. 6; Stuttgart, 1935).

152. Favreau-Lilie, Marie-Luise, *Die Italiener im Heiligen Land vom ersten Kreuzzug bis zum Tode Heinrichs von Champagne (1098–1197)* (Amsterdam, 1989).

153. *Die Geistlichen Ritterorden Europas*, ed. Josef Fleckenstein *et al.* (VuF 26; Sigmaringen, 1980).

154. Godfrey, John, *1204—The Unholy Crusade* (Oxford, 1980).

155. Hamilton, Bernard, *The Latin Church in the Crusader States* (London, 1980).

156. Heinemann, Hartmut, 'Untersuchungen zur Geschichte der Zähringer in Burgund', *ADipl* 29 (1983), 42–192; 30 (1984), 97–257.

157. Herde, Peter, *Karl I. von Anjou* (Stuttgart etc., 1979).

158. *A History of the Crusades*, ed. Kenneth M. Setton, vol. i (Philadelphia, 1958); vol. ii (Philadelphia², 1969).

159. Hoffmann, Hartmut, *Gottesfriede und Treuga Dei* (Schriften der MGH 20; Stuttgart, 1964).

160. Lilie, Ralph-Johannes, *Handel und Politik zwischen dem byzantinischen Reich und den italienischen Kommunen Venedig, Pisa und Genua in der Epoche der Komnenen und der Angeloi (1081–1204)* (Amsterdam, 1984).

161. Mayer, Hans Eberhard, *The Crusades*, tr. John Gillingham (Oxford, 1972).

162. Niederkorn, Jan Paul, 'Die Mitgift der Kaiserin Irene, Anmerkungen zur byzantinischen Politik König Konrads III.', *RHMitt* 28 (1986), 125–39.

163. Prawer, Joshua, *Histoire du royaume latin de Jérusalem*, vols. i–ii (Paris, 1969, 1970).

164. Queller, Donald E., *The Fourth Crusade. The Conquest of Constantinople 1201–1204* (Leicester, 1978).

165. Riley-Smith, Jonathan, *The First Crusade and the Idea of Crusading* (London, 1986).

166. Runciman, Steven, *A History of the Crusades*, vols. i–iii (Cambridge, 1951, 1952, 1954).

167. Setton, Kenneth M., *The Papacy and the Levant (1204–1571)*, vol. 1 (Memoirs of the American Philosophical Society, 114; Philadelphia, 1976).

I. 2. The Spread of Latin Christendom in Continental Europe

168. Boockmann, Hartmut, *Der Deutsche Orden* (Munich, 1981).
169. Favreau, Marie-Luise, *Studien zur Frühgeschichte des Deutschen Ordens* (Kieler Hist. Stud. 21; Stuttgart, n.d. [1975]).
170. Kluger, Helmuth, *Hochmeister Hermann von Salza und Kaiser Friedrich II. Ein Beitrag zur Frühgeschichte des Deutschen Ordens* (Quellen und Studien zur Geschichte des Deutschen Ordens, 37; Marburg, 1987).
171. Neitmann, Klaus, *Die Staatsverträge des Deutschen Ordens in Preussen 1230–1449. Studien zur Diplomatie eines spätmittelalterlichen deutschen Territorialstaates* (Neue Forschungen zur brandenburgisch-preussischen Geschichte, 6; Cologne, 1986).

I. 3. The Creation of New Kingdoms and Forms of Lordship

172. *Die Anfänge der Landgemeinde und ihr Wesen*, vols. i–ii (VuF 7–8; Constance etc., 1964).
173. Baldwin, John W., *The Government of Philip Augustus* (London, 1986).
174. Barrow, Geoffrey W. S., *The Anglo-Norman Era in Scottish History* (Oxford, 1980).
175. Becker, Alfons, *Studien zum Investiturproblem in Frankreich* (Saarbrücken, 1955).
176. Brooke, Christopher N. L., *The Saxon and Norman Kings* (London, 1978).
177. Brühl, Carlrichard, *Fodrum, Gistum, Servitium regis* (Kölner Hist. Abh. NS 14; Cologne etc., 1968).
178. Buisson, Ludwig, *König Ludwig IX. der Heilige und das Recht* (Freiburg, 1954).
179. Caspar, Erich, *Roger II. (1101–1154) und die Gründung der normannisch-sizilischen Monarchie* (Innsbruck², 1904).
180. *La France de Philippe Auguste: Le temps des mutations*, ed. Robert-Henri Bautier (Colloques internationaux du Centre national de la Recherche Scientifique, 602; Paris, 1982).
181. Grundmann, Herbert, 'Rotten und Brabanzonen', *DA* 5 (1942), 419–92.
182. *Histoire de la France religieuse*, ed. Jacques le Goff, vol. 1 (Paris, 1988).
183. *Histoire de la France rurale*, ed. Georges Duby *et al.*, vol. i (Paris, 1975).
184. *Histoire de la France urbaine*, ed. Georges Duby, vol. ii (Paris, 1980).

185. Hoffmann, Erich, *Königserhebung und Thronfolgeordnung in Dänemark bis zum Ausgang des Mittelalters* (Beitr. zur Gesch. und Quellenkde. des Ma 5; Berlin etc., 1976).

186. Hoffmann, Hartmut, 'Die Anfänge der Normannen in Süditalien', *QFIAB* 49 (1969), 95–144.

187. Hoffmann, Hartmut, *Der Kirchenstaat im hohen Mittelalter*, *QFIAB* 57 (1977), 1–45.

188. Hole, Andalus (E. C.), *Spain under the Muslims* (London, 1958).

189. Kaiser, Reinhold, *Bischofsherrschaft zwischen Königtum und Fürstenmacht* (Pariser Hist. Stud. 17; Bonn, 1982).

190. Kamp, Norbert, *Kirche und Monarchie im staufischen Königreich Sizilien*, vol. i. 1–4 (Münstersche MA-Schriften 10, i. 1–4; Munich, 1973–82).

191. Kamp, Norbert, 'Kirchenpolitik und Sozialstruktur im staufischen Königreich Sizilien' [100: ii. 948–58].

192. Krieger, Karl-Friedrich, *Geschichte Englands. Von den Anfängen bis zum 15. Jahrhundert* (Munich, 1990).

193. Mitteis, Heinrich, *Lehnrecht und Staatsgewalt* (Weimar, 1933).

194. Mitteis, Heinrich, *Der Staat des hohen Mittelalters* (Cologne[9], 1974).

195. Norwich, John J., *The Normans in the South, 1016–1130* (London, 1967).

196. Petit-Dutaillis, Charles E., *The French Communes in the Middle Ages* (Paris, 1947).

197. Prinz, Friedrich, 'Zur französischen Nationwerdung', *Bohemia, Jb. des Collegium Carolinum*, 16 (1975), 51–68.

198. Richard, Jean, *Saint Louis roi d'une France féodale, soutien de la Terre Sainte* (Paris, 1983).

199. Riis, Thomas, *Les Institutions politiques centrales du Danemark 1100–1332* (Odense, 1977).

200. Stenton, Frank M., *The First Century of English Feudalism 1066–1216* (Oxford[3], 1972).

201. Ullmann, Walter, 'Von Canossa nach Pavia', *HJb* 93 (1973), 265–300.

202. Werner, Karl Ferdinand, 'Königtum und Fürstentum im 12. Jahrhundert' [126: 177–227].

I. 4. Population Increase, Settlement Density, and Economic Growth

203. Genicot, Léopold, 'Sur les témoignages d'accroissement de la population en Occident du XIe au XIIIe siècle', *Cahiers d'histoire mondiale* 1 (1953), 446–62; 2 (1954), 445–62.

204. Gimpel, Jean, *Die industrielle Revolution des Mittelalters* (Zürich etc., 1980).

205. Goehrke, Carsten, 'Die Anfänge des mittelalterlichen Städtewesens in eurasischer Perspektive', *Saeculum* 31 (1980), 194–220, 221–39.

206. Harvey, Alan, *Economic expansion in the Byzantine Empire, 900–1200* (Cambridge, 1989).

207. *A History of Technology*, ed. Charles Singer *et al.*, vol. ii (Oxford, 1972).

208. Lopez, Robert S., *The Commercial Revolution of the Middle Ages 950–1350* (Englewood Cliffs, NY, 1971).

209. Moxó, Salvador de, *Repoblación y sociedad en la España cristiana medieval* (Cuestiones Fundamentales, 18; Madrid, 1979).

210. Schaube, Adolf, *Handelsgeschichte der romanischen Völker des Mittelmeergebietes bis zum Ende der Kreuzzüge* (Munich etc., 1906).

211. Schulte, Aloys, *Geschichte des mittelalterlichen Handels und Verkehrs zwischen Westdeutschland und Italien mit Ausschluß von Venedig*, vols. i–ii (Leipzig, 1900).

212. Slicher van Bath, Bernard Hendrik, *The Agrarian History of Western Europe,* AD *500–1850*, O. Ordish (London, 1963).

213. Straus, Raphael, *Die Juden in Wirtschaft und Gesellschaft* (Frankfurt am Main, 1964).

214. White, Lynn jun., *Medieval Religion and Technology* (Publications of the Center for Medieval and Renaissance Studies, 13; Berkeley etc., 1978).

215. White, Lynn jun., *Medieval Technology and Social Change* (Oxford, 1962).

I. 5. Poverty, Penitence, and Heresy

216. Borst, Arno, *Die Katharer* (Schriften der MGH, 12; Stuttgart, 1953).

217. Brooke, Rosalind and Christopher, *Popular Religion in the Middle Ages. Western Europe 1000–1300* (London, 1984).

218. Grundmann, Herbert, *Ketzergeschichte des Mittelalters* (Göttingen, 1963).

219. Grundmann, Herbert, *Religiöse Bewegungen im Mittelalter* (Darmstadt[3], 1970).

220. *Hérésies et sociétés dans l'Europe préindustrielle (11e–18e siècles)*, ed. Jacques Le Goff (Civilisations et Sociétés, 10; Paris, 1968).

221. *Istituzioni monastiche e istituzioni canonicali in Occidente (1123–1215)*, Milan, 1980 (pub. as No. 89, 9).

222. Koch, Gottfried, *Frauenfrage und Ketzertum im Mittelalter* (Forsch. zur ma. Gesch. 9; Berlin, 1962).

223. Mollat, Michel, *Les Pauvres au moyen âge* (Paris, 1978; German edn. Munich, 1984).
224. Molnár, Amedeo, *Die Waldenser* (Berlin, 1980).
225. Schneider, Martin, *Europäisches Waldensertum im 13. und 14. Jahrhundert* (Arbeiten zur Kirchengesch. 51; Berlin etc., 1981).
226. Selge, Kurt Victor, *Die ersten Waldenser*, vols. i–ii (Arbeiten zur Kirchengesch. 37. i–ii, Berlin, 1967).
227. van Mingroot, Erik, 'Ramihrdus de Schere alias Ramihrd d'Esquerchin, gest. 1077', in *Studies voor Prof. J. M. de Smet*, ed. R. Lievens *et al.* (Louvain, 1983), pp. 75–92.
228. Werner, Ernst, *Häresie und Gesellschaft im 11. Jahrhundert* (Sitzungsber. der Sächs. Akad. der Wiss. zu Leipzig, phil.-hist. Kl. 117, H. 5; (East) Berlin, 1975).
229. Werner, Ernst, *Pauperes Christi* (Leipzig, 1956).
230. Werner, Ernst, and Erbstößer, Martin, *Ketzer und Heilige. Das religiöse Leben im Hochmittelalter* (Berlin, 1986).

I. 6. The Papacy, the Church, and Monasticism

231. Beck, Hans-Georg, *Geschichte der orthodoxen Kirche im Byzantinischen Reich* (Die Kirche in ihrer Gesch. 1; Göttingen, 1980).
232. Becker, Alfons, *Papst Urban II (1088–1099)*, vol. ii, *Der Papst, die griechische Christenheit und der Kreuzzug* (Schriften der MGH, 19; Stuttgart, 1988).
233. Benzinger, Josef, *Invectiva in Romam* (Hist. Stud. 404; Lübeck etc. 1968).
234. Chazan, Robert, *Daggers of Faith. Thirteenth Century Christian Missionizing and Jewish Response* (Berkeley etc., 1989).
235. *Die Cistercienser*, ed. Ambrosius Schneider *et al.* (Cologne³, 1986).
236. Cowdrey, Herbert E. J., 'The Papacy, the Patarenes and the Church of Milan', *Transactions of the Royal Historical Society*, 18 (1968), 25–48.
237. Elm, Kaspar, 'Franziskus und Dominikus', *Saeculum* 23 (1972), 127–47.
238. Elm, Kaspar, 'Italienische Eremitengemeinschaften des 12. und 13. Jahrhunderts' [99: 491–559].
239. Engen, John van, 'The "Crisis of Cenobitism" Reconsidered: Benedictine Monasticism in the Years 1050–1150', *Speculum* 61 (1986), 269–304.
240. Fuhrmann, Horst, *Einfluss und Verbreitung der pseudoisidorischen Fälschungen*, parts i–iii (Schriften der MGH 24. i–iii; Stuttgart, 1972–4).

241. Fuhrmann, Horst, 'Quod catholicus non habeatur, qui non concordat Romanae ecclesiae', *Fs. für Helmut Beumann* (Sigmaringen, 1977), pp. 263–87.

242. Fuhrmann, Horst, 'Papst Gregor VII. und das Kirchenrecht. Zum Problem des Dictatus Papae', *La riforma Gregoriana e l'Europa. Congresso Internazionale, Salerno, 20–25 maggio 1985* [261, 13 (1989): 123–49].

243. Fuhrmann, Horst, 'Das Reformpapsttum und die Rechtswissenschaft' [115: 175–203].

244. Hallinger, Kassius, *Gorze-Kluny*, vols. i–ii (Studia Anselmiana, 22–5; Rome, 1950, 1951).

245. Hoffmann, Hartmut, 'Die beiden Schwerter im hohen Mittelalter', *DA* 20 (1964), 78–114.

246. Hoffmann, Hartmut, 'Von Cluny zum Investiturstreit', *AKG* 45 (1963), 165–209.

247. Hüls, Rudolf, *Kardinäle, Klerus und Kirchen Roms 1049–1130* (Bibl. des DHI in Rom, 48; Tübingen, 1977).

248. *Le istituzioni ecclesiastiche della 'societas christiana' dei secoli XI e XII* (Milan, 1974) (publ. as No. 89, 7).

249. Klewitz, Hans-Walter, *Reformpapsttum und Kardinalkolleg* (Darmstadt, 1957).

250. *I laici nella 'societas christiana' dei secoli XI e XII* (Milan, 1968) (publ. as No. 89, 5).

251. Maccarone, Michele, *Studi su Innocenzo III* (Italia sacra, 17; Padua, 1972).

252. Maleczek, Werner, *Papst und Kardinalskolleg von 1191 bis 1216. Die Kardinäle unter Coelestin III. und Innocenz III.* (Publ. d. Hist. Instituts beim Österreichischen Kulturinstitut in Rom, 1, 6; Vienna, 1984).

253. *Il monachesimo e la riforma ecclesiastica (1049–1122)* (Milan, 1971) (publ. as No. 89, 6).

254. Morris, Colin, *The papal Monarchy: the western church from 1050 to 1250* (Oxford history of the Christian Church; Oxford, 1989).

255. *Neue Forschungen über Cluny und die Cluniacenser*, ed. Gerd Tellenbach (Freiburg, 1959).

256. Pacaut, Marcel, *Alexandre III* (L'église et l'état au moyen âge, 11; Paris, 1956).

257. Parisse, Michel, *La Lorraine monastique au moyen âge* (Nancy, 1981).

258. Partner, Peter, *The Lands of St. Peter* (Berkeley etc., 1972).

259. *La Riforma Gregoriana e l'Europa. Congresso internazionale, Salerno, 20–25 maggio 1985, vol. 1: Relazioni*, ed. A. M. Stickler *et al.* [261, 13 (1986)].

260. *Stellung und Wirksamkeit der Bettelorden in der städtischen Gesellschaft*, ed. Kaspar Elm (Berliner Hist. Stud. 3; Ordensstud. 2; Berlin, 1981).

261. *Studi Gregoriani per la storia di Gregorio VII e della Riforma Gregoriana*, ed. Giovanni Battista Borino, vols. i–vii (Rome, 1947–60); vols. viii– : *Studi Gregoriani per la storia della 'Libertas Ecclesiae'*, ed. Alfonso M. Stickler *et al.* (Rome, 1970–1990–); vol. viii, indexes to vols. i–vi, rev. by Zelina Zafarana (Rome, 1970).

262. Szabó-Bechstein, Brigitte, *Libertas ecclesiae. Ein Schlüsselbegriff des Investiturstreits und seine Vorgeschichte, 4.–11. Jh.* [261, 12 (1985)].

263. Tellenbach, Gerd, *Libertas* (Forsch. zur Kirchen- und Geistesgesch. 7; Stuttgart, 1936).

264. Tellenbach, Gerd, *Die westliche Kirche vom 10. bis zum frühesten 12. Jahrhundert* (Die Kirche in ihrer Geschichte. Ein Handbuch, Lfg. F 1, vol. 2; Göttingen, 1988).

265. Töpfer, Bernhard, *Das kommende Reich des Friedens* (Forsch. zur ma. Gesch. 11; (East) Berlin, 1964).

266. Violante, Cinzio, *Studi sulla cristianità medioevale* (Cultura e storia, 8; Milan², 1975).

267. *La vita comune del clero nei secoli XI e XII*, vols. i–ii (Milan, 1962) (publ. as No. 89, 3).

268. *Die Zisterzienser*, ed. Kaspar Elm *et al.*; suppl. vol. ed. Kaspar Elm *et al.* (Schriften des Rhein. Museumsamtes 10, 18; Cologne, 1980).

I. 7. Education and Learning

269. *Abélard et son temps* (Paris, 1981).

270. *Albertus Magnus. Ausstellung zum 700. Todestag* (Cologne, 1980).

271. *Albertus Magnus*, ed. Gerbert Meyer *et al.* (Walberger Stud., Philos. Reihe, 6; Mainz, 1980).

272. *Antiqui und Moderni*, ed. Albert Zimmermann (Misc. Mediaevalia, 9; Berlin etc., 1974).

273. *Die Auseinandersetzungen an der Pariser Universität im XIII. Jahrhundert*, ed. Albert Zimmermann (Misc. Mediaevalia, 10; Berlin etc., 1976).

274. Berschin, Walter, *Griechisch-lateinisches Mittelalter* (Bern, 1980).

275. Chenu, Marie-Dominique, *La théologie au XIIᵉ siècle* (Etudes de la philosophie médiévale, 45; Paris², 1976).

276. Curtius, Ernst Robert, *European Literature and the Latin Middle Ages*, tr. W. R. Trysk (London, 1954).

277. Fried, Johannes, *Die Entstehung des Juristenstandes im 12.*

382   Bibliography

        Jahrhundert (Forsch. zur neueren Privatrechtsgesch. 21;
        Cologne, 1974).
278.   Götze, *Castel del Monte. Gestalt, Herkunft und Bedeutung* (Sb. der
        Heidelb. Ak. d. Wiss.1984, Ber. 2; Heidelberg, 1984).
279.   Grabmann, Martin, *Gesammelte Akademieabhandungen, Munich
        1922–1944* (Münchner Universitätsschriften, Veröffentl. des
        Grabmann-Instituts NF 25. i–ii; Paderborn etc., 1979).
280.   Grabmann, Martin, *Die Geschichte der scholastischen Methode
        nach gedruckten und ungedruckten Quellen*, vols. i–ii (Freiburg,
        1909, 1911).
281.   Grabmann, Martin, *Thomas von Aquin* (Munich⁷, 1946).
282.   Haskins, Charles H., *The Renaissance of the Twelfth Century*
        (New York¹⁶, 1972).
283.   Haverkamp, Alfred, 'Zur Sklaverei in Genua während des 12.
        Jahrhunderts', *Geschichte in der Gesellschaft, Fs. for Karl Bosl*
        (Stuttgart, 1974), pp. 160–215.
284.   Heidelberger, Michael, and Thiessen, Sigrun, *Natur und Er-
        fahrung* (Reinbek bei Hamburg, 1981).
285.   *A History of Twelfth-Century Western Philosophy*, ed. Peter
        Dronke (Cambridge, 1988).
286.   Morris, Colin, *The Discovery of the Individual 1050–1200*
        (Church History Outlines 5; London, 1972).
287.   *Petrus Abaelardus (1079–1142)*, ed. Rudolf Thomas *et al.*
        (Trierer Theol. Stud. 38; Trier, 1980).
288.   *Philosophie im Mittelalter. Entwicklungslinien und Paradigmen*, ed.
        Jan P. Beckmann *et al.* (Hamburg, 1987).
289.   Podlech, Adalbert, *Abaelard und Héloisa oder Die Theologie der
        Liebe* (Munich, 1990).
290.   *Renaissance and Renewal in the Twelfth Century*, ed. Robert L.
        Benson *et al.* (Oxford, 1982).
291.   *Die Renaissance der Wissenschaften im 12. Jahrhundert*, ed. Peter
        Weimar (Züricher Hochschulforum, 2; Zürich, 1981).
292.   Sauerländer, Willibald, *Das Jahrhundert der großen Kathedralen,
        1140–1260* (Munich, 1990).
293.   *Science in the Middle Ages*, ed. David C. Lindberg (Chicago,
        1978).
294.   Sprandel, Rolf, *Gesellschaft und Literatur im Mittelalter* (Pader-
        born, 1982).
295.   Stock, Brian, *The Implications of Literacy* (Princeton, 1983).
296.   *Thomas von Aquin. Werk und Wirkung im Licht neuerer
        Forschungen*, ed. Albert Zimmermann (Miscellanea Medi-
        aevalia, 19; Berlin etc., 1988).
297.   Wellas, Michael B., *Griechisches aus dem Umkreis Kaiser Friedrichs*

II. (Münchener Beiträge zur Mediävistik und Renaissance-Forschung 33; Munich, 1983).

298. Werner, Ernst, *Stadt und Geistesleben im Hochmittelalter* (Forsch. zur ma. Gesch. 30; Weimar, 1980).

I. 8. Social Change

299. Bosl, Karl, 'Die "familia" als Grundstruktur der mittelalterlichen Gesellschaft', *ZBLG* 38 (1975), 403–24.
300. Classen, Peter, *Burgundio von Pisa* (Sitzungsber. der Heidelberger Akad. der Wiss., phil.-hist. Kl. 1974, 4; Heidelberg, 1974).
301. Classen, Peter, 'Kodifikation im 12. Jahrhundert' [129: 311–17].
302. *Curialitas. Studien zu Grundfragen der höfisch-ritterlichen Kultur*, ed. Josef Fleckenstein (Veröffentlichungen des Max-Planck-Instituts für Geschichte, 100; Göttingen, 1990).
303. Dilcher, Gerhard, 'Rechtshistorische Aspekte des Stadtbegriffs', *Vor- und Frühformen der europäischen Stadt im Mittelalter*, part 1, ed. Herbert Jankuhn *et al.* (Abh. der Akad. der Wiss. in Göttingen, phil.-hist. Kl., 3. Folge 83; Göttingen, 1973), pp. 12–33.
304. Duby, Georges, *Les Trois Ordres ou l'imaginaire du féodalisme* (Paris, 1978).
305. Duby, Georges, *Guerriers et paysans, VIIe–XIIe siècles; Premier essor de l'économie européenne* (Paris, 1977).
306. Duby, Georges, *La société aux XIe et XIIe siècles dans la région mâconnaise* (Paris, 1971).
307. *Famille et parenté dans l'occident médiéval*, ed. Georges Duby *et al.* (Coll. de l'Ecole Franç. de Rome, 30; Rome, 1977).
308. Fleckenstein, Josef, 'Über den engeren und weiteren Begriff von Ritter und Rittertum (*miles* und *militia*)', in *Person und Gemeinschaft im Mittelalter. Fs. für Karl Schmid*, ed. Gerd Althoff *et al.* (Sigmaringen, 1988), pp. 379–92.
309. *Höfische Literatur, Hofgesellschaft, höfische Lebenformen um 1200*, ed. Gert Kaiser *et al.* (Düsseldorf, 1986).
310. Hyams, Paul Raphael, *King, Lords and Peasants in Medieval England* (New York etc., 1980).
311. Matheus, Michael, *Adelige als Zinser von Heiligen. Studien zu Zinsverhältnissen geistlicher Institutionen im hohen Mittelalter*. Habilitationsschrift, typescr. (Trier, 1989).
312. *La noblesse au moyen âge, XIe–XVe siècles, Essais à la mémoire de Robert Boutruche* (Vendôme, 1976).

313. Oexle, Otto Gerhard, 'Die funktionale Dreiteilung der "Gesellschaft" bei Adalbero von Laon', *Frühmittelalterliche Studien*, 12 (1978), 1–54.
314. Parisse, Michel, *Noblesse et chevalerie en Lorraine médiévale* (Nancy, 1982).
315. Tellenbach, Gerd, 'Mentalität' [104: 11–30].
316. *Das ritterliche Turnier im Mittelalter. Beitrag zu einer vergleichenden Formen- und Verhaltensgeschichte des Rittertums*, ed. J. Fleckenstein (Veröffentlichungen des Max-Planck-Instituts für Geschichte, 80; Göttingen, 1985).
317. Verlinden, Charles, *L'Esclavage dans l'Europe médiévale*, vol. i (Bruges, 1955); vol. ii (Ghent, 1977).

I. 9. Typology and Transmission of Sources

See also under Sources and General Literature

318. Eisenlohr, Erika, 'Paläographische Untersuchungen zum Tafelgüterverzeichnis des römisches Königs (Hs. Bonn UB S. 1559). Schreibgewohnheiten des Aachener Marienstifts in der zweiten Hälfte des 12. Jdt.', *Zeitschrift des Aachener Geschichtsvereins* 92 (1985), 5–74.
319. Esch, Arnold, 'Überlieferungs-Chance und Überlieferungs-Zufall als methodisches Problem des Historikers', *HZ* 240 (1985), 529–70.
320. Fehring, Günter P., *Einführung in die Archäologie des Mittelalters* (Darmstadt, 1987).

II. GERMANY FROM THE MIDDLE OF THE ELEVENTH TO THE MIDDLE OF THE TWELFTH CENTURY

II. 1. Imperial Rule from Henry III to Barbarossa (1056–1152)

321. Bernhardi, Wilhelm, *Konrad III.*, vols. i–ii (Jb. der dt. Gesch. 16. i–ii; Leipzig, 1883).
322. Beumann, Helmut, 'Das Reich der späten Salier und der Staufer 1056–1250' [59: 280–382].
323. Blumenthal, Uta-Renate, *Der Investiturstreit* (Urban-Taschenbücher, 335; Stuttgart etc., 1982).
324. Boshof, Egon, Die Salier (Stuttgart, 1987).
325. *Geschichte Thüringens*, ed. Hans Patze *et al.*, vol. ii (Mitteldt. Forsch. 48; Cologne, 1974).
326. Giesebrecht, Wilhelm von, *Geschichte der deutschen Kaiserzeit,*

vol. v, sections 1, 2; vol.vi, contin. and ed. by Bernhard von Simson (Braunschweig, 1880; Leipzig, 1888, 1895).

327. Haverkamp, Alfred, 'Italien im hohen und späten Mittelalter 1056–1454' [59: 546–681].

328. Hoffmann, Hartmut, 'Zum Register und zu den Briefen Papst Gregors VII.', *DA* 32 (1976), 86–130.

329. Jasper, Detlev, *Das Papstwahldekret von 1059. Überlieferung und Textgestalt* (Beiträge zur Geschichte der Quellenkunde des Mittelalters, 12; Sigmaringen, 1986).

330. Kienast, Walter, *Deutschland und Frankreich in der Kaiserzeit (900–1270)* (Monographien zur Gesch. des MA 9. i–iii; Stuttgart, 1975).

331. Lechner, Karl, *Die Babenberger (976–1246)* (pub. of IOG 23; Vienna etc., 1976).

332. Meyer von Knonau, Gerold, *Jahrbücher des Deutschen Reiches unter Heinrich IV. und Heinrich V.* (Jb. der dt. Gesch. 14. i–vii; Leipzig, 1890–1909).

333. Müller-Mertens, Eckhard, *Regnum Teutonicum* (Forsch. zur ma. Gesch. 15; Berlin, 1970).

334. Müller-Mertens, Eckhard, 'Reich und Hauptorte der Salier: Probleme und Fragen' [338: 1. 139–58].

335. Overmann, Alfred, *Gräfin Mathilde von Tuszien* (Innsbruck, 1895).

336. Prinz, Friedrich, 'Die Grenzen des Reiches in frühsalischer Zeit: ein Strukturproblem der Königsherrschaft' [338: 1. 159–73].

337. *Rheinische Geschichte*, ed. Franz Petri *et al.*, vol. i (Düsseldorf, 1983).

338. *Die Salier und das Reich*, parts I–III, ed. Stefan Weinfurter (Sigmaringen, 1991).

339. Schieffer, Rudolf, 'Von Mailand nach Canossa', *DA* 28 (1978), 333–70.

340. Schieffer, Rudolf, *Die Entstehung des päpstlichen Investiturverbots für den deutschen König* (Schriften der MGH 28; Stuttgart, 1981).

341. Schmidt, Ulrich, *Königswahl und Thronfolge im 12. Jahrhundert* (Forschungen zur Kaiser- und Papstgeschichte, 7; Cologne etc., 1987).

342. Schultze, Johannes, *Die Mark Brandenburg*, vols. i–ii (Berlin, 1961).

343. Servatius, Carlo, *Paschalis II. (1099–1118)* (Stuttgart, 1979).

344. Struve, Tilman, 'Kaisertum und Romgedanke in salischer Zeit', *DA* 44 (1988), 424–54.

345. Thomas, Heinz, 'Julius Caesar und die Deutschen. Zu

386   *Bibliography*

Ursprung und Gehalt eines deutschen Geschichtsbewußtseins in der Zeit Gregors VII. und Heinrichs IV' [338: iii. 245–77].

346. Töpfer, Deinhard, 'Tendenzen zur Entsakralisierung der Herrscherwürde in der Zeit des Investiturstreites', *Jb. für Gesch. des Feudalismus* 6 (1982), 163–71.

347. Vollrath, Hanna, 'Konrad III. und Byzanz', *AKG* 59 (1977), 321–65.

348. Wadle, Elmar, 'Heinrich IV. und die deutsche Friedensbewegung' [115: 141–73].

349. Weinfurter, Stefan, *Herrschaft und Reich der Salier. Grundlinien einer Umbruchzeit* (Sigmaringen, 1991).

350. Ziese, Jürgen, *Wibert von Ravenna* (Päpste und Papsttum, 20; Stuttgart, 1982).

II. 2. The Power Structure and its Evolution

351. Bosl, Karl, 'Die Entstehung der bürgerlichen Freiheit im süddeutschen Raum', *Les libertés urbaines et rurales du XIᵉ au XIVᵉ siècle* (Brussels, 1968), pp. 81–95.

352. Bosl, Karl, *Die Reichsministerialität der Salier und Staufer*, parts i–ii (Schriften der MGH 10. i–ii; Stuttgart, 1950, 1951).

353. Brunner, Otto, *Neue Wege der Verfassungs- und Sozialgeschichte* (Göttingen², 1968).

354. Büttner, Heinrich, 'Die Bischofsstädte von Basel bis Mainz in der Zeit des Investiturstreites' [115: 351–61].

355. Büttner, Heinrich, *Schwaben und Schweiz im frühen und hohen Mittelalter*, ed. Hans Patze (VuF 15; Sigmaringen, 1972).

356. *Burgen der Salierzeit*, parts 1–2, ed. Horst Wolfgang Böhme (Römisch-Germanisches Zentralmuseum: Monographien, 26; Sigmaringen, 1991).

357. *Die Burgen im deutschen Sprachraum*, vols. i–ii, ed. Hans Patze (VuF 19. i–ii; Sigmaringen, 1976).

358. Castorph, Bernward, *Die Ausbildung des römischen Königswahlrechtes* (Göttingen, 1978).

359. Classen, Peter, 'Das Wormser Konkordat in der deutschen Verfassungsgeschichte' [115: 411–60].

360. Claude, Dietrich, *Geschichte des Erzbistums Magdeburg bis in das 12. Jahrhundert*, vols. i–ii (Mitteldt. Forsch. 67. i–ii; Cologne etc., 1972, 1975).

361. Diederich, Toni, 'Coniuratio Coloniae facta est pro libertate', *AHVN* 176 (1974), 7–19.

362. Diestelkamp, Bernhard, *Gibt es eine Freiburger Gründungsurkunde aus dem Jahre 1120?* (Berlin, 1973).

363. Diestelkamp, Bernhard, 'König und Städte in salischer und staufischer Zeit' [137: 247–97].

364. Falck, Ludwig, *Geschichte der Stadt Mainz*, vols. ii–iii (Düsseldorf, 1972, 1973).

365. Faussner, Hans Constantin, 'Die Verfügungsgewalt des deutschen Königs über weltliches Reichsgut im Hochmittelalter', *DA* 29 (1973), 345–449.

366. Fenske, Lutz, *Adelsopposition und kirchliche Reformbewegung im östlichen Sachsen* (pub. of MPIG 47; Göttingen, 1977).

367. Ficker, Julius von, *Forschungen zur Reichs- und Rechtsgeschichte Italiens*, vols. i–iii (Innsbruck, 1868–72).

368. Ficker, Julius von, *Vom Reichsfürstenstande*, vols. i–ii, ed. Paul Puntschart (Innsbruck, 1861–1923).

369. Fleckenstein, Josef, 'Hofkapelle und Reichsepiskopat unter Heinrich IV.' [115: 117–40].

370. Fleckenstein, Josef, 'Zum Begriff der ottonisch-salischen Reichskirche' [104: 61–71].

371. Gawlik, Alfred, *Intervenienten und Zeugen in den Diplomen Kaiser Heinrichs IV. (1056–1105)* (Münchner Hist. Stud., Abt. Gesch. Hilfswiss. 7; Kallmünz, 1970).

372. Gernhuber, Joachim, *Die Landfriedensbewegung in Deutschland bis zum Mainzer Reichslandfrieden von 1235* (Bonner rechtswiss. Abh. 44; Bonn, 1952).

373. *Geschichte der Erzbistums Köln*, ed. Wilhelm Neuss, vol. i (Cologne, 1964).

374. *Geschichte der Stadt Speyer*, pub. by the city of Speyer, vol. i (Stuttgart etc.², 1983).

375. Giese, Wolfgang, *Der Stamm der Sachsen und das Reich in ottonischer und salischer Zeit* (Wiesbaden, 1979).

376. Glaeske, Günter, *Die Erzbischöfe von Hamburg-Bremen als Reichsfürsten (937–1258)* (Quellen und Darstellungen zur Gesch. Niedersachsens, 60; Hildesheim, 1962).

377. Hausmann, Friedrich, *Reichskanzlei und Hofkapelle unter Heinrich V. und Konrad III.* (Schriften der MGH, 14; Stuttgart, 1956).

378. Haverkamp, Alfred, 'Die "frühbürgerliche" Welt im hohen und späten Mittelalter', *HZ* 221 (1975), 572–602.

379. Haverkamp, Alfred, '"Heilige Städte" im hohen Mittelalter', in *Mentalitäten im Mittelalter*, ed. František Graus (VuF 35; Sigmaringen, 1987), pp. 119–56.

380. Haverkamp, Alfred, 'Die Städte im Herrschafts- und Sozialgefüge Reichsitaliens' [137: 149–245].

381. Haverkamp, Alfred, 'Die Städte Trier, Metz, Toul und

Verdun. Religiöse Gemeinschaften im Zentralitätsgefüge einer Städtelandschaft zur Zeit der Salier' [338: iii. 165–90].

382. Hirsch, Hans, *Die hohe Gerichtsbarkeit im deutschen Mittelalter* (Darmstadt², 1958).

383. Hirsch, Hans, *Die Klosterimmunität seit dem Investiturstreit* (Weimar, 1913).

384. Jakobs, Hermann, 'Stadtgemeinde und Bürgertum um 1100' [76: 14–54].

385. Jenal, Georg, *Erzbischof Anno II. von Köln (1056–1075) und sein politisches Wirken*, vols. i–ii (Monographien zur Gesch. des MA 8. i–ii; Stuttgart, 1974).

386. Keller, Hagen, 'Über den Charakter Freiburgs in der Frühzeit der Stadt', in *Fs. für Berent Schwineköper* (Sigmaringen, 1982), pp. 249–82.

387. Keller, Hagen, '"Kommune": Städtische Selbstregierung und mittelalterliche "Volksherrschaft" im Spiegel italienischer Wahlverfahren des 12.–14. Jahrhunderts', in *Person und Gemeinschaft im Mittelalter, Fs. für Karl Schmid*, ed. Gerd Althoff *et al.* (Sigmaringen, 1988), pp. 573–616.

388. Keller, Hagen, 'Schwäbische Herzöge als Thronbewerber: Hermann II. (1002), Rudolf von Rheinfelden (1077), Friedrich von Staufen (1125). Zur Entwicklung von Reichsidee und Fürstenverantwortung, Wahlverständnis und Wahlverfahren im 11. und 12. Jahrhundert', *ZGO* 131 (1983), 123–62.

389. Keller, Hagen, 'Der Übergang zur Kommune' [76: 55–72].

390. Köbler, Gerhard, 'Zur Entstehung des mittelalterlichen Stadtrechts', *ZRG, GA* 86 (1969), 177–98.

391. Körner, Theodor, *Juramentum und frühe Friedensbewegung (10.–12. Jahrhundert)* (Abh. zur rechtswiss. Grundlagenforsch. 26, Münchener Universitätsschriften; Berlin, 1977).

392. Kottje, Raymund, 'Zur Bedeutung der Bischofsstädte für Heinrich IV.', *HJb* 97/98 (1978), 131–57.

393. Lewald, Ursula, 'Köln im Investiturstreit' [115: 373–93].

394. Maurer, Helmut, *Der Herzog von Schwaben* (Sigmaringen, 1978).

395. Mayer, Theodor, *Fürsten und Staat* (Weimar, 1950).

396. Metz, Wolfgang, *Das Servitium Regis* (EdF 89; Darmstadt, 1978).

397. Metz, Wolfgang, 'Städte als Stützpunkte salischer Reichspolitik', in *Gesch. Landeskde.* 7 (Wiesbaden, 1972), 34–50.

398. *Ministerialität im Mittelrheinraum* (Gesch. Landeskde. 17; Wiesbaden, 1978).

399. *Ministerialität im Pfälzer Raum*, ed. Friedrich Ludwig Wagner

(publ. of the Pfälz. Ges. zur Förderung der Wiss. in Speyer, 64; Speyer, 1975).

400. Minninger, Monika, *Von Clermont zum Wormser Konkordat* (Forsch. zur Kaiser- und Papstgesch. des MA, 2; Cologne, 1978).

401. Patze, Hans, 'Christenvolk und Territorien' [89: 146–212].

402. Patze, Hans, 'Klostergründung und Klosterchronik', *BDLG* 113 (1977), 89–121.

403. Planitz, Hans, *Die deutsche Stadt im Mittelalter* (Vienna etc.[3], 1973).

404. Prinz, Friedrich, 'Bayerns Adel im Hochmittelalter', *ZBLG* 30 (1967), 53–117.

405. Reuling, Ulrich, *Die Kur in Deutschland und Frankreich* (pub. of MPIG, 64; Göttingen, 1978).

406. Schlesinger, Walter, 'Das älteste Freiburger Stadtrecht', *ZRG*, *GA* 83 (1966), 63–116.

407. Schlesinger, Walter, *Mitteldeutsche Beiträge zur deutschen Verfassungsgeschichte des Mittelalters* (Göttingen, 1961).

408. Schmid, Peter, *Regensburg* (Regensburger Hist. Forsch. 6; Kallmünz, 1977).

409. Schulte, Aloys, *Der Adel und die deutsche Kirche im Mittelalter* (Stuttgart[2], 1922).

410. Schulz, Knut, 'Die Ministerialität als Problem der Stadtgeschichte', *Rhein Vjbll* 32 (1968), 184–219.

411. Schulz, Knut, *Ministerialität und Bürgertum in Trier* (Rhein. Archiv, 66; Bonn, 1968).

412. Seeliger, Gerhard, *Die soziale und politische Bedeutung der Grundherrschaft* (Abh. der phil.-hist. Kl. der Sächs. Akad. der Wiss. 20; Leipzig, 1903).

413. Stehkämper, Hugo, 'Die Stadt Köln in der Salierzeit' [338: iii. 75–152].

414. Stoob, Heinz, 'Gedanken zur Ostseepolitik Lothars III.', in *Fs. für Friedrich Hausmann* (Graz, 1977), pp. 531–51.

415. Stoob, Heinz, 'Westfalen und Niederlothringen in der Politik Lothars III.', in *Tradition als historische Kraft* (*Fs. für Karl Hauck*) (Berlin etc., 1982), pp. 350–71.

416. Stoob, Heinz, 'Zur Königswahl Lothars von Sachsen im Jahre 1125' [101: 438–61].

417. Strait, Paul, *Cologne in the Twelfth Century* (Gainesville, 1974).

418. Vogt, Herbert Walter, *Das Herzogtum Lothars von Süpplinburg 1106–1125* (Quellen und Darstellungen zur Gesch. Niedersachsens, 67; Hildesheim, 1959).

419. Voltmer, Ernst, *Reichsstadt und Herrschaft* (Trierer Hist. Forsch. 1; Trier, 1981).

420. Wadle, Elmar, *Reichsgut und Königsherrschaft unter Lothar III. (1125–1137)* (Schriften zur Verfassungsgesch. 12; Berlin, 1969).

II. 3. The Basis and Development of the Economy

421. Abel, Wilhelm, *Geschichte der deutschen Landwirtschaft vom frühen Mittelalter bis zum 19. Jahrhundert* (Dt. Agrargesch. 2; Stuttgart², 1967).

422. *Altständisches Bürgertum*, vols. i–iii, ed. Heinz Stoob (WdF 302, 417, 646; Darmstadt, 1978, 1989).

423. Blaschke, Karlheinz, *Bevölkerungsgeschichte Sachsens bis zur industriellen Revolution* (Weimar, 1967).

424. Borchers, Hertha, 'Untersuchungen zur Handels- und Verkehrsgeschichte am Mittel- und Oberrhein bis zum Ende des 12. Jahrhunderts', Diss. typescript (Marburg, 1952).

425. Curschmann, Fritz, *Hungersnöte im Mittelalter* (Leipziger Stud. aus dem Gebiet der Gesch. 6. i; Leipzig, 1900).

426. Despy, Georges, and Billen, Claire, 'Les marchands mosans aux foires de Cologne pendant le XIIᵉ siècle', in *Recherches sur l'histoire des finances publiques en Belgique*, ed. Maurice-Aurélien Arnould et al., vol. 3 (Acta historica Bruxellensia, 3; Brussels, 1974), pp. 31–61.

427. Dilcher, Gerhard, 'Die mittelalterliche deutsche Stadt in ihrer Heraushebung aus der grundherrschaftlich-agrarischen Welt des Hochmittelalters', in *Sozialwissenschaften im Studium der Rechtswissenschaften*, vol. iv, *Rechtsgeschichte*, ed. Gerhard Dilcher et al. (Jus-Didaktik, H. 6; Munich, 1978), pp. 95–107.

428. Dollinger, Philippe, 'Der Aufschwung der oberrheinischen Bischofsstädte in salischer Zeit (1025–1125)' [76: 134–48].

429. Dollinger, Philippe, *Der bayerische Bauernstand vom 9.–13. Jahrhundert*, ed. Franz Irsigler (Munich, 1982).

430. Dopsch, Alfons, *Herrschaft und Bauer in der deutschen Kaiserzeit* (Quellen und Forsch. zur Agrargesch. 10; Stuttgart², 1964).

431. Dopsch, Alfons, *Naturalwirtschaft und Geldwirtschaft* (Vienna, 1930).

432. Engel, Gustav, *Herrschaftsgeschichte und Standesrecht* (Bielefeld, 1976).

433. Ennen, Edith, and Janssen, Walter, *Agrargeschichte Deutschlands bis zum Beginn der industriellen Revolution* (Wiss. Paperbacks, Sozial- und Wirtschaftsgesch. 12; Wiesbaden, 1978).

434. Franz, Günter, *Geschichte des deutschen Bauernstandes vom frühen Mittelalter bis zum 19. Jahrhundert* (Dt. Agrargesch. 4; Stuttgart, 1970).

435. Haverkamp, Alfred, 'Die Mosellande im 12. Jahrhundert', *Zs. für siebenbürgische Landeskde.* 4 (75) (1981), 21–39.

436. *Gilden und Zünfte. Kaufmännische und gewerbliche Genossenschaften im frühen und hohen Mittelalter*, ed. Berent Schwineköper (VuF 29; Sigmaringen, 1985).

437. Hess, Wolfgang, 'Münzstätten, Geldverkehr und Handel am Rhein in ottonischer und salischer Zeit' [76: 111–33].

438. Kaminsky, Hans H., *Studien zur Reichsabtei Corvey in der Salierzeit* (Cologne etc., 1972).

439. Kamp, Norbert, 'Probleme des Münzrechts und der Münzprägung in salischer Zeit' [76: 94–110].

440. Kluge, Bernd, *Deutsche Münzgeschichte von der späten Karolingerzeit bis zum Ende der Salier* (Sigmaringen, 1991).

441. Lamprecht, Karl, *Deutsches Wirtschaftsleben im Mittelalter*, vols. i–iii (Leipzig, 1885, 1886).

442. Linck, Eberhard, *Sozialer Wandel in klösterlichen Grundherrschaften des 11. bis 13. Jahrhunderts* (pub. of MPIG, 57; Göttingen, 1979).

443. Lütge, Friedrich, *Deutsche Sozial- und Wirtschaftsgeschichte* (Berlin etc.³, 1966).

444. Lütge, Friedrich, *Geschichte der deutschen Agrarverfassung vom frühen Mittelalter bis zum 19. Jahrhundert* (Dt. Agrargesch. 3; Stuttgart², 1962).

445. Maschke, Erich, 'Die Brücke im Mittelalter', *HZ* 224 (1977), 265–92.

446. Metz, Wolfgang, 'Marktrechtfamilie und Kaufmannsfriede in ottonisch-salischer Zeit', *BDLG* 108 (1972), 28–55.

447. Mitterauer, Michael, *Markt und Stadt im Mittelalter* (Monographien zur Gesch. des MA, 21; Stuttgart, 1980).

448. Mottek, Hans, *Wirtschaftsgeschichte Deutschlands*, vol. i (Berlin⁵, 1973).

449. Oexle, Otto Gerhard, 'Die mittelalterliche Zunft als Forschungsproblem', *BDLG* 118 (1982), 1–44.

450. Perrin, Charles-Edmond, *Recherches sur la seigneurie rurale en Lorraine d'après les plus anciens censiers (IXᵉ–XIIᵉ siècle)* (Paris, 1935).

451. Pitz, Ernst, *Wirtschafts- und Sozialgeschichte Deutschlands im Mittelalter* (Wiss. Paperbacks, Sozial und Wirtschaftsgesch. 15; Wiesbaden, 1979).

452. Rey, Manfred van, *Einführung in die rheinische Münzgeschichte des*

Mittelalters (Beitr. zur Gesch. der Stadt Mönchengladbach,17; Mönchengladbach, 1983).

453. Schmitz, Hans-Jürgen, *Faktoren der Preisbildung für Getreide und Wein in der Zeit von 800–1350* (Quellen und Forsch. zur Agrargesch. 20; Stuttgart, 1968).

454. *Siedlungen und Landesausbau zur Salierzeit*, parts 1–2, ed. Horst Wolfgang Böhme (Sigmaringen, 1990).

455. *Die Stadt des Mittelalters*, ed. Carl Haase, vols. i–iii (WdF 243–5; Darmstadt, 1972).

456. *Die Städte Mitteleuropas im 12. und 13. Jahrhundert*, ed. Wilhelm Rausch (Beitr. zur Gesch. der Städte Mitteleuropas, 1; Linz, 1963).

457. Stein, Walter, *Handels- und Verkehrsgeschichte der deutschen Kaiserzeit* (Berlin, 1922).

458. Stoob, Heinz, 'Die hochmittelalterliche Städtebildung im Okzident', in *Die Stadt*, ed. Heinz Stoob (Städtewesen, 1; Cologne, 1979), 131–94.

459. Suhle, Arthur, *Deutsche Münz- und Geldgeschichte von den Anfängen bis zum 15. Jahrhundert* (Berlin[4], 1970).

460. *Über Bürger, Stadt und städtische Literatur im Spätmittelalter* (Göttingen, 1980).

461. *Zwei Jahrtausende Kölner Wirtschaft*, vol. i (Cologne, 1975).

II. 4. The Church, Piety, and Education

462. Beumann, Helmut, 'Zur Verfasserfrage der Vita Heinrici IV.' [114: 305–19].

463. Bogumil, Karl-Otto, *Das Bistum Halberstadt im 12. Jahrhundert* (Mitteldt. Forsch. 69; Cologne etc., 1972).

464. Bosl, Karl, *Regularkanoniker (Augustinerchorherren) und Seelsorge in Kirche und Gesellschaft des europäischen 12. Jahrhunderts* (Abh. der Bayer. Akad. der Wiss., phil.-hist. Kl., NF 86; Munich, 1979).

465. Brucher, Günter, *Die sakrale Baukunst Italiens im 11. und 12. Jahrhundert* (Cologne, 1987).

466. Classen, Peter, *Gerhoch von Reichersberg* (Wiesbaden, 1960).

467. Ehlers, Joachim, *Hugo von St. Viktor* (Frankfurter Hist. Abh. 7; Wiesbaden, 1973).

467a. Fried, Johannes, 'Die Rezeption Bologneser Wissenschaft in Deutschland während des 12. Jahrhunderts', *Viator* 21 (1990), 103–45.

468. Fuhrmann, Horst, ' "Volkssouveränität" und "Herrschaftsvertrag" bei Manegold von Lautenbach', in *Fs. für Hermann Krause* (Cologne etc., 1975), pp. 21–42.

469. Grundmann, Herbert, *Geschichtsschreibung im Mittelalter* (Göttingen, 1965).

470. Hallinger, Kassius, 'Das Phänomen der liturgischen Steigerungen Clunys (10.–11. Jahrhundert)', in *Studia historica ecclesiastica, Fs. für Luchesius G. Spätling OFM* (Rome, 1977), pp. 183–236.

471. Hauck, Albert, *Kirchengeschichte Deutschlands*, part iii (Berlin etc.[6], 1952).

472. Haverkamp, Alfred, 'Tenxwind von Andernach und Hildegard von Bingen' [114: 515–48].

473. *Heidenmission und Kreuzzugsgedanke in der deutschen Ostpolitik des Mittelalters*, ed. Helmut Beumann (WdF 7; Darmstadt[2], 1973).

474. Jakobs, Hermann, *Der Adel in der Klosterreform von St. Blasien* (Kölner Hist. Abh. 16; Cologne, 1968).

475. Jakobs, Hermann, *Die Hirsauer* (Kölner Hist. Abh. 4; Cologne etc., 1961).

476. Kurze, Dietrich, *Pfarrerwahlen im Mittelalter* (Forsch. zur kirchl. Rechtsgesch. und zum Kirchenrecht, 6; Cologne etc., 1966).

477. Lotter, Friedrich, *Die Konzeption des Wendenkreuzzugs* (VuF, extra ser. 3; Sigmaringen, 1977).

478. Märtl, Claudia, 'Regensburg in den geistigen Auseinandersetzungen des Investiturstreites', *DA* 42 (1986), 145–91.

479. *Norbert von Xanten. Adliger, Ordensstifter, Kirchenfürst*, ed. Kaspar Elm (Cologne, 1984).

480. Petersohn, Jürgen, *Der Südliche Ostseeraum im kirchlich-politischen Kräftespiel des Reichs, Polens und Dänemarks vom 10. bis 13. Jahrhundert* (Ostmitteleuropa in Vergangenheit und Gegenwart, 17; Cologne etc., 1979).

481. Rösener, Werner, *Reichsabtei Salem* (VuF, extra ser. 13; Sigmaringen, 1974).

482. Ruh, Kurt, *Geschichte der abendländischen Mystik*, vol. 1: *Die Grundlegung durch die Kirchenväter und die Mönchstheologie des 12. Jahrhunderts* (Munich, 1990).

483. Schmid, Karl, 'Adel und Reform in Schwaben' [115: 295–319].

484. Semmler, Josef, *Die Klosterreform von Siegburg* (Rhein. Archiv, 58; Bonn, 1959).

485. Weinfurter, Stephan, 'Neuere Forschungen zu den Regularkanonikern im Deutschen Reich des 11. und 12. Jahrhunderts', *HZ* 224 (1977), 379–97.

486. Weinfurter, Stephan, 'Norbert von Xanten', *AKG* 59 (1977), 66–98.

487. Weinfurter, Stephan, 'Reformkanoniker und Reichsepiskopat im Hochmittelalter', *HJb* 97/98 (1978), 158–93.

394   Bibliography

488. Weinfurter, Stephan, *Salzburger Bistumsreform und Bischofspolitik im 12. Jahrhundert* (Kölner Hist. Abh. 24; Cologne etc., 1975).
489. *Zisterzienser-Studien*, vols. i, iii (Stud. zur europäischen Gesch. 11, 13; Berlin, 1975, 1976).

II. 5. Groups and Communities in Transformation

490. Agus, Irvin A., *Urban Civilization in Pre-crusade Europe*, 2 vols. (Leiden², 1968).
491. Bosl, Karl, 'Die Sozialstruktur der mittelalterlichen Residenz- und Fernhandelsstadt Regensburg' [143: 93–213].
492. Bumke, Joachim, *Studien zum Ritterbegriff im 12. und 13. Jahrhundert* (Euphorion, suppl. 1; Heidelberg², 1977).
493. Chazan, Robert, *European Jewry and the first crusade* (Berkeley, 1987).
494. Dollinger, Philippe, 'Aspects de la noblesse allemande, XIᵉ– XIIIᵉ siècles', in *La noblesse au moyen âge, XIᵉ–XVᵉ siècles*, ed. Philippe Contamine (Paris, 1976), pp. 133–49.
495. Epperlein, Siegfried, *Bauernbedrückung und Bauernwiderstand im hohen Mittelalter* (Forsch. zur ma. Gesch. 6; (East) Berlin, 1960).
496. Fischer, Herbert, *Die verfassungsrechtliche Stellung der Juden in den deutschen Städten* (Gierkes Unters. 140; Breslau, 1931).
497. Fleckenstein, Josef, 'Die Entstehung des niederen Adels und das Rittertum', in *Herrschaft und Stand*, ed. Josef Fleckenstein (publ. of the MPIG, 51; Göttingen, 1977).
498. Fleckenstein, Josef, 'Zum Problem der Abschließung des Ritterstandes' [101: 252–71].
499. Fleckenstein, Josef, 'Zur Frage der Abgrenzung von Bauer und Ritter' [145: 246–53].
500. *Germania Judaica*, ed. Ismar Elbogen *et al.*, vol. i (Tübingen, 1963).
501. Irsigler, Franz, 'Freiheit und Unfreiheit im Mittelalter', *Westf. Forsch.* 28 (1976/7), 1–15.
502. Johrendt, Johann, *'Milites' und 'militia' im 11. Jahrhundert*, Diss. phil. (Erlangen, 1971/2).
503. Lambert, Malcolm D., *Medieval Heresy. Popular Movements from Bogomil to Huss* (London, 1977).
504. Leyser, K(arl), 'The German Aristocracy from the Ninth to the Early Twelfth Century', *Past and Present* 41 (1968), 25–53.
505. Liebeschütz, Hans, *Synagoge und Ecclesia*, ed. Alexander Patschovsky (Heidelberg, 1983).
506. Maier, Johann, 'Il Hassidismo aškenazita e il suo ambiente', in *Atti del congresso tenuto a S. Miniato dal 12 al 15 novembre 1984*

(Associazione italiana per lo studio del Giudaismo, testi e studi; Rome, 1987), pp. 203–25.

507. Mitterauer, Michael, and Siedler, Reinhard, *Vom Patriarchat zur Partnerschaft* (Munich², 1980).

508. *Monumenta Judaica*, ed. Konrad Schilling, vols. i–ii (Cologne, 1963).

509. Oexle, Otto Gerhard, 'Die mittelalterlichen Gilden' [135: i. 203–26].

510. Reuter, Hans G., *Die Lehre vom Ritterstand* (Neue Wirtschaftsgesch. 4; Cologne etc., 1971).

511. Rösener, Werner, 'Bauer und Ritter im Hochmittelalter' [114: 665–92].

512. Schmid, Karl, 'Zur Problematik von Familie, Sippe und Geschlecht', *ZGO* 105 (1957), 1–62.

513. Schreckenberg, Heinz, *Die christlichen Adversus-Judaeos-Texte (11.–13. Jh.). Mit einer Ikonographie des Judenthemas bis zum 4. Laterankonzil* (Europäische Hochschulschriften, ser. xxiii: Theologie, 335; Frankfurt/Main etc., 1988).

514. Schreiner, Klaus, *Sozial- und standesgeschichtliche Untersuchungen zu den Benediktiner-Konventen im östlichen Schwarzwald* (pub. of the Komm. für gesch. Landeskde. in Baden-Württemberg, series B, 31; Stuttgart, 1964).

515. Schulz, Knut, 'Zum Problem der Zensualität im Hochmittelalter', in *Beiträge zur Wirtschafts- und Sozialgeschichte des Mittelalters, Fs. für Herbert Helbig* (Cologne etc., 1976), pp. 86–127.

516. Schulz, Knut, 'Reichsklöster und Ministerialität. Gefälschte Dienstrechte des 12. Jahrhunderts. Ursachen und Absichten', in *Gesellschaftsgeschichte, Fs. für Karl Bosl*, ed. Ferdinand Seibt, vol. ii (Munich, 1988), pp. 37–54.

517. Schulze, Hans K., 'Rodungsfreiheit und Königsfreiheit', *HZ* 219 (1974), 529–50.

518. Schulze-Dörrlamm, Mechtild, *Der Mainzer Schatz der Kaiserin Agnes aus dem mittleren 11. Jahrhundert* (Sigmaringen, 1991).

519. Schwer, Wilhelm, *Stand und Ständeordnung im Weltbild des Mittelalters* (Görres-Ges. zur Pflege der Wiss., pub. of the Sektion für Wirtschafts- und Sozialwiss. 7; Paderborn², 1952).

520. Stemberger, Brigitte, 'Zu den Judenverfolgungen in Deutschland zur Zeit der ersten beiden Kreuzzüge', *Kairos*, NF 20 (1978), 53–72, 151–7.

521. Töpfer, Bernhard, 'Ursachen für Fortschritte und Stagnationserscheinungen in der Feudalgesellschaft', *ZfG* 31 (1983), 132–46.

III. GERMANY UNDER THE STAUFEN:
NEW FORMS AND LIMITATIONS

III. 1. Imperial Rule in the Staufen Period

522. Berg, Beverly, 'Manfred of Sicily and the Greek East', *Byzantina* 14 (1988), 263–89.
523. Berg, Dieter, 'Staufische Herrschaftsideologie und Mendikantenspiritualität. Studien zum Verhältnis Kaiser Friedrichs II. zu den Bettelorden', *Wissenschaft und Weisheit* 51 (1988), 26–51, 185–209.
524. Borst, Arno, *Reden über die Staufer* (Vienna, 1978).
525. Cleve, Thomas C. van, *The Emperor Frederick II of Hohenstaufen* (Oxford, 1972).
526. Csendes, Peter, *Die Kanzlei Kaiser Heinrichs VI.* (Österr. Akad. der Wiss., phil.-hist. Kl., Denkschriften, 151; Vienna, 1981).
527. Engels, Odilo, 'Zum Konstanzer Vertrag von 1153', in *Deus qui mutat tempora! Menschen und Institutionen im Wandel des Mittelalters, Fs. für Alfons Becker*, ed. Ernst-Dieter Hehl *et al.* (Sigmaringen, 1987), pp. 235–58.
528. Engels, Odilo, *Die Staufer* (Stuttgart etc.[4], 1989).
529. Engels, Odilo, *Stauferstudien. Beiträge zur Geschichte der Staufer im 12. Jahrhundert* (Sigmaringen, 1988).
530. *Federico Barbarossa nel dibattito storiografico in Italia e in Germania*, ed. Raoul Manselli *et al.* (Bologna, 1982).
531. Fleckenstein, Josef, 'Friedrich Barbarossa und das Rittertum' [100: ii. 1022–141].
532. *Friedrich Barbarossa. Handlungsspielräume und Wirkungsweisen des staufischen Kaisers*, ed. Alfred Haverkamp (VuF 40; Sigmaringen, 1991).
533. Hamilton, Bernard, 'Prester John and the Three Kings of Cologne', in *Studies in Medieval History presented to R. H. C. Davis*, ed. Henry Mayr-Harting *et al.* (London, 1985), pp. 177–91.
534. Haverkamp, Alfred, 'Friedrich I. Barbarossa', in *Die Großen der Weltgeschichte*, vol. iii (Zürich, 1973), pp. 418–39.
535. Herkenrath, Rainer Maria, *Die Reichskanzlei in den Jahren 1174 bis 1180* (Abh. der Österr. Akad. der Wiss., phil.-hist. Kl., Denkschriften, 30; Vienna, 1977).
536. Hucker, Bernd Ulrich, *Kaiser Otto IV.* (Schriften der MGH, 34; Hanover, 1990).
537. Jordan, Karl, *Henry the Lion*, tr. P. S. Falla (Oxford, 1986); orig. pub. as *Heinrich der Löwe* (Munich, 1979).

538. Kantorowicz, Ernst, *Kaiser Friedrich der Zweite*, vol. i (Berlin[4], 1936); vol. ii (suppl. vol.) (Berlin, 1931).
539. Koch, Walter, *Die Reichskanzlei in den Jahren 1167 bis 1174* (pub. of the Hist. Komm. der Österr. Akad. der Wiss., phil.-hist. Kl., Denkschriften, 115; Vienna, 1973).
540. Lamma, Paolo, *Comneni e Staufer*, vols. i–ii (Rome, 1955, 1957).
541. Opll, Ferdinand, *Friedrich Barbarossa* (Gestalten des Mittelalters und der Renaissance; Darmstadt, 1990).
542. Rieckenberg, Hans Jürgen, 'Arnolt Walpot, der Initiator des Rheinischen Bundes von 1254', *DA* 16 (1960), 228–37.
543. Rösener, Werner, 'Südwestdeutsche Zisterzienserklöster unter kaiserlicher Schirmherrschaft', *ZWLG* 33 (1974), 24–52.
544. Schaller, Hans Martin, 'Endzeit-Erwartung und Antichrist-Vorstellungen in der Politik des 13. Jahrhunderts' [100: ii. 924–47].
545. Schaller, Hans Martin, *Kaiser Friedrich II. Verwandler der Welt* (Persönlichkeit und Gesch. 34; Göttingen[2], 1971).
546. Schaller, Hans Martin, 'Die Kanzlei Kaiser Friedrichs II.', parts i–ii, *AfD* 3 (1957), 207–86; 4 (1958), 264–327.
547. Wolter, Heinz, 'Die Verlobung Heinrichs VI. mit Konstanze von Sizilien im Jahre 1184', *HJb* 105 (1985), 30–51.
548. Zinsmaier, Paul, 'Die Reichskanzlei unter Friedrich II.' [127: 135–66].
549. Zinsmaier, Paul, *Die Urkunden Philipps von Schwaben und Ottos IV. (1198–1212)* (pub. by the Komm. für gesch. Landeskde. in Baden-Württemberg, series B, Forsch. 53; Stuttgart, 1969).

III. 2. Continuity and Change in Lordship

550. Angermeier, Heinz, 'Landesfriedenspolitik und Landfriedensgesetzgebung unter den Staufern' [127: 167–86].
551. Berthold, Brigitte, 'Sozialökonomische Differenzierung und innerstädtische Auseinandersetzungen in Köln im 13. Jahrhundert' [138: 229–87].
552. Büttner, Heinrich, 'Zähringerpolitik im Trierer Raum während der zweiten Hälfte des 12. Jahrhunderts', *Rhein Vjbll* 33 (1969), 47–59.
553. Diestelkamp, Bernhard, 'Welfische Stadtgründungen und Stadtrechte des 12. Jahrhunderts', *ZRG, GA* 81 (1964), 164–224.
554. Eckhardt, Albrecht, 'Das älteste Bolander Lehnsbuch', *AfD* 22 (1976), 317–44.
555. Engel, Evamaria, 'Beziehungen zwischen Königtum und

Städtebürgertum unter Wilhelm von Holland (1247–1256)'
[138: 63–107].

556. Engel, Evamaria, 'Finanzielle Beziehungen zwischen
deutschen Königen und Städtebürgern von 1250 bis 1314',
JbWG (1975), iv. 95–113.

557. Engel, Evamaria, 'Städtebünde im Reich von 1226 bis 1314',
in *Bürgertum, Handelskapital, Städtebünde* (Hansische Stud. 3.
Abh. zur Handels- und Sozialgesch. 15; Weimar, 1975),
pp. 177–209.

558. Fein, Hella, *Die staufischen Städtegründungen im Elsaß*, phil.
Diss. (Schriften des wiss. Instituts der Elsass-Lothringer im
Reich, NF 23; Frankfurt am Main,1939).

559. Fried, Johannes, 'Die Wirtschaftspolitik Friedrich Barbarossa
in Deutschland', *BDLG* 120 (1984), 195–239.

560. Friedland, Klaus, Goez, Werner, and Müller, Wolfgang J.,
Politik, Wirtschaft und Kunst des staufischen Lübeck (Lübeck,
1976).

561. Gattermann, Günter, 'Die deutschen Fürsten auf der Reichs-
heerfahrt', Diss. typescript (Frankfurt am Main, 1956).

562. Goez, Werner, *Der Leihezwang* (Tübingen, 1962).

563. Helbig, Herbert, *Der wettinische Ständestaat* (Mitteldt. Forsch.
4; Münster etc., 1955).

564. Holbach, Rudolf, *Stiftsgeistlichkeit im Spannungsfeld von Kirche
und Welt*, parts i–ii (Trierer Hist. Forsch. 2. i–ii; Trier, 1982).

565. Kuhn, Walter, 'Die deutschen Stadtgründungen des 13. Jahrhunderts im westlichen Pommern', *ZOF* 23 (1974), 1–58.

566. Martin, Thomas, 'Die Pfalzen im 13. Jahrhundert', in
Herrschaft und Stand, ed. Josef Fleckenstein (pub. 07 MPIG, 51;
Göttingen, 1977), pp. 277–301.

567. Maschke, Erich, *Städte und Menschen* (VSWG, suppl. 68; Wiesbaden, 1980).

568. Metz, Wolfgang, *Die staufischen Güterverzeichnisse* (Weimar,
1933).

569. Rabe, Horst, 'Frühe Studien zur Ratsverfassung in den
deutschen Reichslandstädten bzw. Reichsstädten Oberdeutschlands' [77: 1–17].

570. Rösch, Gerhard, *Venedig und das Reich* (Bibl. des DHI in Rom,
53; Tübingen, 1982).

571. Rübsamen, Dieter, *Kleinere Herrschaftsträger im Pleissenland.
Studien zur Geschichte des mitteldeutschen Adels im 13. Jh.* (Mitteldeutsche Forschungen, 95; Cologne etc., 1987).

572. Schlesinger, Walter, 'Die mitteldeutsche Ostsiedlung im
Herrschaftsraum der Wettiner und Askanier', in *Deutsche Ost-*

siedlung in Mittelalter und Neuzeit (Stud. zum Deutschtum im Osten, 8; Cologne etc., 1971).

573. Schlunk, Andreas Christoph, *Königsmacht und Krongut. Die Machtgrundlage des deutschen Königtums in 13. Jahrhundert — und eine neue historische Methode* (Stuttgart, 1988).

574. Schmid, Karl, *Gebetsgedenken und adliges Selbstverständnis* (Sigmaringen, 1983).

575. Schwind, Fred, 'Nachstaufische Reichsministerialen in der Wetterau und am Oberrhein' [77: 72–93].

576. Schwind, Fred, 'Zur Verfassung und Bedeutung der Reichsburgen vornehmlich im 12. und 13. Jahrhundert' [357: i. 85–122].

577. Steinbach, Hartmut, *Die Reichsgewalt und Niederdeutschland in nachstaufischer Zeit (1247–1308)* (Kieler Hist. Stud. 5; Stuttgart, 1968).

578. Stoob, Heinz, 'Formen und Wandel staufischen Verhaltens zum Städtewesen' [139: 51–72].

579. *Südwestdeutsche Städte im Zeitalter der Staufer*, ed. Erich Maschke *et al.* (Stadt in der Gesch. 6; Sigmaringen, 1980).

580. Töpfer, Bernhard, 'Stellung und Aktivität der Bürgerschaft von Bischofsstädten während des staufisch-welfischen Thronstreits' [138: 13–62].

581. Troe, Heinrich, *Münze, Zoll und Markt und ihre finanzielle Bedeutung für das Reich vom Ausgang der Staufer bis zum Regierungsantritt Karls IV. (VSWG,* suppl. 32; Stuttgart, 1937).

582. Voltmer, Ernst, 'Formen und Möglichkeiten städtischer Bündnispolitik in Oberitalien nach dem Konstanzer Frieden: Der sogenannte Zweite Lombardenbund', in *Kommunale Bündnisse Oberitaliens und Oberdeutschlands im Vergleich*, ed. Helmut Maurer (VuF 33; Sigmaringen, 1987), pp. 97–116.

583. Voltmer, Ernst, 'Der Rheinische Bund (1254–1256). Eine neue Forschungsaufgabe?', in *Der Rheinische Städtebund von 1254/56. Katalog zur Landesausstellung in Worms* (Koblenz, 1986), pp. 117–43.

584. Weibels, Franz, *Die Großgrundherrschaft Xanten im Mittelalter* (Niederrhein. Landeskde., Schriften zur Natur und Gesch. des Niederrheins, 3; Krefeld, 1959).

585. Zillmann, Sigurd, *Die welfische Territorialpolitik im 13. Jahrhundert (1218–1267)* (Brunswick, 1975).

III. 3. The Expansion of the Economy

586. Benl, Rudolf, *Die Gestaltung der Bodenrechtsverhältnisse in Pommern vom 12. bis zum 14. Jahrhundert* (Mitteldeutsche Forschungen, 93; Cologne, 1986).

587. Chorley, Patrick, 'The cloth exports of Flanders and northern France during the thirteenth century: a luxury trade?', *EconHR* 40 (1987), 349–79.

588. Dirlmeier, Ulf, *Mittelalterliche Hoheitsträger im wirtschaftlichen Wettbewerb* (VSWG, suppl. 51; Wiesbaden, 1966).

589. Dollinger, Philippe, *Die Hanse* (Stuttgart⁴, 1989).

590. Ennen, Edith, 'Aachen im Mittelalter', *Zs. des Aachener Geschichtsvereins* 86/87 (1979/80), 457–87.

591. Fryde, Natalie, 'Arnold Fitz Thedmar und die Entstehung der großen deutschen Hanse', *HGBll* 107 (1989), 27–42.

592. *Die Grundherrschaft im späten Mittelalter*, parts i–ii, ed. Hans Patze (VuF 27. i–ii; Sigmaringen, 1983).

593. *Die Hanse. Lebenswirklichkeit und Mythos*. Eine Ausstellung des Museums für Hamburgische Geschichte in Verbindung mit der Vereins- und Westbank, 2 vols. (Hamburg, 1989).

594. Kamp, Norbert, 'Moneta regis', phil. Diss. typescript (Göttingen, 1957).

595. Kamp, Norbert, 'Münzprägung und Münzpolitik der Staufer in Deutschland', *Hamburger Beitr. zur Numismatik*, 17 (1963), 517–44.

596. *Pommern und Mecklenburg, Beiträge zur mittelalterlichen Städtegeschichte*, ed. Roderich Schmidt (pub. of Hist. Komm. für Pommern, series V, Forsch. zur Pommerschen Gesch. 19; Vienna, 1981).

597. Schildhauer, Johannes, Fritze, Konrad, and Stark, Walter, *Die Hanse* ((East) Berlin, 1974).

598. Schulze, Hans K., 'Der Anteil der Slawen an der mittelalterlichen Ostsiedlung nach deutschen Recht in Ostmitteldeutschland', *ZOF* 31 (1982), 321–36.

599. Schulze, Hans K., 'Die Besiedlung der Mark Brandenburg im hohen und späten Mittelalter', *JGMODtI* 28 (1979), 42–178.

600. Sprandel, Rolf, 'Flandrisch-lübeckischer Fernhandel und die deutsche Ostsiedlung' [92: 130–43].

601. *Studien zur Geschichte des sächsisch-magdeburgischen Rechts in Deutschland und Polen*, ed. Dietmar Willoweit *et al.* (Rechts hist. Reihe, 10; Frankfurt am Main etc., 1980).

602. Thiele, Augustinus, *Echternach und Himmerod* (Forsch. zur Sozial- und Wirtschaftsgesch. 7; Stuttgart, 1964).

III. 4. Church Life, Piety, and Education

603. Bertau, Karl, *Deutsche Literatur im europäischen Mittelalter*, vols. i–ii (Munich, 1972, 1973).
604. Bumke, Joachim, *Mäzene im Mittelalter* (Munich, 1979).
605. Dickson, Gary, 'The flagellants of 1260 and the crusades', *Journal of Medieval History* 15 (1989), 227–67.
606. Freed, John B., *The Friars and German Society in the Thirteenth Century* (Medieval Academy of America, Publication 86; Cambridge, Mass., 1977).
607. *Hildegard von Bingen 1179–1979*, ed. Anton Philipp Brück (Quellen und Abh. zur mittelrhein. Kirchengesch. 33; Mainz, 1979).
608. Höing, Norbert, 'Die "Trierer Stilübungen"', *AfD* 1 (1955), 257–329; 2 (1956), 125–249.
609. Holladay, Joan A., 'Hermann of Thuringia as patron of the arts: a case study', *Journal of Medieval History* 16 (1990), 191–216.
610. Köhn, Rolf, 'Die Verketzerung der Stedinger durch die Bremer Fastensynode', *Bremisches Jb.* 57 (1979), 15–85.
611. Lorenz, Sönke, *Studium generale Erfordense: zum Erfurter Schulleben im 13. und 14. Jh.* (Monographien z. Geschichte des Mittelalters, 34; Stuttgart, 1989).
612. MacDonnell, Ernest W., *The Beguines and Beghards in Medieval Culture* (New Brunswick, 1954).
613. *Ornamenta ecclesiae. Kunst und Künstler der Romanik*, vols. i–iii (Cologne, 1985).
614. Patschovsky, Alexander, *Der Passauer Anonymus* (Stuttgart, 1968).
615. Patschovsky, Alexander, 'Zur Ketzerverfolgung Konrads von Marburg', *DA* 37 (1981), 641–93.
616. Pitz, Ernst, 'Schrift und Aktenwesen der städtischen Verwaltung im Spätmittelalter', *Mitteilungen aus dem Stadtarchiv von Köln* 45 (1959), 3–483.
617. Pixton, Paul B., 'Die Anwerbung des Heeres Christi', *DA* 34 (1978), 166–91.
618. *Sankt Elisabeth* (pub. by the Philipps-Universität Marburg with the Hessische Landesamt für gesch. Landeskde.; Sigmaringen, 1981).
619. Sauerländer, Willibald, 'Die bildende Kunst der Stauferzeit' [147: iii. 205–47 and further articles in 147: v].
620. Schmidt, Hans-Joachim, *Bettelorden in Trier. Wirksamkeit und Umfeld im hohen und späten Mittelalter* (Trierer Hist. Forsch. 10; Trier, 1986).

621. Segl, Peter, *Ketzer in Österreich. Untersuchungen über Häresie und Inquisition im Herzogtum Österreich im 13. und beginnenden 14. Jahrhundert* (Paderborn etc., 1984).

622. Simons, Walter, *Bedelordenkloosters in het graafschap Vlaanderen: Chronologie en topografie van de bedelordensverspreiding voor 1350* (Bruges, 1987).

623. Simons, Walter, *Stad en apostolaat: De vestiging van de bedelorden in het graafschap Vlaanderen* (ca. *1225*–ca. *1350*) (Verhandelingen van de Koninklijke Academie voor Wetenschappen, Letteren en Schone Junsten van België, Klasse de Letteren, Jaargang 49, nr. 121; Brussels, 1987).

624. *Stauferzeit*, ed. Rüdiger Krohn *et al.* (Karlsruher kulturwiss. Arbeiten 1; Stuttgart, 1979).

625. Störmer, Wilhelm, ' "Spielmannsdichtung" und Geschichte', *ZBLG* 43 (1980), 551–74.

626. Wolf, Gunther, 'Die Anfänge des sogenannten "Konziliarismus" als Indiz eines Bewußtseinswandels zur Zeit Kaiser Friedrichs II.', *ZRG, KA* 106 (1989), 155–76.

627. Wriedt, Klaus, 'Das gelehrte Personal in der Verwaltung und Diplomatie der Hansestädte', *HGbll* 96 (1978), 15–37.

III. 5. New Beginnings in the Social System

628. Awerbuch, Marianne, 'Weltflucht und Lebensverneinung der "Frommen Deutschlands" ', *AKG* 60 (1978), 35–93.

629. Chazan, Robert, 'Emperor Frederick I, the Third Crusade, and the Jews', *Viator* 8 (1977), 83–93.

630. Fleckenstein, Josef, 'Vom Stadtadel im spätmittelalterlichen Deutschland', *Zs. für siebenbürgische Landeskde.* 3 (74) (1980), 1–13.

631. Ignor, Alexander, *Über das allgemeine Rechtsdenken Eikes von Repgow* (Rechts- und staatswissenschaftliche Veröffentlichungen der Görres-Gesellschaft, new ser. 42; Paderborn, 1984).

632. Jordan, William Chester, *The French monarchy and the Jews. From Philip Augustus to the last Capetians* (University of Pennsylvania Press Middle Ages ser.; Philadelphia, 1989).

633. Klinkenberg, Hans Martin, ' "Bürgerliche Bildung" im Mittelalter', in *Studien zur deutschen Literatur des Mittelalters*, ed. Rudolf Schützeichel *et al.* (Bonn, 1979), 334–70.

634. Kurze, Dietrich, 'Häresie und Minderheiten im Mittelalter', *HZ* 229 (1979), 529–73.

635. Schmidt, Hans Joachim, 'Arbeit und soziale Ordnung. Zur Wertung städtischer Lebensweise bei Berthold von Regensburg', *AK* 71 (1989), 261–96.

636. Schulz, Knut, 'Stadtrecht und Zensualität am Niederrheim (12.–14. Jahrhundert)', in *Soziale und wirtschaftliche Bindungen im Mittelalter am Niederrhein*, ed. Edith Ennen *et al.* (Klever Archiv, 3; Kleve, 1981), pp. 13–36.

637. *Stadt und Ministerialität*, ed. Erich Maschke *et al.* (pub. of the Komm. für gesch. Landeskde. in Baden-Württemberg B, Forsch. 76; Stuttgart, 1973).

638. Stroll, Mary, *The Jewish pope: Ideology and Politics in the Papal Schism of 1130* (Brill's Studies in Intellectual History, 8; New York, 1987).

INDEX

Index

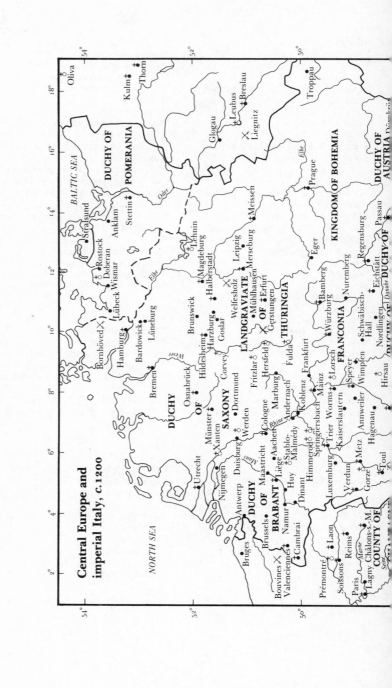

Central Europe and imperial Italy, c. 1200

BALTIC SEA

NORTH SEA

DUCHY OF POMERANIA

Oliva

Thorn
Kulm
Leubus
Breslau
Glogau
Liegnitz
Troppau

Stralsund
Rostock
Doberan
Anklam
Wismar
Stettin
Lübeck
Hamburg
Bardowick
Lüneburg

DUCHY OF SAXONY

Bremen
Osnabrück
Brunswick
Hildesheim
Harzburg
Goslar
Corvey
Werden
Dortmund

Chimin
Magdeburg
Halberstadt
Welfesholz
Mühlhausen
Leipzig
Merseburg
Meissen

KINGDOM OF BOHEMIA

Prague
Eger
Regensburg
Passau

DUCHY OF AUSTRIA

LANDGRAVIATE OF THURINGIA

Erfurt
Gerstungen
Fritzlar
Hersfeld
Fulda

Bornhöved
Utrecht
Münster
Xanten
Duisburg
Nijmegen
Maastricht

Frankfurt
Koblenz
Andernach
Mainz
Worms
Speyer
Wimpfen

FRANCONIA

Bamberg
Würzburg
Schwäbisch-Hall
Nordlingen
Hirsau
Eichstätt

DUCHY OF BRABANT

Antwerp
Brussels
Bruges
Liège
Huy
Namur
Dinant
Cambrai
Valenciennes
Bouvines

Aachen
Stablo-Malmédy
Himmerod
Luxemburg
Trier
Kaiserslautern
Metz
Gorze
Verdun
Toul

Lorsch
Annweiler
Hagenau
Springiersbach

COUNTY OF

Prémontré
Laon
Soissons
Reims
Paris
Lagny
Châlons-s.-M.

Rhine
Maas
Weser
Elbe
Oder
Marne
Seine
Danube

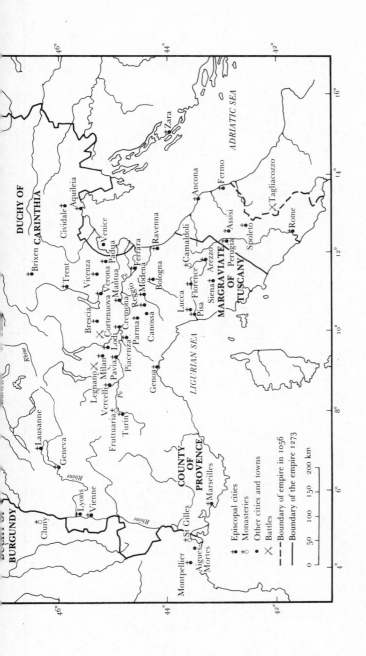

DUCHY OF CARINTHIA

Brixen† †Cividale †Aquileia

Trent† Venice †Zara

DUCHY OF BURGUNDY

Lausanne†

Geneva†

Lyons† Vienne†

Cluny

St Gilles† Montpellier

Aigues-Mortes †Marseilles

COUNTY OF PROVENCE

Fruttuaria Turin† Vercelli† Milan Pavia† Legnano Lodi Piacenza† Cremona Brescia† Vicenza† Cortenuova Verona Mantua Padua†

Genoa†

LIGURIAN SEA

Canossa Parma† Reggio Modena† Ferrara† Bologna

Ravenna†

Lucca† Pisa† Florence† Siena† Arezzo† Camaldoli† Perugia† Assisi† Spoleto† Ancona† Fermo† Tagliacozzo Rome†

MARGRAVIATE OF TUSCANY

ADRIATIC SEA

Rhine Rhône Po

† Episcopal cities
†ₒ Monasteries
• Other cities and towns
✕ Battles
– – Boundary of empire in 1056
——— Boundary of the empire 1273

0   50   100   150   200 km

46° 44° 42°

46° 44° 42°

4° 6° 8° 10° 12° 14° 16°